FINANCIAL INSTITUTIONS AND MARKETS IN THE SOUTH PACIFIC

Also by Michael T. Skully

MERCHANT BANKING IN AUSTRALIA
AMERICAN DEPOSITARY RECEIPTS: Internationalizing
  Australian Fund Raising and Securities Trading
ASEAN FINANCIAL CO-OPERATION: Developments in
  Banking, Finance and Insurance
DIVIDEND REINVESTMENT PLANS: Their Development and
  Operations in Australia and the United States
MERCHANT BANKING IN ASEAN: A Regional Examination
  of its Development and Operations
MERCHANT BANKING IN THE FAR EAST
FINANCING EAST ASIA'S SUCCESS: Comparative Financial
  Development in Eight Asian Countries (*co-author*)
CREDIT UNIONS FOR AUSTRALIANS (*co-author*)
CAPITAL MARKET DEVELOPMENT IN THE ASIA
  PACIFIC REGION (*editor*)
FINANCIAL INSTITUTIONS AND MARKETS IN THE
  SOUTHWEST PACIFIC: A Study of Australia, Fiji, New
  Zealand and Papua New Guinea (*editor*)
FINANCIAL INSTITUTIONS AND MARKETS IN
  SOUTHEAST ASIA: A Study of Brunei, Indonesia, Malaysia,
  Philippines, Singapore and Thailand (*editor*)
FINANCIAL INSTITUTIONS AND MARKETS IN THE FAR
  EAST: A Study of China, Hong Kong, Japan, South Korea and
  Taiwan (*editor*)
A MULTINATIONAL LOOK AT THE TRANSNATIONAL
  CORPORATION (*editor*)
HANDBOOK OF AUSTRALIAN CORPORATE FINANCE
  (*co-editor*)
CAPITAL MARKET EFFICIENCY: The Empirical Evidence
  (*co-editor*)

FINANCIAL INSTITUTIONS AND MARKETS IN THE SOUTH PACIFIC

A Study of New Caledonia, Solomon Islands, Tonga, Vanuatu and Western Samoa

Michael T. Skully
Senior Lecturer in Finance
University of New South Wales, Australia

St. Martin's Press   New York

First published in the United States of America in 1987

Printed in Hong Kong

ISBN 0–312–00529–6

Library of Congress Cataloging-in-Publication Data
Skully, Michael T.
Financial institutions and markets in the
South Pacific.
Bibliography: p.
Includes index.
1. Financial institutions—Oceania—Case studies.
2. Finance—Oceania—Case studies. I. Title.
HG190.A2S58 1987   332.1′099   87–4506
ISBN 0–312–00529–6

Contents

List of Maps

List of Tables

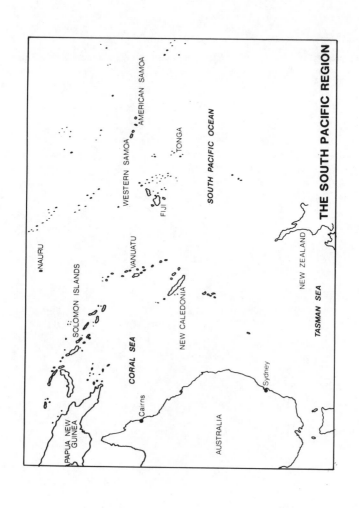

THE SOUTH PACIFIC REGION

Preface

One of the more interesting aspects of the 1970s was the growth and development of financial institutions and markets within the Asia Pacific region. Early in the decade few countries had financial markets of any significance: commercial banks dominated the domestic financial sectors and, in some cases, were virtually the only institutions. Today the capitalist countries of the region have the beginnings of, if not a well-developed range of financial institutions and instruments and in many cases money markets, securities markets, and foreign exchange markets as well. This book represents the fourth of a series of titles which provide an in-depth, country-by-country coverage of these developments and the respective financial institutions and markets as they exist today.

In many respects the coverage of these relatively smaller countries of the Solomon Islands, Tonga, Vanuatu and Western Samoa and the French Territory of New Caledonia present an interesting contrast to the other countries covered by this series, as their financial sectors are still very much in the development stage and many institutions have only recently been established. Similarly, any financial markets in operation are limited largely to foreign exchange and interbank transactions and a more formal money or securities market is at best only in the planning stages. There is nevertheless considerable interest in financial development within these countries and it is likely that the material presented may be outdated faster than any of the previous titles in the series. Hopefully this prediction will prove true, as much can be done to improve the operations of the existing financial systems and enhance their contribution to their respective country's economy.

The research associated with this title was conducted with the assistance of the National Centre for Development Studies of the Australian National University and the Australian Government's Australian Development Assistance Bureau. Their support and co-operation in this effort has been most appreciated. Similarly, special mention must be given to the Westpac Banking Corporation and the

Australian Trade Commission whose offices and affiliates assisted in the scheduling of the various appointments in the countries concerned.

The information presented, unless otherwise noted, is derived from interviews and correspondence with government officials, academic researchers, and business leaders within the country concerned. In particular, special thanks must go to Thomas Bayer, Pacific International Trust Co.; W. M. Beith, John Briggs, Russell Leitch, David Olley, Clive Smith, and Colin Wise, Westpac Banking Corporation; Mark Bidus, US Agency for International Development; Wayne Bornemeier, Volunteers in Overseas Co-operative Assistance; Andrew Brett and L. G. Peeters, Australian Trade Commission; Damien Cash, Australia and New Zealand Banking Group; A. S. Chan Ting, Western Samoa Life Assurance Corporation; Rodney Cole, Australian National University; R. H. Dean, World Bank; Dr Bronwen Douglas, La Trobe University; Marie-Noelle Ferrieux, Banque Indosuez Vanuatu; Edward Fillingham, Central Bank of Vanuatu; Carson Flint; Tua Hansell and Martin Kleis, Western Samoa Accident Compensation Fund; George Hazelman, Development Bank of Western Samoa; Ko-kwang Huh, Asian Development Bank; R. H. Griffin, Bank of New Zealand; P. B. Jones, Bank of Tonga; George Kejoa, Minister of Finance of the Solomon Islands; Charles Kick, Development Services Exchange; Daniele Lerable, French Embassy (Canberra); E. S. Mason, Government Shareholding Agency; Peter McShane, Pacific Commercial Bank; Tom Parry, University of New South Wales; Leumaga Pita, Samoa Credit Union League; Brian A. Ponter, Massey University; J. D. Russell, New Zealand Insurance Co.; C. R. Rye, International Monetary Fund; Fred Shanaman, Bank of Hawaii; Peter Starr, Australian Financial Review; T. Tapavalu, Commodities Board, Tonga; Cyrus Towfiq, Central Bank of Samoa; F. Tuipeatau, Tongan Registrar of Co-operative Societies; P. Vea and R. Yoder, Tonga Development Bank; H. J. Walker, National Pacific Insurance Ltd; Alan Ward, La Trobe University; A. W. White, National Bank of New Zealand; E. D. Williams, Post Office Savings Bank; and to Joyce L. Burcham for the translation of the New Caledonia material. The views expressed, however, remain solely those of the author.

June 1986   MICHAEL T. SKULLY

CORAL SEA

LOYALTY ISLANDS

Koumac

Touho

NEW CALEDONIA

Noumea

Goro

ISLE OF PINES

NEW CALEDONIA

1 Financial Institutions and Markets in New Caledonia

INTRODUCTION: THE SETTING

Located some 1500 kilometres due east of Australia and 1700 kilometres north of New Zealand, the French Overseas Territory of New Caledonia covers a land area of 19,103 square kilometres. It is comprised of the islands of New Caledonia, Walpole, Isle of Pines, and the Loyalty, Belep, Huon and Surprise and Chesterfield island groups.[1] The island of New Caledonia, la grande terre, is the largest and comprises 16,750 square kilometres or some 88 per cent of the Territory's total land mass and the major portion of its population of 145,368. The population itself is comprised of different races and cultures of which the native Melanesians are the largest group. The most recent statistics indicated that they comprised 42.6 per cent of the population compared to 37.1 per cent for Europeans, 8.4 per cent Wallisians and Futunians (another French Pacific Territory), 3.8 per cent Tahitians, 3.5 per cent Indonesians, 1.6 per cent Vietnamese, and the remainder from a mixture of other races to include Chinese and ni-Vanuatu.

Relatively little is known of the islands pre-European history. La Perouse reported signs of land in this general area but did not sight any of the islands. This was left to Captain James Cook. He visited the islands on 4 September 1774 and named the main island, New Caledonia, as well as the Isle of Pines. The French explorer, Bruni d'Entrecasteaux, also visited the area in 1792. In practice, however, there was little interest in the land other than for some sandalwood trading. Missionaries brought about the first extended European contact. British missionaries from the London Missionary Society, for example, arrived in the Loyalty island group in the 1830s, and were followed by French Catholic missionaries in 1840. The first missionaries on the island of New Caledonia itself were Protestants from Polynesia in 1841, and they were joined in late 1843 by French

Catholic priests who landed at Balade supported by French naval forces. The latter on 21 January 1844 raised the French flag over the island where it continued to fly until 1846, when an official French presence was withdrawn. Apparently France had intended to take New Caledonia after having lost the opportunity to claim New Zealand but, following problems with the British over other matters, the claim was never pressed. The British too seemed interested in the islands but, like the French, seemed unwilling to push the issue. The French interest in New Caledonia resumed in 1851 when the government considered its possibilities as a convict settlement and finally an alliance, in 1853, between France and England against Russia removed the last obstacle for annexation.[2] Thus, in response to numerous incidents in which French missionaries, and even the crew of a survey ship, were killed and eaten by the local islanders, France sent naval forces to the area. Febvrier Despointes raised the flag and annexed the islands for France on 24 September 1853. This, however, did not solely resolve the fighting between natives and Europeans and conflicts with local islanders continued at least up to 1917 with some serious fighting in 1878 and 1917.

The Territory was used as a French penal colony from 1864 to 1897, but even before annexation some European cattle ranches were already in operation. The early settlers tried many other crops and a range of cash crops, such as sugar, tobacco, coffee, and cotton were all grown with some success, only to fail later due to pests, disease, or other natural problems. There was also difficulty in obtaining sufficient labor when required, even while a penal colony. The labor problems for agriculture were compounded in 1863 when a French mining engineer, Jules Garnier, discovered commercial nickel deposits and the later gold rush in 1870. As the mineral sector paid much higher wages, it similarly depleted the potential for an agricultural work force, and this problem remains largely the same today.

Much of New Caledonia's mineral industry owes its origins to the work of John Higginson, an Australian, born of Irish parents. He was responsible in 1877 for establishing the world's first nickel ore smelter in Noumea. Later, on 18 May 1880, the major operators in mining business, Garnier, Higginson and Henri Marbeau, effectively merged their operations to create the Société le Nickel: the company which still today dominates New Caledonia's economy.

With the Second World War, and the occupation of France by Germany, there was concern that New Caledonia's mineral resources might be used by the Axis powers, and the islands' future particularly worried Australia and New Zealand. Fortunately the Petainist Governor was overthrown and in 1940 New Caledonia was one of the first territories to join the Free French government under General Charles de Gaulle. The Free French subsequently invited the Australians, American and New Zealand forces to establish local bases.

As elsewhere in the Pacific, the American occupation resulted in a major construction boom, and even today US military-built airfields, ports, roads and buildings are still very much in evidence. The South Pacific Commission, for example, uses the former US Pacific Headquarters building for its main offices. The American forces also caused a marked change in local attitudes. By 1946, for example, Melanesians were finally permitted to leave their reserves without special permission, and in 1951 they generally received the right to vote.

Similarly, in local politics there was a movement toward multi-racialism, and in 1951 a multiracial party, the Union Calédoniènée, was formed to campaign on the slogan, 'two colours, one people' for moderate reform and a devolution of control from Paris to New Caledonia residents. Local autonomy was actually introduced in 1957 with a Territorial Assembly and a Governing Council chosen by elections. In 1958 the residents voted to remain part of France, and in 1959 it was incorporated as an Overseas Territory within the French Republic. New Caledonians thus have a say in the French government through their election of two deputies (voting representatives) to the French National Assembly, as well as one senator to the French Senate: a position it still holds today. Unfortunately, following the assumption of power by Charles de Gaulle in 1958 and the Algerian crisis, local control was withdrawn and the 1957 constitution abolished. The French government again assumed direct power.[3]

Following the economic expansion of the nickel boom, New Caledonia residents began to seek greater political and economic control. As a result the Territory's self-governing powers were expanded. In 1976, for example, the elected Territorial Assembly in turn chose a Council of Government responsible for the Territory's primary education system, taxation, internal commerce and other domestic matters, but the French High Commissioner retained control over such matters as foreign affairs, defence, money and credit, justice, and secondary and tertiary education.

In March 1979, however, the local government was dismissed and the Territory again put directly under French rule from Paris. This dismissal, coupled with the election of the socialist president,

François Mitterrand, in May 1981, served as a catalyst to the current independence moves. Tension between the various local political factions were further worsened with the September 1981 assassination of a pro-independence leader, Pierre Declercq.

The Mitterrand government took direct control of local government in 1982 and implemented by decree a number of economic and social reforms, particularly in the areas of landownership and legal matters. It also established a Land Reform Board, the Office for the Development of the Interior and the Islands, and an Office of Kanak Science and Culture.

In attempt to resolve the local conflict, the French government sponsored the Nainville-les-Roches Round Table discussions near Paris, 8–12 July 1983, between New Caledonian political leaders. These talks, though, failed to reach an actual compromise solution between the parties but the French government nevertheless recognized the rights of the Kanak people to independence.

The French Minister for Overseas Territories, Georges Lemoine, visited New Caledonia in November 1983 with a five-year proposal under which New Caledonia could chose its own future (to include independence) in 1989. While the 'Lemoine Plan' was rejected by both the pro-independence parties (as it postponed independence) and the pro-French parties (because it had an option for independence), the French government proceeded with the basic concept and held new elections to a revised Territorial Assembly on 18 November 1984.

By then the pro-independence movement had announced a boycott of the elections and moved to disrupt the proceedings. Road blocs and other measures also helped keep voter turnout at the 50 per cent level, and these measures were continued after the elections, generally disrupting the flow of supplies and people into Noumea. Outlying properties were damaged and some deaths resulted. This, coupled with the victory of the anti-independence parties, caused the Kanak Socialist National Liberation Front (FLNKS)[4] to declare a provisional government on 1 December 1984, and resulted in the French government's appointment of special High Commissioner, Edgard Pisani, on 4 December. Commissioner Pisani, under the Prime Minister Laurent Fabius's socialist government, favoured independence for New Caledonia as soon as possible, but in association with France. Under the Pisani Plan, France retained responsibility for New Caledonia's defense, internal security, justice system, currency and banking system, transport and communications – a position not unlike its arrangements with Monaco. He argued that a French presence was necessary to 'maintain and guarantee the new equilibrium; to accompany the new institutions (still without experience) in their first steps toward the development of human and economic resources; to guarantee the statute and the interests of those non-Kanaks, who would fear for their safety and belongings'.[5]

Under legislation passed on 12 August 1985, New Caledonia was to receive self-government (which could include independence) no later than 31 December 1987. In the meantime the Territory was divided into four autonomous regions as a transitional measure. These regional divisions are administered by regional councils which have extensive powers in matters of economic development and regional planning, education, and cultural and social policies. Each region is to have its own budget with some 80 per cent of its funding coming through the Territorial government. Each region elects its own council members. These members in turn also comprise the Territorial Congress of 46 members. The regions and their respective populations and council positions are as follows: the North region (19,000) with 9 counsellors; South (25,000) with 9 counsellors; Noumea (85,000) with 21 counsellors; and the Loyalty Islands (15,500) with 7 counsellors.[6]

Each council is headed by a President elected from the council members. There is also a President elected to head the Territorial Congress. These five Presidents in turn comprise the Territory's Executive Council which assists the High Commissioner (the French government-appointed local governor) in administering the Territorial government.

Elections for these regional council positions were held on 29 September 1985. The Melanesian party, the Kanak Socialist National Liberation Front (FLNKS), won control of the North, South and Islands regions with pro-French parties, the Rassemblement pour la Calédonie dans la République (RPCR) and the Front Nationale controlling the Greater Noumea region.

Despite the three council results, the over-all voting was very much against straight independence. The pro-independence parties received only 37 per cent of the votes compared to 59 per cent for the anti-independence group. Some 80 per cent of the electors voted. Of the 46 seats, the two largest parties were the anti-independence party, the RPCR, with 25 seats, and the pro-independence party, the FNLKS, with 16.

With the victory of conservatives in the March 1986 French

national elections, the position has again changed it terms of French national policy toward New Caledonia and, as of April 1986, the four regional councils will be retained, but only in form, as most of their former powers have been centralized again under the control of the High Commissioner and the anti-independence-led Territorial Assembly, and the regions will retain responsibilities for cultural activities and local public works. It has also closed the Land Office which had been purchasing land from Europeans for return to Melanesian ownership.

In marked contrast to many of its neighbours, New Caledonia is not at all dependent on agricultural exports, and even a large portion of its exports are subject to some industrial processing. Unfortunately this difference has not made it any more immune to the effects of swings of commodity prices. It is only in this case that economy depends on nickel prices rather than copra. As one local saying suggests of the local economy, 'when nickel goes . . . all goes'.

A quick examination of New Caledonia exports justifies this view as, in 1984, nickel products comprised 97 per cent of the Territory's export income. Most of the ore is treated locally by the Société le Nickel and then exported, mainly to France, with some less-processed material sent to Japan. In addition it also produces copper, iron, cobalt, and silver as by-products of the smelting process to produce ferro-nickel and is active in chrome mining. Its success in minerals is a function of its rich natural endowments whose nickel deposits alone account for some 30 per cent of the world's known reserves and it is generally second only to Canada in nickel exports.

The importance of nickel and related mineral processing is reflected throughout New Caledonia's economy. Indeed, the mining workers' relatively high salary levels alone provides a market within Noumea for shopping and restaurant facilities equivalent to a metropolitan French town with a population of 300,000.

While mineral discoveries and changes in commodity prices have historically caused major swings in New Caledonia's economic fortune, the most recent was a nickel boom from 1969 to 1974. The nickel boom is the force that expanded the economy and attracted most of the financial institutions and other commercial operations now operating within the Territory. Some indication of the boom conditions can be founded in the growth of wages and work force size, 'from 1961 to 1969 wages multiplied by 2.4 while wage-earners multiplied by 2. However, from 1969 to 1976 wages multiplied by 6.4 while wage-earners multiplied by only 2.5'.[7] New Caledonia's *per capita* income likewise grew accordingly, and thus by 1974 New Caledonia was 'by far the richest and most industrialized of the islands in the South Pacific'[8] – a position it holds even today.

While this produced a tremendous increase in living standards for local miners, it also attracted many French citizens from all over the world. This migration was responsible for a major change in the composition of the local population with European and other non-Melanesians becoming much more significant. As a result the percentage of Melanesians declined sharply in the early 1970s from 51.1 per cent of the population in 1956, 47.6 per cent in 1963, 47 per cent in 1967 and only 41.7 per cent in 1976.[9]

This migration and the resulting changes in the composition of the local population, however, were not simply a matter of economics. In a recently-made-public letter dated 19 July 1972, the then French Prime Minister, Pierre Messmer, argued that 'in the long term, a nationalist upsurge can only be avoided if the non-Pacific communities and European French represent the demographic majority and it goes without saying that this can only be achieved by the systematic migration of women and children and the setting up of small middle-class enterprises'.[10] While the French government could not create the nickel boom and its resulting effects, it seems likely they assisted the process and achieved many of the results Messmer had suggested.

While the mineral sector still dominates the economy, it is not the sole activity, and since 1974 tourism has started to play a more important role both as a source of foreign exchange and of employment. The government encourages the visits of both shipboard visitors and those staying at hotels, and since 1981 has provided substantial incentives for new facilities to be established. As a result of newer hotels and good public relations, New Caledonia showed relatively good growth both in tourist numbers and in the average length of stay through most of 1984.

The tourists also provide money for Noumea's more fashionable shops, but most of these items are imported from France or elsewhere overseas. Indeed, New Caledonia produces relatively little of even its basic food items, and relies particularly on France for most processed foods and other consumer items. It does, however, produce some cement, soap, plastics, beer, soft drinks, handicrafts, building materials, furniture, printings, and chemicals.

Agricultural products are an important part of New Caledonia's 5 per cent non-nickel-related exports with fish, coffee and copra being the most important. Other domestic production concentrates on beef and dairy cattle, potatoes, corn, bananas, copra and coconut oil, and vegetable market gardening. The Territory also has some timber resources but is a net importer.

Finally the French naval, air force and army personnel permanently stationed at various bases throughout the Territory, as well as other French civil servants, are also an important source of foreign exchange.

While New Caledonia had had some success in developing the tourist industry, chrome mining, and other smaller enterprises, as an offset to its dependence on nickel, much of its success has been more than offset by the impact of the events of November 1984. The building industry has slumped as people were not keen to invest, given the Territory's uncertain political future, and tourists were frightened due to a few well-publicized terrorist attacks. Indeed, over-all tourist numbers in 1985 declined by 44 per cent from the 1984 figures and Australian tourist numbers dropped even more sharply from 26,532 to 5413.

Despite this initial set-back in tourist numbers, the Territorial government nevertheless plans to centre its development efforts on tourism, an expansion of nickel mining and processing, commercial fishing, and agricultural products. In this regard, it, and its Paris counterparts, has established a number of tax and loan concessions for investments in appropriately productive areas. The financial sector currently plays an important role in this process and will no doubt expand its involvement in line with current government policy.

Overview of the Financial Sector

As shown in Table 1.1, the Territory of New Caledonia has a well diversified financial sector comprised of a wide range of institutions, only some of which are officially controlled by the Territory's central banking institution, the Institut d'Emission d'Outre-Mer. As of late 1985, these other institutions included: the banking facilities run by the Territory's postal service, a number of non-registered leasing companies, the general and life insurance companies, investment companies, and the Territorial government's workers' compensation, medical and pension scheme body, CAFAT.

Not surprisingly, the commercial banks account for the bulk of the Territory's credit facilities, and in 1985 provided some 60 per cent of local lending. As shown in Table 1.2, development finance institu-

TABLE 1.1   Financial institutions in New Caledonia, by type, 1985

Institut d'Emission d'Outre-Mer*
Commercial banks*
Co-operative agricultural banks*
Savings banks*
Postal banking services
SICNC[a]*
Other development institutions*
Finance companies*
General insurance companies
Life insurance companies
CAFAT[b]
Superannuation funds
Investment companies
Other lending bodies

---

[a] Société Immobilière et de Crédit de Nouvelle-Calédonie.
[b] Caisse de Compensation des Prestations Familiales des Accidents du Travail et de Prévoyance des Travailleurs de la Nouvelle-Calédonie et Dépendances.
* Officially controlled by the Institut d'Emission d'Outre-Mer.

Source: Industry interviews (1985).

tions, namely the Société Immobilière et de Crédit de la Nouvelle-Calédonie, were the next in importance with 20 per cent of the total. Specialist financial institutions, such as the Caisse Centrale de Coopération Economique and the Société de Développement et d'Expansion du Pacifique, were next, followed by the other finance companies and the co-operative savings bank, Caisse de Crédit Agricole Mutuel.

TABLE 1.2   Lending in New Caledonia, by institutional type, September 1985

	CFP (m)	%
Commercial banks	29,234	60.5
Co-operative banks	762	1.6
Development finance companies	9,673	20.0
Other finance companies	3,155	6.6
Specialized financial inst.	5,466	11.3
Total lending	48,290	100.0

Source: Institut d'Emission d'Outre-Mer (1985) *Nouvelle-Calédonie Bulletin Trimestriel*, 45, December, p. 18.

In addition to the formal financial system, there are a number of other sources of finance to include merchant houses and family members. Another informal alternative, the agents d'affaires, are like a form of private money-lender who provides inventory finance and relatively short-term loans. There are also a few private financiers operating in conjunction with car dealers.

FINANCIAL INSTITUTIONS

Institut d'Emission d'Outre-Mer

The Institut d'Emission d'Outre-Mer (Institute for Currency Issue Overseas) provides the note-issuing and most other central banking functions for the Territory of New Caledonia. The Institut is actually headquartered in Paris, and operates through three branch offices (New Caledonia, French Polynesia and Mayottee) and one agency in Mata Utu in the Wallis and Futuna Islands. At the end of 1984 the Institut had a total of 80 field staff, of which 37 are located in Noumea. Of these 37, 5 were expatriate French and 32 were locally-hired personnel.

The Institut is responsible for the implementation of local monetary policy, the regulation of reserve requirements and other banking regulations, banking services to the Territory and other government agencies, and the provision of statistical information and economic advice. As in metropolian France, monetary policy in New Caledonia has traditionally favoured certain industries or economic objectives as well as affecting the over-all economy.

The Institut is also responsible for the local legal tender, the Colonies Françaises du Pacifique or CPF. Interestingly, the CPF is technically not a currency at all, but rather a note which is in turn convertible at a fixed rate of exchange into French francs. Since 1 January 1960 this conversion rate has been that 1 CPF equals 0.055 French francs. Besides its note issuing and regulatory functions, the Institut d'Emission is also an important source of funding for the commercial banks and other institutions through its conditional and automatic rediscount schemes. The Institut d'Emission was also responsible for the establishment of the Interbank Guarantee Fund (FGI). As shown in Table 1.3, such lending activity accounts for approximately half of its assets.

TABLE 1.3 Institut d'Emission d'Outre-Mer: assets and liabilities, 31
December 1984

Assets	French francs
French franc notes	952,070.00
Coins	2,660.63
Correspondent bank balances	32,998.72
Public Treasury operations	506,115,250.81
Advances and rediscounted loans	566,635,906.24
Net fixed assets	31,240,017.12
Other assets	17,691,227.53
Total assets	1,122,670,131.05
Liabilities	
Notes on issue	604,661,228.99
Short term creditors	425,972,852.74
Transfers and collections	7,285,596.06
Settlements of Treasury accounts	8,440,199.17
Equipment reserves	660,582.09
Other reserves	38,615,852.21
Statutory reserves	4,309,655.02
Capital	22,000,000.00
Other liabilities	10,784,164.77
Total liabilities	1,122,670,131.05

Source: Institut d'Emission d'Outre-Mer (1984) *Exercice 1984 Rapport d'Activité*, pp. 50–1.

Commercial Banks

The commercial banking industry in New Caledonia is the most developed among the South Pacific countries, with five major French banks having either branches or local subsidiaries. They provide a full range of traditional banking services as well as support Territorial government development policies through the Institut d'Emission d'Outre-Mer's special loan rediscounting facilities.

(i) *Development*

Commercial banking in New Caledonia commenced in 1871 with the opening of the Banque Marchand. Although operating mainly in the Territory, it was headquartered in Paris, and later its main shareholders sold out and on 14 July 1874 opened for business in Noumea as the Banque de Nouvelle-Calédonie.[11] This bank was initially quite successful, and apparently well respected among banking circles. One Australian banker in 1875, for example, explained that 'it is very prudently managed, and is not only a first class concern but is one which will be of great value to this bank (Bank of New South Wales) in every way'.[12] Unfortunately, by late 1876 the Banque de Nouvelle-Calédonie was having difficulties meeting its obligations and came close to insolvency. It again had difficulties in late 1877, but this time was forced into bankruptcy on 27 November 1877.[13]

With its closure came the opportunity for Australian banks, which had lost money through the Banque de Nouvelle-Calédonie's closure, to open branches in New Caledonia. Indeed, by the end of 1877 Australian bankers were already in Noumea trying to salvage some of their losses.[14]

A Noumea branch had previously been considered by at least some bankers. In 1874, for example, what was then the Union Bank (now the Australia and New Zealand Banking Group (ANZ) had received petitions from merchants and planters in New Caledonia to open branches within the Territory. This suggestion, though, was rejected by the Bank's directors as the Bank's charter then allowed it only to operate in British colonies.[15] Later, in 1877–8 the Union Bank's directors requested the management to reconsider a branch in New Caledonia in 'response to an approach by French merchants there, following the collapse of a local bank, the Bank of Caledonia'. A Union Bank official apparently 'discussed an approach to the French government for facilities in opening in Noumea, but abandoned it'.[16]

The Bank of New South Wales (now Westpac Banking Corporation) had received similar petitions in 1877, and was subsequently approached in March or April 1878 by John Higginson and other prominent New Caledonia businessmen. Higginson apparently sought

> an assurance that if he will get the Bank of New South Wales the monopoly of the banking business in New Caledonia for 10 . . . years and the purchase right of all the government Treasury drafts on Paris now £420,000 a year and increasing 20 d/st at franc for franc we will let him have Treasury drafts at same rate as we get them from government not exceeding the amount of the money coming from him monthly from government for contracts and not exceeding in any one month 20 per cent of the total received by us.[17]

Seemingly in return for lobbying the French government, Higginson wished favourable credit for his various enterprises. It is not known if the Bank of New South Wales agreed, but nothing eventuated from this proposal.

The failure to open was seemingly not due to the lack of profit potential for one banker described the rates on local business as 'very high and tempting'.[18] More likely the French government was reluctant to let foreign institutions gain what would be a *de facto* monopoly in a French colony. In any event, the Banque de l'Indochine eventually opened a branch in Noumea in September 1888.

The Banque de l'Indochine had, in 1875, received the note issuing rights for the French possessions in Indo-China, India, and the Pacific, but did not begin issuing local currency notes in Noumea until 15 October 1888, and these notes gradually became important in the New Hebrides as well. There were no special regulations that the bank cover the notes on issue with any specific reserves, and their resulting liabilities were simply offset by the bank's general assets. The amount of currency on issue was subject to agreement between the Banque and the Bank of France, but was generally related to demand for currency within the local economy. It effectively retained this note issue as well as other quasi central bank functions until 1966 when the Institut d'Emission assumed these roles.

Though the Australian banks did not open in Noumea, there was nevertheless important trading links between New Caledonia and Australia. Indeed, as what is now the Banque Nationale de Paris had had offices in Melbourne and Sydney since the late 1880s, it is surprising that it did not similarly open a branch in Noumea. Likewise, as there were then no specific restrictions on foreign bank entry, the Banque de l'Indochine could have similarly opened branches in Sydney and Melbourne to handle the Australian side of these transactions. While economically this would have greatly expanded the trading relations, neither bank saw the potential competition as desirable and so simply agreed not to compete in each other's markets.

It would be difficult to overstate the importance of the Banque de l'Indochine during New Caledonia's early development for it, together with the Rothschilds, successfully restructured the Territory's early mining operations when they first experienced financial difficulties in the late 1800s. It acted similarly during subsequent recessions and gain additional financial power in the process. As one study commented, the Banque de l'Indochine's 'single office at Noumea exercised almost absolute control over large sectors of the economy in both territories and used this to preserve some trading companies, while eliminating others, during the depression of the 1930s'.[19] The Banque similarly made many loan foreclosures during New Caledonia's major recession after the 1960s nickel boom.

In any case, there were few other alternatives. For example, 'money orders, payable in Paris at 1.25 per cent, can be obtained at the Treasury at Noumea'.[20] Likewise, 'a certain amount of banking business is carried on and banking facilities are given by local merchants',[21] but these merchants, too, 'were generally dependent on loans from [Banque de l'Indochine]'.[22]

This position of power and control apparently made the Banque de l'Indochine 'very unpopular with Caledonians because of its long monopoly of local credit facilities and its failure to invest more in the Territory'.[23] Similarly, the lack of adequate credit to smaller businesses no doubt hampered any economic diversification efforts. As one writer commented on bank financing in the early 1960s, the way to raise finance

> is to have a working arrangement either with the local branch of the Banque de l'Indochine or with some similar institution in France. But both these arrangements are beyond the scope of the small business man seeking to expand; he is working on too small a scale to be able to interest any organisations in France, and the local branch of the Banque de l'Indochine is simply not concerned to help people who operate on a one man scale.[24]

The rapid development of the local economy in the 1960s, particularly with the nickel boom from 1966 onwards, attracted many new French settlers and businesses. There was similar increase in the demand for banking services and the Banque de l'Indochine was unable to respond adequately to these new requirements. This, in 1969 the Banque Nationale de Paris opened for business. As shown in Table 1.4, Société Générale followed in 1971, Banque de Paris et des Pay-Bas (now Banque Paribas Pacifique) in 1974, and Banque de Nouvelle-Calédonie, a consortium venture involving Crédit Lyonnais, the Bank of Hawaii, Jean Breaud and local investors among its shareholders, also in 1974.

Though these arrivals set the structure of the local industry, there have since been a number of changes. For example, on 1 October 1975 the Banque de l'Indochine merged with the Banque de Suez et de l'Union des Mines to form the current Banque de l'Indochine et

TABLE 1.4   Commercial banks in New Caledonia, 1985

Bank	Established locally
Banque de l'Indochine et Suez	1888
Banque Nationale de Paris/Nouvelle-Calédonie	1969
Société Générale Calédoniènne de Banque	1971
Banque Paribas Pacifique	1974
Banque de Nouvelle-Calédonie–Crédit Lyonnais	1974

Note: Date when the parent bank initially established local operations.

Source: Industry interviews (1985).

Suez or Banque Indosuez. In 1978 the Banque Nationale de Paris converted its operations in New Caledonia from a branch to a wholly-owned subsidiary. Similarly, Paribas operates through a local company, which is in turn a 70-per-cent-owned subsidiary of another local company, CALDEV (a firm 70-per-cent-owned by Paribas of France and 30-per-cent by local shareholders) and 30-per-cent-owned directly by the Paribas group. Banque Indosuez likewise considered transferring its operations to a local subsidiary a few years ago, but this was postponed due to the local political situation. It was felt that under the circumstances that a branch status would have a better standing in the community than a locally-incorporated subsidiary.

Another significant aspect of the local market is that all five banks are either government owned or have the French government among their major shareholders. In some cases, such as the Banque Nationale de Paris and the Société Générale, these banks have been government owned since their nationalization in 1945 following the end of the Second World War. Crédit Lyonnais has been nationalized even longer. The remainder, Banque Indosuez and Banque Paribas, were only nationalized in 1981 by the socialist-lead Mitterrand government. Surprisingly, given this common government ownership, the banks still compete with each other in much the same manner as they might if privately owned. It is important, perhaps, to suggest why neither Banque Indosuez or Banque Paribas were nationalized earlier with the other major firms. The reason is, at least partly, that both are generally considered banques d'affaires or the French equivalent of a merchant bank. In addition to the corporate finance functions normally expected by merchant banks,[25] the banques d'affaires are also active in a venture capital sense and most hold extensive share investment portfolios among their assets.

(ii) *Regulation*

As part of France, the commercial banks in New Caledonia are subject to much the same degree of regulation as banks in metropolitan France. Within metropolitan France the Banque de France (Bank of France) is the bank of issue and regulator of the financial sector. It is managed by the Conseil National de Crédit (National Credit Council) which has representatives from the banks, government, unions, business and farmers. The Commission de Controle des Banques (Banking Control Commission) assists the Banque de France in establishing liquidity, solvency and credit ratios for all banks and financial institutions. Within New Caledonia, the Institut d'Emission d'Outre-Mer performs most of these same functions.

In terms of local regulations, the commercial banks in New Caledonia are required to keep non-interest bearing deposits with the Institut d'Emission d'Outre-Mer equal to 4.25 per cent on their cheque account deposits and 0.25 per cent on their savings accounts and term deposits. The banks must also maintain similar reserves in regard to certain types of lending. For example, they must have ordinary lending reserves of an amount equal to 5 per cent of those bank loans outstanding which would not be eligible for rediscounting with the Institut d'Emission d'Outre-Mer. In addition, they must also maintain special reserves based on those advances made over and above a limit set by the Institut d'Emission as per a specific reference date. Finally the banks must keep an amount equal to at least 60 per cent of their current account deposits and term deposits with less than a three months maturity remaining in the form of either Institut d'Emission deposits, Treasury securities, or rediscountable loans.

The bank lending is also subject to certain minimum and maximum lending rates set for various types of business as shown in Table 1.5. Since 13 August 1984 the Comité de la Règlementation Bancaire has published the mid-month rate of the money market. In October 1985, this stood at 9.34 per cent. As indicated in Table 1.5, this rate is used to calculate the maximum lending rate allowable on certain loans. There is also a general interest rate ceiling, the usary rate, over which lending is not permitted. Since 2 September 1985 this rate has been 24.42 per cent.

The Comité also controls the rates paid on certain types of deposits.

TABLE 1.5   Interest rate guidelines in New Caledonia, 1985

	Rediscountable		Non-rediscountable	
	Minimum	*Maximum*	*Minimum*	*Maximum*
Business loans:				
commercial bill facilities	9.50	19.00	13.25	22.50
overdraft facilities	9.50	17.50	13.75	22.50
medium term loans	9.50	18.00	13.75	22.50
medium and long-term loans to development bodies	9.50	TTM+3	7.5	TTM+3
Personal loans:	–	–	13.75	24.00
Real estate loans:				
to normal borrowers	13.00	17.75	14.00	19.25
to development bodies	8.00	14.00	8.00	14.00

Note: TTM – taux moyen mensuel (money-market mid-month rate).

Source: Institut d'Emission d'Outre-Mer (1985) *Nouvelle-Calédonie Bulletin Trimestriel*, 45, December, p. 23.

Since 30 September 1985, for example, the maximum payable on savings accounts was 6 per cent per annum. Deposits of less than the equivalent of less than 500,000 French francs and for less than one year are subject to maximum interest rate ceilings, as are deposits of over 500,000 French francs, but for less than six months.

(iii) *Assets*

The commercial banks hold the bulk of their assets in the form of loans to clients, bills of exchange and other securities, and deposits with the Institut d'Emission d'Outre-Mer and other government bodies.

   Due to the industry's regulatory and rediscounting provisions, commercial bank loans should be divided into three types: those which are of little economic interest to the government or unsound and hence not rediscountable; conditional rediscountable loans; and automatic rediscountable loans. The latter are loans to those sectors such as agriculture, forestry, fishing, small and medium industry, hotels, handicrafts, tourism, and energy conservation. To be acceptable for automatic discounting, any equipment financed must be of French origin. However, even if the loan is in the automatic category, the Institut d'Emission d'Outre-Mer still rediscounts on a case-by-case basis and may choose not to rediscount if it considers the advance unsound or the project uneconomic.

In terms of charges, bank rates for commercial borrowers in late 1985 ranged from 15 to 18 per cent on equipment finance of less than two years, to 16.75 to 18.5 per cent on equipment finance for over two years, and Institut d'Emission refinanced lending, 9.5 per cent. There is an insurance expense in addition to the charges for equipment finance. Overdraft facilities are available to very good companies at the base lending rate, but most customers would pay a margin over this figure with an end cost of 15 to 17 per cent. In addition, there is a quarterly overdraft usage fee calculated at a rate of 0.25 per cent per annum on the highest overdrawn point over each quarter.

In terms of maturity, commercial bank advances can be divided between short-term advances of up to two years, medium up to seven years, and longer-term from seven to ten years. Generally the maximum terms available for commercial finance on small equipment purchases would be for up to two years. Investment finance might be for two to five years. An indication of the relative importance of short-term to medium- and long-term lending is provided in Table 1.6.

TABLE 1.6   Commercial bank in New Caledonia: loans, by type (figures in million CPF)

Short-term loans	15,254
Medium- and long-term loans	14,540
Total loans	29,794

Source: Institut d'Emission d'Outre-Mer (1985).

Where the borrower is unable to justify the loan on his own financial position, the banks will sometime provide the advance if supported by a third party guarantee. A larger firm, for example, will sometimes guarantee a bank loan to a smaller customer. Also, since 1982 an Interbank Guarantee Fund has operated to assist banks, the SICNC and Crédit Agricole in making advances to cottage industries, small and medium business, hotels, and fishing. The Fund can guarantee up to 70 per cent of the participating financial institution's advance up to 10 million CPF. The Fund is financed by mandatory contributions from both lenders and borrowers and is assisted with government subsidies.

In the case of a fairly large loan, a commercial bank may provide the finance in conjunction with other lenders. This is often via a local loan syndication or 'pool of banks'. In the case of a new hotel construction, establishing a new industry, or other purposes supported by SICNC lending, the SICNC will provide the longer-term finance and the bank the working capital.

In addition to industrial and commercial lending, the commercial banks also provide some funds to individual customers both for housing finance and as straight consumer lending. Visa, Master Card and American Express card facilities are also available through the banking system. The commercial bank involvement in housing finance is somewhat limited by the low rates available through the government support development institution and, to a much lesser extent, Crédit Agricole. The terms over which the banks can lend also limits their exposure to housing finance and most would require repayment generally within five to seven years. Other personal loans would be over one to three years.

In late 1985 banks charged 19.5 per cent for short-term personal loans under a year, 18.65 to 21.65 per cent for motor vehicle finance under three years, 20.65 per cent for ordinary personal loans of under three years, and 15.75 to 16.75 per cent for real estate finance of less than seven years. In addition to these costs, a life and disability insurance policy is required for the amount of the loan.

Given their long standing presence in the Territory, Banque Indosuez and Banque Nationale de Paris are the most important in terms of bank lending. As shown in Table 1.7, together they accounted for close to 60 per cent of all bank advances. Similarly as the most recent bank entry, Banque de Nouvelle-Calédonie has the smallest portfolio. The Banque Paribas Pacifique's figures, however, possibly understates its local importance. Traditionally Paribas takes a somewhat more selective approach in its banking business with its client base structured more like a merchant bank or wholesale banker than a traditional commercial bank. It also makes use of equity investment, board representation and associate companies to maximize its influence on customer performance.

In addition to direct lending, some French banks also provide some equity capital to their client firms. Of those banks in New Caledonia, Banque Paribas Pacifique is the most active and holds a number of shareholdings directly, as well as indirectly, through its local investment company parent, Société Néo-Calédoniènne de Développement et de Participations (known as CALDEV). At the end of 1984

TABLE 1.7   Commercial bank advances in New Caledonia, by bank, October 1985

	Short term	Longer term	Total CPM (m)	% of total
Banque Indosuez	6,264	4,681	10,945	36.7
Banque Nationale de Paris/Nouvelle-Calédonie	2,935	3,345	6,280	21.1
Société Générale Calédoniènne de Banque	2,691	2,397	5,088	17.1
Banque Paribas Pacifique	1,950	2,562	4,512	15.1
Banque de Nouvelle-Calédonie	1,414	1,555	2,969	10.1
Total	15,254	14,540	29,794	100.0

Source: Institut d'Emission d'Outre-Mer (1985).

these included 81.74 per cent of Société Havraise Calédoniènne, 96 per cent of Caldmin, 2.19 per cent of SA Touristique des Mers du Sud, 2.17 per cent of SCI Residence du Rocher, 2.63 per cent of Savexpress, 1.25 per cent of Société du Relais de Fayaoue, 3.33 per cent of Société d'Exploitation des Entrepôts Frigorifiques, 3.64 per cent of Air Calédonie International and 0.016 per cent of Soproner.

(iv) *Funding*

The commercial banks in New Caledonia raise their funding through a range of deposit accounts, their own capital funding, and the rediscounting facilities provided through the Institut d'Emission d'Outre-Mer. Of these the deposits and rediscounting facilities are the most important.

The deposits may come in the form of demand deposits or cheque accounts, savings deposits and term deposits. The latter can be provided by certificates with either bearer or registered. The negotiable certificates of deposits are bearer security. Of these forms, demand deposits have traditionally been the most important and still account for 42 per cent of commercial bank deposits. Term deposits, however, are also now very important and provide 40 per cent of the funding: the remaining 18 per cent comes from savings account deposits.

TABLE 1.8   Bank deposits in New Caledonia, by type and bank,
October 1985 (in million CPF)[1]

	Demand deposits	Savings deposits	Term deposits	Total deposits	% of total
Banque Indosuez	8,736	4,335	5,610	18,681	37.7
Banque Nationale	5,104	2,472	5,159	12,735	25.7
Société Générale	3,201	1,334	3,757	8,292	16.8
Banque Paribas	2,483	499	3,362	6,344	12.8
Banque de Nouvelle-Calédonie	1,294	299	1,868	3,461	7.0
Totals	20,818	8,939	19,756	49,513	100.0

Source: Institut d'Emission d'Outre-Mer (1985).

In terms of the local deposit raising, Banque Indosuez understandably is the market leader and it together with the Banque Nationale de Paris accounted for over half of total bank deposits. As shown in Table 1.8, Banque Indosuez's importance is particularly noticeable in both the demand and savings deposit areas where its extensive branch structure, compared to the other banks, has proved an advantage. In term deposits, however, where interest rates levels would be more important, it is only slightly larger than Banque Nationale de Paris.

Traditionally the commercial banks raise much more in deposits than required for their loan operations. Indeed, industry interviews suggest that there are just insufficient loan demands within New Caledonia to utilize the deposits raised and thus a large portion are sent to Paris for reinvestment by the banks' head offices. Recent political problems within New Caledonia, though, have also affected bank deposit raising. In late 1984, for example, the banking system lost some 2.5 billion CPF in deposits between December 1984 and January 1985. Most of these funds are deposited directly in metropolitan France although some were apparently invested in Tahiti. While no doubt some funds were also placed in various off-shore financial centres, these flows to other French areas do not require exchange control approval.

As discussed earlier, the Institut d'Emission d'Outre-Mer provides an important source of bank funding through its rediscount programme. In late 1985 these funds were provided at 6 per cent interest, but with the provision that a maximum of 9.5 per cent be charged to the end lender. In addition to these refinancing facilities, the Institut d'Emission may also provide the banks with short-term loans against the guarantee of their French parent bank.

The final area of importance is that of capital. Each bank, whether incorporated locally or operating as a branch, is required to allocate a certain portion of its capital in support of its New Caledonia operations. As shown in Table 1.9, the Banque Nationale de Paris's local subsidiary in 1984 actually had the largest paid-up capital.

TABLE 1.9   Commercial banks in New Caledonia, by local capital, 1984

	CPF
Banque Indosuez	1,000,000,000
Banque Nationale de Paris Nouvelle-Calédonie	1,278,400,000
Banque de Nouvelle-Calédonie	150,000,000
Banque Paribas Pacifique	400,000,000
Société Générale Calédoniènne de Banque	275,000,000

Source: Institut d'Emission d'Outre-Mer (1984) *Nouvelle-Calédonie Exercice 1984 Rapport d'Activité* pp. 69–70.

(v) *Representation*

Commercial banks operating in New Caledonia operate through branch offices both in Noumea and elsewhere in Territory. These branches accept deposits and make limited personal loans and other small lending: larger applications require head office evaluation and approval. All trade finance and similar banking business is centralized at head office.

The banks' branch structure reflects the concentration of the population and commerce within the capital. As shown in Table 1.10, their 26 branches in Noumea comprise 60 per cent of their total branches. Table 1.10 also reflects the importance of the Banque Indosuez which has 56 per cent of the total branches and 70 per cent of bank branches in rural areas.

In addition to full-time branches, some banks also operate small bank-staffed agencies on a part-time basis. The Banque Indosuez, for example, operates four or five of these facilities at employer offices and one island location. The Banque Nationale de Paris, too, operates a small agency for two hours a week in Periodique at the Nepoui mining site. It also, when required, operates a foreign exchange

TABLE 1.10   Commercial bank representation in New Caledonia, 1985

	Noumea branches*	Other branches	Total branches
Banque de Nouvelle-Calédonie	2	–	2
Banque Indosuez	12	12	24
Banque Nationale de Paris/NC	5	2	7
Banque Paribas Pacifique	2	1	3
Société Générale Calédoniènne	5	2	7
Totals	26	17	43

* Includes main branch or head office.

Source: Industry Interviews (1985).

facility on cruise ships when they visit the port. Banque Paribas similarly operates a foreign exchange office at the Surf Hotel.

Though there is little question that Banque Indosuez will retain its dominance in the local market, the maintenance of its present branch structure has been under question ever since the 1975 merger of Banque de l'Indochine into Banque Indosuez. The merged institution has subsequently adopted Indosuez's approach to banking and has concentrated on business or wholesale rather than retailing banking. In contrast Banque de l'Indochine was active in both areas. In 1985 Banque Indosuez was active in retail banking only in New Caledonia, French Polynesia and Saudia Arabia. Within metropolitan France, it had gradually closed or sold off most of its remaining branches other than its head office. Banque Indosuez had been intended to conduct a major rationalization of its branch network within New Caledonia and close all marginal offices. This process would have shut at least half the present branches but, as with the creation of a local subsidiary, the matter was postponed due to the local political situation.

(vi) *Staffing*

In 1985 the level of Melanesian participation within the banking industry was relatively small, given New Caledonia's over-all population, but possibly there is a greater percentage of Melanesians in those branches outside of New Caledonia. Banque Indosuez – as both the largest and oldest bank – had the highest percentage of Melanesian staff with approximately 15 to 20 per cent of the total. What is perhaps not so obvious is the relatively high level of French-born persons among the banking staff. For example, of some 30 senior officers within Banque Indosuez's operations, there was only one Melanesian and one locally-born New Caledonian. This is due to the major migration of French settlers in the early 1970s rather than bank policy. Only five of Banque Indosuez's 350 staff, for example, were on secondment from metropolitan France: the rest were locally hired. The other banks have similar staff compositions. Industry interviews suggest that relatively few New Caledonians or Melanesians seemed interested in banking as a career, and, despite recruitment at the school level, the industry had seen little change in the over-all mix of employees.

TABLE 1.11   Commercial bank staffing in New Caledonia, 1985

Banque de Nouvelle-Calédonie	n.a.
Banque Indosuez	350
Banque Nationale de Paris/NC	180
Banque Paribas Pacifique	63
Société Générale Calédoniènne	n.a.
Total	n.a.

Source: Industry interviews (1985).

Caisse de Crédit Agricole Mutuel

The Caisse de Crédit Agricole Mutuel de la Nouvelle Calédonie et Dépendances was established in 1931 and commenced operations in 1934. It is a co-operative agricultural savings bank designed to provide finance for agricultural purposes and operates under a name similar to one of metropolitan France's largest banking institutions. New Caledonia's Crédit Agricole is a somewhat more modest operation but is nevertheless important in providing short- and medium-term financing for agricultural development. Over 1984, for example, Crédit Agricole provided slightly more than the SICNC to the agricultural sector with 50.9 per cent of the total compared with 48.2 per cent for SICNC. The remaining 0.9 per cent came directly from the Territorial government.

The bank was created following the same basic provisions as co-operative agricultural savings banks in France, and initially received substantial government assistance. The Territorial government has subsequently provided other funds from time to time, but no additional money has been forthcoming since 1978. In addition to its own funds, the government 'arranged for a loan of 1 million francs to it by the Banque de l'Indochine, but this sum was so small that it could not meet more than a small fraction of the local needs'.[26] Indeed, the demand for agricultural finance was significant for as one study commented, 'until it was established, the only source of loans to individual farmers were the Banque de l'Indochine and some of Noumea's trading firms'.[27]

It should be stressed, although operating with a similar name as the major co-operative banking institution in France, the New Caledonia company is a totally separate entity and has no relationship with its mainland counterpart. It was suggested in some interviews, though, that the competition in retail banking would be greatly increased if a merger was arranged between these Territorial and metropolitan institutions.

(i) *Assets*

As shown in Table 1.12, Crédit Agricole holds the bulk of its assets in the form of loans to members: some 82 per cent of total assets in 1984. These for short- , medium- and long-term maturities. Short-term loans are generally over 3 to 24 months while medium-term finance is available for periods of from two to seven years and longer-term advances are for over seven years. As shown in Table 1.12, medium-term advances are the most important and in 1984 accounted for some 64 per cent of Crédit Agricole's total assets.

The interest rate charged on all loans is currently 9.5 per cent per annum. This rate is based on the interest rate allowed under the Institut d'Emission's rediscounting scheme.[28] As with the commercial banks, Crédit Agricole can rediscount its advances at a rate of 6 per cent, provided it charges no more than a 3.5 per cent margin to its customers. Though Crédit Agricole only discounts approximately 30 per cent of its advances, it uses the same 9.5 per cent on all rural advances. Those borrowers with more than 50 per cent of their income from non-agricultural sources, however, are charged 11.5 per cent. In addition to interest, all borrowers must pay an additional 0.5 per cent per annum life insurance charge based on the initial advance.

Crédit Agricole's advances are generally either unsecured or made

TABLE 1.12   Caisse de Crédit Agricole Mutuel: assets and liabilities,
31 December 1984

Assets:	
Net fixed assets	2,349,136
Other assets	21,050
Long-term loans	16,431,833
Medium-term loans	578,488,367
Short-term loans	86,335,880
Loans in arrears	69,896,808
Other debtors	478,269
Comptes de régularisation	24,830,791
Deposits with IEOM[a]	1,068,172
Deposits with Banque Indosuez	9,249,481
Deposits with Cheques Postaux	42,536
Deposits with Caisse des Dépôts et Consignations	89,838,932
Deposits with Treasury	26,418,571
Cash	839,619
Total assets	906,289,445
Liabilities:	
Capital	90,782,400
Statutory reserves	159,929,781
Earnings carried forward	1,366,229
Provisions	13,141,322
Treasury donations	26,418,571
Long-term borrowings	18,580,192
Medium-term borrowings	413,485,883
FDEB borrowings[b]	36,000,000
Funds managed for the Territory	3,897,937
Short-term IEOM borrowings[a]	24,329,000
Medium-term IEOM borrowings[a]	78,086,000
Deposits at 4 per cent	2,085,210
Demand Deposits	12,966,042
SICNC – FGI funds	2,480,266
Approved loans not fully drawn	12,276,015
Other creditors	69,359
Regular accounts	4,643,645
Social organizations	1,274,991
Dividends payable	4,476,602
Total liabilities	906,289,445

[a] Institut d'Emission d'Outre-Mer (Institute for Currency Issue Overseas).
[b] Fonds de Concours pour le Développement de l'Elevage Bovin (Development Fund for Cattle Raising).

Source: Caisse de Crédit Agricole Mutuel de la Nouvelle-Calédonie et Dépendances (1984) *Rapports du Conseil d'Administration et des Commissaires aux Comptes sur l'Exercice 1984*, pp. 24–5.

TABLE 1.13   Caisse de Crédit Agricole Mutuel: new loans in 1984, by type

	Short-term	Medium-term	Total lending
Beef cattle	36,660	70,100	106,760
Pigs	1,500	3,850	5,350
Sheep	–	500	500
Poultry	17,088	–	17,088
Grains	7,450	11,670	19,120
Market gardening	2,068	7,797	9,865
Supplies	250	1,565	1,815
Fruit	–	2,160	2,160
Timber	520	–	520
Coffee	8,000	–	8,000
Dairy cattle	560	2,380	2,940
Aquaculture	–	1,000	1,000
Potatoes	30,305	4,180	34,485
Others	–	26,000	26,000
Total	104,401	131,202	235,603

Source: Caisse de Crédit Agricole Mutuel (1985).

against a warrant over cattle or fixed assets. Loans of one million CPF or more normally require mortgage security. Much of its lending is to finance agricultural equipment purchases, but Crédit Agricole frequently finances cattle purchases, crop financing, and piggeries: as shown in Table 1.13, beef cattle is the most important activity with some 45 per cent of the advances made over 1984. It will also provide finance for housing purposes or for land purchase in rural areas. Housing loans must be repaid within seven years, but land purchase finance can have terms of up to 15 years and a deferral of repayments of up to three years. These loans are normally made in conjunction with the Territorial government purchase plans. As shown in Table 1.13, there were no long-term advances made over 1984.

The advance may be for as high as 80 per cent of the project's requirements. As the borrower needs to provide the remainder, plus the 5 per cent worth of shares, before receiving the loans, their equity is about 24 per cent of the total. The repayment terms are somewhat flexible and can be arranged to suit the borrowers' requirements. Approximately a third of borrowers repay their loans through monthly repayments while the remainder pay on an annual basis.

In addition to its own operations, Crédit Agricole also manages some lending activities on the behalf of other bodies. Its Co-operative Fund for the Development of Cattle Farming is one such example. The fund is financed by levy of 5 francs per kilo on all meat slaughtered in the Territory. The Fund specifically finances government-agency-approved farm development plans for better pasture areas, irrigation, fencing, farm building, breeding stock and otherwise improving conditions for local cattle raising.

(ii) *Funding*

Crédit Agricole obtains its funds from three major sources: its own retained earnings and member capital and borrowings. It also raises deposits from members.

As was shown in Table 1.12, Crédit Agricole obtained some 31.8 per cent of funds in 1984 from its own capital, reserves and provisions. Its shares have a par value of 200 CPF each. Besides any shares purchased when joining Crédit Agricole, its members are required to purchase additional shares in line with any borrowings. These must be purchased before the loan is made and be the equivalent of 5 per cent of the amount borrowed from Crédit Agricole: in the case of short-term loans, the maximum share purchase required is for 100,000 CPF. When the loan is repaid, the borrower can sell his shares to other potential borrowers. Crédit Agricole is not directly involved in the sale of existing shares, but can issue new shares for sale directly to members if no existing shares are available for purchase. These shares do pay dividends and over 1982–4 Crédit Agricole paid a dividend of 9.86 to 9.99 on its capital.

Borrowings account for some 51.5 per cent of Crédit Agricole's funding. In addition to normal arrangements, the Territorial government has also provided some funding without interest, but there has been no additional Territorial money since 1978.

While Crédit Agricole may accept deposits, it has not been particularly aggressive in this regard. Traditionally it has paid relatively low rates of interest and this has not encouraged depositors. On 1 July 1984 it raised the rate from 4 to 6 per cent per annum, but even the new rates have not been sufficient to attract much money and in 1984 deposits comprised only 1.3 per cent of Crédit Agricole's total funding.

(iii) *Representation and staffing*

Crédit Agricole operates from only one office, its headquarters in Noumea, and with some five staff members. This is made possible by the use of the Territory's agricultural department service to help evaluate the borrower's proposal and the postal system or commercial banks for the repayments: about 80 per cent of repayments are paid direct via the banking system.

Loan applications may also be made by mail and Crédit Agricole estimates that approximately half of its business is accomplished in this manner. Access to its head office, however, still seems important in the mix of business as most borrowers are located on the west coast of the main island where a good road network allows easy access to Noumea.

Caisse d'Epargne

As in metropolitan France, the government-owned savings bank, the Caisse d'Epargne, provides basic savings facilities for Territory residents both from its own head office in Noumea and outside of Noumea through agency arrangements with Post Offices throughout the Territory. As a member of the Groupement Regional d'Epargne et de Prévoyance (Regional Savings Bank and Provident Society Group, sometimes referred to as 'squirrel' syndicate after their common corporate logo), accounts with the Caisse d'Epargne in New Caledonia can be accessed through special arrangements elsewhere in France and in some cases through the French Embassy service.

Caisse d'Epargne is one of New Caledonia's older institutions. As one report commented, 'a local savings bank had been created by the decree of October 5, 1923 but a limit on 5000 francs was placed on the amount that any single person could deposit'.[29] This understandably limited its competitive position. Caisse d'Epargne in its current form dates back to 1928 and over time its position has been improved through the introduction of special tax concessions.

Since 1985 Caisse d'Epargne has raised deposits both through savings passbook accounts and savings bonds or certificates. Each of these in turn are structured to provide two different types of taxation arrangements.

In terms of savings passbook accounts, Caisse d'Epargne offers an 'A' account and a 'B' account. The 'A' accounts have a minimum deposit of 200 CPF and a maximum level of 1,250,000 CPF. They pay interest currently at 6 per cent, but this interest is not subject to taxation. The 'B' accounts also have a minimum deposit of 200 CPF, but have no upper limit. The 6 per cent interest paid on these deposits is fully taxable, but at a special tax rate of only 12 per cent. As an additional incentive, an insurance premium of 273 CPF per year deducted from one's account provides an accidental death coverage for 'A' account depositors. This will pay one's estate an amount double the then balance with a minimum payment of 90,000 CPF and a maximum of 1,000,000 CPF. As of September 1985 the savings bank had 24,274 accounts.

The savings bank's bonds or savings certificates also come in two forms: either as inscribed stock and subject to a 12 per cent withholding tax, or in a bearer form where a 27 per cent withholding tax is applied. Otherwise these securities are the same in other respects. They are sold in denomination of 20,000, 100,000 and 200,000 CPF, as well as in their French franc equivalent (1100; 5500; 11,000). These certificates are similar to US savings bonds, in that to gain the full 10.5 per cent interest rate, they must be held for their full maturity. Thus, in late 1985, savers would earn the full rate only if they hold the bonds for 5 years. The bonds will then continue to pay interest at that rate for an additional five years if desired. After ten years, however, interest is no longer paid. Earlier redemption would result in a lower interest rate: 6 per cent after one year, 7 per cent after two years, 8 per cent after three years and 9 per cent after four years.

Centre de Chèques Postaux

As in metropolitan France, the government's postal system plays an important role in providing basic financial services through its offices. They have been in operation within New Caledonia since 1924. These services are provided both directly in the case of cheque accounts and postal money orders, and indirectly as agents for the government savings bank, Caisse d'Epargne.

In New Caledonia the Post Office has 39 offices throughout the Territory so that even where commercial banks are not represented, smaller towns still receive basic banking services. It offers its own current accounts, cheque books, money orders and direct payment facilities throughout the Territory and savings bank services in all post offices but the main office in Noumea – Caisse d'Epargne's own Noumea office handles this business.

Except for the General Post Office in Noumea, these postal banking services are operated by normal postal workers rather than special banking staff.

Société Immobilière et de Crédit de Nouvelle-Calédonie (SICNC)

The Société Immobilière et de Crédit de Nouvelle-Calédonie (SICNC) was established in 1955 as a 50-50 joint venture between the French government development bank, Caisse Centrale de Coopération Economique and the Territorial government. It was initially a development banking and housing finance institution which provided medium- and long-term finance for housing, agriculture, industry and tourism at concessional rates of interest. In 1966, however, when the massive immigration accompanying the nickel boom required a substantial expansion of the Territory's housing facilities, SICNC also became a property developer, builder and property manger. It still builds, owns and rents out its own stock of residential properties, and in late 1985 owned 2570 apartments.

(i) *Assets*

While property ownership and development finance are the SICNC's dual operational role, this is not reflected in the asset figures where in 1984 real estate holdings account for some 18 per cent of total assets compared to 57 per cent for the loan portfolio. The other major holding shown in Table 1.14 is that of cash and demand deposits which accounted for an additional 18 per cent.

The SICNC provides finance for a range of purposes to include both housing, agriculture and commercial projects. It will also provide some trade finance. As a rule, productive projects receive the lower rates. Housing projects might also receive lower rates if viewed as fulfilling a social welfare purpose. In the case of residential housing, it will provide 80 per cent of the costs financed over a period of 15 years at an interest rate of 8 to 13 per cent. Commercial or agricultural loans would be made similarly with a charge of 8 to 12 per cent.

Most SICNC advances are for long maturities. Of its 1984 advances of the equivalent of 2,273,814,000 million French francs, for example, 85.6 per cent were for long-term loans. In terms of loan numbers, the breakdown of lending over 1984 was 329 long-term, 49 medium-term and 25 short-term advances. Since the late 1970s it has typically made 400 to 500 loans per year.

As shown in Table 1.15, loans relating to real estate was the largest lending category with 42.8 per cent of 1984 advances. These loans typically finance the construction of new houses and the SICNC is the

TABLE 1.14   Société Immobilière et de Crédit de la Nouvelle-Calédonie: assets and liabilities, 31 December 1984

Assets	Fr F (m)
Planning expenses	1,041,667
Land	316,913,278
Urban rental properties	2,910,279,408
Other rental properties	66,443,624
Service buildings	150,625,718
Furniture and equipment	67,851,489
Transport equipment	10,362,230
Buildings for sale	734,760
Share investments	23,840,909
Secured deposits	2,066,883
Supplies and maintenance products	8,729,994
Houses for sale	4,608,000
Loans to clients	9,420,271,315
Doubtful loans	102,393,552
Disputed loans	168,032,763
Irrecoverable funds	311
Funds due from tenants	33,682,344
Other debtors	29,735,871
Cheques awaiting collection	5,174,879
Cash at bank and on hand	3,021,655,141
Prepayments	3,712,653
Receivables	271,359,517
Variations on asset values	925,548
Total assets	16,620,441,854

Liabilities	
Capital	420,000,000
Statutory reserves	57,766,814
Reserves on buildings	137,591,229
Revaluation reserves	176,028,200
Resultat en instance d'affection	(490,466,051)
Endowment for agricultural loans	10,000,000
Endowment for agric. rediscounting	294,066,744
Endowment for problem businesses	120,000,000
Guarantee fund	230,703,117
Provisions	1,773,086,154
Long-term borrowing – real estate	3,322,801,368
Long-term borrowing – lending	8,968,358,471
Subordinate borrowings – EIB[a]	49,278,498
Participations – EIB[a]	14,895,264
Medium-term rediscounting – IEOM[b]	189,413,487
French fund for Vanuatu refugees	3,348,945

Territory Fund for lending	133,831,276
Territory Fund for real estate	35,667,281
Guarantee Fund	56,076,245
Money owed suppliers	10,964,665
Deposits from tenants	55,210,502
Other personal borrowings	115,660,851
Other creditors	160,585,135
Short-term borrowings – IEOM[b]	26,458,725
Short-term borrowings – real estate	187,098,542
Short-term borrowings – lending	423,219,371
Accrued expenses	137,273,872
Prepayments by others	656,851
Variations on liabilities values	866,298
Total liabilities	16,620,441,854

[a] European Investment Bank.
[b] Institut d'Emission d'Outre-Mer.

Source: Société Immobilière et de Crédit de la Nouvelle-Calédonie (1984) *Report d'Activité Exercice 1984*, pp. 76–7.

TABLE 1.15   Société Immobilière et de Crédit de la Nouvelle-Calédonie: advances, by type, over 1984

	F Fr (m)	%
Real estate finance – Noumea	426,564	18.8
Real estate finance – interior	425,262	18.7
Real estate finance – tribal	121,036	5.3
Loans for agriculture and fishing	313,009	13.8
Loans for commerce and hotels	560,580	24.6
Loans for industry and handicrafts	132,836	5.8
Local government	144,847	6.4
Public collectives	149,680	6.6
Total advances	2,273,814	100.0

Source: Société Immobilière et de Crédit de la Nouvelle-Calédonie (1984) *Report d'Activité Exercice 1984*, p. 14.

major source of construction finance within the Territory. Generally a family would require an income of between 100,000 and 500,000 CPF per month to qualify for SICNC real estate financing. Those with higher incomes are expected to seek finance through the commercial banks or finance companies.

Some SICNC lending is done in conjunction with other bodies. In the purchase of land, for example, the SICNC provides 50 per cent of the financing, the Territorial government will lend another 20 per cent, and the purchaser is expected to have the remainder as a deposit. The SICNC loan is over 15 years at 7.5 per cent interest and the Territory loan is for 20 years at 4.5 per cent: repayments on the Territory loan do not start for 15 years.

In addition to its own funds, the SICNC also helps clients to raise funds through the banking system by providing loan guarantees. These funds are organized as separate guarantee pools within SICNC, with each allocated a specific amount and purpose. The Tribal Habitat Guarantee Fund is the largest fund, and at the end of 1984 accounted for close to 50 per cent of all guarantee funds. Other purposes include agriculture, fishing, handicraft, commerce and debt reconstruction.

Despite its social and development emphasis, the SICNC, like the commercial banks, has indicated that it has had more than adequate funds available for lending requirements. The real problem was to find the suitable projects and the right borrowers.

In addition to its lending operations, the SICNC can also provide equity finance to clients. Some of these investments are funded under a special credit facility provided by the European Investment Bank. In addition the SICNC also holds shares on behalf of the Territory of New Caledonia in some commercial ventures. At the end of 1984 these holdings included a 70 per cent interest in Air Calédonie. SICNC also invests on its own behalf and has shares in the Société de Développement et d'Expansion du Pacifique, Sedecal, Secal, Savexpress, Sodacal, Relais de Fayoue, and Aquamon. At the end of 1984 these investments had a cost of 4,450,909 CPF and a market value of 23,840,909 CPF.

(ii) *Funding*

As was shown in Table 1.14, the SICNC obtains the major portion of its funds from longer-term borrowings. In 1984, for example, its borrowing for real estate purposes accounted for 20.9 per cent of its total liabilities and borrowing for commercial purposes another 53.9 per cent.

The SICNC can fund its advances by refinancing its loans through special lines of credit provided by the Caisse Centrale de Cooperation Economique and the Institut d'Emission d'Outre-Mer. As a rule, Caisse Central provides the financing for the larger and longer advances while the Institut d'Emission finances the smaller, short- to medium-term projects. It also received some funds through the European Investment Bank.

The funds from Caisse Central are provided over a 15-year period with a 5-year grace period and at only 5.5 per cent interest. Each loan refinanced under this facility must be justified before Caisse Central will release the funds. Each year Caisse Central establishes a new facility, and in 1985 some 2.53 billion CPF were provided. In contrast, the Institut d'Emission concentrates its refinancing in the medium term with 5- to 7-year funding.

In addition to its own capital and the various endowment and guarantee funds shown in Table 1.14, the SICNC may accept deposits from its loan clients but since late 1985 it had not done so.

(iii) *Staffing and representation*

In late 1985 the SICNC had a staff of approximately 200, of which 50 to 70 worked in the banking side of the business and the remainder in the housing activities. It was not possible for SICNC to provide a specific breakdown as many administrative positions service both divisions.

In terms of representation, the SICNC has branches in Poindimié and Kone, in addition to its Noumea headquarters. In 1985 it seemed quite likely that given the economic development powers planned for the four regional councils, the SICNC branch representation in each region would be desirable and other offices opened accordingly.

In the meantime, SICNC also works in conjunction with the Territory's Rural Development Office and Lands Office. The latter is involved in the transfer of land from European to Melanesian ownership while the former advises on how these properties can be best utilized.

Other Development Institutions

In addition to the SICNC two financial institutions headquartered in Paris also provide development finance funds and maintain offices within New Caledonia. These are the French-government-owned Caisse Centrale de Cooperation Economique, and the private-sector-sponsored consortium, Société de Développement et d'Expansion du Pacifique.

(i) *Caisse Centrale de Cooperation Economique*

The Caisse Centrale de Cooperation Economique (CCCE) is the French government's development bank designed to assist Third World countries and French overseas territories through concessional long-term lending and financial advisory assistance.

Caisse Central was established in London by the Free French forces during the Second World War to serve as the government's central bank. At that time Free France consisted mainly of the French colonies in Africa, and slightly later New Caledonia. The Banque de France has since resumed the government's central banking functions, but Caisse Central was retained for development purposes.

In terms of its lending, the concessional rates are dependent on the purpose, and the borrowing country's state of development. In the case of New Caledonia lending, for example, these rates range between 6 and 8 per cent and those to developing countries may be even lower. In terms of maturity, New Caledonia loans are typically for 8 to 15 years.

Though most Caisse·Centrale loans are to finance infrastructure, its lending is designed for those projects that can in turn provide revenue through which the loan can be repaid. In New Caledonia, for example, Caisse Centrale finances productive and public infrastructure projects such as electricity supply, water supply, and irrigation services. Its customers are confined to public sector institutions. Thus it will lend to the Territory government, statutory corporations, local governments and possibly, depending on their end structure, the regional council governments.

Caisse Centrale importance, however, is not confined to public sector lending. It is also an important source of private financing, but these funds are provided indirectly through government development banks. Indeed, Caisse Centrale has been instrumental in establishing many such institutions in former French possessions. In the case of New Caledonia, Caisse Centrale was instrumental in the establishment of the Société Immobilière et de Crédit de Nouvelle-Calédonie (SICNC), the Territory's development and housing finance institutions, as a 50-50 joint venture with the Territorial government. Caisse Centrale's private sector lending is then conducted indirectly through refinancing facility with SICNC.

In addition to concessional finance, the Caisse Centrale will also provide market rate loans to large projects which are raised from commercial sources under a French government guarantee. It may also raise money from borrowings in other currencies, but all lending is conducted in French francs.

(ii) *Société de Développement et d'Expansion du Pacifique*

The Société de Développement et d'Expansion du Pacifique (SODEP) was established in Paris in 1961 as a development banking venture between a mixture of commercial banks and government agencies. In 1985 some of its major shareholders included the Banque Indosuez, Banque Nationale de Paris, Société Générale, Crédit Lyonnais, Cofimerle (a Paribas affiliate), the Banque de Tahiti, and the SICNC. It is intended to provide medium- and long-term development finance to projects in the French Pacific territories which create employment and competition, innovation, saving energy or promote greater efficiency.

These special investment loans may provide up to 70 per cent of the finance required within the project, and have a maturity of 6 to 10 years for medium-term advances, and of 12 to 15 years for longer-term finance. In some cases certain projects which do not meet the SODEP's normal investment requirements, may still receive a SODEP finance at a market rate of interest but receive an interest rate concession of 2 per cent from SODEP's operations. Finally, in addition to its lending activities, SODEP may also undertake equity positions in client companies.

SODEP obtains its funding from commercial loans and concessional government funding. It sometimes also receives a subsidy from the government which allows it to provide a concessional lending subsidy to the end borrower.

In terms of the Pacific region, SODEP has become relatively inactive and made its last loan in New Caledonia in 1982, but is still an active lender in Tahiti. This is partly a function of lower demand for funds within New Caledonia, increased local interest rates, and competition from government lending agencies. In late 1985 it was mainly a holding operation which collected the payments on its outstanding loans and managed a small equity portfolio of holdings in local companies. It does maintain a small office in Noumea on a shared basis with various Banque Indosuez affiliates. Banque Indosuez also provides much of SODEP's management on a management contract basis.

TABLE 1.16   Finance and leasing companies in New Caledonia, 1985

Firm	Affiliation
Société Financière pour le Crédit Bail	Société Générale
Crédit Calédonien et Tahitien	Banque Indosuez
Crédit Commercial de Noumea	Banque Indosuez
Crédit Foncier et Immobilier de la Nouvelle-Calédonie et de Polynésie	Banque Indosuez
Crédit du Pacifique	Crédit Lyonnais
Sud-Pacifique Location	Banque Indosuez
et Noumea Bail	Crédit Lyonnais
Sogener	Société Générale
Sofinauto	Société Générale

Source: Industry interviews (1985).

Finance Companies

The finance companies are the other major group of financial institutions within New Caledonia. Their activities vary considerably from company to company but include real estate finance, consumer credit and business loans. At present some companies are active in the leasing business as well, but most have affiliated leasing companies for that purpose. Some firms also use affiliates to keep their real estate and consumer finance operations under separate corporate structures. This position, though, is expected to change over 1986 as new financial institution legislation, which requires finance companies to have a paid-up capital of some 135 million CPF, will more than offset any benefits afforded under the older multicorporate structure. As a result, there should be a significant rationalization of existing consumer, real estate and leasing companies under the one corporate structure. Another area of legislative-caused changes in 1986 will come when the Territory's new consumer credit protection regulations take effect.

As shown in Table 1.16 there is substantial room for rationalization, particularly among those non-bank financial institutions affiliated with Banque Indosuez. It is the majority shareholder in all but Crédit Commercial de Noumea. Its main operation, Crédit Calédonien et Tahiti, is 68 per cent owned by Banque Indosuez, 13 per cent by its affiliate, Banque Francis de l'Asie; 4 per cent by Uneca; 2 per cent by the Comptoir de Représentation Industrièlles Minières et Commerciale, 2 per cent by Ballande, and the remaining 11 per cent by many smaller shareholders.

(i) *Development*

As with many other aspects of New Caledonia finance, most finance companies trace their origins to the nickel boom and high prosperity of the late 1960s and early 1970s. As the mineral expansion required a major increase in the work force, there was substantial immigration and the new settlers needed to establish their own households as soon as possible. The commercial banks were not so active in this type of consumer lending and thus the finance companies developed to meet the need. They were very successful in this respect and helped both to consumerize the local economy and make it more dependent on metropolitan France.

As the banks could refinance equipment loans at a special rate with the Institut d'Emission and, as most finance companies were owned by the banks, the finance companies were initially given similar treatment in terms of rediscounting facilities. Up until 1976 the finance companies could borrow most of their funds from the commercial banks and the Institut d'Emission. The former provide the funds at around 9 per cent interest and the latter at a 7 per cent fixed rate. At the end of 1976, however, the Institut's rediscounting facility was withdrawn and the industry became almost solely dependent on bank financing.

As with many businesses in the French Pacific, most finance companies operate both in New Caledonia and Tahiti. This is reflected in the name of Crédit Calédonien et Tahitien, but most finance companies have a similar dual exposure: Crédit Calédonien held approximately 57 per cent in Tahiti loans compared with 43 per cent in New Caledonia.

(ii) *Regulations*

In 1984 there was a major reform in metropolitan France of the financial sector in which the finance companies were required to have a much higher level of paid-up capital and placed under direct central bank control. Thus, as with banks, finance companies are now authorized to conduct business by the National Committee of Credit.

Under the new regulations, finance companies are limited as to the growth of their receivables. For example, the amount outstanding as of the end of 31 December 1985 could only be a certain percentage of those outstanding as of 1 January 1985. In the case of leasing companies this was set at 109.5 per cent and 110 per cent for ordinary finance companies. Each year a new limit is set based on the then outstanding amount. There are quarterly reference points as well.

In addition to these lending limitations, the finance companies are also subject to reserve deposit requirements. These include deposits equal to 5 per cent of their non-refinanceable outstanding receivables in a non-interest bearing account with the Institut d'Emission. In addition, a finance company must also deposit a further percentage for every 0.5 per cent of advances made over and above the allowable reference figures.

(iii) *Consumer and business lending*

The finance companies traditionally charge much more than commercial banks for their finance. In late 1985, for example, Credit du Pacifique charged 19 to 23 per cent with an average of 21 per cent. Crédit Calédonien charged fairly similar rates with a range of 17 to 25 per cent for personal loans and 15 to 21.5 per cent for businesses. While finance company loans are made with adjustable interest rates, these rates cannot be varied without government approval: a process which takes approximately 2 months.

Most finance company advances are on terms of 24 to 36 months, except for motor vehicles, for which finance is provided on terms up to 48 months. The repayments must normally be less than 35 per cent of the borrower's salary and are typical secured by a warrant over the consumer durable purchased with the advance.

These advances are funded through borrowings from the commercial banks with each finance company raising the bulk of its funding from its affiliated commercial bank. These vary according to company and market conditions but are typically tied to the wholesale money-market rates. Crédit Calédonien, for example, raises its money both through borrowings with the local Banque Indosuez branch as well as some Paris-based raisings. These funds were borrowed at a margin over the one-month money-market rate in Paris.

(iv) *Real estate financing*

Banque Indosuez's non-bank real estate financing in New Caledonia is conducted by Crédit Foncier et Immobilier de la Nouvelle-Calédonie et de la Polynésie (CFI). It is a wholly-owned subsidiary of the Banque Indosuez group and 73.11 per cent of the shares are owned directly by the Banque. As its name implies, it operates in both New Caledonia and Tahiti, but its business in New Caledonia accounts for some 60 per cent of its 1.3 billion CPF in outstanding loans. It is the only finance company specializing in real estate financing.

CFI obtains much of its funds through borrowings in the French money market. These are raised (depending on market conditions) on terms of one to five years, and normally structured to allow spread liability maturity. While the amount and maturity are determined by CFI in New Caledonia, the rates are a function of the market and it uses Banque Indosuez's Paris office to arrange the actual borrowings in return for a one-eighth of a per cent margin over the commercial loan rate. In its last major borrowings three years ago, it paid 14.75 to 15 per cent.

CFI relends these funds at rates of 16.5 to 17 per cent on terms of up to four years in the case of land purchase or development, or up to seven years for construction finance or the purchase of an existing home. Most of its business is with individuals for residential properties. It also tends to be more active in financing the purchase of existing homes as financing for new homes can generally be arranged at less cost through SICNC.

(v) *Leasing*

Leasing companies' major growth started in the early 1980s when the refinancing rates rose above the industry's interest rate ceilings so that the finance companies were exposed to almost negative margins and thus forced to stop lending. Finance company money in June 1981, for example, cost approximately 19.93 per cent compared to an average customer loan rate of 20.5 per cent. In contrast, leasing companies were providing finance at rates of 24 to 26 per cent.

Since late 1985 the major leasing companies in New Caledonia have included et Noumea Bail, Sud-Pacifique Location and Société Financière pour le Crédit Bail (SOFINBAIL). Each of these companies are in turn affiliated with one of the major banking groups. Société Financière pour le Crédit Bail, for example, is a Société Générale subsidiary. Sud-Pacifique is a Banque Indosuez affiliate but only indirectly: 92.7 per cent of its shares are held by Crédit Calédonien and Tahitian (CCT) and remainder are held by small New

Caledonia and Tahiti shareholders, but CCT plans to purchase these smaller holdings in order to consolidate the operations into one corporate structure. Finally, et Noumea Bail is a division of Tahiti Bail du Pacifique which trades under the former name in New Caledonia. This company is owned 69 per cent by Crédipac, 20 per cent by the Banque de Tahiti, 5 per cent by Slibail and the remainder by individuals: Crédipac in turn is a Crédit Lyonnaise affiliate.

In terms of their respective operations, leasing companies effectively finance consumer durables (mainly cars) whereby in return for a monthly rent the consumer has the option to purchase the leased item at its residual value at the end of the lease. As leasing was not then considered finance company business, the leasing companies operated free from the controls placed on finance companies. This allowed them to charge relatively higher rates for their effective advances. In late 1985, for example, et Noumea Bail's lease finance rates ranged from between 21 to 24.5 per cent with an average of 23.5 per cent, while Sud-Pacifique Location charged an effective 24 to 25 per cent per annum on its car lease finance.

General Insurance

The insurance industry in New Caledonia is well developed in terms of available services, but there are no locally incorporated insurance companies. As with other Pacific countries, motor vehicle insurance is the major source of local premium income. Third party motor vehicle insurance is compulsory, and those drivers who for some reason are not insured are covered through a guarantee fund operated jointly by all local insurers. Fire insurance is next in importance, followed by marine insurance. Workers' compensation coverage, together with sickness or medical insurance, is effectively a monopoly under a local government scheme, CAFAT, and hence is not a source of premiums.

There is still considerable scope for expanding the level of premium income as many people within the Territory are inadequately covered against even the most basic risks. It is apparently common, for example, for those people living in brick homes not to insure them.

Little reinsurance business is conducted within the Territory as this is done at the head office level in Paris, or elsewhere overseas. There is, however, some spreading of risks between local insurers, with one company endorsing the policy of another for a percentage of the

TABLE 1.17   General insurance companies in New Caledonia: 1984
(New Caledonia sales in French francs)

Groupement Français Assurances (GFA)[a]	29,448,111
Les Mutuelles de Mans Accidents (MFG)*	16,464,874
Assurances Générales de France (AGF)[a]*	13,003,964
Commercial Union[b]	10,302,525
La Mutuelle Capma	9,897,059
QBE Insurance[c]	9,749,822
L'Union des Assurances de Paris Urbaine (UAP)*	9,173,663
La Concorde	8,492,402
New Hampshire Insurance[d]	7,713,679
Assurances du Groupe de Paris (AGP)	6,503,661
Le Secours Assurances	4,575,703
Préservatrice Foncière Assurances (PFA)	3,710,251
La Providence Assurances	3,418,475
Guardian Royal Exchange Assurance (GRE)[b]	2,897,605
Saint Paul Fire and Marine Insurance[d]	843,375
Cie Européene d'Assurance	283,304
General Accident[b]	ceased 1984
Yorkshire[b]	commenced 1984
Royal Insurance[b]	n.a.

* Government-owned.
[a] Branch operation.
[b] Owned by British insurer.
[c] An Australian insurer.
[d] A US insurer.

Source: Comité des Assureurs (1985).

coverage risk, in return for a somewhat similar percentage of the premiums.

On receipt of the premiums there is no obligation to invest the funds locally. Thus, after retaining a sufficient amount to cover potential claims, typically three to four months worth of premiums, most companies remitted the rest to France for investment. The general insurance industry is thus not a particularly important source of local investment and its assets held in New Caledonia are confined largely to bank deposits.

As shown in Table 1.17, the French company, Groupement Français Assurances or GFA, is by far the largest firm. French-government-owned companies, if combined, would have created the largest company, but in practice the government ownership does not create any specific co-operation between these companies or any particular marketing benefit in the local market. As indicated, most companies operate through local agents, but a few firms, such as Yorkshire, New Hampshire and General Accident, rely on New Caledonia's two insurance brokers, Assurim Courtage d'Assurances and Cabinet Courtage Assurance R. Paradis, for most of their business.

As with many aspects of New Caledonia business, most insurance firms now represented commenced local business in the early 1970s during the mining boom period. A few companies, however, have a much longer history. UAP, for example, has traditionally sold its policies through the Ballande group and the Groupe de Paris has also been long established. Interestingly, QBE Insurance, an Australian-based insurer, is one of the oldest companies operating within the Territory, reflecting the importance of Australian trade in New Caledonia's early days.

Under local regulations, insurance coverage of risks within New Caledonia can only be obtained from a company which is registered with the Territorial government. The insurance industry, itself, though, is regulated both at the French and Territorial level. In France the firm must be a registered insurer with the French Finance Department. The French Finance Minister then sets the various reserves and other regulations relating to insurance company operations. Each company, for example, must hold a prescribed amount of French government bonds and Treasury securities. In addition, any policies sold in New Caledonia, as elsewhere in France, must be registered with the Director of Insurance in Paris. Each policy must be approved before they can be sold to the public. In practice, though, it is not a particular problem as most companies follow a fairly standard coverage within specific policy types.

In addition to government regulations from Paris, insurance operations within the Territory are also heavily influenced by the French Committee of Insurers. This body, together with the Minister of Finance, produces a set of indicative rates and a manual stating what charges and coverage is appropriate under different circumstances. It is effectively the 'operational bible' for all French insurers and is followed accordingly.

Within New Caledonia insurers registered with Paris must nevertheless also register with the Territorial government and pay annual fees. Foreign companies are also required to place a certain deposit with the Territorial government based on a percentage of local premium income.

There is also a local insurance industry body within New Caledonia, the Comité de Assurer (the Committee of Insurers). This committee is comprised of representatives of almost all companies operating with the Territory. It acts as a consultation vehicle between the insurers and the Territorial government as well as a means of settling small disputes and other local matters. At its monthly meetings, for example, it frequently acts as arbitrator to settle small claims between member companies, rather than resorting to the time and expense of a court settlement. It also produces the local code of insurance, recommendations on changes in traffic law, co-ordinates new policies types, guidelines for local premium rates and collects local claim statistics. The Code de Assurance (Code of Insurance) is a particularly important document as it also provides details of all past claim experiences and appropriate court cases. At one time the rates recommended by the Committee and those charged to clients were effectively the same and there was no local price competition. This has now changed and most companies will discount to some degree for better customers.

Life Insurance

As with general insurance, the life insurance industry in New Caledonia is characterized by a large number of firms represented by local branches and agents. There are no locally-incorporated life insurance companies. The companies provide ordinary life coverage, savings or endowment policies, mixed life and endowment policies, and temporary or term life insurance. In addition to these major types, customers may also purchase these policies with either a guaranteed return or with the end benefits linked to the investment performance of the life office's investments. Annuities are also available.

Given the local government's CAFAT and its compulsory retirement benefit programme, as well as sickness and medical coverage, there might seem limited local potential for life insurance business. In practice, however, the benefits afforded under CAFAT are generally not adequate for retirement purposes, and most residents have had to establish their own longer-term savings programmes, typically through life company policies.

In addition there is an added incentive toward life policy investment as for income tax purposes a deduction of 200,000 CPF per family, and an additional 50,000 CPF per child, is available on premiums paid on savings or mixed life insurance policies (not term

TABLE 1.18   Life insurance companies in New Caledonia: 1984 New
Caledonia sales figures in French francs

L'Union des Assurances de Paris Urbaine (UAP)*	9,467,335
Assurances Générales de France (AGF)*	3,560,457
Préservatrice Foncière Assurance (PFA)	912,759
Les Mutuelles du Mans Vie (MFG)*	467,565
Presence Vie	409,530
Eagle Star Vie	[a] [b]
Euravie	[a]
Assurances du Groupe de Paris (AGP)	unknown
La Mondiale	unknown
Abeille Paix Vie	unknown

* Government-owned.
[a] Commenced business over 1984.
[b] Owned by a British insurer.

Source: Comité des Assureurs (1985).

insurance). As a rule life policies are written in French francs rather
than CPFs and the premiums, while paid locally in CPF, are also set
in French francs.

Some indication of the relative importance of the various life
offices is shown in Table 1.18, but it is not truly reflective of the total
market share. In particular, industry interviews suggest that La
Mondiale is the largest insurance company in terms of New Caledonia business but, as it is not a member of the local insurance committee, its local sales figures are not publicly available. Similarly,
although only recently established, Eagle and Euravie are said to be
very active in the current market.

CAFAT

The Caisse de Compensation des Prestations Familiales des Accidents du Travail et de Prévoyance des Travailleurs de la Nouvelle-Calédonie et Dépendances, commonly known by the initials,
CAFAT, is a private, non-profit, company which under a management contract with the Territorial government administers certain
social welfare schemes to include the old age pension, medical
insurance, and child endowment for Territorial residents.

(i) *Development*

CAFAT initially developed to administer the family allowance payments and so it basically had no investments. With its expansion into workers' compensation insurance and retirement benefits, however, this position changed, and CAFAT soon became an important source of potential funding within the Territory. As one study described,

'the scheme is designed in such a way that payments at any time should be covered by contributions, but the existence of a qualifying period for contributions means that in the years before payments begin, a huge capital sum can be amassed. Theoretically neither this money, nor the return on it, will be needed by the Caisse, and it is intended to use it in investments to promote social welfare'.[30]

These funds were duly invested in low interest loans for housing finance and similar type advances as well as bank deposits and other liquid assets.

(ii) *Funding*

CAFAT obtains most of its funding through contributions. The required premium is substantial, and since 1 June 1985 amounted to 35.17 per cent of an employee's wage, plus a variable amount (depending on occupational risk) for workers' compensation coverage, which can bring the total to between 35.93 and 42.01 per cent of a worker's basic salary up to a maximum of CPF 175,000 per month for full coverage. This money is then paid to CAFAT each quarter. The employer in return may deduct a portion of these payments from the employee's wage. The specific breakdown is provided in Table 1.19.

(iii) *Assets*

While these premiums certainly assist New Caledonia residents, the payments in themselves are not sufficient to cover all expenses. Indeed, even the sickness coverage pays 100 per cent of the costs only of major illness and those of children, otherwise it refunds only a portion of the total medical expenses. Similarly in the case of retirement, the benefit level is generally considered too low, so in practice

TABLE 1.19   CAFAT contributions, June 1985

Type of benefit	Employer premium	Employee premium	Total premium
Family allowances	10.50	–	10.50
Article 14 charges	0.20	–	0.20
Retirement	8.17	3.33	11.50
Sickness and hospital	5.98	2.99	8.97
Unemployment insurance	1.50	0.50	2.00
Fonds Social de l'Habitat	2.00	–	2.00
Subtotal	28.35	6.82	35.17
Workers' compensation	0.76 to 6.84	–	0.76 to 6.84
Total	29.11 to 35.19	6.82	35.93 to 42.01

Source: CAFAT (1986).

it is supplemented privately by employer-run pension scheme, or personal savings – often through life insurance policies.

In addition to these directly funded benefits, the CAFAT coverage also contains a large element of social welfare, in that those unemployed workers, particularly in rural areas, can still qualify for the medical treatment as well as the minimum old age retirement benefit.

These costs and the scheme's intention to break-even on its operations, has meant that there is no longer an ever-increasing investment portfolio. Even so, CAFAT still holds considerable assets within the Territory. As shown in Table 1.20, of its assets of 8911 million CPF in 1984, some 23.8 per cent were held in the form of advances, another 17.8 per cent in securities investments, and 30.5 per cent in uncommitted funds. This latter category represented money held on deposit in varying amounts with each of the five banks, the post office, the savings bank and in cash: of these deposits, commercial bank term deposits were the most important category.

Though not specifically reflected in the accounts, CAFAT also maintains some of its deposits in the form of Australian dollars. This is to cover medical expenses incurred in Australian hospitals: more specialized hospital cases are treated in New South Wales under an intergovernment agreement.

Superannuation Funds

Given that most people consider CAFAT's retirement benefits in-

TABLE 1.20   CAFAT assets and liabilities, December 1984

Assets:	
Cash at bank	37,690
Land	160,905,745
Work under construction	476,648,089
Tools and equipment	34,400,854
Transport equipment	2,319,776
Office furniture	39,563,075
Furnishings	555,163
Fittings and fixtures	12,921,503
Loan agreements	2,122,207,045
Other advances	77,998,994
Securities investments	1,582,143,640
Secured deposits	881,560
Funds due from clients	650,007
Funds due from Territory govt	1,236,458
Other short-term assets	913,494
Other debtors	50,670,409
Prepayments	6,486,375
Receivables	41,385,722
Uncommitted funds	2,714,798,253
Contributions collected	832,487,251
Contributions remaining	751,926,571
Total assets	8,911,137,674

Liabilities:	
General reserves	2,405,508,306
Reserves on investment	40,592,564
Reserves on real estate	727,351,859
Reserves on loan pledges	11,000,000
Reserves on loan agreements	2,122,207,045
Reserves on other advances	77,998,994
Reserves on securities	1,582,143,640
Reserves on secured deposits	881,560
Balance carried forward	5,494,476
Provisions	76,695,810
Short-term borrowings	276,849,562
Contributions paid in advance	832,487,251
Payments due on judgements	751,926,571
Total liabilities	8,911,137,674

Source: Caisse de Compensation des Prestations Familiales des Accidents du Travail et de Prévoyance des Travailleurs de la Nouvelle-Calédonie et Dépendances (1984), *Rapport d'Activité Exercice 1984*, Annex, p. 1.

adequate, employees seek to supplement these funds through their own arrangements. As a result, some larger employers operate their own pension or superannuation schemes. New Caledonia's largest employer, the Société le Nickel, for example, operates one such scheme. Similarly, French and Territorial government employees are exempt from CAFAT and covered under their own benefit scheme.

Co-operatives

Other than Crédit Agricole, the co-operative movement has not been particularly strong in New Caledonia. One exception was in the fishing industry where there was a 'cooperative society whose members can now borrow the sums needed to buy improved equipment'.[31]

Investment Companies

As mentioned in the commercial banking section, the banques d'affaires have traditionally taken equity interests in their client companies as well as advance loans. They may also take board of director representation on these firms. While each bank would make some equity investments directly, they also generally hold shares indirectly through affiliated investment companies which work on behalf of the group. In the case of New Caledonia, both Banque Indosuez and Paribas have such investment company affiliates with substantial local interests: Banque Indosuez uses the Société d'Etudes et de Participations Minières de la France d'Outre-Mer (SEPAMIFOM) and SOCAFIM for this purpose while Paribas uses the Société Néo-Calédoniènne de Développement et de Participations (CALDEV).

(i) *Société d'Etudes et de Participations Minières de la France d'Outre-Mer*

The Société d'Etudes et de Participations Minières de la France d'Outre-Mer (SEPAMIFOM) is a wholly-owned subsidiary of Banque Indosuez and acts mainly as a holding company for the Group's local shareholdings in New Caledonia. It is apparently one of the Territory's older companies and was established in the 1800s. It initially commenced its mining investment operations in Vietnam and then later transferred to New Caledonia.

SEPAMIFOM has investments in the mining industry and is part of a syndicate with the Société le Nickel. Its share portfolio has around 15 to 20 companies. Most of these holdings are small but for Ballande where it owns a 20 per cent shareholding.

(ii) *SOCAFIM*

SOCAFIM is another Banque Indosuez subsidiary. It was initially a major construction company within the Territory, building roads and other public construction contracts. It was financed by Banque Indosuez but, unfortunately, experienced financial problems. In the end Banque Indosuez was forced to take control, and in 1985 owned approximately 90 per cent of the company. The remaining shares are held by the initial shareholders, many of whom are local residents.

It is no longer active in public works contracting but still does some land subdivision. Its main activities are the owning and rental of buildings and landholdings, as well as selling local real estate.

(iii) *Société Néo-Calédoniènne de Développement et de Participations*

The Société Néo-Calédoniènne de Développement et de Participations (CALDEV) is basically a combination of a venture capital firm and a holding company for Banque Paribas within the French Pacific Territories. It is owned 70 per cent by Paribas of France and 30 per cent by local shareholders.

CALDEV's first, and still largest, investment is a 70 per cent shareholding in Banque Paribas Pacifique. Initially this was a joint venture with the Bank of America holding the remaining 30 per cent, but in the mid-1970s the Bank of America changed its policy on participating in companies where it held less than a controlling interest, and so it sold this 30 per cent holding directly to Banque Paribas in France.

The rest of CALDEV's portfolio generally consists of fairly small, usually only 3 to 5 per cent, shareholdings in existing customers of Paribas and the shareholdings are often done in conjunction with Paribas France as well as Banque Paribas Pacifique. In the case of Sofrana, for example, CALDEV owns 3 per cent of the shares and the Paribas Group owns 17 per cent. Some of CALDEV's other holdings include SNICR-Chateau Royal, SCI Les Madrepores, SCI Residence du Rocher, Société Touristique des Mers du Sud, Savaexpress, Blanchisserie Industrièlle de Noumea, Société Française des Viandes et Salaisons du Pacifique, Socaba, Société d'Exploitation des

Entrepôts Frigorifiques, Relais de Fayahoue, Groupe Sofrana, Tiare Hotel SA, and Air Calédonie International.

Other Lending Bodies

In addition to normal financial institutions and those government schemes operated by the SICNC, some government departments or agencies are also active as lenders in their own right. Perhaps not surprisingly the Ministry of Agriculture offers the widest range of these plans; the Fonds d'Investissement de Développement Economique et Social, Le Fonds d'Aide au Développement des Iles et de L'Intérieur, and the Caisse de Dépôts et Consignations.

Fonds d'Investissement de Développement Economique et Social, (FIDES) is a state development fund used to acquire land for Melanesian native use within New Caledonia.

The Caisse de Dépôts et Consignations is another important French government-owned development finance institution. It complements Caisse Centrale's lending operations by providing concessional long-term finance to those development projects which do not in themselves produce revenue. In New Caledonia, for example, Caisse de Dépôts et Consignations has provided finance for schools and other public infrastructure which is not linked directly with production. While it has no office in New Caledonia, it is nevertheless still an important source of public sector development finance.

Le Fonds d'Aide au Développement des Iles et de L'Intérieur (the Development Funds for the Islands and the Interior) (FADIL) was established in 1975 with the assistance of the French government to provide financial and technical help in cattle, coffee, fishing and other rural projects. These were to be combined with land repurchase for Melanesian use to assist rural development. As a rule it generally prefers to lend to group or community projects with Melanesian participation rather than to individuals.

FINANCIAL MARKETS

As with the other smaller Pacific countries, New Caledonia has no local financial markets of significance. There is some interbank trading in deposits and in foreign exchange, but this is relatively minor within New Caledonia: most financial market business is conducted directly within the Paris market through parent companies or agents.

Corporate Equities

There is a very strong incentive for local investment, for an equity participation in local firms within certain industries (particularly agriculture, fishery and tourism) may be fully deductible for personal tax purposes up to 1,500,000 CPF per annum. Thus far, though, these benefits have attracted only a small degree of individual investor participation and as yet proved insufficient for local stock exchange trading.

Foreign Exchange

Foreign exchange dealing is conducted only by commercial banks although facilities for tourists are readily available. Traditionally there has been little competition in foreign exchange business between the banks. Banque Indosuez calculates the major rates daily and then prints copies for its own branches and four other banks.

On 26 December 1945 the franc of the Colonies Françaises du Pacifique (CPF) was made the official currency of the French colonies in the Pacific to include the New Hebrides (now Vanuatu), New Caledonia, and French Oceania. It was created by General de Gaulle and the Free French government in London to separate the currency of those areas recognizing the de Gaulle government from those of occupied France. The choice of separate currencies for Africa and for the Pacific reflected the differing economic conditions. The major presence of American and other Allied forces in the Pacific region caused substantial economic growth and this was reflected in part by a conversion rate of 100 CPF equalling 240 French francs compared to the African currency's conversion of 100 CFA to 170 French francs. Since 1 January 1960 the conversion rate has been 1 CPF equals 0.055 French francs or one French franc is equal to 18.18 CPF.

ANALYSIS

Any evaluation of New Caledonia's financial sector must consider that New Caledonia, as a French Overseas Territory, is an integral part of the French financial sector, and what happens there to a large extent is subsequently reflected in New Caledonia, the only difference being the impact of these measures on a developing, rather than a fully-developed, economy. It is not just a matter of the key interdependence between the Territory and metropolitan France. As one paper commented, the French 'government has very extensive controls over the Territory's fiscal and monetary operations. It controls capital spending, interest rates, trade policies, foreign exchange allocations' and other important matters.[32] While some powers have been delegated to local institutions, the government can and does take direct action where desired. Some particular measures which might assist in local development would include the establishment of a separate development bank, the creation of an investment company, and greater competitive freedom and innovation within the existing commercial banks.

Development Banking

For purposes of this Chapter the SICNC has been classified as a development bank and it not only has the power but also fulfils many such functions. In practice,though, the Institut d'Emission classifies it as a finance company. Similarly, in the Territory's 1981 development plan, one recommendation is for the creation of a development bank. Thus while the SICNC should be providing these functions, neither the Institut nor the Territory seemingly feel that this is the case, and thus a new institution might well be needed.

The reason for this position is probably that the SICNC has been given too many responsibilities to perform. Those skills required for real estate development,for rental property management, for mortgage lending, and for development banking, are all different. Unfortunately the development banking staff are outnumbered within SICNC's existing framework, and thus it would be more effective to split SICNC's operations into at least a separate real estate development and management operation and a separate lending business. The latter in turn might be even more effective if further divided into a mortgage lending and a development banking operation. If this division of SICNC takes place, the lending business side might then assume the title of the Banque de Développement du Nouvelle-Calédonie.

It should be remembered that good development banking is not simply mortgage lending. It entails specialized lending and project management skills as well as the ability to provide financial and managerial advice to client firms. These are not services particularly well provided by the SICNC, nor is it likely that SICNC will provide them under the current structure. A development bank status would also be important in the case of New Caledonia independence, for this institution could serve as a conduit for international concessional aid sources (such as the Asian Development Bank and the World Bank) which are not readily available as part of France.

A further incentive, which may no longer be so important under the French conservative government, was the expansion in the SICNC's development finance business caused by its management of the 'fonds special pour le développement economique'. These funds were to be established as part of the newly-formed regional council administration system.

Investment Companies

As discussed, New Caledonia has the advantage of having a number of investment companies in operation within the local economy. These are mainly affiliates of the existing banks, but the SICNC has also made some equity investments. There were also plans that under the four-regional council system each regional government would receive some grant funds to help support local projects and that these funds could be used as part of the equity funding in local joint venture projects. The regional councils therefore might create local investment companies to hold the shares in these ventures as well as to conduct other commercial undertakings.

There would certainly be some advantages in obtaining more venture type capital, and it is interesting that the Territorial government development plan also called for the creation of a Territorial investment bank which could be financed by tax rebatable donations. No action, however, has been taken to create any such institutions.

Improved Banking Services

At present most observers feel there are too many banks within Noumea and with the Banque Indosuez current branch structure and the postal chequeing and savings bank agency services, most of New Caledonia is relatively well provided with basic banking services. Whether these services are conducive to lending and promoting economic growth, however, is another matter.

As mentioned in the commercial banking section, each of the five banks at present are either owned or controlled by the French government. In two cases this ownership is relatively recent, but in other cases nationalization dates to after or before the Second World War. Over time this has resulted in these institutions adopting a very conservative approach to banking, and similarly has reduced the level of competition and innovation within the system.

Thus, although economic uncertainty is no doubt the key problem between the banks' failure to relend their deposits within the local market, the banking system itself could well take part of the blame. Indeed, even given a number of special concessional finance plans, the banks have only lent out some 60 per cent of the funds raised in New Caledonia. In October 1985, for example, the five commercial banks had raised some 49,518 million CPF in deposits but had lent only 29,794 million.

The denationalization moves planned by the current French conservative government might help free these institutions from some of their present conservatism, but financial innovation and competition may well require some additional incentives. One measure might be to allow further commercial bank entry from countries other than France. This would encourage the inflow of new ideas into the local market and help encourage New Caledonian trade with other markets. Initially this would probably have to be through foreign bank branches in Noumea rather than as a shareholder in a foreign bank – French bank joint venture. The Bank of America, for example, was at one time a partner in the Banque Paribas Pacifique and the Bank of Hawaii is still a passive shareholder locally through its shareholding in the Banque de Nouvelle-Calédonie. A direct presence will be required if the full benefits are to be achieved. Ideally, Japanese and American as well as Australian and New Zealand, institutions could be encouraged to apply.

TRENDS AND PREDICTIONS

As stressed throughout this paper, the future of New Caledonia's economy, and hence its financial sector, is a function of its political future, and given the current uncertainty it is difficult to be successful with either economic or financial development. As indicated, the bankers claim, and rightly so, an inadequate supply of worthwhile lending proposals, and hence they are unable to relend the deposits they collect within the Territory. The funds are instead invested in the Paris money-market. Unfortunately, until the political position is resolved, there will be little change in this position. Indeed, if domestic violence resumes, the problem may well become worse.

It should also be stressed that today's political problems are hardly a new development. As one French government publication explains, 'five different statutes have been enacted since 1958. None succeeded in solving the imbalances which characterise the political life of the Territory'.[33]

The saddest part of this process is that if any of the early measures, such as those introduced in the early 1950s, had been allowed to continue, it is possible that the Melanesians would have become integrated into the existing local political system, and any current political problems would be strictly idealogical rather than racially based. Even as late as 1969 the idea of independence was being raised only by students and radicals. It was only in 1979 that political parties became involved, and then only in 1984 that they began to show substantial power. Even had the French government fulfilled its plans of 1981, there might well be less problems. The problem is that by announcing one set of plans and then changing them later, few residents now believe government pronouncements. It is now highly unlikely that any plan which entails French ownership of New Caledonia will work in the long run. Indeed, it would seem no longer a question as to whether New Caledonia will receive independence, it is a matter of when and under what conditions.

From both a French and New Caledonian viewpoint, probably the best alternative would be a version similar to that initially proposed by Edgard Pisani in 1985. It would entail New Caledonia gaining full independence from France but then choosing to govern the country in association with France: Article 88 of the French constitution already provides for such an 'independence-association with France' status. From the practical standpoint, the relationship between the Cook Islands and New Zealand provides a good example of how such an arrangement might work. In that instance the Cook Islands first gained its independence from New Zealand. It then passed legislation which established a treaty with New Zealand whereby New Zealand would provide for the country's defense and assist in its foreign policy matters outside the region. This independence in association concept might well be packaged appropriately to gain the support of both Melanesians and pro-French interests.[34] Industry interviews at least suggest that the more realistic Europeans and other non-Melanesians within New Caledonia have realized that independence is just a matter of time and would support that plan which achieved it with the minimum decline in their living standards.

While to some the election of Jacques Chirac's conservative government in April 1986 might suggest that the independence is no longer an option, it is doubtful that the new government will fulfil all of its stated promises. For example, in regard to the four regions, the conservative parties had promised to abolish the system. In practice, however, interviews in late 1985 suggested that such an action would be too dangerous and a more gradual approach should be applied. France's new conservative-led government has followed exactly this approach and removed much of the powers previously afforded the regional councils, but not the councils themselves. This measure was further offset by the promise that France would provide an additional 7 billion CPF to finance development projects, tax cuts and to compensate those property losses suffered during the disturbances.

Political problems aside, while nickel did relatively well over 1985, a decline in tourism, building, cement and chrome has meant that unemployment has become a growing problem within the Territory, and that in itself could prove a potential source of further political problems. This could perhaps be avoided if the government were to take action now to diversify the economy's current dependence on nickel and other minerals. As the then French Prime Minister, Georges. Pompidou commented, the 'wealth and the tragedy of New Caledonia is to have an economy based solely on the essential rich nickel'.

As mentioned, the Territorial government in 1981 created a three-year economic plan starting in 1984 to achieve greater balance in the local economy. It centres on the encouragement of increased agricultural and maritime production, more small- and medium-size business, greater processing of current mineral exports, and the expansion of the tourist industry.[35]

The most obvious area for improvement is in agriculture, where the plan has defined some seven objectives: cattle-raising, cereals, coffee, timber, vegetables, tropical fruit, meat and dairy products. At present New Caledonia imports a large portion of its food requirements, but there are more than adequate land resources and climatic conditions to produce much of these items locally. In addition, there might be the possibility of exporting certain products such as coffee, beef and timber. More traditional tropical exports such as copra and vanilla could also have some limited potential. As one government official explained, in the past 'the development of agriculture, forestry and cattle raisings has not been favoured, soil and climate have only been exploited up to 10 or 20 per cent of their potential'.[36] Similarly in terms of primary products there is also potential for aquaculture, fishing, and the utilization of other sea resources. Hence the government's other priorities include 'the exploitation of underground resources; the exploitation of sea resources and the exploitation of natural sites for tourism'.[37]

Tourism is the other major area where some significant diversification might be possible. The three-year economic plan, for example, set a goal for the Territory to attract some 120,000 tourists per year. This would be accomplished through the provision of more resort standard hotels, a higher standard of tourist services, and using Noumea as a starting point for other travel within the Territory. At present most tourists confine their visit to the urban areas in New Caledonia, but there is much more to see within the Territory. In particular, the reef surrounding the main island is as attractive and has much easier access than its nearby Australian counterpart, the Great Barrier Reef. Little as yet has been done to promote this aspect of New Caledonia holidays, and such promotions might also help diversify the Territory's current dependence on Australian, Japanese and New Zealand visitors.

Unfortunately, tourism is the one area most sensitive to political problems. Not only are tourist numbers down considerably following the domestic disturbances in late 1984, but the construction of at least one major tourist resort was suspended. This project, the Taire Resort, was to have a major new tourist golf course, marina, 200-room hotel, a condominium (or home unit) development and casino. It was sponsored by a consortium of American, Japanese and French interests, and involved an investment of over 10,000 million CPF.

In conclusion, a quick resolution of New Caledonia's political future would do much to resolve the current level of uncertainty that has caused the postponement of much investment within the Territory. There is much that can be accomplished in development outside of the existing nickel industry, but it is unlikely that any government incentive will prove effective while the question of independence remains unresolved.

NOTES

1. Since 1975 both New Caledonia and Vanuatu have also claimed the Hunter and Matthew islands.
2. William McTaggart (1963) 'Noumea: a study in social geography', Ph.D. thesis, Australian National University, March, pp. 7–8.
3. Alan Ward (1983) *New Caledonia – the immediate prospects*, (Canberra: Parliament of Australia Legislative Research Service).
4. The FLNKS is a coalition group of four political parties and two independent groups.
5. Edgard Pisani, a speech dated 7 January 1985, p. 2.
6. Initially under the Pisani plan, the Noumea region had only 18 places.
7. Myriam Dornoy (1984) *Politics in New Caledonia* (Sydney: Sydney University Press) p. 137.
8. J. T. Macrae (1974b) 'The New Caledonia Economy, 1967–72', *New Zealand Economic Papers*, 8:23.
9. Sturt Inder (1983) 'New Caledonia's Future', *The Bulletin*, 26 July 1983, pp. 66–7.
10. Jean-Pierre Lehmann (1985) 'The second front', *Far Eastern Economic Review*, 24 January, p. 10.
11. Pierre Gascher (1974) *La Belle au bois Dormant: regards sur l'administration coloniale en Nouvelle-Calédonie de 1874 à 1894* (Noumea: La Société d'Etudes Historiques de la Nouvelle-Calédonie) p. 246.
12. Bank of New South Wales, General Manager, Extracts from private letters from the Managing Director, London, 29 October 1875. Both the Bank of Australasia and the Union Bank held similarly high opinions.
13. Pierre Gascher (1974) *La Belle au bois Dormant: regards sur l'administration coloniale en Nouvelle-Calédonie de 1874 à 1894*, (Noumea: La Société d'Etudes Historiques de la Nouvelle-Calédonie) p. 246.
14. Bank of New South Wales, General Manager, Extracts from private letters to the Managing Director, London, 22 December 1877. What is now the Australia and New Zealand Banking Group also sent an officer to Noumea to salvage whatever assets possible.
15. J. S. Butlin (1961) *Australia and New Zealand Bank: the Bank of Australasia and the Union Bank of Australia, 1828–1951* (Sydney: Longmans) p. 207.
16. J. S. Butlin, *Australia and New Zealand Bank*, p. 246.
17. Bank of New South Wales, General Manager, Extracts from private letters to the Managing Director, London, 12 April 1878 (second letter on that day).
18. Bank of New South Wales, General Manager, Extracts from private letters to the Managing Director, London, 22 December 1877.
19. H. C. Brookfield and Doreen Hart (1971) *Melanesia: a geographical interpretation of an island world*, (London: Methuen) p. 253.
20. *French Possessions in Oceania* (1920) (London: HMSO) p. 39.
21. *French Possessions in Oceania*, p. 30.
22. Virginia Thompson and Richard Adloff (1971) *The French Pacific Islands: French Polynesia and New Caledonia* (Berkeley: University of California Press) p. 475.

23. Thompson and Adloff *The French Pacific Islands*, p. 408.
24. William McTaggart (1963) 'Noumea: a study in social geography', Ph.D. thesis, Australian National University, March, p. 43.
25. For a discussion as to what constitutes a merchant bank and its traditional functions see Michael T. Skully (1987) *Merchant Banking in Australia* (Melbourne: Oxford University Press).
26. Thompson and Adloff, *The French Pacific Islands*, p. 39.
27. Thompson and Adloff, *The French Pacific Islands*, p. 39.
28. In order to use the Institut d'Emission facility for equipment financing, the items purchased must originate from EEC countries. It may also not rediscount any finance provided for the purchase of land or homes.
29. Thompson and Adloff, *The French Pacific Islands*, p. 476.
30. McTaggart 'Noumea', p. 40.
31. Thompson and Adloff, *The French Pacific Islands*, p. 399.
32. J. T. Macrae (1974a) 'New Caledonia: a summary of recent economic developments with special reference to "le problème Melanesian"', *Pacific Viewpoint*, 15 (1), May:49.
33. *New Caledonia: a background* (1985) (Canberra: French Embassy) p. 1.
34. A speech dated 25 July 1964 as cited in Alan Ward (1982) *Land and Politics of New Caledonia* (Canberra: Department of Political and Social Change, Australian National University) p. 145.
35. 'New Caledonia and Dependencies Three Year Plan, 1981', a one page, undated English summary, provided by the French Embassy, Canberra, Australia, May 1986.
36. Edgard Pisani, a speech dated 7 January 1985, p. 10.
37. Pisani, p. 11.

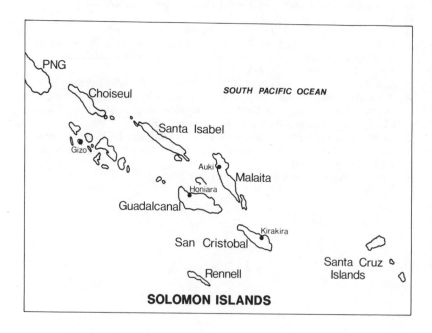

PNG

Choiseul

SOUTH PACIFIC OCEAN

Santa Isabel

Gizo

Auki

Malaita

Honiara

Guadalcanal

Kirakira

San Cristobal

Santa Cruz
Islands

Rennell

SOLOMON ISLANDS

2 Financial Institutions and Markets in the Solomon Islands

INTRODUCTION

Located approximately 1900 kilometres north-east of Australia, the Solomon Islands cover an area of some 27,560 square kilometres and, with a population of 267,000, is the third most populous of the Pacific island countries after Papua New Guinea and Fiji. In addition to its six main islands, Choiseul, New Georgia, Santa Isabel, Guadalcanal, Malaita and San Cristobal, there are many smaller inhabited and uninhabited islands stretching some 1450 kilometres in an east by south-east direction from Papua New Guinea to slightly north of Vanuatu.

The great distances between many of the islands and the rugged, mountainous, often inaccessible, terrain of the large islands, has caused the people to develop their own languages, customs and traditions, and today there are some 87 vernacular languages spoken in the country. As a result English has been chosen as the official language and pidgin English is widely used as the working language within the country. In addition to the Melanesians, which account for some 93.3 per cent of the population, there are also Polynesians (4 per cent), Micronesians (1.5 per cent),[1] as well as some resident Chinese and Europeans.

The islands gained their present name in 1568 when the first European, the Spanish explorer, Alvaro de Mendaña de Neyra, visited many of the major islands and he is also responsible for their Spanish sounding names. Mendaña's choice of 'Isles of the Solomons', 'supposing them to be those islands where Solomon fetched gold to adorn the Temple in Jerusalem',[2] was intended to encourage Spain to colonize the area, and in 1595 he returned to establish a colony in Guadalcanal. He landed instead in the Santa Cruz islands.

Unfortunately the islanders were not friendly and shortly after Mendaña's own death the colony was abandoned in November 1595.

The islands were subsequently visited by many other explorers, and later whalers and missionaries established outposts on some islands. It was not until 1885, however, that the European powers took a formal control. Initially this was limited to the Germans in the northern portion of the present country, as part of their New Guinea Territory. In 1893, however, the British formalized their claim over the southern portion and proclaimed a protectorate over Guadalcanal, Savo, Malaita, San Cristobal and the New Georgia group. Santa Cruz and the Rennell islands were subsequently added to the British claims in 1898 and 1899 respectively and in 1900 the Choiseul, Santa Isabel, and Shortland islands were transferred from Germany to British control under the Samoan Tripartite Convention of 1899: the British relinquished all claims to German Samoa in return.

From then until the Japanese invasion in 1942, the British Protectorate of the Solomon Islands was managed by a Resident Commissioner under the control of the Western Pacific High Commission based in Fiji.[3] With the end of hostilities in 1945,[4] the Solomons began rebuilding as most of its plantations and other economic infrastructure were destroyed during the war and, unlike Malaysia, no war damages or reparations were paid to the previous owners: many therefore did not return.

The war period also changed local attitudes toward British rule, and from 1946 the 'marisna ruru' or 'marching rule' movement pushed for independence. In 1953 participation in local government councils commenced the process and was gradually introduced at the national level. The country assumed its present name in June 1975 and over-all selfgovernment on 2 January 1976. The Solomon Islands became fully independent on 7 July 1978.

As with the other Pacific island countries, its economy is characterized by a high level of subsistence agricultural activities and its foreign exchange earnings is dependent on primary product exports. However, while it has a lower Gross Domestic Product (GDP) *per capita* than many of its neighbours, it does have the advantage of a somewhat broader-based economy. To a large extent this broadening has been a function of the government's joint ventures with foreign enterprises. Prior to the 1970s, for example, copra was virtually the only export, but gradually fishing and timber have become important, and for many years (excepting 1984) copra has rated third in export values. Palm oil and palm kernels has been another recent growth area as has cocoa. Rice, tobacco products, marine shells and gold, comprise the other major categories. In addition to more diversified exports, the Solomons' balance of payments has also been assisted from a variety of foreign aid grants and soft loans – primarily from the UK, Australia, New Zealand, the European Development Fund, the Asian Development Bank, the World Bank and a range of UN agencies.

These various benefits have helped the Solomon Islands economy grow rapidly, and over 1971–9 it had a growth rate averaging 5.0 per cent per annum. In 1984 the Solomon Islands had a real growth in GDP of some 9 per cent. This impressive record, however, has been somewhat offset by a high population growth. As the World Bank commented, 'the real GDP has grown at a reasonable rate, but the rapid population growth has limited the improvement in *per capita* incomes'.[5] Indeed, as the Central Bank governor warned, 'it may not be possible to do more than keep pace with a population growth of over 3 per cent and we may actually lose ground'.[6]

The government hopes to overcome this problem with increased investment in employment generating projects, particularly accomplishing more in processing its primary products and generally expanding local manufacturing beyond its present soap, boats, biscuits, beverages, wood and rattan furniture, clothing, shell jewellry, fiberglass water tanks, canoes, and handicrafts.

As one government leader's report commented, 'to achieve the target output will require higher and more rational investment . . . [an] average of 14–15 per cent of GNP'.[7] This investment programme will require substantially greater fund raising both within the Solomons and from foreign sources. Thus savings mobilization will play a more important role in the future and the government's current plan aims to 'promote the development of a sound banking and financial system; ensure that the system and its services are relevant and responsive to the needs of the country; [and] increase banking and financial services in rural areas'.[8]

Overview of the Financial Sector

Little is known of the earlier financial history of the Solomons. Local commerce was conducted by barter and to a lesser extent with shell and feather money. Even today barter remains a common means of trade in villages. Similarly, traditional money is still used in remote areas to settle claims between tribal groups and to pay the price of a bride.

Some money obviously came into circulation as a by-product of the sandalwood trade, and by the early 1900s Burns Philp steamers were plying between islands for copra and trading purposes. Shortly afterwards a number of major firms established local plantations: Levers (1905); Burns Philp (1906); and the Queensland Malayta Co. (1909). As elsewhere in the islands, these trading firms also effectively acted as bankers for their clients and for a short time Burns Philp's Pacific notes were not uncommon as local tender. These notes were later removed from circulation 'by an official regulation of 1910 which required that custom duties and other charges levied by the government, and also wages due to labourers be paid in British coin'.[9]

The effective end of its Pacific notes, though, did not terminate Burns Philp's involvement in early Solomon Island finance, for in 1917 it established the first formal banking operation within the islands by opening agencies of the Commonwealth Bank's savings department (Commonwealth Savings Bank after 1927) in its offices at Faisa, Gizo and Makamba (later Tulagi). Accounts opened by these agencies were administered from the Commonwealth's Sydney office and periodically inspected by Commonwealth Bank personnel.[10] In contrast to one government report which mentions that 'there are no banks in the Protectorate except a branch of the Commonwealth Savings Bank which transacts savings bank business',[11] they were never run by the Commonwealth Bank nor did they obtain branch status. Instead, as with other agency agreements, Burns Philp received a commission on deposits and withdrawals as well as an incentive payment for new accounts. These operations were never particularly significant and were simply an additional service provided for Burns Philp's clients. For the fiscal year ending 1938, for example, the agencies together had handled only 408 deposits worth some £6374 and 165 withdrawals worth £3372. Furthermore, these agencies primarily serviced the expatriate community 'with little encouragement being given to indigenous depositors'.[12]

Following the Second World War's commencement in the Pacific, these operations officially closed on 6 February 1942. However, as Burns Philp did not resume operations in the Solomons after the war, it was not until 1951, when the Commonwealth Trading Bank opened a Honiara branch for its savings and trading banks, that local banking services were again established. In more recent years other foreign

TABLE 2.1   Financial institutions in the Solomon Islands, by type, 1985

Central Bank of Solomon Islands
Commercial banks
Development Bank of Solomon Islands
Provincial development corporations
Other development institutions
Finance companies
General insurance companies
Life insurance companies
National Provident Fund
Other provident funds
Commodities Export Marketing Authority
Co-operatives
Credit unions
Postal agencies
Government Shareholding Agency
Solomon Island Housing Authority

banks have established branches, and in 1981 the Commonwealth transformed its Solomon Islands operations into a joint venture with the Solomon Island government, the National Bank of Solomon Islands.

A number of other institutions, as shown in Table 2.1, have also been created, many of which are statutory financial institutions. As one government plan commented, these 'institutions have a vital role to play in national economic growth, by managing, promoting, safeguarding and providing the kind of finances and financial services that national development needs, at the time and place that it needs them'.[13] In addition some 'non-governmental organizations, co-operatives, small rural businesses, and individuals also provide credit in rural areas'.[14]

FINANCIAL INSTITUTIONS

Central Bank of Solomon Islands

The Central Bank of Solomon Islands is wholly owned by the government via the Government Shareholding Agency and performs most traditional central bank functions. These include acting as a banker to the government, commercial banks and, to a lesser extent, other financial institutions; designing, printing and distributing the country's coins and currency; managing the exchange rate and the country's external reserves; administering the foreign exchange controls; regulating banks and other financial institutions; operating the clearing system; managing the money supply; collecting financial statistics; and advising the government on financial matters. The Bank also acts as the registrar and selling agency for the various government securities issues, and, since 1980, has represented the Solomon Islands on both the World Bank's International Development Agency and International Finance Corporation operations. In addition to these more normal functions, the Bank is also an important lender (directly and indirectly) to the government and to the government statutory bodies. Since January, 1984 it has held 10 per cent of the shares of the Development Bank of Solomon Islands.

The Bank's operations are supervised by a Board of Directors comprised of the Bank's Governor and Deputy Governor, the Permanent Secretary of the Ministry of Finance, and three to six other directors appointed by the Minister of Finance. The Governor serves as both the Chairman of the Board and the Bank's chief executive. Interestingly, neither the names (other than the Governor), nor the number of directors are disclosed in the Bank's reports.

(i) *Development*

The Central Bank of Solomon Islands was created on 24 January 1983 under the Central Bank of Solomon Islands Act 1976 and assumed the operations of its predecessors, the Solomon Islands Monetary Authority, as well as the powers of a central bank.

The Solomon Islands Monetary Authority was established on 21 June 1976 under the Solomon Islands Monetary Authority Act 1976 (the earlier version of the current central bank legislation), and commenced operations in October 1976. The Authority was created to manage the issue and international exchange of the Solomon Islands currency, oversee the banking system, provide certain banking services, prepare statistics, and advise the government on economic and financial matters, and promote the country's economic growth and development.[15]

The Authority's initial function was to replace the Australian dollar (which was used as the local currency) with the Solomon Island dollar. As part of this process, the Authority's first action was to assume control of the country's foreign exchange control system in May 1977. The currency itself was subsequently launched on October 1977, and Australian dollars were to be phased out as legal tender by 30 June 1978. The dual currency period, though, was later extended to 30 September 1978, but since then the Solomon Island dollar has been the sole legal tender within the country. The Bank is responsible for the production and distribution of the currency and coinage and, as they are produced overseas, normally maintains 'reserve stocks of notes and coins sufficient for two to three years ahead'.[16]

Following the currency's introduction, the Authority took on additional functions. In 1978, for example, it commenced limited banking services to the local commercial banks; in 1979 it accepted deposits from statutory corporations, the government and commercial banks. Later it made short-term advances to the government and statutory bodies to cover temporary financial deficiencies and in September 1980, it also assumed the operations of the local clearing system.

As the Bank expanded its operations additional powers were required, and in 1983 amendments to the Authority's legislation finally changed the Authority into a central bank. The new organization, under Section 4, was also given the following objectives:

(a) to regulate the issue, supply, availability, and international exchange of money;
(b) to advise the government on banking and monetary matters;
(c) to promote monetary stability;
(d) to supervise and regulate banking business;
(e) to promote a sound financial structure; and
(f) to foster financial conditions conducive to the orderly and balanced economic development of the Solomon Islands.

(ii) *Operations*

Thus today the Central Bank has extensive control over banking operations to include (Section 28A) setting the maximum and minimum (lending and deposit rates), specifying the calculating interest on loans and deposits, and determining the institutions' service charges, commissions and other fees. It can also set the minimum cash margins or security on certain lending and the maximum maturities, all of which can be applied selectively to certain classes of borrowers or types of financial institutions. It has tended to limit direct use of these powers to special schemes, relying more on moral suasion and policy measures. For example, when commercial bank deposit rates rose by 1 to 3 per cent in 1983 without a significant corresponding rise in overdraft rates, this was achieved through discussions rather than directives.

The Bank does make strong use of qualitative controls and, in late 1985, had restricted new lending commitments only to projects that increase foreign exchange earnings, employment, government revenues, Solomon Islander participation in the cash economy, or new dwellings.

Under its legislation the Central Bank may also set reserve requirements for the commercial banks and other financial institutions of up to 40 per cent of their total deposits. These requirements must be uniform for all institutions within the same class and 30 days notice must be given in the case of any changes. The first of the reserve requirements came in 1981 when commercial banks were required to deposit an amount equal to 5 per cent of their deposit liabilities in the account with the Authority. Though these funds earned no interest, any excess deposits earned 4 per cent per annum. This requirement was replaced in May 1983 with a 15 per cent liquidity ratio, and subsequently raised to 25 per cent in February 1985.

Besides its normal deposit facilities, the Bank has also provided commercial banks with special deposit facilities during periods of excessive liquidity. In 1984, for example, it permitted banks with liquid asset holdings in excess of 30 per cent of their liabilities to place additional deposits in a special account earning 8 per cent interest.

(iii) *Assets*

In terms of the Central Bank's assets, as shown in Table 2.2, the bulk of these are held in the form of foreign exchange reserves – comprising gold, foreign currencies, international reserve assets, foreign bills of exchange and promissory notes and foreign government Treasury bills. At one time the reserves were almost exclusively in Australian dollar-denominated government and bank securities. However, since severing the Solomon Island dollar from its Australian link, these investments have diversified and comprise primarily commercial bank deposits within the Asia-Pacific region. The Bank in managing these reserves, 'is expected to ensure the convertibility of the currency, avoid exchange rate losses, and given the above, maximize the interest income and trading profits from this portfolio'.[17]

TABLE 2.2   Central Bank of Solomon Islands: assets and liabilities, 30 June 1985

		Assets *SI$ (000)*
2.2	Special drawing rights	1,565
35.7	Foreign call and term deposits	24,968
35.7	Foreign securities	24,971
5.7	Advances to domestic banks	4,000
6.7	Advances to central government	4,698
–	Development Bonds	25
0.8	Treasury Bills	538
1.9	Other securities	1,333
0.8	Non-government securities/investments	500
5.0	Fixed assets (less depreciation)	3,462
5.5	Other assets	3,844
100.0	Total Assets	69,904

		Liabilities *SI$ (000)*
11.1	Foreign international organizations	7,752
10.9	Deposits from domestic banks	7,635
20.3	Currency issued	14,193
27.9	Deposits from central government	19,509
9.1	Capital accounts	6,374
20.7	Other liabilities	14,441
100.0	Total Capital and Liabilities	69,904

Source: Central Bank of Solomon Islands (1985) *Mid-Year Economic Review*, pp. viii–ix.

Advances to the central government and to the domestic banks are also important Bank assets, particularly as the amounts shown in Table 2.2 represent new levels for both categories. Previously, advances to the central government had been at a low level. Over 1984–5, however, the government's deficit began a major expansion, and with it came a marked increase in local borrowings both from the Central and commercial banks. These deficit problems have since continued and in December 1985 were presenting considerable difficulties for the government administration.

The Central Bank's involvement as a lender both directly and indirectly has been paramount in funding government affiliated statutory corporations through both back-to-back loan facilities and refinancing schemes with commercial banks. Over 1982–3, for example, the Central Bank indirectly provided SI$ 2 million in term loans to Solomon Tanyo and the National Fisheries Development through back-to-back term deposits with the commercial bank lenders. The Bank also assisted the Government Shareholding Agency in the same period through a loan of SI$ 5 million secured by promissory note facility. Under the scheme, the GSA then acquired loans by the commercial banks to GSA affiliated companies. Thus the banking system funds were freed to finance additional lending.

In addition to these specific refunding operations the Central Bank operates a general purpose deposit/advance facility by which the banks can effectively refund their lending. The specific rates and conditions depend on local monetary conditions and in late 1985 they were made both less attractive and less available to the banks. First, on 5 December the Central Bank changed its general purpose lending rate for commercial banks from a stepped system, initially starting at 12 per cent, to just one rate set at 14 per cent. Secondly, it began reducing the funds available through this facility. On 19 December 1985, for example, these funds were limited to an amount equal to 18 per cent of the commercial bank's deposit liabilities, this was reduced to 16.5 per cent on 9 January 1986 and finally on 30 January 1986, to 15 per cent. Such advances, however, are still not counted as deposit liabilities for purposes of the liquid asset ratio.

(iv) *Liabilities*

In terms of liabilities, the Central Bank's traditional funds have come from central government deposits, followed by Solomon Island currency on issue. The commercial banks are also major depositors, particularly during periods of high liquidity. Over 1984, for example, when copra exports caused a huge increase in the local money supply, their deposits with the Central Bank reached a new high of SI$ 19,626,000. Central government deposits also reflect local economic conditions and they too were at much higher levels in 1984, reaching a high of SI$ 30,616,000. The lower levels shown in Table 2.2 in part reflect the outflow of foreign exchange that has occurred over 1985.

Under recent amendments to its legislation, the Central Bank is now enpowered to issue its own securities which gives it an instrument for open market operations in addition to government securities and, at the same time, not directly affecting the government's financing position.

(v) *Staffing*

Initially, the Bank's staff levels were minimal, as most work related to planning rather than administrative duties. Even with the release of the Solomon Island dollar in 1977 there were only 11 employees. Since then the numbers have grown in line with the Bank's new activities and at the end of 1984 it had 40 staff, including two expatriates serving as the managers of the banking and the research departments.

In encouraging the development of local staff, the Bank now sponsors courses throughout the year for its own, and sometimes other financial institutions' staff. In 1984, for example, these included in-house courses on foreign exchange, bank supervision, and rural banking. The Bank also has an arrangement with the New Zealand Technical Correspondence Institution through which Bank and other institutions staff can enroll in specialist banking subjects. Finally, it also participates in a range of international and regional seminars and training programmes.

Commercial Banks in the Solomon Islands

The commercial banks are both the oldest and most significant financial institutions in the Solomon Islands as well as major employers within the private sector. As with other Pacific island banks, they provide a full range of commercial and savings bank services with a marked specialization in foreign trade finance and related matters. This section examines the recent history, regulation, assets, sources of funds, representation and staffing of the industry.

(i) *Development*

Modern banking in the Solomon Islands dates to 23 July 1951, when what is now the Commonwealth Bank of Australia opened a trading and savings bank branch in Honiara. This branch was apparently 'established at the request of the local Administration as a medium of assistance to local residents and for the promotion of trade between the Protectorate and Australia'.[18] The Bank subsequently established a sub-branch in Gizo on 17 March 1969 and, as shown in Table 2.3, a considerable number of savings bank agencies throughout the country.[19]

The Commonwealth's direct operations in the Solomons was

TABLE 2.3   Commonwealth Savings Bank Agencies in the Solomon
Islands, 1952–81

Place	Opened	Closed	Operator
Atoifi	1969*	1981	Adventist Hospital
Auki	1970*	1981	District Crown Office, Malaita
Buala	1966	1981	Santa Isabel Council
Gizo	1972	1979	S.I. Govt Touring Department
Gojurur[a]	1956	1957	Unknown
Graciosa Bay	1971*	1981	District Commissioner's Office
Kirakira	1953*	1981	Solomon Islands Govt
Kolombangara	1968	1981	CHV Hodges Pty Ltd[b]
Liapari[c]	1960*	1981	CHV Hodges Pty Ltd[b]
Lutee	1952	1954	Unknown
Maluu	1954	1981	Solomon Islands Govt
Munda Airport	1974*	1981	Post & Telecommunications Dept
Nila	1967	1981	Catholic Mission
Papuru	1967	1979	General Trading Store
Pigeon Island	1967	1981	General Trading Store
Rendova Island	1963	1978	Unknown
Sasamungga	1969	1981	United Church
Sirovanga	1967	1981	Catholic Mission
Tegano[d]	1980	1981	East Rennell Council
Tulagi	1969	1981	Solomon Island Govt
West Rennell	1972	1979	Unknown
Yandina	1971	1981	Lever's Pacific Plantation

* Estimated date.
[a] Santa Isabel.
[b] Assumed later by Liapari Ltd.
[c] Vella Lavella Island.
[d] East Rennell Island.

Source: Commonwealth Banking Corporation, correspondence dated 17 February
1986.

particularly interesting for only here and in Papua New Guinea did
the Bank establish local banking operations.[20] In Papua New Guinea
the Commonwealth Bank's involvement was a direct function of the
Australian administration of the Territories of Papua and New
Guinea,[21] but in the Solomons the direct connection between the
Australian government interests in what was a British colony or
protectorate and those of the Bank are difficult to determine. It is
interesting, though, that due to inadequate war loss compensation to
British planters following the Second World War, many former
residents chose not to return and Australian interests filled the

TABLE 2.4   Commercial banks in the Solomon Islands, by establishment
dates

Australia and New Zealand Banking Group	3 October 1966
Hongkong and Shanghai Banking Corporation	17 December 1973
National Bank of Solomon Islands Ltd[a]	31 October 1980
Westpac Banking Corporation	15 October 1985

[a] Established initially on 23 July 1951 as a branch of the Commonwealth Bank and, commenced operations as the National Bank of Solomon Islands on 2 March 1981.

Source: Correspondence with respective banks (1983 and 1985).

vacuum. Similarly, at least some Australian politicians in the post-war period suggested that the British might give Australia responsibility for the Solomons, and that possibly the Solomons might later be merged with the Papua and New Guinea territories into a Melanesian Federation.[22] While there is no direct relationship between these events and the Commonwealth Bank's branch opening, such discussions may well have influenced the decision.

The Australia and New Zealand Banking Group (ANZ) was the next bank to open in the Solomons and, as with the Commonwealth, its establishment differed slightly from its traditional overseas operations. It had been approached by several local businessman to offer an alternative banking service in the country, but rather than a normal branch, 'the initial consideration was for a joint venture between ourselves [(the ANZ)] and Hongkong and Shanghai Banking Corporation'.[23] The rationale was that the joint venture would gain access to the profitable local Chinese merchant import finance as well as Australian business. The joint venture did not proceed, however, and the ANZ and the Hongkong and Shanghai, as shown in Table 2.4, eventually both opened separate branches in 1966 and 1983 respectively.

Following independence, the Solomon Island government held discussions with the Commonwealth Bank to acquire its local operations within the country and in late 1980 agreement was finally reached to transfer these operations over to a new company, the National Bank of Solomon Islands Ltd. The National was owned 51 per cent by the Commonwealth Bank and 49 per cent by the Solomon Island government via the Government Shareholding Agency. In practice, however, the government's investment was effectively funded via a A$ 900,000 joint venture scheme grant under Australia's aid program.

The National was established

> to expand and develop operations so as to extend the availability of
> banking services throughout the Solomon Islands, subject to sound
> commercial banking criteria; and to operate a progressive, efficient
> and competitive commercial banking undertaking in the best inter-
> ests of the Solomon Islands people[24]

Its operations, though, are still managed via senior Commonwealth
Bank staff under a management contract arrangement. In addition to
the direct salary costs of these staff, the National also pays the
Commonwealth Bank the greater of 7.5 per cent of the National's
after-tax profits or SI$ 12,500.

The Westpac Banking Corporation is the most recent entry into
local banking. It opened for business in 1985 as part of what the
Australian Financial Review described 'a strategy to expand its operations in the Pacific region'.[25] It was specifically invited by the government to encourage greater competition and financial innovation
within the commercial banking sector. From Westpac's viewpoint the
Honiara branch should prove a valuable addition to its Pacific island
operations for, in addition to any local banking business, trade and
project finance work, it should also provide additional support for its
Australian, Papua New Guinea, Fiji, Vanuatu, and New Zealand
banking operations as well as its affiliates in other Pacific countries.

(ii) *Regulation*

Commercial banks are currently licensed and regulated under the
Banking Ordinance 1976. It sets out the basic provisions for licensing, and the operational and regulatory requirements of banking and
other financial institutions within the country.

Under its provisions local banks are expected to maintain paid-up
capital and reserves in excess of the greater of SI$ 500,000 or 5 per
cent of its total deposit liabilities. Overseas incorporated banks must
hold the equivalent of SI$ 40 million. Other capital related regula-
tions include a maximum loan to any single group of borrowers
limited to 25 per cent of a local bank's paid-up capital and reserves or
2.5 per cent in the case of an overseas incorporated bank. There are
other restrictions on the lending to directors and bank employees and
on engaging in non-banking business activities.

As mentioned in the Central Bank section, the major operational control on the commercial banks is the liquidity asset ratio. This ratio was introduced in 1983 to replace the 5 per cent reserve requirement initially placed on banks. It is set at an amount equal to 25 per cent of the bank's total liabilities. Liquid assets for this purpose include currency, deposits with the Central Bank of Solomon Islands, deposits with other local banks, government securities, and short-term foreign assets.

The Central Bank can also significantly affect bank operations by changing its rediscounting provisions as well as its actions with government securities and statutory corporations funding and investment.

The degree of bank, as well as other financial institutions, regulation is expected to increase substantially over 1986–87 with the passing of a new Financial Institution Act. It is expected to include a number of new or more restrictive prudential requirements. The new Act will also introduce an annual licensing system through which the Central Bank will place a greater emphasis on Solomon Islander training and rural banking representation.

While the ideas behind the Act are hardly new (it was first raised in parliament in 1984), the Act itself is still in the drafting process and it was significant that as of late 1985 no bankers had actually seen a copy nor would the Central Bank provide a summary of its main provisions.

(iii) *Assets*

As shown in Table 2.5, local advances comprised some SI$ 45,449 or 65.8 per cent of commercial bank assets. This, however, was not always the case, and prior to the introduction of the Solomon Island dollar in October 1978, the bank's overseas asset holdings typically equalled around 60 per cent of their deposit liabilities.[26]

As shown in Table 2.6, the fishing industry is the largest of the various borrowers for 1985, reflecting the strong investment by Solomon Islands government corporations in this area. Much of the agricultural borrowing, too, also relates to government-owned or GSA-affiliated corporations. Likewise, government affiliation was equally important in the manufacturing and service sector. Indeed, a study in 1983 found that loans to statutory corporations and GSA affiliated companies accounted for some 51 per cent of over-all

TABLE 2.5   Commercial banks in the Solomon Islands, by type of assets
(figures for 30 June 1985)

Per cent	Type	SI$ (000)
2.9	Foreign assets	2,000
1.7	Currency	1,177
12.0	Due from other banks	8,298
7.2	Central govt. securities	4,964
3.3	Advances to central govt.	2,264
7.6	Advances to statutory corpn.	5,279
54.9	Advances to others	37,906
10.4	Other domestic assets	7,144
100.0	Total assets	69,032

Source: Central Bank of Solomon Islands (1985) *Mid-Year Economic Review*, p. x.

commercial bank lending. Significantly, in terms of loan numbers, though, these government- and GSA-affiliated borrowers accounted for only 3 per cent.[27]

Another interesting aspect of the study was the relatively small portion of loan funds advanced to Solomon Islanders. In 1983, for example, 10 per cent of lending went to Solomon Islanders or other native people, compared with 39 per cent to non-Solomon Islander private businesses.[28] This relative low importance of Solomon Islanders has sometimes been suggested to reflect that a 'racial bias might be affecting loan decisions'. A detailed investigation by the Central Bank in 1982, however, found 'no evidence of prejudice or bias on racial grounds'.[29] It is simply the relatively small loan size of the average Solomon Islander advance, usually much less than SI$ 3800. If examined on terms of numbers, Solomon Islanders accounted for 65 per cent of loans.[30]

As shown in Table 2.7, another aspect of local commercial bank lending is the increased growth of central government and, more recently, other borrowing categories. The former is a function of a greater need for working capital finance by the government as its costs have expanded rapidly while its collection of revenue and aid program refunds have slackened. The other change reflects the marked increase in consumption demand following the good prices for copra over 1984; since late 1985 there was an over-demand for import financing.

TABLE 2.6   Commercial banks in the Solomon Islands: advances by types of borrowers, 1982–5 (figures in SI$ (000) for year ending 30 June)

	1982	1983	1984	1985[a]
Manufacturing	833	1,572	2,884	2,746
Agricultural[b]	5,340	6,164	3,324	4,921
Fishing	4,664	4,865	9,990	9,949
Construction	377	200	759	632
Mining	25	–	10	9
Transport	2,098	1,775	1,562	1,830
Retail distribution	3,573	3,173	3,461	1,475
Other distribution	2,280	1,703	3,209	6,194
Other services[c]	5,227	6,840	6,161	2,878
Persons	1,658	2,023	4,493	3,807
Total	26,075	28,315	35,853	34,441

[a] Figures for the end of March 1985.
[b] Includes forestry.
[c] Includes public utilities, governments, professional, scientific and financial.

Source: Central Bank of Solomon Islands (1985) *Mid-Year Economic Review*, p. xvi and (1984) *Annual Report*, p. xv.

TABLE 2.7   Commercial banks in the Solomon Islands: total advances, bill receivables, term loan investments and securities, 1982–5

	1982	1983	1984	1985
Central government	1,677	4,923	6,570	7,228
Statutory corporations	5,996	6,723	4,633	5,279
Others	22,159	23,991	24,422	37,906
Total	29,832	35,637	35,625	50,413

Source: Central Bank of Solomon Islands (1985) *Mid-Year Economic Review*, p. xiv and (1984) *Annual Report*, p. xiii.

In terms of the costs, bank interest charges vary with the type of borrower and loan as well as the borrower's specific financial position and banking history. The ANZ Bank's normal rates, for example, ran between 14 and 17.5 in late 1985 while the Westpac Banking Corporation charges ranged between 15 and 18.5 with 16 to 16.5 most common.

Most of the lending is done either through an overdraft (usually secured with a first charge over property for at least 70 per cent of the loan's value), or via a fully-drawn advance. In the latter category, small- to medium-term lending was probably the most common, with the funds repayable in monthly principle and interest components over two to three years. Few of these loans would be in excess of SI$ 200,000. In addition to these commercial and normal trade financing, the local bank advances also include housing finance and personal loans.

Thus far housing finance, other than for bank staff, has not been a major area of bank lending. All the banks offer this facility but the terms and conditions vary considerably. The Hongkong and Shanghai Banking Corporation was seemingly the least interested as it would lend for periods of only up to five years. Thus those moneys lent were almost exclusively for investment rather than personal housing purposes. The Bank indicated a desire to lend on the more traditional 15-year basis but considered its local funding base too small and short term, to commit funds for that purpose.

In contrast, the National Bank of Solomon Islands was pleased to provide housing finance over 10 years at 17 per cent daily reducible. It normally required a 20 to 30 per cent down payment and would allow the repayments to equal as much as 50 to 60 per cent of the applicant's salary. This contrasts with approximately 30 to 35 per cent in Australia – the much higher rate reflects the lower cash requirements of most Solomon Islanders as they often receive their basic food items from visiting relatives or 'wantoks' from their local village.

The two remaining banks, Westpac Banking Corporation and the Australia and New Zealand Banking Group, both take a more traditional approach to housing finance with Westpac lending over 12 years or more at 15 per cent and the ANZ lending over 15 to 20 years at 14.5 per cent. While the latter rates and conditions are certainly more favourable, it should not be implied that either banks were actively bidding for housing loans. All banks in practice quite correctly agree with the Hongkong and Shanghai Banking Corporation's view on the funding position. Hopefully the revitalization of the Solomon Island Housing Authority into an active housing lender will allow the banking sector to concentrate any longer-term lending toward more productive economic purposes.

The banks also did some small personal lending with the loans generally between SI$ 1000 and 5000 and with consumer good items, small home repairs or improvement, and travel being the major purposes. Most personal lending is charged a flat interest rate with some banks, like the ANZ, making a distinction between secured and unsecured, 9.5 and 10 per cent flat respectively. The rates also varied somewhat with the customers past banking history, with 10.5 per cent flat seemingly the highest rate charged. Interestingly a number of personal loans are made against the security of the customer's existing bank deposits. The considerable difference between deposit and loan rates would not normally justify such applications, but apparently some customers find it easier to collect debts from the relatives or 'wantoks' if they show the funds are being used to repay a bank loan rather than going into their own bank account.

Over 1984 there was a major expansion in the banks' personal lending activities and one bank's outstandings in this area tripled in size over their 1983 totals. The motor vehicle finance was a major factor in this growth and one in which all the banks are active. Typically this lending requires a 30 to 50 per cent down payment on the vehicle and the rest is provided by the bank under a registered bill of sale. These loans are typically for three to five years and charged a flat rate of interest ranging from 9.5 to 10.5 per cent: 10 per cent flat seemed the most common.

Another reason for the increase in personal lending is the Small Loan Guarantee Scheme. This scheme was established in October 1983 to assist Solomon Islanders with the start up or working capital necessary to establish themselves in the monetary economy. Under this plan, the government, via the Central Bank, would provide a guarantee of up to 80 per cent of the unsecured funds lent by the banks under this scheme up to a maximum loan of SI$ 50,000. By the end of 1984 there were some 200 loans outstanding worth some SI$ 1.5 million ranging from SI$ 5000 to 10,000 each. The National Bank of Solomon Islands accounted for around 60 to 70 per cent of this business. More recent lending has been for somewhat smaller amounts with loans over SI$ 5000 being the exception rather than the rule.

It is difficult to judge the scheme's success without a detailed survey, but the impression gained from local interviews was that the funds were used mainly to finance import-based consumption rather than for the scheme's intended productive purposes. The major productive category over 1984, during the period of high copra price, was working capital finance for small individual copra traders buying copra in the more remote areas of the country.

It is a fair comment to suggest that the banks are not particularly enthusiastic participants in the scheme. Obviously one reason is that the costs of such loans are high, and despite the government guarantee the banks themselves have a 20 per cent risk exposure on these advances: advances they would probably not have otherwise made, but for the scheme. Some bankers also expressed concern over the lack of a written government guarantee on these advances. By December 1985 the banks had only received an understanding from the Central Bank that it would cover 80 per cent of the loss after all avenues for collection are pursued. This suggests that court action will be needed before any government repayment is forthcoming. For the banks, the shortage of local lawyers generally means substantial delays and some gave instances of waiting over two years for a case to be heard.

Perhaps not surprisingly, the banks generally try to collect through their own staff or via discussions with the borrower's employer. Interestingly, if and when a court action is taken and the matter does come to a hearing, the debt is apparently sometimes paid in full by the borrowers' relatives to avoid the adverse publicity that a judgment might entail.

The banks' other asset holdings are largely reflective of their liquid asset ratio requirements. The government securities are held for this purpose, as are deposits with the Central Bank. Since December 1985 the commercial banks have received 8 per cent per annum on their daily balance with the Central Bank. These interest bearing facilities, though, are often limited to certain conditions. At present, for example, a bank's liquid asset holdings must exceed an amount equal to 30 per cent of its total liabilities before using the Central Bank deposit facility.

(iv) *Funding*

As shown in Table 2.8, deposits comprise the vast majority of commercial bank funding with SI\$ 53,239 or 77.1 per cent of the total funds as of mid-1985.

As shown in Table 2.9, although the private sector is the major source of deposits, statutory corporations are nevertheless significant. Of these, the National Provident Fund and the Commodities Export Marketing Authority are the most important. The deposits, when placed, are generally offered to all the banks with the funds allocated to the bank offering the highest rate. Interestingly, due to its later start in the market, the National does not handle all the

TABLE 2.8 Commercial banks in the Solomon Islands, by types of liabilities, 30 June 1985 (figures in SI$ (000)

Capital	2,000
Demand deposits – central government	295
Demand deposits – statutory corporations	1,760
Demand deposits – provincial governments	556
Demand deposits – others [a]	10,310
Savings deposits	12,019
Time deposits – central government	228
Time deposits – statutory corporations	13,875
Time deposits – others [a]	14,196
Due to other banks	4,000
Bills payable	294
Other domestic liabilities	5,861
Foreign liabilities	3,638
Total liabilities and capital	69,032

[a] Includes non-resident deposits.

Source: Central Bank of Solomon Islands (1985) *Mid-Year Economic Review*, p. xi.

TABLE 2.9 Commercial bank deposits, by source, 1983–5 (figures in SI$ (000) for year ending 30 June)

	1983	1984	1985
Central govt	2,195	2,091	295
Statutory corpn	10,223	18,054	15,635
Provincial govt	261	822	784
Private sector	21,597	30,422	36,525
Total	34,276	51,389	53,239

Source: Central Bank of Solomon Islands (1985) *Mid-Year Economic Review*, p. xiii.

banking business of the various statutory bodies. The National Provident Fund, for instance deals with the Hongkong and Shanghai Banking Corporation as has the Solomon Island Housing Authority.

One of the more interesting aspects of the mid-1980s was the marked increase in the level of deposits resulting from the high commodity prices. This produced extremely liquid conditions for most bank customers as well as for the banking system itself. As a result overdraft facilities were used less, demand for new loans declined, and other outstanding loans repaid.

As with many countries, commercial banks generally do not pay interest on demand deposits within the Solomons. The exception are those accounts run by church groups, clubs and other non-profit organizations. Interest is normally paid at the rate for savings bank deposits. The ANZ Bank, for example, pays 6 per cent interest on such cheque account balances.

In addition, there is also an overnight interbank market between the four banks. In recent times, however, it has not been very active.

Passbook savings accounts are the traditional means of savings in the Solomon Islands and still account for around 22 per cent of total bank deposits, an amount similar to demand deposits. Individually, these accounts are quite small and expensive to operate. In 1984, for example, the banks had 53,000 savings accounts with deposits of SI$ 8 million or an average of only SI$ 150 an account. This compared with some 34,000 accounts in 1974 of which only 29,000 were held by Solomon Islanders.[31]

To encourage depositors to keep their account balances at more economically worthwhile levels, many of the banks have resorted to split interest rates for these accounts. Of these Westpac Banking Corporation is the most forceful in that it pays no interest on accounts with balances of under SI$ 49.99; 6 per cent on those with balances of SI$ 50 to 1999; and 10 per cent on those with SI$ 2000 or more. The National Bank of Solomon Islands similarly splits its interest with 4 per cent per annum compounded daily on savings passbook accounts with balances up to SI$ 299 and 9 per cent on amounts of SI$ 300 or more. In contrast, the ANZ Bank pays 6 per cent per annum on the minimum monthly balance for passbook accounts, but now offers 9.75 per cent compounded daily on its savings investment accounts, with the hope that more business will be directed to this less active type of deposit business.

In addition to the normal savings accounts, the National also operates a special school savings passbook account system initially established by the Commonwealth Bank in line with its traditional practice in Australia. It is seemingly the only bank to do so.

As was shown in Table 2.10, time or fixed-term deposits are the largest single source of commercial bank deposits, averaging slightly over half of total deposits over the last few years. For the banks, these monies represent the most competitive area of funding and the rates, terms and conditions vary considerably among the different institutions. In the case of minimum deposits, for example, the National is pleased to accept time deposits for as little as SI$ 300.

TABLE 2.10   Commercial bank deposits, by type, 1983–5

	1980	1981	1982	1983	1984	1985
Demand deposits	6,333	10,724	7,846	8,561	14,163	12,921
Savings deposits	6,770	6,999	7,121	7,627	9,336	12,019
Time deposits	21,525	13,254	14,617	18,088	27,890	28,299
Total	34,628	30,977	29,584	34,276	51,389	53,239

Source: Central Bank of Solomon Islands (1985) *Mid-Year Economic Report*, p. xiii and (1982) *Annual Report*, p. 39.

TABLE 2.11   Commercial bank deposits rates for SI$ 25,000 or less

	Australia and New Zealand Banking Group	National Bank of Solomon Islands	Westpac Banking Corporation
30 up to 90 days	9.00	10.00	10.00
3 up to 6 months	9.50	10.25	10.25
6 up to 12 months	9.75	11.00	10.75
12 up to 18 months	10.25	11.75	11.50
18 up to 24 months	11.25	12.25	12.00
24 months	11.50	–	12.50

Source: Industry interviews (December 1985).

In theory the interest rates on time deposits of up to SI$ 25,000 are controlled under an informal agreement among the commercial banks, but in practice this agreement has not been followed for sometime, and it is interesting to note the marked differences in deposit rates among the different banks in Table 2.11.

Over SI$ 25,000 the banks bid more actively with the rates for the various terms changing often on a daily basis in line with the banks' projected needs for funds. By December 1985 most banks were highly liquid and did not perceive a major change in their position or an increase in lending demand in the near future. Thus they were generally less aggressive for funds than might normally be the case. It is also interesting to note in Table 2.12 the marked difference in short rates between that of the ANZ Bank and Westpac Banking Corporation and those of the other banks. The lower rates of the former two suggesting a short-term oversupply of money.

TABLE 2.12   Commercial bank term deposit rates for amounts of
SI$ 100,000

	Australia and New Zealand Banking Group	Hongkong and Shanghai Banking Corporation	National Bank of Solomon Islands	Westpac Banking Corporation
7 days	8.00	12.00	10.00	7.5–8
30 days	12.00	12.00	13.50	10.5
3 months	13.50	14.00	13.50	10.5
12 months	13.50	14.00	13.50	11.5
24 months	12.00	14+	–	12.5

Source: Industry interviews (December 1985).

In addition to normal deposit raisings, the Central Bank has also been an important source of funds for some bank lending. Since mid-1983 it has provided a special refinancing scheme to direct credits to the productive areas of the economy. Currently Central Bank 'back-to-back' financing is available on a set margin with the rate declining rather than rising with maturity. Thus a bank could effectively borrow from the Central Bank at 1 per cent less than what the customer was charged on a one- to three year-loan, at 0.75 per cent on a four- to six-year loan, and at a 0.5 per cent margin on a seven- to ten-year loan.

In addition, up until 5 December 1985 the Central Bank would provide on-lending facilities at 12 per cent for the first 0.5 million, raising by 0.5 per cent with every additional 0.5 million up to a ceiling of 14 per cent. This has since been changed to a straight 14 per cent regardless of the amount. In addition, where as previously there was no set limit as to the funds available, on 19 December 1985 the Central Bank directed the banks to limit such borrowings to an amount equal to 18 per cent of their other deposit liabilities and then to reduce this further to 16.5 per cent by 9 January 1986 and to only 15 per cent by 30 January.

Given that three of the four commercial banks operate as branches of foreign banks, the paid-up capital reflected in Table 2.8 is the SI$ 2 million paid-up capital of the National Bank of Solomon Islands and thus any ratio calculations using industry figures would be very misleading. It is understood that each of the foreign banks, though, do have a *de facto* capital position in terms of their respective local

TABLE 2.13   Commercial bank staffing in the Solomon Islands, 1985

	Expatriate	*Local*	*Total*
Australia and New Zealand Banking Group	5	30	34
Hongkong and Shanghai Banking Corporation	9[a]	41	50
National Bank of Solomon Islands	14	98	112
Westpac Banking Corporation	4	10	14

[a] The Hongkong and Shanghai Banking Corporation normally operates with three European and three Chinese expatriate staff but has required additional assistance in the computerization of their operations.

Source: Industry interviews (December 1985).

position. The ANZ Bank and Hongkong and Shanghai Banking Corporation, for example, were believed to increase their effective local paid-up capital in line with that of the National in 1984, and the Westpac Banking Corporation was to start operations with an allocation of SI$ 1.25 million. It is not known where these amounts are reflected in the Table 2.8 figures.

(v) *Staffing*

As shown in Table 2.13, Solomon Islanders account for most commercial bank staff, but the key managerial and technical positions are still filled by expatriate staff on secondment from either Australia or, in the case of the Hongkong and Shanghai Banking Corporation, Hong Kong.

In the ANZ Bank, for example, the five expatriate staff serve as the Bank's manager, accountant, office supervisor, loans supervisor, and international department supervisor. Its most senior local staff have around five to seven years' service and occupy the position of accounting supervisor and, until recently, a loan officer. The loss of the latter staff member to other employment required an additional expatriate to be brought in the short term. It is intended that the loans position will again be filled by local staff in 1987, the office supervisor by 1988 and the international department by 1989.

It seems the most senior Solomon Islander among the banks was a sub-branch manager with the National Bank: he had been with the

Commonwealth, and then the National, for a total of 12 years. By late 1985 the National had 14 expatriates serving as the manager, accountant, foreign exchange dealer, financial controller, company secretary, branch operations, loans officer, operations officer, and six front office supervisors in the main branch.

Finally Westpac Banking Corporation's four expatriates serve as the manager, accountant, manager's assistant, and training officer. The latter two positions will be gradually phased out once the Bank's local operations are fully established.

Considerable training and experience will be required before these more technical positions can be localized. At present, each bank conducts its own training both locally in clerical duties, or overseas. The Central Bank would like to encourage more combined training efforts, but the potential for this is limited by the different administrative systems adopted by each bank. There would still be scope, however, for more general training on banking topics. The Central Bank, for example, has organized a training course to help local staff sit for the New Zealand Bankers' Institute examinations, and the commercial banks are welcome to send staff to these special sessions. Similarly, when the Development Bank has had overseas specialists giving courses locally, the other banks have been invited to send representation. The financial arrangements or the degree of success of these efforts is not known.

In addition to any local training, each of the banks send a couple of local staff each year for a few months training overseas, usually a combination of residential and on-the-job training. The emphasis of the former is normally on commercial lending practice and international banking and the latter is conducted, in the case of the Australian banks, at their branches in Queensland. The Queensland branches are thought to have both climatic and transport cost advantages for this purpose, as well as a historically-strong commercial connection between Brisbane and the Solomons.

The National Bank, with the largest staff, is very active in terms of training local staff.[32] Typically, they send four staff a year to Australia for three months training, with the on-the-job training done in branches in the Brisbane area. As with the other banks, the concentration has been on international banking, lending, and other specialist areas. In addition, it sends six to eight staff per year to Papua New Guinea for training, to the former Commonwealth Bank operations in that country, the Papua New Guinea Banking Corporation: Papua New Guinea has proved particularly helpful for these purposes as the level of local banking services are more similar to those used in the Solomons and the similarities in culture causes less problems for staff. The Bank also has six staff attending university on a full-time basis at the University of Papua New Guinea and the University of the South Pacific (in Fiji).

Finally, in addition to training and experience, the banks must also pay sufficiently high salaries to attract local staff. In late 1985, SI$ 8000 to 9000 per annum was generally considered a good salary for a local bank officer. Some indication of the higher ranges were reflected in a recent National Bank advertisement. It called for a 'manager international' who should have 'extensive international banking experience and possess a comprehensive knowledge of international exchange legislation and documentation' and for a 'manager administration & secretary' with 'tertiary qualification in accounting and have had considerable administrative and secretarial experience preferably in banking'. The salaries afforded potential applicants were both in the range of SI$ 12,000 to 15,000.[33]

There will undoubtedly be a considerable expansion in local training as the localization of expatriate positions will certainly be a condition of the annual license renewal requirements expected under the Financial Institution Act. Localization is not expected to replace the expatriate staff totally, and the managerial position of each of the foreign banks will remain expatriate staffed.

(vi) *Representation*

As mentioned earlier, the bank representation is concentrated within the area of Honiara with only the National Bank of the Solomon Islands operating branches in provincial towns. Thus far only three of the National's branches shown in Table 2.14 are outside of Honiara, but it plans to open two additional branches over 1986: one at Buala in Isabella Province and Noro in Western Province. The difficulties of opening such provincial branches should not be under estimated. For example, plans for the National to open a branch in Munda in Western Province was announced as early as 1982. Unfortunately though, after long delays, in 1984 the opening was 'deferred due to the unavailability of suitable land for a branch office and staff housing'.[34]

Despite the various physical and administrative problems associated with additional provincial branches, there seems no question that each of the banks will soon be more active in rural areas, as such

TABLE 2.14   National Bank of Solomon Islands: branches, 1985

Honiara[a]	2 March 1981
Gizo[b]	2 March 1981
Auki	9 July 1981
Chinatown-Honiara	4 August 1981
Kirakira	September 1984

[a] Initially opened by the Commonwealth Bank on 23 July 1951.
[b] Initially opened by the Commonwealth Bank on 17 March 1969.

Source: National Bank of Solomon Islands (1985).

an expansion is expected as a prime condition of renewal under the forthcoming annual licensing. Similarly, the government's current plan calls for bank branches in all provincial capitals by the end of 1986.[35]

Though branches in name, the actual operations of these facilities are really more like a sub-branch or bank staffed agency with their basic business restricted to accepting deposits and making withdrawals. There is some trade finance related work, as well as some small overdraft and personal loan business conducted at the branch level, but any actual loan applications, as well as any other significant decisions, must be forwarded to the head office for action.

In addition to the full-time branches, there are also some sub-branches or bank agencies operated on a part-time basis. The Hong-kong and Shanghai Banking Corporation's mini-branch in Kukum near Honiara, for example, is open only in the mornings. The Hongkong and Shanghai also operates two employer-located faci-lities one afternoon a week for Solomon Islands Plantations at Tettre and Mbalisuna, while the National Bank also operates a school banking service at the Woodford School (mainly expatriates' stu-dents) in Honiara.

The private agencies are the other category of bank representation in the Solomons. They are run by non-bank staff, usually in conjunc-tion with the agents' other business activities. Small trading stores, for example, offer the banking business to encourage shoppers to visit their retail facilities. The agents will open passbook savings accounts and accept deposits or handle withdrawals. For this they receive a commission of so much on deposits, withdrawals and a

TABLE 2.15   Commercial bank representation in the Solomon Island, 1985

	Branches	*Bank agencies*	*Other agencies*
Australia and New Zealand Banking Group	1	–	1
Hongkong and Shanghai Banking Corporation	1	1	–
National Bank of Solomon Islands	5	–	35
Westpac Banking Corporation	1	–	–

Source: Industry interviews (December 1985).

payment on new accounts. The specific commissions vary from bank to bank but typically would be from 0.6 to 1.0 per cent on deposits and 0.4 to 1.0 per cent on withdrawals, as well as SI$ 2.00 per new account. The actual business conducted varies considerably from 'a handful per week, to several hundred' transactions.[36]

As shown in Table 2.15, the National Bank of Solomon Islands has an extensive savings bank agency network throughout the country, and customers can use their National savings passbook to make cash withdrawals of up SI$ 200 at any of these agencies. Of its 35 agencies in mid-1985, 16 were in Western Province, 6 in Choiseul, 1 in Guada canal (ex Honiara), 5 in Malaita (ex Auki) and 1 in San Cristobal/ Mikira (ex Kirakira). Another was operated in conjunction with the Development Bank of Solomon Islands on the latter's inter-island ship, the MV Rainbow.

Given their relatively simple operations, it would seemingly be a relatively simple matter to fulfill government plans for at least 70 bank agencies by 1987/89.[37] In practice, however, agency establishments have not proved quite so easy. The ANZ Bank, for example, in the past had operated as many as seven agencies outside of Honiara but 'six were closed down in April 1978, two at the request of the agencies and four at the bank's own instigation. The reason these four were closed down was economic, plus problems with forgery and fraud'.[38] Besides the economics, one difficulty following independence was the replacement of expatriate missionaries and district officials with Solomon Island nationals. These officials often lacked the same degree of administrative skills as their predecessors and consequently required greater supervision and support from the banks. Unfortunately the remoteness of most agencies and their business generation could not justify the additional expense. Even the National has experienced this problem, and whereas the Commonwealth Bank had 18 agencies as well as Gizo sub-branch in 1979,[39] the National Bank opened operations with only 10 agencies and did not exceeds its 19 position again till 1983.

Regardless of such problems, the number of bank agencies will be greatly expanded over the next couple of years in an effort to bring the most basic of banking services within a day-trip of most Solomon Islanders. These agencies are also hoped to offer an expanded range of services. In particular, it is hoped that they will act as disbursement and payment agents for the Development Bank in addition to their own business. In the long run, it is hoped that eventually, when the business justifies, that many agencies will be upgraded to fully-fledged bank branches.

Development Bank of Solomon Islands

The Development Bank of Solomon Islands was established on 16 December 1977 under the provision of the Development Bank of Solomon Islands Ordinance 1977 and commenced operations on 1 January 1978. It was created to assume the operations of the Agricultural and Industrial Loans Board and to assist in economic and social development with particular emphasis (Section 4):

(a) to promoting the participation of Solomon Islanders in that economic development;
(b) to rural development; and
(c) to stimulating processing and industrial activities which might be expected to strengthen the economic independence of Solomon Islands.

The Bank has been granted a wide range of powers (Section 6) to include: granting short-, medium- and long-term loans; guaranteeing loans from other sources; making equity investments, providing technical, managerial and financial advice; identifying, formulating and promoting new projects; underwriting new issues of securities; drawing, accepting, endorsing and discounting bills of exchange; accepting deposits, administering funds; acquiring, managing and dispensing of real estate and securities; and forming corporations and partnerships.

(i) *Development*

The Development Bank's predecessor, the Agricultural and Industrial Loans Board was established by the government in 1955 with an authorized capital of A$ 355,000. It was intended to finance 'the development, maintenance and improvement of land, for the promotion and development of crafts and industries'.[40] Unfortunately these ambitions were not matched with adequate resources. The Board lacked permanent staff during most of its life and hence was a passive rather than an active lender. In 1966, for example, it made a total of 11 loans, another 13 in 1967 and 20 loans in 1970.[41] Of equal concern was that most lending was to expatriate run commercial and plantation interests rather than to Solomon Islanders. These loans were also commonly of a short-term nature, and as one government evaluator complained, 'tend to overlap with those of the commercial banks'.[42]

While the Board was allowed to borrow its own funds in 1967 to expand its lending programme, there was little change in its operations until May 1972 with the launching of its Small Business Credit Scheme. This A$ 200,000 programme was to provide Solomon Islander business advice as well as funding, and was run with the support of three US Peace Corp volunteers. The Board further expanded its operations in September 1972 by purchasing A$ 25,000 of shares in Solomon Island Investment Ltd, the Solomons' first and, thus far, only, public share issue.[43] In August 1973 the Board also received its first assistance from the Asian Development Bank.

Unfortunately, despite these various efforts the Board did not achieve its initial aims. Indeed, over its 22 years of existence it made a total of only 753 loans worth some A$ 2.6 million. Worse still, few of these advances actually assisted the country's rural development. As one study commented, it 'has not made an input in the rural areas, most of its lending being in the Honiara area'.[44]

Given this performance, the government sought to transform the Board into a more viable project and in 1974 the Asian Development Bank began to examine expanding the Board's operations into a development bank. This concept was well received and by the late 1970s two development finance institutions were under consideration: a

TABLE 2.16   Development Bank of Solomon Islands: assets and liabilities, 1984

%		SI$
	Assets	
–	Deposits with domestic banks	3
92.1	Loans & investments – private sector[a]	10,235
7.9	Other assets[b]	876
100.0	Total assets	11,114
	Liabilities:	
41.3	Loans from overseas	4,590
–	Loans from domestic banks	64
53.2	Loans from Central government[c]	5,916
6.2	Loans from Statutory corporations[d]	689
1.3	Other liabilities[e]	(146)
100.0	Total liabilities[f]	11,114

[a] Net provision of doubtful debts.
[b] Including net fixed assets.
[c] Intermediated by Central government.
[d] Issued capital intermediated by Government Shareholding Agency.
[e] Reserves, undistributed profits and all current liabilities.
[f] Discrepancy in total due to rounding.

Note: Figures in ( ) = negative numbers.

Source: Central Bank of Solomon Islands (1984), *Annual Report*, p. xvii.

government development bank to assume and expand the Board's operations; and a private development institution owned by the then three commercial banks. The latter body would assist the banks to expand into medium- to long-term lending. Eventually though, only the government development bank was created.

(ii) *Assets*

As shown in Table 2.16, loans and investments account for the bulk of the Development Bank's assets. For the most part these are medium- to long-term advances designed to finance the acquisition of fixed assets. The Bank may also provide working capital and performance guarantees, and in the agricultural sector, seasonal and short-term funds as well. Ideally though, the Bank lends in conjunction with a commercial bank providing the working capital finance.

In its lending, the Development Bank is considered 'a risk lender relying on the personal qualities of borrower/guarantors plus the medium to long term prospects of success for the venture financed'.[45] In practice, however, its loan evaluations take in a wide range of factors. First, the borrower is expected to provide a reasonable equity in the proposal, either through assets or physical labor, and have sufficient management and technical abilities to implement the proposal.

Once these factors and the loan security is determined the proposal is also evaluated to ensure it is technically feasible, commercially viable, economically desirable, serves a satisfactory market or demand, has reasonable capital and operating costs and complies with the Solomons' over-all economic and social development plan. Such factors as the use of local materials, local employment and training, broadening local entrepreneurship, expanding exports or decreasing imports, lowering costs or improving the standard of goods and services within the country, are also very important. Though the Bank will lend to any one, anywhere in the Solomons, it also 'gives preference to Solomon Islanders, and to projects in areas other than Honiara'.[46] This position is particularly reflected in more recent lending. In 1983, for example, 82 per cent of loan approvals were for outside Honiara and 95 per cent were to Solomon Islanders.

Development Bank advances are also subject to some size qualification. First, in terms of Bank's own exposure, its total loans, guarantees and equity investments to any one company cannot exceed an amount equal to the Bank's unimpaired paid-up capital and reserves. These funds likewise must not exceed an amount equal to 75 per cent of the client enterprise's fixed assets in industrial ventures (80 per cent for agricultural projects).

In terms of sectors, loans to commerce and industry are by far the most important, and in 1984 accounted for 64 per cent of the outstandings. Real estate development funding is believed to be a large component of these advances and most new buildings in the Solomons are financed either by the Development Bank or the National Provident Fund. Development Bank finance has also been instrumental in the establishment of the local furniture, soap production and steel fabrication industries as well as improving the level of inter-island shipping (see Table 2.17).

The Micro-loans program is by far the most important source of loan applicants, and by 1983 accounted for 83 per cent of the Bank's loan numbers. These loans are designed to assist Solomon Islanders and are generally far less than SI$ 1000; the average is around SI$ 300.

TABLE 2.17   Development Bank of Solomon Islands: lending, by
classification (figures in SI$ (000))

Classification	End of December			
	1981	*1982*	*1983*	*1984*
General	989	1,394	2,028	1,940
Plantations	175	236	247	226
Commercial & industrial	4,642	5,726	6,638	6,869
Rural trading	47	54	51	65
Co-operatives	275	331	347	347
Micro-loans	753	636	571	592
Cattle Development Authority	295	363	359	346
Staff	40	129	264	339
Total	7,216	8,869	10,505	10,724

Source: Central Bank of Solomon Islands (1984), *Annual Report*, p. xviii.

Unfortunately, the Micro-loan scheme, while successful in expanding
Development Bank lending into rural areas, has not been a financial
success. Indeed, by their very nature, the processing expense can
easily exceed the interest earned. The government-set 5 per cent
margin allowed on this lending has further added to the problem. At
present, for example, the Development Bank borrows its funds at 5
per cent from the government for lending at 10 per cent. As a result,
the micro-loan business has been very costly, and in 1981 at least
'expenses are estimated to have exceeded income by more than
$80,000'.[47] Their administrative costs, though, have been sub-
sequently overshadowed by a serious arrears problem resulting from
this programme, and by 1983 some 77 per cent of the micro-loans
outstanding were in arrears.

In terms of its loan administration, the Development Bank is
expected to maintain doubtful debts provisions equal to 10 per cent
of its total loans, guarantees and equity portfolio. In practice, however, the 10 per cent figure has proved insufficient. In 1981, for
example, the Bank reported that 'more than half of DBSI's 3300
active loans being in arrears'.[48] In portfolio terms, at the end of 1983
the arrears rate still stood at 12 per cent of its loan portfolio, or some
SI$ 1.2 million in overdue payments.

As mentioned above, the Bank may make equity investments as
well as loans. Its share purchases, though, are restricted to new
shares that assist new companies or help existing operations expand.

To minimize its risk exposure, the Bank's maximum single equity investment is limited to an amount equal to 10 per cent at the Bank's unimpaired paid-up capital and reserves. Its total equity investments, though, are subject to an over-all limit of 20 per cent of paid-up capital and reserves. Similarly, from a client viewpoint the Bank's investment should not exceed more than 25 per cent of the client's paid-up capital. The intention is that the Bank should not have control of the enterprise but rather dispose the shares as soon as feasible.

As early as 1977, it had been suggested that the Development Bank might use the shares held by the Government Shareholding Agency, together with its own equity holdings, as the basis of a unit trust to be managed by the Bank. While this is still a worthwhile goal, it does not appear under active consideration. The Bank's over-all equity investment operations have also taken a low profile, and the results of its investment operations are given no specific mention in the most recent (1983) General Manager's Report.

In spite of this the Bank was active during the period, and in 1983 added SI$ 134,700 to its equity portfolio (104,700 in over-the-counter shares and SI$ 30,000 in other shares) and sold SI$ 117,699 worth of shares (104,700 in over-the-counter shares and SI$ 12,999 in other shares); this meant a net increase of SI$ 17,001, and resulted in an equity portfolio of SI$ 294,203.[49] The Bank's investment portfolio at the end of December 1985 is shown in Table 2.18. In addition, the Bank also had a wholly-owned subsidiary, Staco Ltd. It would be useful if the Bank resumed practice of reporting the names, percentage of shares held, value and performance of its 1980 equity investments as part of the notes to its accounts.

(iii) *Funding*

Table 2.16 suggests that the Development Bank effectively obtains all its funding from borrowings, with such traditional sources as paid-up capital or retained earnings not even receiving a direct mention in the accounts. An examination of the footnotes, however, reveals a much different picture, for the loans from the Central government are in fact the Development Bank's issued capital. The category 'loans from statutory corporations' also surprisingly contains the Bank's reserves and undistributed profit accounts. Finally, the loans which are listed as from overseas are in fact loans that have been made to the

TABLE 2.18   Development Bank of Solomon Islands: equity investment, 1985

Firm name	Type of business	Amount SI$
Solomon Soaps Ltd	soap production	97,001
Fab Block Co. Ltd	building materials	5,000
South New Georgia Dev. Corp.	boat transport	12,500
Marau Shipping Co. Ltd	boat transport	20,000
Horikiki Develop. Co.	coconut production	20,000
Solomons Rice Co. Ltd[a]	rice business	1
Mendana Hotel Ltd[a]	hotel business	1
Solent Ltd – laundry	laundry	5,000
Flexible Packaging (SI) Ltd	packaging	30,000
Property Development Co. Ltd	real estate dev.	104,700
Asian Paints (SI) Ltd	paints	28,000

[a] Holding due to company law requirements as to the number of shareholders required. Effectively 100 per cent owned by the Government Shareholding Agency.

Source: Development Bank of Solomon Islands (1985).

Solomon Islands' government which it has in turn lent to the Bank. It is not known why these accounts are presented in such a strange fashion.

Thus, despite initial appearances, the Bank's own equity accounts for over half its funding. While this would suggest a very substantial level of government support, in practice most of the Solomon Island government funding, via the Government Shareholding Agency, has resulted from specific purpose aid grants made by the Australian and New Zealand government. As overseas aid can be expected to become more difficult in the future, the Bank will rely increasingly on its own internal funds generation. Over 1985–9, for example, the Bank expects an internally operated cash flow of SI$ 2 to 2.3 million per year, plus additional equity contributions for Government Shareholding Agency and the Central Bank of SI$ 0.5 to 0.75 million.[50]

The Central Bank of Solomon Islands made its first investment in Development Bank shares (some SI$ 0.5 million worth) in 1984. The rationale was seemingly to expand the Development Bank's local funding sources. Under its Act, for example, it can sell shares to non-government bodies provided the Solomon Islands government owns at least 51 per cent of the total shares. The real benefits from the Central Bank's shareholding, however, must be questioned. First, for the Central Bank to hold shares in an institution over which it is the potential regulatory authority seems to invite potential conflicts of interest, particularly if the practice is expanded to cover other institutions. Secondly, it fragments the government ownership, a monitoring role supposedly performed by the Government Shareholding Agency. Thirdly, the exercise is little more than a pen-and-ink accounting measure. There has been no real improvement in the Bank's funding sources as the Central Bank itself is wholly owned by the Government Shareholding Agency. While it is difficult to argue against the Development Bank expanding its shareholder base, this should be a real diversification and expansion. The present moves are simply window-dressing, and would be more effective if the Central Bank had paid higher dividends to the Government Shareholding Agency and it in turn then increased its annual investment in the Development Bank. It is doubtful that the Central Bank's international credit standing is particularly improved by providing the equity finance directly as an investment.

In terms of borrowings, the Development Bank has been well supported by a number of multilateral agencies to include the Asian Development Bank, European Development Fund and the World Bank's International Development Agency. These monies are typically lent in support of certain projects or activities and are made at concessional rates of interest. Many loans also contain an element of technical assistance. Although those loans are denominated in foreign currencies, the Bank is not permitted to assume for foreign exchange risk. Thus the potential losses must either be absorbed by the government, as part of its on-lending conditions, or by the end borrower. In addition to these foreign borrowings, the Development Bank also obtains loan financing through the National Provident Fund and to a much less extent, the National Bank of Solomon Islands.

(iv) *Representation*

In many countries development bank financing is in high demand, and such lending is subject to rationing. This has not been the case with the Solomon Islands. As the Bank has often admitted, 'credit lines available to DBSI through the government were not fully utilized because of a lack of suitable requests for financing'.[51] This position is similarly supported in the most recent development plan which states that the Bank 'has never had to decline a loan proposed for a lack of funds and expects to be able to finance all viable proposals'.[52] The reason for this position is believed to be, not the interest rates charged, but rather the potential borrower 'not knowing how, when or where to approach the DBSI, or a mistaken feeling that DBSI will insist on taking his land as security for a loan'.[53]

To overcome this problem the Bank has had to rely on the support of other government agencies to promote the Bank's services and help with loan applications. The Cattle Development Officers, Agriculture Field Assistants, Co-operative Officers, Forestry and Fishery Officers, and Business Advisory Service staff, are particularly important in this process.[54] Ideally, though, the gradual expansion of the Bank's branch offices and field officers will greatly reduce this reliance on other agencies, particularly in the appraisal area.

A strong Bank presence in rural areas is important for a number of reasons, not the least of which is the heavy demands already placed upon these other government agencies. Bank staff-customer contact at the appraisal stage would also help avoid future misunderstandings about the Bank's expectations, and the client's obligations. Of equal importance is for Bank staff to inspect the project at its various development stages and to supervise loan collection. Though perhaps fairly obvious objectives, the difficulties they present cannot be overstated. This is particularly true given the Bank's commitment to expand its rural lending. Even now most Bank 'travel is by canoe powered by outboard motors, small ships and four wheel drive jeeps'.[55] The Bank's new branch network is then only part of the solution, more trained field officers are required.

The Bank opened its first branch in 1979 and today, as shown in Table 2.19, has five branches and two sub-branches. The initial expansion involved expatriate managers, but by mid-1981 local managers had assumed their positions. Each branch now has around six to ten staff. They are responsible for processing the loan applications, the appraisal reports, and the follow-up and loan supervisions within their area. Each branch is headed by a loans officer who has loan approval power up to SI$ 3000 with larger amounts approved at head office; loans of SI$ 20,000 or more require Board approval. While these delegated amounts may appear small, they adequately handle most applications.

Ideally the Bank should expand its operations further and the current development plan calls for 'representation in Temotu, New Georgia' over 1987/89.[56] It also suggests that the Bank will 'collaborate with commercial banks to economize on capital and operating

TABLE 2.19   Development Bank of Solomon Islands: branch representation

Type	Location	Province
Head Office	Honiara	n.a.
branch	Honiara	Guadalcanal & Central
branch	Auki	Malaita
branch	Gizo	Western
branch	Kirakira	Makira
branch	Buala	Isabel
sub-branch	Tulagi	Central
sub-branch	Munda	Western
planned		Taemoto

Note: Over 1985–9 representation planned for South Malaita, Choiseul and New Georgia.

Source: Development Bank of Solomon Islands (1985).

costs of remote area branches and agencies'.[57] The Central Bank's rural financial study called for even greater rural representation with 'a permanent Development Bank presence at Provincial sub-level, e.g. Taro Island, Munda, Seghe, Lambi Bay, Mara'u, Afio, Malu'u, etc, reporting to Development Bank and bank offices at Provincial head quarters which in turn would be competent to make loan approvals and direct loan after care operations'.[58]

(vi) *Staffing*

By December 1985, the Development Bank had a staff of 83 including three expatriate staff, two of whom are on secondment from the Commonwealth Development Bank of Australia. While the expatriate number may not appear high, these officers occupy the two key operational positions after the general manager: the assistant general manager (administration) and the assistant general manager (lending). The third officer is the Bank's financial controller and has been instrumental in the Bank's computerization programme. All these officers are funded by the Australian Development Assistance Bureau. Until recently the Bank had two additional expatriates: a training officer and an agricultural consultant.

Other Development Bodies

In addition to the Development Bank there are a number of other, mainly foreign-supported, bodies which have some development finance role within the country. The most important of these is the British government's Commonwealth Development Corporation, but various independent non-profit agencies such as the Foundation for Peoples of the South Pacific, the International Human Assistance Program and the Solomon Island Development Trust, all offer some financial support as part of their self-help rural development programmes.

(i) *Commonwealth Development Corporation*

Though not directly represented in the Solomons in an operational sense, the Commonwealth Development Corporation has nevertheless been an important factor in local development work through technical assistance work and direct investment. Its two major projects at present include the Naha Valley Housing estate and Solomon Islands Plantations Ltd. The latter, the country's largest single employer, is owned 57 per cent by the Commonwealth Development Corporation, 40 per cent by the Government Shareholding Agency, and 3 per cent by local landowners. This shareholding, representing a SI$ 8.2 million investment, is further reinforced by a 7.1 million pound sterling loan to the company.

By 1984 Solomon Islands Plantations owned 3538 hectares of oil palms and 81 hectares of cocoa in mature production, but with substantial plans for expansion of both crops.

The Commonwealth Development Corporation also sponsored the Naha Valley housing estate. It is a 200-residential housing scheme near Honiara, which was intended primarily for middle-income earners. The CDC provided a 2 million pound sterling loan for this project.

(ii) *Foundation for Peoples of the South Pacific*

The Foundation is another private agency which acts as a conduit for non-government Assistance from Australia, Holland, New Zealand and the United States. It has operated in the Solomon Islands since 1980 under the guidance of a National Commission or board comprised of seven members: a representative each from the Development Bank of Solomon Islands, National Provident Fund, Economic Planning Office, YMCA, National Council of Women, and the Solomon Islands Christian Association, as well as an Anglican priest, Father John Garern.

The Foundation's 27 full-time and part-time staff within the Solomons work toward improving the quality of village life and the Foundation has been active in the development of rural community fisheries, water supply, women's interests and the creation of the Solomon Island Development Trust. Its most significant programme, the Small Commercial and Community Projects Program, is designed to encourage village groups to engage in small-scale business activities to include fisheries, poultry, piggeries, coconut oil, charcoal stoves, furniture and boat building.[59]

In support of its development program, the Foundation operates an incentive deposit scheme to encourage villages to borrow from the banking system to finance worthy projects. Basically, the Foundation will deposit an amount equal to 15 per cent of the loan (usually between SI$ 500 to 2000) in a bank account on the behalf of the village. When the loan is repaid, this deposit will then become the property of the village. The Foundation has used this scheme since 1984 to encourage both fishery and local boat building projects.

(iii) *International Human Assistance Program*

The International Human Assistance Program is a New-York-based non-profit organization which was initially established in 1952 to assist in self-help programmes in rural areas of Korea. It has since expanded its operations to cover a wide range of developing countries and first opened in the Solomons in August 1980.

Its operations are concentrated at village self help efforts with an emphasis on 'sanitation and primary health, crop diversification and marketing, income generation and training for women and out-of-school youth'.[60] It provides some financial or material support for approved projects which entail community 'sweat equity'.

(iv) *Solomon Island Development Trust*

The Solomon Island Development Trust is another non-government aid body funded primarily from US sources which was established in 1981 and is managed by five to seven trustees appointed by specific national organizations.

At the end of 1985 the Trust employed some 22 full-time and 71 part-time staff.[61] Its activities are primarily of an educational nature and through its Village Outreach program promotes self-reliance at the village level. In addition to some 22 teams of three to four local staff each, the Trust also operates a small loan scheme whereby each of its six operational centres may lend up to SI$ 500 per year in support of village projects. These loans are for a maximum of SI$ 100 each and must be repaid at 6 per cent interest within six months. Most help finance local poultry and piggery operations. The loan scheme, though, is intended more as an education tool to show villagers how credit can be used for productive purposes, than as a significant source of development finance.

Provincial Development Corporations

As mentioned in the Government Shareholder Agency discussion, each of the Solomon's provincial governments also have the ability to establish an agency through which to hold shares in their commercial undertakings. These institutions, for example, were planned to hold the provincial government's shares in the proposed National Insurance Co. They were similarly suggested as shareholders in a restructured Government Shareholding Agency, to be known as the Investment Corporation of the Solomon Islands. As yet, none of these suggestions have been implemented, and not all of the provincial governments have established development authorities or corporations. Nevertheless, at least one company for each province can be expected.

To date, the Makira Economic Development Authority is by far the most developed of these bodies, and has had the longest operating history as well. It was apparently established by the provincial government in 1979, only shortly after the Solomons received independence. Initially, though, it operated through a normal corporate structure and only assumed its current statutory authority position on 7 November 1983 by virtue of a provincial government ordinance. As indicated, the main purpose of these enterprises were to assume control of those commercial activities run by the provincial governments. In the case of Makira, these included the rest house that had been established by the Colonial government and a few other similar enterprises. These activities have since been expanded to include a restaurant (an outgrowth of the rest house operations), a butchery shop, a fish marketing agency, and a shipping service with offices in

Honiara as well as the province. At present its major operation is in shipping where it operates two boats to ensure the provision of supplies within the province. The boats also operate as mobile purchasing units for copra purchasing and the Authority operates as an agent for the Commodities Export Marketing Authority for this purpose. As a result of these efforts, local producers have generally received better prices and the over-all copra production is thought to have increased as a result of both this and the greater certainty of service. In the longer term, though, the Authority hopes to play an even greater role by acting as the local joint venture partner with foreign enterprises wishing to invest within the province. This could see the Authority acting either directly or on behalf of the customary landowners concerned.

Finance Companies

The most recent financial institution type established in the Solomon Islands is the local finance company. The first firm, AGC Finance (SI) Ltd, was incorporated on 20 August 1985, and commenced operations in late November 1985.[62] It is a wholly-owned subsidiary of the Australian Guarantee Corporation which is in turn affiliated with the Westpac Banking Corporation.

The new firm's entry is in response to government efforts to encourage more competition and a wider range of financial services within the Solomons. It is also likely that AGC will not be the only finance company operating locally, for according to the government, it has 'indications by existing commercial banks that finance companies affiliated to them should like to offer services in Solomon Islands'.[63]

From the government's viewpoint it is hoped that the finance companies will complement local banking lending by providing greater medium-term finance than is currently the case. In addition the finance companies are seen to have 'greater flexibility available . . . in structuring loan packages, mainly because of their longer-dated liabilities is expected to benefit the balance sheets of many Solomon Islands enterprises'.[64]

AGC will operate primarily in the areas of motor-vehicle and agricultural finance, as well as providing some business equipment finance. This will be provided by means of normal commercial loans, hire purchase and lease finance. Its hire purchase activities will be mainly in the area of motor vehicles (mainly buses and trucks), with a

50 per cent down payment and the balance secured by a chattel mortgage/registered bill of sale.

As within Australia, lease finance is expected to comprise a major portion of AGC's local business. Thus far there has been little leasing in the Solomons and the government, to date, has done little to encourage its development. The Central Bank, though, apparently sees some merit in leasing for it has commented that 'some of the services developed elsewhere by finance companies, for example leasing of equipment, certainly have a place in Solomon Islands development'.[65] Finance seems particularly applicable to the logging equipment business, and in certain cases AGC may be able to provide virtually 100 per cent financing as a result.

At present AGC expects to have in excess of SI$ 1 million in lease and hire purchase receivables by the end of 1986, and given the present lack of local alternatives for either lease or hire purchase finance, it should have little difficulty in achieving this local portfolio. In terms of funding, the company, in addition to a SI$ 500,000 in paid-up capital, also has local overdraft facilities with the Westpac Banking Corporation. In the longer run, however, it can be expected that AGC will follow its practice adopted in Australia and overseas of raising a large portion of its funds through medium-term debenture or unsecured note issues.

In addition to the more traditional finance company activities, the government also expects that they will perform some merchant-banking-styled services. For example, it expects an increase in syndicated lending between Solomon Island institutions with the finance companies 'acting as catalyst and organiser'.[66] Similarly, AGC also plans its affiliate will provide 'assistance with establishment of small business'.[67]

As with the Westpac Banking Corporation, AGC has a particular advantage over other potential operators in that it has long operated in the Papua New Guinea market and has much experience in dealing with Melanesian business. In addition, the AGC manager, just as most of the Westpac expatriate staff, has worked some years in Papua New Guinea and can speak the Solomon Island version of pidgin English with little difficulty.

General Insurance

The insurance industry in the Solomon Islands is still poorly developed. Local requirements are fulfilled by a variety of foreign-owned companies, mostly through local agents. As one study in 1978 found, there were ten companies operating within the country with 'all the funds being sent abroad'.[68] While the number of firms has since become smaller, little else has changed from a 1980 study, which characterized the industry as 'fragmented, costly and directed entirely from outside'.[69] Indeed, the local market has changed only recently.

A strong local insurance industry could play an important role in retaining foreign exchange reserves within the country and developing local institutional investment. Though its premium income, estimated at around SI\$ 2.5 million per annum,[70] is small by international standards, a redirection of even part of this flow could add significantly to local investment and foreign exchange.

The Solomon Islands government is aware of this potential, and in its 1980–5 development plan stated that 'the primary role of insurance in national development is to provide a means of reducing loss to individual persons, companies and institutions, so that they are not deterred from making investments, creating new productive assets, and playing an active part in national economic life'. The insurance industry also provides 'financial reserves, made up of insurance changes (premiums) and set aside against future claims, which can meanwhile be re-invested in suitable development activities'.[71] Finally it found that the insurance companies account 'for a larger proportion of overseas' transfer of funds'[72] and that government action here might assist the country's balance of payment position.

Given the market's poor development, there was little justification for government regulation. In 1972, however, the largest sub-market of the industry, motor-vehicle insurance, was given some control under the Motor Vehicle (Third Party Insurance) Act 1972. In practice, though, it did little to regulate the industry.

Finally on 3 September 1985, Parliament passed the Insurance Act 1985. It was designed to regulate the insurance business in the Solomons; create a Controller of Insurance; require all insurers, brokers and agents register under the Act; and protect the rights of policy holders. In addition, the Act was to help ensure the industry's 'responsiveness to the needs of national development'.[73]

The Controller of Insurance, under the Minister of Finance's supervision, is the key to the Act's implementation. He has the power to register and supervise the local insurance industry , formulate local standards of conduct, approve the standard policy terms and conditions, determine (with Ministerial approval) local premium rates, prohibit certain transactions, and generally advise the government on insurance matters. He can also direct insurers to modify, or not renew, terms and conditions of reinsurance contracts, provide certified copies of any documents, and be examined under oath on insurance matters. The Controller can also limit management expenses, particularly payments to overseas head offices, commissions and overseas travel.

While the Act states that only registered parties can conduct insurance (other than reinsurance) business in the Solomons, or provide coverage for Solomon Island risks, certain classes of insurance may be exempted where the existing facilities are inadequate or the exemption is otherwise in the public interest: aircraft insurance and certain marine coverage is already so exempted.

Registered foreign companies must have paid-up capital equivalent to SI\$ 500,000 while locally-incorporated insurers need only SI\$ 100,000. In terms of local assets, foreign companies must hold at least SI\$ 50,000 in the Solomons and domestic incorporated companies, SI\$ 20,000. These moneys may be held in real estate or other approved investments. In addition, the insurer must deposit SI\$ 5000 (or the equivalent in Solomon Island government securities) with the Central Bank for each of the six major classes of insurance, shown in Table 2.20, it may wish to underwrite. While technically there are no restrictions on a firm offering all six, the government would prefer to avoid dual life and general licensing.

TABLE 2.20   Insurance business classes in the Solomon Islands

Employers' liability insurance business
Fire insurance business
Long-term insurance business
Marine insurance business
Miscellaneous insurance business
Motor insurance business

Source: The Insurance Act (1985).

In addition to the deposits, registered insurers must maintain a solvency margin position equal to the greater of one-tenth of their premium income or SI\$ 100,000. The insurer's other assets in respect to Solomon Island business should also be invested in the country. However, given the relatively few local investment opportunities, at present only 35 to 40 per cent of an insurer's Solomon Island assets need be held locally. This percentage is expected to rise in line with local opportunities.

In terms of reporting, each insurer must provide an audited balance sheet, and profit and loss account, of their total business in the Solomons, as well as a separate revenue account for each of the six insurance classes. The Controller can also require separate accounts for certain sub-categories.

By late 1985, the Act was still being implemented, and not all general insurance companies had decided whether to remain in the Solomons. For example, both QBE and New Zealand Insurance were active in local underwriting but ceased writing local business in 1985. Both companies expressed concern that the Solomon Island investment requirements proposed under the new Act exceeded their Solomon Island premium income and that, an overly competitive local market, coupled with reinsurance difficulties for this business, did not warrant expanding their business. The firms remaining in late 1985 are shown in Table 2.21.

TABLE 2.21   Insurance companies in the Solomon Islands, 1985

Firm	Home country	Representation
Commercial Union	UK	agent
General Accident Fire & Life	UK	agent
GRE Pacific Insurance Pty Ltd	PNG*	agent
Insurance Company of North America**	USA	branch
National Insurance of New Zealand	New Zealand	branch
Sun Alliance Insurance	Australia	agent

* Indirectly UK-owned.
** Soon to be known as Cigna.

Source: Industry interviews (December 1985).

The use of a branch, rather than an agent, is relatively new in the local market. As a branch can issue policies directly rather than cover notes, this could have a major impact on local market shares. This is because when a local agent writes a policy, the policy itself is not issued in the Solomons.[74] Instead the local agent issues a cover note which, as the name suggests, covers the insured against risk until the policy is issued. It is always possible though, but not common, that the overseas insurer will reject the application and force the customer to seek coverage elsewhere. This may not seem important, but from a lending standpoint a financial institution would obviously prefer immediate cover by way of a policy when the asset serves as loan collateral. As much of the local insurance business relates to loan collateral requirements, companies, which can issue their own policies locally, would seemingly have a considerable competitive advantage.

No doubt the most interesting development within Solomon Island insurance is the attempt to establish a local company, probably with some government equity participation. A World Bank study published in 1980, for example, commented that, 'an insurance company that will mainly transact non-life business is to be set up shortly'.[75] To this end the Solomon Islands government approached most major insurance companies within the region to act as the foreign partner and manager of this national company. The proposal was seriously considered by many firms, but the low level of foreign participation offered (usually 30 per cent), and other conditions, coupled with the Solomons' small national premium base and the poor underwriting experience among the island countries failed to attract a partner.

By far the most interesting proposal to date was from the National Insurance of New Zealand, and its affiliate, the National Insurance Co. of Western Samoa. Unfortunately its plan set only 20 per cent ownership for the Solomon Island government which the government felt insufficient. It wished both greater local ownership as well as control of the new company. In the end these demands, particularly the control issue, proved unsatisfactory to the foreign partners.

Another major problem area in these negotiations (one common to all financial institutions) was the degree of expatriate participation in the new company. Initially the National had wanted four expatriates (manager, claims settlement, administration and reinsurance, and marketing) in the new company, but would replace these with local staff once they were adequately trained and the operation was running smoothly. The government, however, felt only two expatriates should be allowed.

A local insurance company remains a stated goal of the Solomon Island government and its most recent national development plan calls for a 'National Insurance Co.' to be established in 1986.[76] This National Insurance Co. of the Solomon Islands proposal has since developed a more complex ownership structure with each of the seven provincial governments having a 2 per cent shareholding (totalling 14 per cent), the Development Bank of Solomon Islands possibly taking another 16 per cent and the remaining shares split between the foreign company or companies and the Government Shareholding Agency, probably 30 per cent foreign and 40 per cent GSA.

As yet no foreign company has agreed to be the local partner, but there could be some advantages to the successful firm. In an earlier plan, for example, the government concluded that the local insurance market was really 'too small for more than one insurance enterprise to operate economically with adequate quality of on-the-spot management and all-around services' and that as a result 'the new national insurance company will be the sole licensed provider of all insurance except for aircraft, ships and life insurance'.[77] While the new Act suggests the government has since changed this policy, it nevertheless could give any prospective foreign company some significant incentives.

While one might argue that the local ownership and staffing requirements in the National Insurance of New Zealand's negotiations adversely affected the development of a locally-based industry, in some respects the country actually benefited. This is because National Insurance on 1 August 1983 replaced its local agency operations with a local branch. First, as with a local company, the National generally retains the premiums earned, less any reinsurance payments in the country where they are earned. Given this position, the National's branch is really better placed to assist the country. As a branch, for example, its policies have the full backing of the entire National Insurance Group and are not limited to the paid-up capital and reserves of a small Solomon Island incorporated company. Secondly, the National's total portfolio, by covering a wide range of countries, does not require the same degree of reinsurance as a small firm with its policy risks concentrated in the one country. Finally, the National has much more bargaining power in reinsurance treaty negotiations as a major international company than would a small, rather insignificant, local firm.

Turning now to local insurance agencies, insurance agents must register under the Act but presently have no deposit requirements. They must, however, follow a certain code of conduct, and in the case of individual agents, be Solomon Island nationals. There are no actual insurance brokers within the Solomons but both Reed Stenhouse and Melanesian Insurance Brokers (from Vanuatu) have visited the islands from time to time. The latter firm is expanding this regional brokerage role.

There seems substantial room for greater regional participation in insurance among the Pacific Island countries. There are already some discussions in regard to insurance regulation matters and reinsurance with Fiji and, to a lesser extent, Papua New Guinea, but much more could be done in both the government and private sector.

Life Insurance

If the general insurance business in the Solomon Islands is considered undeveloped, then the life industry could be said to be non-existent. Indeed, a study 1978 stated that 'there is no life insurance sold at all'.[78] This was probably true in regards to Solomon Islanders, but not so for expatriate staff. At one time both the Australian Mutual Provident Society and T & G Assurance (now National Mutual) both sold life policies to the local expatriate population, but even prior to independence the expatriate population had declined to the point that they ceased active selling.

There are nevertheless a few foreign companies marketing investment linked policies to expatriates via local agents, such as Australian Eagle and Greater Pacific Life, but these sales amount to only a few dozen policies and are marketed primarily for taxation reasons. INA (Cigna) is also believed to have some life insurance business within the expatriate market and some of the funds generated are now reinvested within the Solomons.

In 1985, however, only one company, Mercantile Mutual Life Insurance Co. Ltd of Australia, was actually writing life policies on Melanesians, as opposed to just expatriates in the Solomon Islands. These were sold through the firm's local agents, BJS Agencies Ltd. At present it has only one local salesman working in Honiara, but another may soon be hired to sell in the provincial capitals.

The policy sales material provides some fairly modest examples of the potential sales. These are general in line with local income levels. Some examples for a person under 35 include: a $ 150 per year for a $ 15,000 policy; $ 200 for $ 20,000; $ 250 for $ 25,000; and $ 300 for $ 30,000. There are also some special policy plans for children.

By December 1985, there were around 500 policies outstanding, most had a coverage at the higher $ 30,000 level and were sold at the rate of approximately 40 per month.

The payments are usually on a monthly basis through salary

deductions arranged with the employers or the policy holder's bank account. The premiums are then periodically remitted by the local agent to the Australian company. Given that these policies are actually written in Australia, both they and their respective premiums are denominated in Australian dollars and hence the value and costs will change in line with currency movements. The premiums are therefore adjusted annually to ensure the proper Australian dollar amount is paid.

The policies, as typical with many life policies, have no cash value if cancelled within the first two years, but after that the policy holder is entitled to at least a 10 per cent return on the money in the policy and most premiums are refunded on a cancellation after five years.

Besides the life coverage benefit and the lack of many other investment alternatives, life insurance payments also offer a substantial tax incentive, for premiums equalling up to 20 per cent of taxable income are eligible for a tax deduction.

While these benefits would seemingly help develop the local life and superannuation business into an important part of the local capital market, not all observers feel the incentives are well placed. The World Bank, for example, found that this 'life insurance and superannuation allowance is too generous and needs to be curtailed'.[79] The government's new insurance regulations, however, may effectively remove most new policy sales potential as interviews with Mercantile Mutual suggest that their local business is not adequate to justify the deposit and other expenses associated with the law's registration requirements.

Solomon Islands National Provident Fund

The Solomon Islands National Provident Fund is intended to 'provide a secure and valuable retirement benefit for its members [and to] create savings out of personal incomes for investment in national development'.[80] It is among the largest of the Solomons' financial institutions and is the major source of long-term debt capital within the country. As a government report explained, the National Provident Fund is 'the largest holder of long-term SI dollar financial assets, with loan securities and other assets totalling $ 36 million in mid-1985'.[81]

The Solomon Islands National Provident Fund was created on 1 January 1976 as a body corporate under the Solomon Islands National Provident Fund Ordinance 1973, and on 16 July 1976 called for registrations of all employers and employees covered by the Fund's legislation. Actual operations, however, did not commence until 1 October 1976, and the first contributions were received in November.[82] This delay between 1973 and 1976 reflected the Fund's administrative requirements: an accounting and administrative system had to be designed; staff recruited and trained; premises found; and the potential employers and employee members educated.

Under the Fund's provisions, any one who employs staff at a rate of SI$ 20 per month, or more, or for six continuous days during any month, must make contributions on the employee's behalf. Employees under 14 years old and those employed under family arrangements (in theory only one's immediate family), however, are exempted from these requirements as are self-employed people. Initially domestic servants were also exempted, but since March 1982 contributions on such employees is also mandatory. As shown in Table 2.22, the Fund now has 1510 employers and 56,874 members.

TABLE 2.22   Solomon Islands National Provident Fund: employers, fund members and employed members, 1977–85[a]

	Employers	Fund members	Members employed
1977	520	18,669	16,549
1978	580	20,000	18,000
1979	640	30,000	22,000
1980	702	36,829	20,618
1981	735	40,848	21,768
1982	844	45,000	20,000
1983	1,177	48,543	21,250
1984	1,357	52,393	24,202
1985	1,510	56,874	23,061

[a] Figures as of June 1986.

Source: Solomon Islands National Provident Fund (1985).

Industry interviews suggest that the Fund now has complete coverage of the national work force in paid employment: casual construction workers are the only area where more work was required. The continuity of this position is ensured through a six-man enforcement unit which visits employers throughout the islands as well as gives public speeches on the Fund and its uses. These inspectors may enter any premises where persons are believed employed, make inquiries, and request copies of all documentation required under the Act. The Fund, as with other government departments, also makes full use of the national radio station to provide details of its operations.

Initially the NPF contribution level was set at an amount equal to 10 per cent of the employee's wages. The employer was legally obliged to make the payment, but could be reimbursed for half the amount (5 per cent) from deductions from the employee's wage. On 1 January 1982, though, the amount was raised to 12.5 per cent. The deduction is now paid as 7.5 per cent by the employer and 5.0 per cent by the employee. The actual payments to the Fund are made monthly by the employers and the employer registers any new employees at that time. The funds can be paid either directly or through bank agencies or the postal services: most employers pay direct. In addition, employers are required to submit much more detailed reports every quarter.

On joining the National Provident Fund each employee receives a membership card, and a nomination form to indicate the member's beneficiaries in case of death, as well as an annual statement of his account. This card is to be presented when seeking employment or changing jobs. This effective portability feature is particularly important in the Solomons as many workers frequently leave the paid employment market to return to their village over their working life. Thus the percentages of employed versus non-employed suggested in Table 2.23 is not reflective of the average Fund members' age.

The Fund operates on a fully-funded basis with members entitled to only those amounts deposited by himself and his employer plus any accumulated interest. The amount of interest paid each year varies with the Fund's performance, but it is precluded from paying more than 2.5 per cent per annum unless the Board is certain of the Fund's ability to fulfill all of its potential obligations. In practice, however, this limitation has not proved a problem. Even so, the interest paid in the early years was generally below the rate of inflation and so it has only been recently that the contributors have experienced a real growth in their balances. The actual amount each year has varied from 5 to 9 per cent.

The members may receive their contributions under five payment categories: to those reaching the age of 50; to emigrants (generally expatriates); to those incapacitated from further employment due to illness or mental disorder; on death to their heirs; and women can withdraw upon marriage (only marriages after the Fund was created). The final category is a special provision granted on a

TABLE 2.23   Solomon Islands National Provident Fund: assets and
interest payments, 1977–85

	Total assets	Percentage paid
1977	875,318	5
1978	2,294,852	5
1979	4,264,808	6
1980	6,716,898	7
1981	9,995,927	8
1982	14,448,658	8
1983	20,292,869	9[a]
1984	27,493,075	9[a]
1985	35,833,282	10[b]

[a] Includes 1 per cent paid as a bonus.
[b] Includes 2 per cent paid as a bonus.

Source: Solomon Islands National Provident Fund (1985).

case-by-case basis to those who, after reaching 40 years of age, wish
to leave the paid work force and return permanently to village life.

In the case of death, a special benefit is paid in addition to the
member's contributions. Initially this amounted to SI$ 500 but was
increased to SI$ 1000 in 1978, and more recently to SI$ 2500; SI$ 5 is
deducted each year to cover these payments.

In addition to these direct payments, Fund members may also use
their balances as collateral for commercial bank loans, as well as
loans from the Development Bank and the Housing Authority.
While many of these loans are for housing, the borrowing can be
made for any purposes. Thus far, the small size of the contributor
balances (three-quarters of them average only SI$ 500) has not made
them suitable for any serious lending.

As shown in Table 2.24, the Fund receives the bulk of its money
from member contributions which it invests on their behalf. According to the Fund, these 'should be invested within Solomon Islands in
such a way as to promote economic development subject to a reasonable rate of return and absolute security being provided'.[83] In its
earlier years, bank deposits comprised the bulk of its investments,
but over the years it has broadened its portfolio to include loans to
the government and quasi government bodies, loans to the private
sector, government securities, and real estate.

As shown in Table 2.24 term deposits comprised some 20 per cent
of Fund assets. This SI$ 7.3 million is the largest single source of

TABLE 2.24   Solomon Islands National Provident Fund: assets and
liabilities, 1985 (unaudited figures (in SI$) as of 30 June)

Assets:	
Cash at bank and in hand	34,912
Accrued interest	821,569
Accrued rent	5,403
Term deposits	7,300,000
Loans – private sector	282,005
Loans – quasi government	10,994,641
Loans – central government	6,717,032
Development bonds	6,878,200
Staff mortgage scheme	150,013
Office and staff quarters	328,791
Capital work in progress	526,346
Real properties	1,794,370
Total assets	38,833,282
Liabilities:	
General reserves	2,110,412
Contributor accounts	33,722,870
Total liabilities	38,833,282

Source: Solomon Islands National Provident Fund (1985).

long-term deposits for the banking system, and not surprisingly its deposits are eagerly sought by the local banks; they are usually invited to bid when a new deposit is made. Interestingly, though, the Fund banks with the Hongkong and Shanghai Banking Corporation, rather than the government joint venture bank, the National Bank of Solomon Islands. This is because the two organizations are located in the same building and hence the movement of cash can be done without difficulty: the National Bank is on the other side of town and, of course, was not government affiliated when the Fund was established in 1976. The Hongkong and Shanghai also provided the most attractive account facilities, with an automatic sweep facility also then into overnight call (now seven-day call) deposits for the Fund's deposit account on balances over a certain level.

Loans to quasi government bodies is the Fund's largest asset category. These include advances to the Government Shareholding Agency, the Development Bank of Solomon Islands, Solomon Island Housing Authority, the Solomon Island Broadcasting Corporation and the Electricity Authority. These are normally medium- to long-term advances at commercial rates of interest. Its advances to the central government are similarly at commercial rates as required under its charter. Its private sector lending has not been active to date. Its major advance (SI$ 400,000 in 1978) was to finance what was then the privately-owned Mendana Hotel. While this is now government owned, the loan is still listed as a private sector advance in the Fund's accounts. As the Central Bank reported, 'the Fund would like to lend more to private corporate sector borrowers but few can offer the high level of security that the Fund is bound by law and by its policy to require'.[84]

Besides its sizable SI$ 6,717,032 in advances to the central government, the Fund holds a slightly larger amount of the government's Development Bonds. Since 1984 these holdings have accounted for some 20 per cent of the government's total loan obligations.

Since 1981 the NPF has been an active investor in real estate. Its major holding is presently Point Cruz House, the five-storey office building in which it is headquartered. It is currently completing another major commercial property, an office and shopping centre on the old Woodford School site in downtown Honiara. In addition to commercial properties, the Fund also built eight residential properties for rental purposes for Solrice employees.

In addition to the above assets, the NPF 'is now diversifying into new forms of assets and is investigating ways in which its member-contributors can use their accumulated contributions for collateral for home-purchase or other long-term assets'.[85] Its purpose could also be expanded. The current national development plan, for example, indicates that 'the possibility of the introduction of a national pensions scheme and its extension to become a full national insurance scheme will be re-examined with a view to its introduction in the late 1980s or early 1990s'.[86].

Other Pension Schemes

There are provisions within the National Provident Fund legislation for employers to offer similar or better benefits to their employees through non-government schemes. At present, however, few employers have used this option and indeed some funds actually closed when the National Provident Fund commenced operations. For example, one of the country's largest employers, Lever Solomons Ltd, previously had a pension scheme covering all its employees but has since phased out its program.[87]

Recently, however, another major local employer, Solomon Islands Plantations Ltd, moved to supplement the government fund's benefits with its own plan. Solomon Islands Plantations did not have a separate pension fund prior to the NPF, but in January 1985 introduced a Non-contributory Long Service Incentive Scheme for its daily-rated and local monthly-salaried staff. It will provide a cash payment to workers calculated by multiplying the employee's number of weeks of continous service by his basic weekly wage on leaving the company by 1/26. Ten years continous service is normally required to obtain the full amount, but workers leaving after five years service may be entitled to half the amount and the amount roughly proportional for additional service until the full ten years is reached. The full amount may also be paid to those workers (with three year continous service) opting to retire at age 50 or being compulsory retired at 55. In addition the scheme provides for a gift to employees after ten years service and a death-in-service payment of $ 3000 after three years service.[88]

Government Shareholding Agency

Though not a financial institution in a formal sense, the Government Shareholding Agency is an exceedingly important feature of the Solomon Islands' financial sector, and is the major source of equity investment capital within the country. The Agency was created as a statutory body on 1 September 1977, under the Government Shareholding Act 1977 (No. 12 of 1977) to acquire a substantial ownership of those commercial operations of strategic importance to the Solomon Islands and to assist (Section 5 (1)) in 'furthering economic development; the promotion of agricultural and industrial expansion and efficiency; and the provision, maintenance or safeguarding of employment'.

Besides the economic development and administrative advantages afforded by consolidating the government's commercial shareholdings into one monitoring vehicle, the GSA also simplified the arrangements for the government's shareholdings. Under the Solomon Islands constitution there is apparently no provision for the government to hold shares directly. Previously the Minister with responsibility for each non-statutory body operation held the shares on behalf of the government. As shown in Table 2.25, while the Government Shareholding Agency does not control all government statutory bodies, it is now the most important.

TABLE 2.25   Statutory corporations, by total assets, 1983

Solomon Islands Electricity Authority	4,793
Solomon Islands Housing Authority	4,913
Cattle Development Corporation	2,137
Copra Board[a]	7,182
Solomon Islands Ports Authority	7,433
Development Bank of Solomon Islands[b]	10,815
National Provident Fund	20,293
Government Shareholding Agency	26,953
Total	
	84,519

[a] Now the Commodities Export Marketing Authority.
[b] Owned by the Government Shareholding Agency and Central Bank.

Source: Central Bank of Solomon Islands (1984) *Annual Report*, p. 40.

When the Agency commenced operations in 1977, it assumed government shareholdings in Solomon Islands Plantations and Solomon Taiyo and has since invested in a range of commercial enterprises as reflected in Table 2.26. These include a copra and cocoa plantation, a rice producer and marketer, an oil palm plantation, tuna fishing and processing, a domestic airline, international communications, hotel, commercial banking, development banking, and stamp sales.

These investments were made for a number of reasons. In some cases, for example, it

> was because the business was likely to be very profitable and the government wanted to obtain dividends as well as tax revenues; in other cases greater importance was attached to participating as a shareholder in the regular decision making of a large company that would affect a large part of the Solomon Island economy.[89]

Ideally the GSA is intended as a minority shareholder with board representations and under its Act (Section 8) cannot hold more than 49 per cent without the consent of the Minister. Those private sector ventures which now have 100 per cent control, particularly Solomons Rice and Mendana Hotels, have resulted from difficulties, often due to operational problems, with their foreign partners. Where possible, the GSA would like eventually to reduce its foreign partners' shareholdings and make these available for sale either to provincial authorities or the general public.

TABLE 2.26   Government Shareholding Agency investments, by type, 1984

	Issued capital ($ m)	% held by GSA	Value at cost ($ m)	1984 sales ($ m)	Employees at year end
Solomon Islands Plantations Ltd	14.4	39.75	3.35	22.0	1712
Solomons Rice Co. Ltd[a]	3.0	100.00	1.35	6.6	300
Lever Solomons Ltd	8.6	40.00	3.81	5.3	1426
Solomon Taiyo Ltd	4.0	50.00	1.75	31.9	966
National Fisheries Development Ltd	1.5	75.00[b]	1.13	4.63	540
Solair Ltd	1.6	49.00	0.78	3.8	108
Soltel[c]	1.2	49.00	0.59	1.5	40
Mendana Hotels Ltd	0.5	100.00	1.18	1.70	115
Development Bank of Solomon Islands	5.3	100.00[d]	5.30	2.6	87
National Bank of Solomon Islands Ltd	2.0	49.00	0.98	8.2	82
Solomon Islands Philatelic Bureau Ltd	0.1	100.00	0.10	0.32	11

[a] Formerly known as Brewer Solomons Agriculture Ltd.
[b] As the other 25 per cent is owned by Solomon Taiyo, the effective ownership is really 12.5 per cent higher or 87.5 per cent.
[c] Full name is Solomon Islands International Communications Ltd.
[d] In 1985 this was reduced to a direct 90 per cent with the Central Bank of Solomon Islands becoming a 10 per cent shareholder.

Note: This excludes the GSA's 70,400 shares in AirPacific Ltd. (SI$ 69,622.94) and 10,000 class A and 53,930 class B shares of the Pacific Forum Line Ltd (56,972.90), as they are minor equity holdings in overseas companies, and its 100 per cent ownership of the Central Bank of Solomon Islands (2,597,000) as it is not an orthodox shareholding.

Source: The Government Shareholding Agency (1984) *Eight Annual Report*, 1 January to 31 December, p. 6.

Although the Agency is not restricted to foreign joint ventures, in practice most locally-owned private enterprises are generally too small for its consideration. Smaller firms are considered more suitable clients for the Development Bank of Solomon Islands and the Agency will not normally invest in a business in which the Development Bank has an interest.

As shown in Table 2.27, loans to affiliated companies is the GSA's second largest asset category. Under its Act the Agency can provide

TABLE 2.27   Government Shareholding Agency: assets and liabilities, 1984

Assets:	
Cash at bank	4,136.27
Bank deposits	550,000.00
Investments	23,038,567.84
Loans to affiliates	5,203,089.76
Accrued interest	3,381.37
Sundry debtors	11,495.84
Equipment	7,504.85
Total assets	
	28,818,175.93
Liabilities:	
Accumulated receipts from:	
Government	21,045,706.76
Accumulated surplus	2,249,042.69
Term loans	5,334,375.00
Interest payable	189,051.48
Total liabilities	
	28,818,175.93

Source: The Government Shareholding Agency (1984) *Eighth Annual Report*, 1 January to 31 December, p. 13.

or assist with debt or equity finance for agricultural and industrial undertakings as well as with the management of its affiliates. At the end of 1984, for example, it had loans outstanding to the Solomons Rice Co. (SI$ 2,167,489.76), Soltel (SI$ 60,600), National Bank of Solomon Islands (SI$ 250,000), and National Fisheries Development (SI$ 2,755,000). These loans represent mainly on-lending of the GSA's own borrowings, primarily from the National Provident Fund, and in such cases charges a 1/2 per cent margin over the costs. Such on-lending allows GSA affiliates access to funds that the National Provident Fund, due to its charter, might not provide directly. Since 1984 The Agency may also provide guarantees itself, or arrange government guarantees on such borrowings.

As was shown in Table 2.27, the vast bulk of the GSA's funding (some 80 per cent in 1984) derived from the government (grants and share transfers) and past revenue. Though technically this percentage represents Solomon Island government money, in practice the bulk of the government funding to the GSA has resulted from special aid grants from British, Australian, New Zealand and other sources. In 1984, for example, SI$ 687,500 came from a UK Special Purpose

TABLE 2.28   Government Shareholding Agency: assets and profits, 1979–84

	Assets	Profits
1979	10,106,833.02	541,211.85
1980	13,483,907.26	154,621.13
1981	16,436,195.04	(97,583.60)
1982	21,702,755.47	(90,493.30)
1983	26,952,750.29	50,432.83
1984	28,818,175.93	1,480,053.06

[a] Figures in parentheses are losses.

Source: The Government Shareholding Agency (1979–84) *Annual Reports*.

Grant, SI$ 77,260 from New Zealand Aid Funds, and only SI$ 300,000 directly from the Solomon Islands government.

As mentioned, most of the GSA's long-term borrowings are for on-lending to its affiliated companies. At the end of 1984, for example these included a SI$ 500,000 ten-year loan from the National Bank of Solomon Islands and three ten-year loans from the National Provident Fund for SI$ 609,375, SI$ 225,000 and SI$ 4,000,000. The latter borrowings each had a grace period of three to five years before any principal repayments were required, but had no provision for early repayment.

The bulk of the GSA's own funds come in dividend payments from its affiliates (SI$ 2,008,571 in 1984) and, to a much lesser extent, interest on loans to affiliates (SI$ 214,132). Ideally the GSA would like a 10 per cent return on its investments. Unfortunately trading difficulties in some GSA affiliates, particularly the rice operations, coupled with the need to reinvest the profits in most of the profitable ventures, has meant the GSA has not always traded with a surplus. In particular, losses shown in Table 2.28 resulted directly from additional GSA borrowings in support of its rice company's operations.

This lack of profits over 1981 and 1982, however, did not preclude a major increase in assets; an increase financed through government and overseas grants.

In addition to its financial functions, the GSA also has an important management role through representation on its affiliates' board of directors. As one report explained, its shareholdings give it 'the right to participate, through the directors it nominates, in policy-making and overall direction of the companies concerned; while also acting as the watchdog of national interests within the company, and a direct and confidential channel of communication between company and government'.[90] The GSA also acts as a training vehicle for its companies. In 1984, for example, it organized a corporate affairs expert under the British Executive Service Overseas Scheme to conduct a formal one-month course for board members of GSA affiliates.

Possibly the GSA may also hold shares in business ventures on behalf of provincial governments or other bodies within the Solomons and in 1985, for example, it was suggested that the GSA might act as the local shareholder and management representative on behalf of the Guadalcanal provincial government in a timber joint venture planned for that province. No such action has yet been taken and some Act amendments might be required before it could act as trustee on behalf of other parties.

Finally, the GSA serves as an advisor to foreign investors and others wishing to commence projects in the Solomon Islands. As with its managerial functions, the GSA's recent move, from the Ministry of Finance building to a commercial office building, has given this advisory role a somewhat more independent and commercial orientation.

In the future, as a major shareholder in the country's largest commercial ventures, the GSA's share portfolio seems a logical basis for encouraging Solomon Islanders to become individual shareholders, but thus far it has taken no action to dilute its ownership via public offering. Significantly, the Agency does have the power (Section 5(3)(u)) 'to establish and make available to the public units trusts'. This would seem a logical first step in introducing the concept of share investing to the local population, and there is a wealth of experience readily available in Papua New Guinea and Fiji in this regard. This was at least partly suggested in August 1981, when the government announced the GSA would be replaced by an 'Investment Corporation' which would 'broaden the base of participation by providing for provincial governments, NPF and other statutory and non-statutory institutions and individual Solomon Islanders to invest in the equity portfolio of the corporations'.[91]

One time it was thought that the GSA, restructured as the Investment Corporation of the Solomon Islands, would also assume the foreign investment control functions currently performed within the Prime Minister's office, and become active in the promotion of foreign investment. Similarly, to make it more responsive to the needs of the provincial governments, each of these would become shareholders in the new body. None of these plans, however, eventuated.

Commodities Export Marketing Authority

The Commodities Export Marketing Authority (CEMA) commenced operations on 1 July 1985 as a statutory corporation under the Commodities Export Marketing Authority Act 1984. It was created to assume the functions of the Solomon Island Copra Board (initially established in 1953 as the British Solomon Islands Copra Board) as well as to promote and market other potentially exportable commodities. Under its Act (Schedule 1), the Authority presently can control the exports of coconut and coconut products, copra, cocoa pods, unfermented cocoa beans, fermented cocoa beans and products, palm oil, palm kernels, palm-based products and spices.

To date the Authority has concentrated on the purchase and marketing of copra (the extracted and dried white meat of the coconut). It is the country's sole exporter of copra and operates buying centres in Lata, Auki and Buala, as well as exporting centres in Noro, Yandina and its headquarters in Honiara. The bulk of its exports are presently sold to Europe (L. M. Fischels & Co.) and Japan (C. Itoh & Co.). The control and export of other crops such as cocoa, ginger, tumeric, and possibly coffee, is also under consideration.

As the Copra Board, the Authority operated three separate trading accounts; one for copra; one for sacks and twine; and one for oil drums. The latter two were materials the Board sold to its customers: the sacks and twine to tie up the copra; and the oil drums for conversion into smallholder copra driers. In fiscal 1984 it earned SI$ 5,197,397 on copra trading, SI$ 40,804 on sacks and twine sales, and broke even on oil drum sales; its over-all operating surplus was SI$ 5,368,385.

Though not a financial institution, the CEMA may grant loans, make guarantees, and provide security for other credit facilities. Its importance in the financial sector, though, relates to its management of its commodity development funds. By December 1985, though, only the Copra Domestic Price Support Fund was in operation. These funds depend on the difference between the price paid for local production and overseas sale prices. The Authority is intended to accumulate sufficient funds by purchasing at lower than world prices during favourable export periods, so that it can subsidize producers

TABLE 2.29   Solomon Islands Copra Board: current and total assets, 1980–84

	Current assets	*Total assets*
1980	8,556,933	9,193,920
1981	5,681,512	6,878,462
1982	4,889,441	6,091,123
1983	7,632,639	8,763,166
1984	14,739,042	16,088,576

Source: Commodities Export Marketing Authority (1985).

with higher than world market prices during poorer periods. The most recent example of the latter was in fiscal 1981 when, as the Copra Board, its average domestic purchase price was $ 260 per ton compared with a London price of $ 235.

Thus copra production levels and the differences between its purchase and sale prices have a marked effect on the Fund and hence the Authority's asset levels. As shown in Table 2.29, for example, the asset levels did not reach that for 1980 until fiscal 1984.

The decision on local versus overseas copra prices has a major impact on the local economy and with a good year the economy will boom accordingly. For example, with good copra prices in 1984 households' operating surpluses rose from SI$ 5.1 million in 1983 to an estimated $ 12.5 million in 1984; SI$ 10.7 million of this represented copra proceeds.[92] Ideally the Authority should try to insulate the local economy from the effects of major price swings in copra and, if other stabilization funds are established (a cocoa fund is planned), other major commodity exports.

In addition to any short-term economic effects, the Authority must also ensure that the rewards from copra production are sufficient to maintain smallholder participation. It is commonly believed that if the local price drops significantly below $ 300 per ton, then many smallholders will cease to improve or even maintain their plantings. At present, local production is about 30 per cent from plantations and 70 per cent from smallholders, but the actual proportions vary dramatically with copra price levels. Plantation production is relatively stable, at from 2300 to 2400 tons per quarter, but smallholder copra products have ranged from a low of 3687 tons in March 1983 to a high of 8950 in June 1984.[93]

Besides its pricing policy, the Authority can also have a major effect on the economy's money supply depending on where it places its deposits. Prior to the early 1980s the then Board traditionally placed its funds in bank deposits and, to a lesser extent, government securities. To the extent that this money enters the banking system, the money supply increases accordingly, and thus the banks can extend more loans; this effect would be multiplied throughout the economy. Unfortunately the Fund's balances move directly in line with local economic conditions. Thus when good copra prices are promoting a strong economy, the Fund's deposit levels increase; in bad times they decline. Thus they magnify economic changes. More recently, to offset some of these effects, the Fund now varies its deposits with the banking sector or the Central Bank in line with local conditions. During the boom period in 1984, for example, it transferred some SI$ 5 million from commercial bank deposits to the Central Bank in order to demonetize their effects. As the Central Bank explained, 'it is intended that about two-thirds of the Copra Board's price support reserves presently [in 1984] around 12 million, should be held in this way outside the money supply'.[94]

The Authority's impact on the local money supply is reflected in Table 2.30 where its SI$ 8.4 million in interest-bearing deposits and SI$ 1.4 million government securities were quite sizeable by Solomon Islands standards. As the Authority was then only involved in copra, there is no separate accounting for the copra stabilization fund. This will probably be reflected, though, under the new Act, particularly if a cocoa or other domestic commodity fund is established.

One fund which is accounted for separately is the Copra Export Duty Stabilization Fund (CEDSF). It was established under an agreement between the Solomon Island government and the then Copra Board signed on 13 November 1975. It states that in any year in which the copra duty paid to the government is less than the average amount for the preceding five years, the Fund will pay the difference. Since 1 September 1984 the export duty on copra has been 20 per cent of the price over $ 300 per ton FOB. However, this obligation, in practice, has been somewhat more flexible. In 1981, for example, when copra export proceeds and hence export duties dropped sharply, the amount payable would have depleted most of the Fund. Thus the two parties compromised on a smaller payment but with an agreement that the bulk of the remaining funds would be invested in Solomon Islands Government Development Bonds. Besides any interest accruing to the CEDSF, the Solomon Island

TABLE 2.30   Solomon Islands Copra Board,[a] assets and liabilities, 1984

Assets:	
Cash on hand and at bank	137,239
Call accounts	500,000
Interest-bearing deposits	8,438,121
Government bonds	1,475,613
C.E.D.S. Fund[b] deposits	354,410
Trade debtors	133,880
Other debtors and prepayments	2,061,305
Accrued interest receivable	168,742
Work in progress	14,791
Stock on hand	1,454,941
Fixed assets	1,349,534
	16,088,576
Liabilities:	
Accumulated funds	11,661,063
Asset revaluation reserve	320,013
C.E.D.S. Fund[b]	997,905
Agent current account	169,738
Other creditors and accruals	2,939,857
	16,088,586

[a] Now known as the Commodities Export Marketing Authority.
[b] Copra Export Duty Revenue Stabilization Fund.

Source: Commodities Export Marketing Authority (1985).

government also contributed money received from the European Development Fund STABEX (Stabilization of Export Earnings) scheme into the CEDSF.

Credit Unions

While the co-operative movement in the Solomon Islands dates to 1957, it is less certain as to when credit co-operatives were first introduced into the country. One Australian source, for example, lists the first credit union, the Bakota Credit Union, as established in 1966 and the Solomon Island Credit Union League as being formed in 1968.[95] The current credit union league cites a Father Loughman as starting the industry in Choiseul in 1968 but that 'with no supporting structures in the country for credit unions, these early efforts fizzled out'.[96] In fact the industry is much older than either source suggests, and in the form of village savings and loan societies (the name also used initially in Papua New Guinea) six small savings and loan societies were established in the Western Province at least as early as 1963–4, and there were eight societies at the end of 1964.[97]

From their initial founding in the early 1960s, the numbers of savings and loan societies grew rapidly to reach 13 societies by 1965, and the movement's assets more than doubled from A\$ 6740 to A\$ 13,368. The number of these societies and their asset figures then stabilized and then declined. Thus by 1977 there were only 10 societies in operation (five in Choiseul, four in Vella Lavella and one in Ranongga – all islands in the Western Province) with assets of A\$ 6270. Unfortunately, by late 1979 even these societies were believed to have effectively ceased operations.[98]

This initial lack of success, however, did not detract from the concept of a Solomon Island credit union industry, and as part of its 1975–9 national development plan, the government policy was

> to encourage the formation of savings and loan co-operatives in selected urban areas, and in areas where there are large employers of labourers, such as on plantations, forestry and fishery projects . . . providing both a means of regular savings and also a source of loan finance from self generated funds.[99]

In line with this goal, an amendment to the Co-operative Societies (Amendment) Bill 1979 was prepared to 'permit the operation of credit unions or thrift and loan societies' in the Solomons. Unfortunately, though, as this legislation was never enacted, the term credit union could not be used legally for a registered co-operative.

By 1981, however, the credit union industry was again active, for in November of that year what is now the Solomon Islands Credit Union League, with the support of the International Human Assistance Program, held a two-week course on credit unions at the Tasia Training Centre in Isabel Province. This rebirth was headed by Dudley Tuti (a retired Anglican bishop), now the League's chairman, and keenly supported by the Foundation for the Peoples of the South Pacific through the Dutch Bishop's Lenten Fund. By the end of 1985, largely as a result of these efforts, there were some 61 credit unions operating in the Solomon Islands with a total of 4736 members and assets of SI\$ 64,762 (some 70 per cent of which was in loans to some 12 to 187 members). Of these 36 credit unions, 4 were in Isabel, 24 in Malaita, and 1 in Temota.[100]

Unfortunately, given the lack of legislation, as one study concluded, 'credit unions in the Solomon Islands have been formed and exist without the benefit of a legislative act'.[101] This position was noted in the recent National Development Plan and 1986 was designated for enacting legislation 'to provide a legal identity for credit unions'.[102] To this end the industry requested a consultant from the US Volunteers in Overseas Co-operation Assistance (VOCA). A model credit union act was subsequently drafted and presented to the government on 29 October 1985. The various proposals have since been accepted by the Ministry of Finance but, as of early December 1985, the draft legislation had not been presented to Cabinet.

If no changes are made to the draft, the Solomon Islands Credit Union League will assume considerable self-regulatory responsibility for the industry, and will become 'the sole organization in the nation to recommend to the Registrar upon the establishment, supervision, and regulation of credit unions/savings clubs'.[103] It will also be active in promoting the over-all industry, conducting training and providing a range of other centralized support facilities. Its own three-year (1986–8) program calls for it to hire a full-time general manager and train four district field officers over 1986 to co-ordinate the growth of credit unions in Guadalcanal Province. By 1989 it hopes to have expanded into the other provinces as well and assumed its secondary society role with a central credit union fund. The League itself will also relocate its operations, currently run from the home of its Chairman to Honiara.[104]

The other change expected for the League is the manner in which it is financed. Rather then rely on government funding or simply assessing each individual credit union a fee to cover its costs, the League will be funded directly through an annual assessment on each member's personal account. As the VOCA consultant stressed, 'the responsibility for building and developing the credit union movement in the country lies with the willingness of the individual members to pay for it'.[105] Each member will have to agree to support the League as a condition of credit union membership, and it is expected that each member, by paying the costs directly, will take a much closer interest in the League's development. Likewise the League itself should prove more responsive to credit union member requests. The funding plan also re-enforces the point that the credit unions movement is owned and run by its members and is not a government agency.

The government will nevertheless be involved in credit union licensing and regulation. This may well be done, though, by the

Central Bank rather than the Registrar of Co-operative Societies. This was recommended in the most recent five-year plan[106] and quite in keeping with the Central Bank's plans to improve financial services in rural areas. Indeed its own study concluded 'a well-established and well run co-operative may act as a mini-financial institution, running current accounts for its members and extending credit, with the assistance of extension staff, being itself the user of Development Bank credit'.[107] In addition it found credit unions were also useful in 'helping to create awareness of thrift and small-scale capital accumulation'[108] and 'offer the best chance of developing financial intermediation quickly and soundly at the village level'.[109]

To assist the credit union industry and general financial services in rural areas, the Central Bank has established a Rural Services Department. This unit will be assisted by a standing committee comprised of representatives from the Solomon Islands Credit Union League and other parties. A similar structure is also planned at the provincial level. If given the proper technical assistance, credit unions should prove very effective at the village level where their co-operative nature is very much in keeping with Melanesian culture.

Co-operative Societies

Co-operative societies play an important role in Solomon Island rural areas in marketing primary produce, consumer retailing, processing of cash crops and other activities. Of these, multipurpose consumer and marketing societies are the most common. The credit co-operatives or credit unions were discussed previously, but some of the other societies also have had some financial functions.

In the case of consumer societies, members wishing to buy an expensive item will sometime make deposits with their society for safe-keeping until they have saved sufficient funds. This is allowable under the Co-operative Societies Act, and around 70 per cent of the multipurpose societies have such facilities. However, as the maximum interest paid on these deposits is set by the Registrar of Co-operatives at only 4 per cent per annum, the over-all level of deposits is not particularly significant. Under Section 27 of the Act the societies also have the power to make loans to members. However, by late 1985 few co-operatives actually provided this service. Advances to members via credit purchases, though, may have been more common previously, for the 1971–4 Development Plan complained that co-operatives' 'credit trading is still rife in all areas and attempts to reduce it are again frustrated by a shortage of ready money in the villages. Such credit trading is bound to wreck the smaller and weaker societies'.[110] Similarly a World Bank study in 1980 remarked that the co-operatives in the Solomons had 'poor recovery of credit sales'.[111]

Postal Savings Agencies

Unlike neighbouring Fiji, the Solomons have not used their postal system significantly for savings mobilization. The colonial government was content to rely on foreign interest to provide the bulk of the country's financial services. Since independence the government has withdrawn further from a direct involvement in banking (district officers, for example, were once a major provider of savings bank services in remote areas) and has relied instead on its more recent commercial banking joint venture, the National Bank of Solomon Islands.

Since November 1985, the postal system has consisted of the general post office (GPO), eight post offices, and 96 postal agencies. As shown in Table 2.31, only two post offices, Munda and Tulagi, act as savings bank agents for the National Bank. Given their government status, permanent buildings and existing staff structure, the government should logically make better use of this already existing office network. Likewise, although postal agencies represent a range of private businesses, churches, schools, co-operatives, and area councils, in order to gain the right to sell stamps (with a 5 per cent commission) and to dispatch and receive mail, they must first have a permanent building and access to a safe and reliable staff. These are the same basic requirements for a private saving bank agency.

Unfortunately, neither the post office nor the banking system seems interested in making more effective use of this existing office/ agency network. First, the private banks viewed any postal agencies as being the National Bank's prerogative, not theirs. Secondly, the postal system viewed the bank agencies as a somewhat bothersome additional duty which they would be pleased to relinquish once the National Bank provides banking services in their remaining towns. Finally the National, as it has had administrative problems with one of its postal agencies, has been less then enthusiastic in expanding this involvement. It has preferred instead to concentrate on establishing its own branch offices. As the government is willing to use its

TABLE 2.31   Post Offices in the Solomon Islands, by town and province

Type	Location	Province
GPO	Honiara	–
PO	Gizo	Western
PO	Taro	Western
PO	Munda[a]	Western
PO	Auki	Malaita
PO	Kirakira	Makira
PO	Lata	Temotu
PO	Tulagi[a]	Central
PO	Yandina	Central

[a] Agent for National Bank of Solomon Islands.

Source: Postmaster, GPO, Honiara (December 1985).

postal system to market its three national savings certificates, it seems strange that it does not use the same system more effectively in promoting its financial development goals.

Solomon Island Housing Authority

The Solomon Island Housing Authority was established in 1970 to assume the ownership and management of the Colonial government's residential real estate holdings, as well as to build and sell houses, and to provide home loans. In addition to on-site building and construction, the Authority also operates a prefabricated housing factory in Honiara. This allows those in more remote areas to purchase homes for erection on their own site.

Specially-designed buildings are also available and the construction of classrooms, rural services offices, local medical clinics and other government-related buildings throughout the country presently dominates the Authority's construction role, and indeed the entire operation. It also accounts for the bulk of the Authority's 140 staff. Thus, today the Authority's home construction and, particularly, its finance functions have become of much less importance.

Some indications of this position is reflected in Table 2.32. Sales revenue, almost exclusively from the prefabrication and construction work, accounted for some 70 per cent of the Authority's income. Of these sales in 1983, 57.5 per cent came from the sale of classrooms and another 36.4 per cent from housing kits.

TABLE 2.32   Solomon Islands Housing Authority: sources of income, 1983

Sales	1,121,974
Rent received	239,105
Interest on loans	154,366
Commission on sales	47,570
Other income	26,845
Total income	1,589,860

Source: Solomon Islands Housing Authority (1985).

In addition to its own operations, the Authority has a 50-50 joint venture with the UK's Commonwealth Development Corporation to provide accommodation for workers at a new development project. The revenue from these loan repayments, however, go to the government who in turn repays the Commonwealth Development Corporation for the initial funding.

(i) *Assets*

As shown in Table 2.33, fixed assets comprise almost half of the Authority's assets. These include a variety of items but are primarily of the Authority's own residential holdings as well as development sites or land held for development. Most of the value relates to the Authority's 60 or so residential rental properties. The Authority also has substantial landholdings for future development, but these assets, and hence importance, are grossly understated for the leasehold land is valued at the lower of the land's cost or its current market value. As most holdings were acquired from the government at no cost, much of them are listed with a zero value on the Authority's books.

In terms of its housing developments, the Authority first applies for land from the government and then sub-divides it into residential blocks, installs the appropriates services, and finally resells the developing property, usually in conjunction with an Authority-built home. As with most local property, the Authority's land is sold with a fixed-term estate title: the ownership reverting to the crown within a specific period. Initially these were set for a period of 99 years but newer grants have been reduced to 55 years.

The Authority is currently developing sites in Baranaba, Vura, and Panatina, but as yet has done no development work on customary

TABLE 2.33   Solomon Islands Housing Authority: assets and liabilities,
30 September 1983

Assets:	
Cash and cash at bank	1,588
Sundry debtors and prepayments	306,873
Inventories and work in progress	494,225
Housing loans	1,526,484
Site development	168,357
Fixed assets	2,356,418
Capital work in progress	9,045
Expenditures carried forward	49,880
Total assets	4,912,870
Liabilities:	
Capital	157,746
Insurance reserves	10,000
Accumulated surplus	51,807
Asset revaluation reserves	1,120,423
Bank overdraft	248,817
Trade creditors and accruals	555,350
Advances from government	50,000
Retention moneys	2,575
Land premium payable	4,200
Secured loans from government	1,717,297
Secured loans from NPF	978,821
Provision for leave	14,354
Bonds on rental properties	1,480
Total liabilities	4,912,870

Source: Solomon Islands Housing Authority (1985).

land: much of its prefabrication work, however, is for customary landholders.

Though the costs vary with the location and customer requirements, the Authority's most expensive house (excluding land) is SI$ 36,000 and the least expensive, a self-assembled prefabricated house, cost SI$ 5000. A prefabricated home of a provincial standard takes approximately two days for Authority staff to complete. Self-assembly obviously varies with the number of local workers and their respective skills. Local workers play an important role in most Authority construction, particularly in provincial areas, but the Authority does have its own staff of skilled workers to connect plumbing, electricity, and supervise the other more technical aspects of the construction.

Authority-built houses can be purchased with a down payment of 7.5 per cent, and are normally repaid over 10 to 15 years with the maximum loan maturity set at 20 years. The actual amount repaid each month depends on the borrower's income, but is approximately a third of his total salary. The interest is set on a fixed basis and presently is being raised from 7 to 8 per cent per annum. By late 1985 there were around 500 home loans outstanding, and a waiting list of 6 to 7 years for an Authority-built house and loan facility.

Though the housing loan terms and conditions are quite reasonable, loan repayments have not proved as important a source of funding as initially planned. This is due largely to the lack of an effective financial management system within the Authority. Thus no proper loan supervision techniques developed and in the process much of the Authority's loan portfolio is now in arrears. Indeed, of the SI\$ 1.5 million in loans outstanding in 1983, some SI\$ 131,000 worth of payments were in arrears. The impact of this on the Authority's cash flow is perhaps more evident when one considers that the total repayments expected were around SI\$ 200,000. Thus roughly 65 per cent of the year's loan receivables were in arrears for 1983. Similarly, in terms of accounts, the arrears position of 251 loans amounted to 56.4 per cent of the Authority's total borrowers.

These problems unfortunately are not new for the Authority. Its financial statements were heavily qualified by its auditors in both fiscal 1980–81 and 1981–82. As a result of this, and its failure to report annually to Parliament as required under its Act, an in-depth investigation of the Authority's affairs was conducted over 1983–4 and many recommendations were forthcoming. As result of these better financial practices and better economic conditions for the country over 1984–5, the Authority's arrears levels has dropped from SI\$ 100,000 to around SI\$ 60,000. Despite this improvement, the levels are still unacceptable, particularly when one considers their relative importance. Indeed, as one report commented, if it fails to correct this problem, the Authority might 'reach the position where it is unable to repay the loans from the government and the National Provident Fund' and, as the authority's debt is government guaranteed, that 'the whole burden will be borne by Treasury for the benefit of a few borrowers and to the detriment of the public at large'.[112]

(ii) *Funding*

As shown in Table 2.33, government borrowings comprise the Authority's largest source of funds, with some 35 per cent of total liabilities and capital. Some SI$ 147,499 of these government loans in 1983 were interest free and SI$ 60,000 is repayable only if the Authority ceases operations. The Authority pays 7 per cent interest on the other government finance but has substantial grace periods on the repayments, and even the interest is capitalized during the grace period. The National Provident Fund is the other major lender to the Authority and its loans account for an additional 20 per cent of the total funds. These borrowings are for a period of 15 years, with an interest rate of 7 to 9 per cent per annum.

The Authority's own capital is the other major source of funding and, together with the various reserves, accounts for some 27 per cent of the total. Interestingly of the SI$ 157,746 shown as capital, some SI$ 117,347 was contributed in the form of government housing. The remainder was mainly in government housing loans transferred to the Authority. This choice of initial funding, which involved so little cash, has adversely affected the Authority's subsequent operations, for inadequate working capital has greatly restricted its development operations. It was probably thought that as the Authority would obtain the basic land for nothing, it had little need for actual cash. Unfortunately, the land cost is only part of the total expense. The Authority had to spend considerably more in subdividing the parcels and installing the appropriate services. Worse still, when the property was sold at a modest profit, the Authority generally received little cash flow as it generally provided the purchase finance. This resulted in the Authority's decision to concentrate mainly on government construction contracts which could be completed much more quickly and produced an immediate cash flow.

Thus for a number of reasons the Solomon Island Housing Authority has failed to achieve its initial purposes. As government itself admits, the Authority 'has ceased to play an effective role in financing and development of housing'.[113] Furthermore, it 'has not utilized the majority of its powers, nor has it undertaken a development role in the provincial centres. Poor management has been the important reason for its poor performance'.[114]

This lack of initial success, however, does not mean that the purpose was incorrect and it is intended that housing construction will soon resume as the Authority's major building function. Indeed, the Authority's new objective will be 'to enable finance to be available at affordable costs to meet housing needs and to make home ownership a reality especially for the urban residents of the lower and middle-income levels'.[115]

To achieve this, the government plans for a 'substantial strengthening of the Authority's staffing, administrative controls and finance and to reestablish it as the principal agent of government housing policy'. In addition 'certain aspects of the Authority's financial activities will need to come within the supervisory scope of the Central Bank and legislative changes are in hand to provide for this'.[116] If these proposals prove effective, the government is hopeful that by 1987 the Authority should become an important financial institution and a 'major source of housing for lower and middle-income residents of Honiara'.[117]

FINANCIAL MARKETS

As yet the Solomons has not developed much in the way of financial markets. There has been some limited amount of interbank dealing in short-term deposits as well as some more frequent interbank activity in foreign exchange dealing. As yet the government bonds and other securities are not available in sufficient numbers, nor are there sufficient holders of these securities to allow for any secondary trading other than resales to the Central Bank.

Government Securities

Unlike many other developing countries, Solomon Island government debt has been issued mostly on market terms. Its raisings are conducted under the Government Loan and Securities Act 1979, and to date consist of Solomon Islands Development Bonds, Treasury bills, and National Savings Certificates. While the Central Bank provides rediscount facilities for both the Development Bonds and Treasury bills, there is no active trading in these securities.

The government is making somewhat more use of government securities as a means of drawing liquidity from the economy, and in June 1985 the Central Bank offered a new issue of government bonds with one-year maturity securities yielding 11 per cent and three-year maturity yielding 12 per cent. These rates were intended to attract local investment from the banking sector and thus help restrain inflation and import consumption. The Central Bank will probably try to make more use of government securities as part of its future monetary policy implementation efforts, and in addition to government securities it may decide to make use of its own powers under the Central Bank legislation to issue its own securities. These would provide an alternative to the existing government securities and broaden the investment choices within the market.

Foreign Exchange Market

In late 1985 there was not an active foreign exchange market in the Solomon Islands dollar. Of the various banks, the National Bank of the Solomon Islands was the most active, and in 1980–81 reportedly established its own foreign exchange dealer as a 'modest trader in the foreign exchange markets of South-East Asia'.[118] While it is true that the National has one officer who now primarily handles foreign exchange business, it is normally conducted in US and Australian dollars via correspondent banks, and could hardly be considered an active trader, particularly in terms of the local market. Perhaps as a result, the other banks tend to look off-shore for their funding via their parents rather than seek the money locally. The ANZ Bank, for example, covers most of its foreign exchange requirements through its Melbourne head office, and the Hongkong and Shanghai Banking Corporation uses Hong Kong largely for the same purpose. Interestingly, there was apparently an attempt to introduce a greater foreign exchange trading between the local banks in late 1985, but for various reasons this did not prove successful.

The banks are active, though, in foreign exchange control matters, for all financial transactions between Solomon Island residents and other countries are subject to foreign exchange controls. As mentioned, these are administered by the Central Bank of Solomon Islands under the Exchange Ordinance 1976, with each of the four commercial banks appointed as 'authorised dealers' and delegated power to approve most personal and commercially related transactions. Capital flows, particularly foreign or overseas investment, generally require additional consideration, and as a general rule direct or portfolio overseas investment by Solomon Island residents is not approved.

In terms of actual foreign exchange, the Solomon Islands dollar is currently linked to a trade-weighted basket of currencies to include US dollar, British pound, Australian dollar, New Zealand dollar, and

Japanese yen. This rate is then converted into US dollars by the Central Bank who will then deal with the commercial banks on this basis. It is also generally willing to deal in some other currencies on this basis.

The Solomon Island dollar, itself, is still a relatively new currency and was introduced on 24 October 1977 to replace the Australian dollar then in local use. The two served as a dual legal tender until 30 September 1978, and parity continued until 18 May 1979 when the Solomon Island dollar was revalued to A\$ 1.05. The current basket method together with more frequent currency rate adjustments was subsequently adopted.

Corporate Securities Market

In the corporate area to date, there has been only one public share issue, that of Solomon Islands Investments Ltd in the early 1970s. In November 1983 Solomon Islands Investments' former property operations were spun off in the form of a new company, Property Development Co. Ltd, and it is that company that has retained the large number of shareholders. Solomon Islands Investment had been an associate of Navita Investments in Fiji and when Burns Philp purchased control of that company, it also gained control of Solomon Islands Investments. Solomon Islands Investments is still held by Burns Philp.

In addition to Solomon Islands Investments, there are some small individual shareholdings associated with Solomon Islands Plantations Ltd. These amount to only 4 per cent of that company's paid-up capital, or 58,000 shares, and were issued by the company to the custom landowners of the area on which its plantations were planted. The initial number of shareholders apparently amounted to several hundred, but the number of current holders is not known. These shareholders are represented on the firm's Board of Directors by one specially appointed director.

ANALYSIS

While the government has had relatively good success in implementing monetary policy measures, its experiences in fiscal management have been less satisfactory and if not improved could seriously affect the potential for financial development. There is much room for improvement in this area as well as the country's bank network representation.

Monetary Policy

Traditionally, the Solomon Islands have three major means of monetary policy implementation: changes in the liquidity ratio; changes in Central Bank deposit and lending arrangements with the commercial banks; and transactions in government securities. More recently it has added a fourth tool, the direction of statutory corporation deposits. Over the boom period of 1983–4, for example, the Central Bank took a number of steps to reduce the over-all liquidity within the country. First, it arranged for the Government Shareholding Agency to refinance a SI\$ 5 million promissory note issue with the commercial banks, previously financed through the Central Bank. Secondly, it requested the Copra Board switch a major portion of its deposits from the commercial banks to the Central Bank. Thirdly, it requested the government also move its main accounts from the commercial banks to accounts with the Central Bank. Finally it raised the liquid asset ratio to 25 per cent of commercial bank liabilities.

Monetary policy has served as the Solomon Island government's main economic tool. It is designed to minimize the country's balance of payments problems, but to ensure adequate finance for productive projects as well as minimize inflation. Rather than rely solely on the market allocation of resources, the government ensures adequate funds through the Government Shareholding Agency, Development Bank and Central Bank support schemes.

Fiscal Management

The impact of improved monetary policy, however, can be quickly offset by poor fiscal policies, and in 1985 the government's fiscal management abilities were very much in question. In many ministries, for example, the budget was apparently not followed and their current account allocations grossly overspent. Indeed, some ministries were seemingly competing to outspend each other, and thus many purchases were poorly planned and, worse still, some made for personal use rather than government business. As the Minister of Finance complained, there are 'fifteen separate ministries, not to mention provincial administrations, all competing to increase their importance and their share of the cake, not just in personnel but also in transport, office equipment, office space and all the other finery of self importance'. Indeed, he characterized the public service as a 'fifteen-headed monster, feeding off our revenues, providing diminishing services and leaving little for development'.[119]

In late 1985 these budgetary problems had reached the point where the government collected all local purchase order books from the various departments and locked them in a safe in the Ministry of Finance. Thus, to purchase even a pencil, required the direct approval of the Ministry of Finance. This step had the desired effect of reducing spending as well as revealing some wasteful and sometimes inappropriate spending, but has not over-come the government's basic administrative problems.

Ironically, one of the major problems should be the government's greatest strengths. This is the diversity and the relative importance of international and bilateral aid. The problem is that each scheme often has its own administrative requirements and each must be met in full before any funds are forthcoming. At the most basic level, for example, there is no uniformity even in claim periods used within each program. France, for example, uses a calendar year for its aid, Australian aid operates from a July to June year, while Japan, New Zealand and the UK use an April to March period. These timing differences can prove very important, for under some programmes, such as those for New Zealand and West Germany, all assistance granted must be fully expended within that respective fiscal year. Many countries also use a reimbursement system by which the recipient government must finance the initial expenses and then claim the money back from the donor: most EC moneys are distributed in this manner. While these very basic conditions may not seem to be overly difficult, in practice they have caused considerable difficulties for the Solomon Islands government. By not spending the aid moneys within the correct period or by failing to claim refunds on its own expenditures, the government has typically under utilized its existing aid approvals as well as failed to take full advantage of all the potential soft lending and grant funds for which it is eligible.

There is little question that the basic cause of these problems has been the too rapid localization of government administrative positions. Local staff have been appointed to positions beyond their present experience levels, and the country's financing is suffering accordingly. As the World Bank expressed it, 'the government itself does not have sufficient skilled manpower to carry out its present functions'.[120] It would seem in the short-term that an expansion rather than a reduction in the level of expatriate staff, particularly in the area of financial administration, is a critical step in improving the government's over-all functioning, and that the additional costs involved, if not funded from bilateral aid directly, would be more than offset by the more timely claiming of genuine aid expenses and the full utilization and expansion of grant and soft loan funding.

These comments do not argue for a permanent expatriate presence within the Solomon Islands government. Solomon Islanders, not expatriates, should be the ones to administer the Solomon Islands. It is just that one must first ensure that there are both adequately trained and experienced local staff available before expatriate positions are eliminated. It would also be helpful to conduct this replacement on a step-by-step basis within each department, rather than to localize all positions within a department at the same time. Similar comments, of course, could be made regarding localizations within the private sector, but the problem there does not appear quite so serious.

If the government has difficulties at present with fiscal management, then its current decentralization plans based on the existing eight provincial governments are of even more concern. Even at their current level of operations, the provincial governments are already having difficulties, and it is very difficult to determine the extent of the current problem. As the Central Bank complained, 'accurate figures for provincial governments' financial performance are not readily available. Most provinces have not presented final accounts for audit in many years'.[121]

In the short run at least, there must a major change in government priorities away from development projects and increased social welfare spending, and toward the training of public sector personnel. Unfortunately many aid programmes are not as keen to fund such technical assistance work as they are not projects with a physical end result. Nevertheless, such funding must be required by the government as a condition for any new project funding. To do otherwise will have a serious impact on the local economy and hence its financial sector.

Bank Representation

As previously indicated, current government plans require a substantial increase in local savings mobilization, and to achieve this requires some major changes in the present financial system. As the Central

Bank indicated, the system must offer a 'more attractive range of financial assets; more effective intermediation between savings and borrowers by the banking system; encourage small holders and large businesses' to invest in productive purposes rather than just consumption.[122]

The continuance of a market-orientated interest rate policy for both the banking sector and government securities is the key to successful savings mobilization and the expected increase in types of government securities and further innovation among existing financial institutions should greatly assist this process. These factors, coupled with a major expansion of the banking system into rural areas, should have a major impact both on savings mobilization and the banking sector's over-all contribution to improved economic growth.

In terms of savings facilities, it is a government policy that 'it should not be necessary to sleep away from home in order to contact the banking system'.[123] At present, other than the National Bank, none of the banks have branches outside Honiara, and likewise it is only the National (with one exception) that has established savings bank agencies in provincial areas. This agency network should be expanded to include the other banks, and it is expected that the Central Bank will provide fairly stong 'informal' guidance to this effect in the near future. The current agency network, however, could be very easily expanded by making more effective use of existing government office facilities in rural areas. As mentioned earlier, in the colonial period the district officers frequently ran a savings bank agency as part of their duties, but in 1985 only one of the National Bank's 35 savings bank agencies involved a (non-postal) government department. It would seem both feasible and logical to reconsider a reintroduction of this past practice.

Probably the most obvious vehicle for a rapid expansion of bank agency facilities is through the better use of the existing post office structure. As previously discussed, two post offices already act as agents for the National Bank and, seemingly, it would not be too difficult to add the receipt and withdrawal of savings to the other post masters' current responsibilities. Indeed, the post offices seem ideally suited for this task in that they are already located in secured buildings and have an existing staff and administrative structure. In addition to the post offices themselves, the postal system also makes use of an extensive network of postal agencies, generally in stores in more remote areas for the sale of stamps, and delivery and receipt of mail. In that they, too, have shown some degree of financial responsibility, they would seem a very convenient group to consider when selecting additional banking agencies.

A major expansion in savings bank agency numbers should certainly improve local savings rates, but it would only resolve part of the problem currently caused by the banks' present capital city orientation. At present, not only are insufficient funds raised in rural areas, but also there is too little money being lent to these areas. As one government study concluded that 'relatively large amounts of money available for lending to rural areas have not been used and manpower and land have remained underutilized'.[124] The lack of a rural branch network is at least one cause for this position as it is difficult to encourage rural applications and to disburse and supervise the resulting loans without rural-based offices.

Unfortunately, it is expensive to establish and operate bank branches in rural areas. Interviews suggest that a local branch in the provincial areas requires at least SI$ 100,000 for the building, as well as a need to provide housing for bank staff. Then operationally, the annual salary costs of the three to four bank staff required would run to at least SI$ 25,000 per year. In addition, there would be the supervisory and training costs as well as the opportunity costs on the funds involved. Initially it is unlikely that these potential branch sites would provide sufficient business to offset these costs. The government too admits that 'the provision of wide-spread services will probably involve individual points that are uneconomic to operate; nevertheless it is essential for public support of the banking system that all people needing to pay or receive cash should be able to make contact with it'.[125]

Given the potential conflict between the government desires on the one hand and the commercial banks' profit requirements on the other, the obvious solution is for the government to fund the establishment costs and possibly some of the operational costs, for those branches considered essential to national development. Fortunately the Central Bank has indicated that it will 'assist with the initial capital and operating costs of approved new branches or sub-branches opened to serve rural areas and with the agreed costs of training and supervising staff and agencies outside Honiara' as well as provide 'a basic cash transfer service between Honiara and certain provincial headquarters'.[126] This position is strongly supported even by the World Bank, which is normally against subsidization. It has instead recommended government financial support for rural banking, and that any subsidy required should be 'regarded as an investment in that country's future'.[127]

Such efforts, together with the planned expansion of the credit union movement and Development Bank representation, should have a most favourable effect, not only on savings mobilization levels but also on rural development.

TRENDS AND PREDICTIONS

As with other island countries, the Solomon Islands faces many potential problems in fulfilling its development goals, and the World Bank has indicated four areas which are particularly serious. These are: creating sufficient employment opportunities for its growing potential work force; the sparsity of cash earning opportunities in rural areas; the major differences in natural resource endowments within the country; and the acute shortage of skilled manpower.[128] Most of these have been discussed previously in some detail, but there seems little question that the future generation of employment, particularly in rural areas, is the most important of these problems.

The government has already take action to create additional employment, and has correctly tried to maintain, if not expand, the country's growing diversity in exports. It thus hopes that the expected increase in the work force will not occur in just one sector, but rather will be spread throughout the economy with particular emphasis on the agricultural, forestry, fisheries, mineral, tourism and manufacturing sectors.

In some respects the government's agricultural policies have been both the most, and the least, successful of its development efforts. The problem is that its current plantation-styled developments, although rational from an economic viewpoint, will do little to create employment opportunities. Instead the greater use of small-holder production is required. While more costly to develop, this production can provide a useful supplement to the present plantation-based output, and through the creation of rural-based employments help stem the current drift of young Solomon Islanders from the rural to urban areas. The current programme has done little to correct this position, and as the World Bank complained, small-holders have 'scarcely participated in the expansion of timber, palm oil, fish and rice exports'.[129]

At present even the country's current agricultural resources remain underutilized. A large portion of the present coconut production, for example, is simply not collected, and left to rot. Similarly, the major expansion in cattle production in the 1970s was never adequately pursued. These are resources which could produce or save valuable foreign exchange, but are underutilized due to lack of manpower and proper direction. Agricultural extension services realize the need to educate smallholders on the best use of their resources, and there has been progress in even such basic items as growing small cash crops of vegetables to supply Honiara rather than flying in produce from Australia and other countries. An expansion in other exports such as a range of tree crops, betel-nuts and peanuts are also considered feasible for small-holder production. Some chilies and tumeric have been exported in small quantities, and coffee is currently grown for local consumption. There appears much potential both in increased and diversified production, as well as for greater local processing of the end products.

Much of the Solomons is covered with potentially commercial forests, and Korean, Hong Kong, and Taiwanese interests have all been active in local logging and exporting. At present little is processed locally, and there is some potential to increase both the local use and value added of these products. Government plans admittedly call for greater processing, at least at sawmill stage, and this may help increase local employment. More work could also be done in the area of replanting, and there is some danger that the current forests are being harvested too quickly to sustain a continued forestry-based industry.

While tuna fishing is already developed to some extent in conjunction with Japanese interests, much more could be done to utilize the country's potential sea resources. The Solomons have already declared a 200-mile economic zone to protect its rich tuna areas: areas that other countries are keen to exploit.[130] Current programmes should increase Solomon Island participation in fishing work as well as greater tuna production. There are also plans to diversify the catch to include more shark and other exotic fish and sea life, as well as to conduct more local processing. Prawn and other seafood breeding is also under consideration for West Guadalcanal. As of 1985, though, the major development was the construction of a new port with fish processing and canning facilities in Noro.

In addition to its agricultural capabilities, the country also has a significant mineral resources potential. Over the years it has been a small but continual exporter of gold and, to a very much less extent, other minerals. Guadalcanal, for example, has known deposits of gold, silver and copper. There are also phosphates, asbestos, bauxite, nickel, copper, chromite, and manganese ores, and similar deposits on other islands. The real potential lies in greater mineral exploration. This is already under way and includes direct exploration or consortium participation by Amoco Minerals Solomons Ltd, Austpac Resources, BHP Minerals, Cyprus Mines, Dominion Gold, Elders Resources, Jason Mining, Kia Ora Gold Corporation, Mitsui Mining and Smelting, Negri River Corporation, Newmount Mining, Sol Exploration, Solomon Pacific Resources and Zanex.

Unlike some of its neighbours, the Solomon Islands has relatively little involvement in tourism, and the Tambea Village Resort in West Guadalcanal, and the Anuha resort are the only real major tourist operations to date. This is unfortunate as the country's significance in the Second World War provides a worthwhile basis for overseas promotional work, and many of the American, Japanese and other visitors to date have at least some relationship with Second World War events. One of tourism's major attractions is that it is very labour intensive as well as a source of foreign exchange. Interestingly, given its self-sufficiency in most foodstuffs and quality handicrafts, the World Bank at least considers 'the Solomon Islands is in a better position to retain most gains from tourism within the country than most other small countries'.[131] Interviews suggest that there is some foreign interest in local tourism projects, and that a number of proposals are in various stages of discussion.

Thus far the least-developed potential source of employment is manufacturing. As the World Bank commented, 'because many opportunities for import substitution remain to be exploited, there is substantial scope for a wide range of small industries catering to the domestic market'.[132] The government has selected a number of areas for potential investment to include food, beverages and tobacco, textiles, timber, pulp and paper, printing and publishing, leather, rubber, plastics, industrial chemicals, fertilizers, clay products, metal and machinery, electrical items, watches and clocks, and other products. The South Pacific Regional Trade and Economic Co-operation Agreement (SPARTECA) and Lomé Agreements, which give Solomon Island manufactured products an advantage in exporting to the Australian, New Zealand and EC markets, might also encourage some export-oriented as well as import-substitution production. In conjunction with these plans, an industrial estate at Kukum, outside Honiara, has been constructed and similar estates are planned for

Auki and Noro. The revitalization of shipbuilding and repair facilities on Florida Island is also under consideration.

In conclusion, the Solomon Islands have been very fortunate in obtaining relatively good economic growth and development since independence, and in diversifying their export base. Much work, though, still needs to be done, and much of this relates to developing local skills and experience in public sector and business management. Just recently, for example, the government failed to act with sufficient strength to control the boom conditions created by 1984's high copra prices. While this money could have been retained through the stabilization fund and either invested overseas or used for local development, most of the benefits were immediately passed through to producers. This resulted in a major expansion in consumption and unfortunately in the Solomons this meant a major growth in import levels. Monetary policy was inadequate to stem this flow and in late 1985 the country's current account was in deficit, and the country's foreign exchange reserves were declining. Indeed, as one financial journal commented, 'without aid the place would undoubtedly sink'.[133] Both positions are expected to get worse, and real decline in GDP is expected over 1986. Hopefully the resulting problems will not have too adverse an affect on present development efforts, and the experience will ensure the government acts more effectively during the next period of high commodity prices.

NOTES

1. Many of these people are Gilbertese (now Kiribati) who were resettled by the British in the 1950s and 1960s from Phoenix Island.
2. Sir Harry Luke (1962) *Islands of the South Pacific* (London: Harrap) p. 122.
3. When a separate High Commission was established in Fiji in 1952, the High Commission of the Western Pacific was moved to Honiara. In addition to the Solomons, the Gilbert and Ellice Islands and the Anglo-French Condominium of the New Hebrides came under his control until 1971 and 1973 respectively. The High Commissioner was subsequently redesignated Governor for the Solomon Islands in 1974.
4. Besides the Battle of Guadalcanal and the exploits of its many coast watchers, the Solomons was also the site, in 1943, of the later famous sinking incident of John F. Kennedy's PT boat 109 near Olasana.
5. *The Solomon Islands: an introductory economic report* (1980) (Washington, DC: World Bank) p. 17.
6. A. R. Hughes (1985) 'Coming back to earth . . . return to economic

reality and prospects for growth', a speech, 19 August, p. 15.

7. *Solomon Islands National Development Plan, 1985–1989* (1985) (Honiara: Ministry of Economic Planning 1985) p. 16.

8. *Solomon Islands National Development Plan* (1985) p. 183.

9. K. Buckley and K. Klugman (1981) *The History of Burns Philp: the Australian company in the South Pacific* (Sydney: Burns Philp & Co.) p. 247. To a lesser extent, Burns Philp was also affected by the Commonwealth Notes Act 1910 in Australia which imposed a prohibitive tax on private bank notes.

10. Commonwealth Banking Corporation, correspondence dated 17 February 1986.

11. *British Solomon Island Protectorate, 1931* (Honiara: HMSO, 1932) p. 12.

12. Commonwealth Banking Corporation, correspondence dated 13 March 1986.

13. *Solomon Islands National Development Plan, 1980–1984* (1980) (Honiara: Ministry of Economic Planning) para. 4.1.

14. *Solomon Islands National Development Plan, 1985–1989* (1985) (Honiara: Ministry of Central Planning) p. 186.

15. *Solomon Islands National Development Plan* (1980), p. 43.

16. *The Money System* (1984) (Honiara: Central Bank of Solomon Islands) p. 14. The currency is presently available in notes $ 2, $ 5, $ 10 and $ 20 denomination and coins of 1, 2, 5, 10, 20, and 100 cents.

17. *The Money System*, p. 16.

18. Commonwealth Bank of Australia (1952) *Annual Report*, pp. 30–1.

19. Commonwealth Banking Corporation, correspondence dated 17 February 1986.

20. The Commonwealth has long had a branch in London but it was established mainly to serve Australian visitors and intending migrants as well as for international banking liaison work rather than local banking. More recently the Commonwealth has established branch operations in New York, Singapore and, soon, Hong Kong, but again these branches are not designed to attract local banking business.

21. See Michael T. Skully (1985) 'Financial Institutions and Markets in Papua New Guinea', in Michael T. Skully (ed.) (1985) *Financial Institutions and Markets in the Southwest Pacific: A study of Australia, Fiji, New Zealand and Papua New Guinea* (London: Macmillan) pp. 257–8.

22. In 1944, for example, Dr Evatt had argued that Australia assume responsibility for the Solomon Islands, and in the mid-1950s the then Minister for External Affairs, R. G. Casey, suggested the idea of a Melanesian Federation of Papua New Guinea and the Solomons. Griffin James (1973), 'Papua New Guinea and the British Solomon Islands Protectorate: fusion or transfusion', *Australian Outlook*, December, pp. 319–28.

23. Australian and New Zealand Banking Group, Honiara, correspondence dated 6 July 1983.

24. National Bank of Solomon Islands Ltd (1981), *Annual Report*, p. 3.

25. *Australian Financial Review*, 26 July 1985, p. 68.

26. *The Solomon Islands: an introductory economic report* p. 60.

27. *Solomon Islands National Development Plan* (1985) p. 184 Honiara; Ministry of Economic Planning.
28. *Solomon Islands National Development Plan* (1985) p. 184.
29. Central Bank of Solomon Islands (1982) *Annual Report* p. 19.
30. *Solomon Islands National Development Plan* (1985) p. 184.
31. *Solomon Islands* (1978) (London: HMSO) p. 19.
32. Another reason for this position is that the National Bank received an interest-free loan of SI$ 250,000 repayable over 10 years, starting in 1986, from the Government Shareholding Agency, to establish a Training and Development Fund for the Bank.
33. *Solomons Toktok*, 18–22 November 1985, p. 16.
34. National Bank of Solomon Islands (1984) *Annual Report*, p. 4.
35. *Solomon Islands National Development Plan* (1985) p. 191. (Honiara: Ministry of Economic Planning).
36. *Rural Financial Services in Solomon Islands* (1984) (Honiara: Central Bank of Solomon Islands) p. 3.
37. *Solomon Islands National Development Plan* (1985) p. 191. (Honiara: Ministry of Economic Planning).
38. George F. Pickering (1978) *Basic Banking Facilities in Rural Areas of the Solomon Islands*, (Suva: United Nations Development Advisory Team for the Pacific) p. 4. The remaining agency was not profitable either. Industry interviews suggest that the ANZ Bank's agency network at one time might have included as many as 12 to 15 outlets.
39. Pickering, *Basic Banking Facilities*, p. 4.
40. *Solomon Islands Fifth Development Plan, 1968–1970* (Honiara: British Solomon Islands Protectorate, 1968) p. 26.
41. *British Solomon Islands 1970* (London: HMSO, 1970) p. 21.
42. *Solomon Islands Sixth Development Plan 1971–73* (Honiara: British Solomon Islands Protectorate, 1971) p. 96.
43. *6th Development Plan, 2nd Review 1973* (Honiara: British Solomon Islands Protectorate, 1973) p. 35.
44. Pickering, *Basic Banking Facilities* p. 7.
45. K. J. Ayton (1982) 'Solomon Islands – the country and its people', *Bankers Magazine of Australasia*, February: 10.
46. *The Money System*, p. 17.
47. Development Bank of Solomon Islands (1981) *Annual Report*, p. 8.
48. Development Bank of Solomon Islands (1981) *Annual Report*, p. 8.
49. Development Bank of Solomon Islands (1983) *6th Annual Report*, p. 18.
50. *Solomon Islands National Development Plan* (1985) p. 188.
51. Solomon Islands Monetary Authority (1981) *Annual Report*, p. 21.
52. *Solomon Islands National Development Plan* (1985) p. 188.
53. *Solomon Island National Development Plan* (1980) p. 45.
54. *The Solomon Islands: an introductory economic report*, p. 28.
55. Ayton, 'Solomon Islands', p. 11.
56. *Solomon Islands National Development Plan* (1985) p. 191.
57. *Solomon Islands National Development Plan* (1985) p.188.
58. Pickering *Basic Banking Facilities*, p. 7.
59. Charles G. Kick (ed.) (1986) *Development Services Exchange of the*

Solomon Islands: directory (Honiara: Development Services Exchange) p. 7.

60. Kick (ed.) *Development Services Exchange*, p. 7.
61. Kick (ed.) *Development Services Exchange*, p. 7.
62. In name at least, the Salaka Finance Co. would pre-date AGC as would another local firm, Jonny Arrow Funding Co. Central Bank interviews, however, indicated that neither of these companies, in fact, were local finance company operations.
63. *Solomon Islands National Development Plan* (1985) p. 186. The Hongkong and Shanghai Banking Corporation has a long history of providing financing services in developing countries and the ANZ Bank, through its recent Grindlays acquisition, now also has a similar ability. Finally, the National Bank, through its Commonwealth Bank affiliations, might draw on the experiences of the Papua New Guinea Banking Corporation in this area. None of the banks, however, mentioned any finance company plans during interviews in December 1985.
64. *Solomon Islands National Development Plan* (1985) p. 186.
65. *The Money System* p. 23.
66. *Solomon Islands National Development Plan* (1985) p. 186.
67. Australian Guarantee Corporation Ltd, correspondence dated 4 April 1986.
68. Pickering, *Basic Banking Facilities*, p. 8.
69. *Solomon Island National Development Plan* (1980) p. 15.
70. Based on industry interviews, December 1985.
71. *Solomon Island National Development Plan* (1980) p. 15.
72. *Solomon Island National Development Plan* (1985) p. 189.
73. *Solomon Islands National Development Plan* (1985) p. 186.
74. Both GRE and General Accident, for example, use their Port Moresby affiliate, whereas others such as Sun Alliance and INA (Sigma) have their policies issued from Australia.
75. *The Solomon Islands: an introductory economic report*, p. 59.
76. *Solomon Island National Development Plan* (1985) p. 191.
77. *Solomon Island National Development Plan* (1980) p. 15.
78. Pickering *Basic Banking Facilities*, p. 8.
79. *The Solomon Islands: an introductory economic report*, p. 58.
80. *Solomon Islands National Development Plan* (1980) p. 46.
81. *Solomon Islands National Development Plan* (1985) p. 185.
82. Solomon Islands National Provident Fund (1977) *First Annual Report*, p. 1.
83. Solomon Islands National Provident Fund, *First Annual Report*, p. 40.
84. Central Bank of Solomon Islands (1984) *Annual Report*, p. 25.
85. *Solomon Islands National Development Plan* (1985) p. 185.
86. *Solomon Islands National Development Plan* (1985) p. 185.
87. Lever Solomons Ltd, correspondence dated 11 February 1986.
88. Solomons Islands Plantations Ltd, correspondence dated 12 February 1986.
89. *The Money System*, p. 20.
90. The Government Shareholding Agency (1980) *Fourth Annual Report*, p. 11.

91. The Government Shareholding Agency (1981) *Fifth Annual Report*, p. 4.
92. Central Bank of Solomon Islands (1985) *Mid-Year Economic Review*, p. 18.
93. Central Bank of Solomon Islands, *Mid-Year Economic Review*, p. 15.
94. Central Bank of Solomon Islands (1984) *Annual Report*, p. 21.
95. Stanley F. Arneil (1979) *Forming and Running a Credit Union*, 2nd edn (Sydney: Alternative Publishing Co-operative) pp. 145, 146.
96. *Some Information for Credit Unions: The Credit Unions Idea is Born, 1854* (Honiara: Solomon Island Credit Union League, 1985) p. 1. The 1854 date refers to the industry's original founding in Germany.
97. *British Solomon Islands, Reports for the years 1963 and 1964* (1965) (Honiara: British Solomon Island Protectorate) p. 40.
98. Interviews and research at the Solomon Islands Department of Co-operative Societies, December 1985.
99. *Solomon Islands National Development Plan, 1975–1979* (1975) (Honiara: Ministry of Economic Planning) p. 111.
100. Wayne M. Bornemeier (1985) *Development Plan for the Solomon Islands Credit Union League 1986–1990* (Washington DC: Volunteers in overseas Co-operative Assistance) p. 3.
101. Bornemeier, *Development Plan*, p. 3.
102. *Solomon Islands National Development Plan* (1985) p. 191.
103. Bornemeier, *Development Plan*, p. 17.
104. Industry interviews, December 1985.
105. Bornemeier, *Development Plan* pp. 17–18 .
106. *Solomon Islands National Development Plan* (1985) p. 190.
107. *Rural Financial Services in Solomon Islands* (1984) (Honiara: Central Bank of Solomon Islands, 1984) p. 6.
108. *Rural Financial Services*, p. 4.
109. *Solomon Islands National Development Plan* (1985) p. 189.
110. *Sixth Development Plan 1971–1974: Second Annual Review* (1973) (Honiara: British Solomon Islands Protectorate) p. 33.
111. *The Solomon Islands: an introductory economic report*, p. 28.
112. J. R. Ringshall (1984) 'Report of the SIHA and overall housing policy and funding', Commonwealth Development Corporation sponsored paper, November, p. 19.
113. *Solomon Islands National Development Plan* (1985) p. 185.
114. *Solomon Island National Development Plan* (1980) pp. 21–7.
115. *Solomon Island National Development Plan* (1985) p. 189.
116. Central Bank of Solomon Islands (1984) *Annual Report*, p. 25.
117. *Solomon Islands National Development Plan* (1985) p. 185.
118. National Bank of Solomon Islands (1981) *Annual Report*, p. 3.
119. George Kejoa (1985) 'Introduction to the 1985 Supplementary Appropriations Bill', speech, p. 2.
120. *The Solomon Islands: an introductory economic report*, p. 3.
121. Central Bank of Solomon Islands (1984) *Annual Report*, p. 22.
122. A. R. Hughes (1985) 'Coming back to earth . . . return to economic reality and prospects for growth', speech, 19 August, pp. 12–13.
123. *Rural Financial Services*, p. 5.

124. *Rural Financial Services*, p. 4.
125. *Solomon Islands National Development Plan* (1980) p. 14.
126. *Rural Financial Services*, p. 10.
127. *The Solomon Islands: an introductory economic report*, p. 62.
128. *The Solomon Islands: an introductory economic report*, pp. i–ii.
129. *The Solomon Islands: an introductory economic report*, p. 9.
130. One violation resulted in the seizure of a US tuna boat, the 'Jeanette Diana', and political conflict with the United States. A US embargo on Solomon Island tuna exports resulted and the boat was eventually resold to its US owners for US$ 700,000 plus a $ 72,000 fine (*Island Business*, February 1985, p. 39).
131. *The Solomon Islands: an introductory economic report*, p. 34.
132. *The Solomon Islands: an introductory economic report*, p. 33.
133. *Asian Banking*, August 1984, p. 104.

Niuafo'ou

Tafahi

VAVA'U GROUP

Vava'u Neiafu

SOUTH PACIFIC OCEAN

Tofua HA'APAI
Pangai GROUP

Nuku'alofa

Tongatapu

TONGATAPU GROUP

Teleki Tonga

TONGA

3 Financial Institutions and Markets in Tonga

INTRODUCTION

The Setting

Located some 3000 kilometres north-east of Sydney and 650 kilometres east of Fiji, the Kingdom of Tonga consists of 171 islands covering some 360,000 square kilometres in area, but with a land area of only 747 square kilometres. Most of this land is divided between three main island groups running from north to south in two parallel chains: the Vava'u group in the north, Ha'apai in the centre and Tongatapu in the south. Of the islands, however, only 36 of the islands are inhabited and the bulk of the population lives on Tongatapu, Vava'u, Ha'apai, 'Eua, and Niuas: Tongatapu alone accounts for some 64 per cent of the Kingdom's 106,000 population.

Tonga is believed to be one of the oldest of the Polynesian nations, and at one time its monarchy had considerable control over its neighbouring countries. At its peak in the thirteenth century Tonga controlled Samoa, as well as having a major influence over events in Fiji and Hawaii.

Tonga was first sighted by Europeans on 16 May 1616 by the Dutch navigator, Jakob Le Maire, as part of the Schouten and Le Maire expedition although another Dutch explorer, Abel Tasman, was the first known European actually to land on the islands on 27 January 1643, and he named many of them after major Dutch cities. Other explorers followed, including Captain Cook, who visited Tonga in 1773, 1774 and 1777 and gave it the name, 'the Friendly Islands'. None of these European names survive today and the islands retain their earlier native name which actually means 'south' in many Polynesian languages.

The Europeans did little to settle or trade in the area but the missionaries, keen to gain converts, arrived in 1797 and again in

157

1822. Of the various religious groups, the Wesleyan Mission proved the most successful and eventually they succeeded in converting many nobles including the King. The King later took the name Siaosi and his consort the name Salote, after the Tongan versions of the then English King George III and Queen Charlotte. After uniting what is now Tonga in 1845, he was proclaimed King George Tupou I, and his family still rule Tonga today.

A combination of Tonga's isolated geographical location, and the fact that it had developed a national government by the time the colonial powers were seeking Pacific island territory, allowed it to be the only Pacific country to retain its local government largely intact from the 1700s. For example, Tonga introduced its first written code of law in 1839, and the constitution it adopted in 1875 is still largely in use today. The King also introduce the system of land tenure whereby every male over the age of 16 is entitled to apply for allotment of 3.4 hectares of land.

It was sufficiently developed to conduct its own foreign policy and by the late 1800s had signed a number of foreign treaties (notably with Germany in 1876, Britain in 1879 and the United States in 1888). These acknowledged the friendship between Tonga and each country and, more importantly, recognized Tonga's independence. The treaties also helped ensure that each of the colonial powers would seek to protect Tonga from losing its independence to a rival. This position, coupled with the colonial powers greater attention to Samoa and other areas, gave Tonga an important respite from direct colonization.

The agreement between the Germans, American and British resolving the ownership of Samoa, though, placed the British in a greater position to influence Tongan affairs, and on 18 May 1900 the King signed a Treaty of Friendship and Protection with the British which provided for British assistance in foreign affairs and other matters. Initially this protectorate status was intended to provide only military protection and the conduct of Tonga's foreign relations. A Supplementary Agreement in 1905, though, allowed the British to nominate the key government officials and required the King to accept the local British agent's advice on all matters of importance.[1]

Tonga's internal political position was assisted over the protectorate period by an extreme degree of political stability. Queen Salote Tupou III, who gained much publicity for the Kingdom through her overseas visits, ruled Tonga from 1918 to 1965. The present King, Taufa'ahau Tupou IV, who succeeded her, had served as the Kingdom's prime minister since 1949. His brother, Prince Fatafehi Tu'ipelehake was subsequently appointed prime minister; a position he too holds today. The importance of the King and the royal family in both political and commercial life cannot be overstated, and under the current three-tiered political system of 'the King, chiefs and matapules, and commoners',[2] he retains considerably more direct power and influence than most other constitutional monarchs. Tonga finally regained full control over its internal affairs in 1967, and the Kingdom resumed full independence on 4 June 1970.

Tonga's government today is an adaptation of the UK parliamentary system with the King and the Privy Council at the top, the Cabinet, and the Legislative Assembly comprised of 9 nobles elected by Tonga's 33 nobles, 9 members elected by the people, and 9 government appointees.

As with other South Pacific countries, Tonga's economy is dependent on agricultural production, with much of this conducted on a subsistence basis. There is also a much smaller, modern portion of the economy confined mainly to the general area of Nuku'alofa. Its exports are therefore dependent on a few agricultural products. Coconut oil, desiccated coconuts and other coconut products comprise the bulk of its exports with vanilla, kava, watermelon, and bananas also important.

This has meant that Tonga's economic health is very dependent on a combination of its local production levels and international commodity prices. For example, coconut production dropped by some 70 per cent in 1982 due to the damage of Hurricane Isaac, and banana production, once one of the largest exports, has declined to minor importance due to a combination of storm damage, disease, and tough price competition in international export markets. In recent years these factors have produced a significant deficit in Tonga's trade account, and today Tonga's exports generally cover only a tenth to a sixth of its import requirements. This trade deficit has only been partially offset by substantial remittances from Tongans resident overseas. The remainder of the funds have had to come from foreign aid, and in most years have been sufficient to produce a surplus in the country's balance of payments.

While at present there seem sufficient foreign aid resources available to raise the necessary offsetting funds, some developed countries have been questioning the value of their aid contributions in general, and Tonga may be forced to compete with other countries for what may prove a decreasing (in real terms at least) pool of funds. The raising of additional aid funds is also constrained by its abilities to process the programmes that these aid funds entail. Already, the government has found that increased foreign aid has put 'added strains on the Ministry of Finance [as] aid donors require detailed and periodic statements accounting for funds made available which government accounts do not normally provide'[3] and it seems questionable in the short run that the government could administer any major increase in these programmes.

Given the problems of its frequently unstable commodity prices, remittances and foreign aid constraints, the government has been working to diversify the economy into greater value-added agricultural exports and manufacturing items. For example, following the opening of a copra crushing factory in 1979, and a desiccated coconut operation, the Kingdom has eventually ceased copra exporting and sells only processed coconut products. An expansion of passion fruit processing is similarly planned to export frozen pulp or fruit drinks rather than simply the fruit itself.

All of these processing efforts have helped to increase the Kingdom's level of manufacturing. Tonga has worked towards this end by granting a range of fiscal incentives[4] as well as providing adequate sites in a small, 12-acre, fully-serviced, industrial estate in Ma'ufanga outside the capital, Nuku'alofa. Since 1986, the Small Industries Centre tenants have included some 14 light industries producing refrigerators, filing cabinets, knitwear, jewelry, bicycles, wheelbarrows, toilet paper, postcards, soccer balls and wooden toys.

The government would like further diversification of the country's commodities and manufacturing exports and considers that 'the development of private enterprises is stressed as a major objective'[5] in this process. A major expansion of the Kingdom's private sector will require considerable capital investment and this is a problem which the government has yet to overcome. Traditionally Tonga has had 'low domestic savings which, in turn, is affected by the high rate of growth of domestic consumption and the incomplete monetization of the economy'.[6] This 'relatively undeveloped nature of the financial sector [also] limits the ability of government to use various policy instruments'.[7]

There is thus a considerable need to expand both the level of monetization as well as domestic savings within the Kingdom. This is reflected in the Kingdom's current plans to establish a National Provident Fund as a means of increasing local savings, as well as the creation of a Central Monetary Authority[8] or Central Bank to 'develop the domestic financial sector'.[8]

Overview of the Financial Sector

As with most Pacific countries, the early financial services in Tonga were initially provided through local European merchants. In the case of Tonga, the Hamburg-based firm of Johann Ceasar Godeffroy and Sohn (commonly called J. C. Godeffroy and Son, or simply Godeffroys) was among the most important. It obtained this position, both in Tonga and Western Samoa, at least partially due to its importation of South American coinage and an extensive foreign exchange trading network. Indeed, within these countries, eventually 'almost all the small Pacific traders were committed to using the Godeffroy banking network because they were too small to arrange their own bills of exchange. Meanwhile Godeffroys were financing their own imports by issuing bills on London or Sydney'.[9]

Godeffroy's real importance in Tonga came in 1869 when they arranged to lend money to the King of Tonga in return for the right to export all the copra that the Tonga government received from local taxations.[10] It similarly gained local influence through its close association with Christian churches. Besides gaining the right to purchase copra collected by the missions, it timed its arrangements to lend Tongan growers money against promises of copra at the critical time before the vigorous church collections'.[11] It also had the missions act as its agents.

The missions, too, as a result became much more involved in island business, and this eventually resulted in Tonga's famed European missionary, Mr Shirley Baker, establishing Tonga's first formal financial institution, the Bank of Tonga, as a joint venture with the Tongan government. The new Bank 'tried to formalise Godeffroy's foreign exchange dealings, by drawing its own bills on Godeffroy's Sydney account and offering them at the old rates to traders'.[12] According to Mr Baker, the venture was a purely philanthropic one and designed to 'advance deposits on something like a building society principle so as to enable natives to build homes and get homes for themselves'.[13] In practice, though, the Bank operated very much for profit, and the venture was considered of 'dubious propriety'.[14] Unfortunately the Bank had poorly selected its manager and it was later forced to cease business.

This left Godeffroys with little local competition, and by the end of the 1870s Godeffroys 'controlled the currency. They ran a network of stores and over half the tonnage of ships calling there, and 1200 acres of plantations' as well as a monopoly on Tonga's copra exports.[15] Unfortunately, though, Godeffroys itself experienced financial problems as a result of events in Europe and went bankrupt in 1879. Deutsche Handels und Plantagen Gesellschaft subsequently assumed Godeffroys' Pacific interests in 1880.

The next banking institution in the Kingdom of Tonga was the Government Savings Bank. It was established under the Savings Bank Act of 1936. Unlike the earlier venture, this institution was solely government owned and operated, and in practice there was little difference made between the Government Savings Bank and the Treasury Department which operated this activity. In addition, the Treasury itself provided a limited range of financial services. As one report commented,

> the Treasury in most respects acts as a trading bank – with the exception that it does not operate individual cheque accounts. Local traders and commercial firms pay in cash to the Treasury which negotiates foreign exchange, drafts, etc., on their behalf. It will also cash travelers cheques.[16]

The Treasury also conducted some lending business in support of special government programmes as well as to government employees through its Government Employee Housing Scheme and Hire Purchase Scheme for Civil Servants. In practice, though, much of the local banking business was conducted through bank accounts in banks in Fiji, New Zealand and Australia.[17]

These facilities were later supplemented at the village level, first by deposit taking and lending by co-operative societies and then by credit unions. These, combined with the government's activities, were apparently adequate, for it was not until 1974 that the new, part-government-owned, Bank of Tonga Ltd, opened for business. It was joined in 1977 by the Tonga Development Bank, and these institutions account for the bulk of financial sector assets. There are also some foreign insurance companies, some small superannuation funds, the stabilization funds of the Commodities Board and a (short-lived) merchant bank. There are plans, however, for a much more diversified structure to include the creation of a Central

TABLE 3.1   Financial institutions in Tonga, by type, 1985

Central Monetary Authority[a]
Bank of Tonga
Tonga Development Bank
Off-shore banks
Commodities Board
National Provident Fund[a]
Tonga Insurance Corporation[a]
Insurance companies
Credit unions
Co-operatives

---

[a] Planned but not in operation.

Monetary Authority, National Provident Fund, Tonga Insurance Corporation and an off-shore banking centre (see Table 3.1).

FINANCIAL INSTITUTIONS

Central Bank

As of early 1986 Tonga did not have a central bank. Instead the country's traditional central banking functions were performed by a number of agencies to include the Commissioners of Currency, the Treasury and the Bank of Tonga.

Commissioners of Currency was established under the Treasury Notes Act, 1935, to control the issue of notes and coins within the Kingdom. Under the Act, Tongan currency must be backed at least 75 per cent by the assets of the note and the coinage security funds. These assets in turn must be invested only in approved securities.

As a part-government-owned institution, the Bank of Tonga at present performs many traditional central banking functions on behalf of the government. For example, it administers the Kingdom's Exchange Control Regulations and, more importantly, manages its foreign exchange reserves. It also acts as the registrar and an underwriter for government securities. In addition the Bank assists in the formulation of local credit policies for it 'liaises regularly with the Ministry of Finance regarding the level and direction of lending'.[18] Thus far its measures have apparently been considered successful for one government report concluded that 'the Bank of Tonga has shown itself to be fully responsible in promoting the economic growth and stability of the Kingdom through its lending policies'.[19]

Understandably the government would like to assume more direct control of the local monetary supply, and in 1984 the first steps were taken toward the creation of a Central Monetary Authority for the Kingdom. It was intended for the new authority 'to regulate the monetary factors in the economy and to hold the national foreign reserves'[20] as well as to consider appropriate 'policies to develop the domestic financial sector and the effective management of public debt'.[21]

It was intended that the monetary authority would commence operations in mid-1986, but in early 1986 there were some indications that a Central Bank might be created instead.

Commercial Banks

The Bank of Tonga, the Kingdom's only commercial bank, operates as a traditional Pacific-island-based commercial bank, and provides overdraft facilities, term loans, housing loans, personal loans, letters of credit and performance guarantees. In addition, it is a minority shareholder in the Tonga Development Bank. Under Section 7, the Bank of Tonga has the power to be an underwriter, executor, trustee, receiver and registrar, and operate pension schemes, unit trusts, trade in bullion, promissory notes, hire purchase lending, travel agencies and other services for travellers. The Bank of Tonga also performs certain duties on behalf of the Ministry of Finance in regard to Exchange Control Regulations, and acts as the custodian of the country's main foreign exchange reserves.

(i) *Development*

While the current Bank of Tonga was formed in 1974, the history of this new institution dates back to as early as 1955, when the now King as Prime Minister visited the Bank of New Zealand to discuss the possibility of establishing a local bank. The Bank of New Zealand subsequently sent an officer to Tonga to conduct a feasibility study initially in 1956 and again in 1958. These studies suggested 'extremely favourable' prospects for a bank.[22] Unfortunately by then the government had higher priority matters to resolve and the Bank of Tonga proposal was shelved. It was revived again in 1967 by the Bank of Hawaii which began discussions on opening a branch in Nuku'alofa.

The government suggested the concept of a consortium banking venture with government participation, and in 1970 the Bank of New Zealand again sent an officer to Tonga for a feasibility study. It was again favourable but did predict that, due to the poor local loan potential, much of the Bank's initial deposits would need to be invested overseas. Finally, the three interested banks, the Bank of Hawaii, the Bank of New South Wales (now Westpac Banking Corporation) and the Bank of New Zealand, met with the government in Nuku'alofa in November 1971.

While the commercial bankers in their negotiations indicated that 'the major concern of everyone concerned with the bank should be the interests of the Tongan people and the extent to which a bank might be able to contribute to the future wealth and prosperity of the Tongan economy', they nevertheless expected 'the bank to be established on a viable basis with reasonable profit expectance'.[23] They thus considered the Government Savings Bank's business and, more importantly, the Treasury's foreign exchange revenue as the basis for the Bank's initial operations and hence required their inclusion within the new institution.[24] Previously most of these assets were invested by the Crown Agents in the UK, or placed in New Zealand government securities.

The Bank of New South Wales was given responsibility

> to handle the detailed organization leading to establishment. This involved the drafting and passage of the Bank of Tonga Act 1972 through the Legislative Assembly of the Kingdom, the drafting and registration of Articles of Association governing the rights of the shareholders and the management of the company, and the drafting of a formal agreement between the government and the participating banks.

It also later handled the construction of the bank's premises and the manager's residence.[25] The government legislation was subsequently passed in 1972, and the Bank's articles and the final joint venture agreement was signed in 1973. The Bank of Tonga finally commenced business on 1 July 1974.

The Bank of Tonga subsequently experienced rapid growth, but as

TABLE 3.2 Bank of Tonga: deposits, loans, investments and total assets, 1979–84 (figures in T$ 000 at 31 December)

	Deposits	Loans & advances	Investment overseas	Total assets
1978	9,998	3,088	8,386	13,539
1979	12,026	4,090	10,179	17,245
1980	13,760	5,159	11,997	19,818
1981	14,526	6,911	12,804	21,951
1982	17,893	9,553	14,541	26,379
1983	22,342	9,527	19,718	31,578
1984	25,895	9,849	24,239	36,699

Source: Bank of Tonga (1985) *Annual Report: balance sheet and profit & loss account for the year ending 31 December 1984 for the twelfth annual general meeting, 25 June 1985*, p. 19 and (1982) p. 17.

shown in Table 3.2, it has been much more successful in collecting deposits than in lending these funds for local purposes.

(ii) *Regulation*

The Bank of Tonga operations are confined by its establishment act. In addition the Ministry of Finance provides direction on the Bank's lending levels, the direction of lending, and overseas reserves.

In 1982, for example, government guidelines caused the Bank of Tonga to limit its total lending to not more than 50 per cent of its foreign reserves and, if the reserves dropped below the equivalent of three months' worth of imports, lending should cease until the reserves could build up to an amount equal to at least four months' worth of exports. In 1983 the Ministry of Finance introduced new lending guidelines to slow economic demand. These allowed the Bank to lend freely when its lending commitments were equal to less than 50 per cent of its foreign exchange reserves. However, if these reserves dropped to less than three months' of imports, then the Bank had to restrict its lending to current levels, and if the reserves dropped to two months' worth of imports, to cease all lending. Where the Bank's loans exceeded 50 per cent of foreign exchange reserves but these were worth more than three months' imports, the Bank could continue to lend on a restrictive basis in line with government economic policies.[26] In addition to the Ministry of Finance guidelines, the terms of the Contract Act limit bank loan rates to a maximum of 10 per cent per annum.

TABLE 3.3   Bank of Tonga: assets and liabilities, 1984

%	Assets	T$
3.3	Notes and coins	1,202,707
11.9	Current deposits with overseas banks	4,383,312
50.1	Term deposits with overseas banks	18,376,950
2.9	Securities held overseas	1,053,999
1.2	Tonga government securities	430,800
0.8	Shares in Tonga Development Bank	310,510
25.1	Loans, bills discounted and receivables	9,193,891
2.6	Net fixed assets	957,786
2.1	Other assets	788,558
100.0	Total assets	36,698,513

%	Liabilities	T$
2.7	Paid-up capital	1,000,000
13.6	General reserve	4,985,000
3.4	Exchange equalization reserve	1,235,310
2.2	Contingency reserve	804,333
1.3	Unappropriated profits	484,207
70.5	Deposits	25,894,847
3.4	Bills payable and other liabilities	1,240,133
0.6	Balances due to overseas banks	207,588
1.5	Provisions for taxes	547,095
0.8	Provisions for dividends	300,000
100.0	Total liabilities	36,698,513

Source: Bank of Tonga (1985) *Annual Report: balance sheet and profit & loss account for the year ending 31 December 1984 for the twelfth annual general meeting, 25 June 1985*, pp. 10–11.

(iii) *Assets*

As shown in Table 3.3, the Bank of Tonga, unlike most developed country banks, holds approximately half of its assets in the form of deposits with overseas banks rather than using these funds for advances to local industry and consumers. This position is in part a lack of local lending opportunities, but mainly reflects the Bank of Tonga's quasi central bank role as the manager of a major portion of the Kingdom's foreign exchange reserves. While these funds have provided substantial profits to the Bank, their relative importance finally resulted in a special agreement in 1981 whereby the Bank of Tonga provides the government an additional share of this revenue. In 1984, for example, the Bank paid some T$ 209,872 under this arrangement.

TABLE 3.4   Bank of Tonga: loans and advances, by purpose,
31 December 1985

%		T$
1.28	Agriculture	131,329
4.46	Manufacturing	457,704
4.14	Transport, storage & communication	425,201
0.17	Retail commerce	17,407
2.41	Wholesale commerce	246,781
7.32	Wholesale and retail commerce	751,095
1.01	Building	103,178
3.72	Other business	381,937
18.22	Government and public authorities	1,869,530
48.11	Housing	4,935,356
6.91	Personal	709,417
2.25	Non-profit organizations	230,442
100.00	Total advances	10,259,377

Source: Bank of Tonga (1986).

Loans, bills discounted and other receivables accounted for 25.1 per cent of the Bank's assets. As shown in Table 3.4, housing loans were the most important lending category with 48.11 per cent of advances. Loans to private sector business were next in importance, accounting for 23.23 per cent of the total. Government bodies amounted to 18.22, personal lending to 6.91, non-profit lending to 2.25, and agriculture, only 1.28.

In 1984 overdrafts have comprised T$ 3,814,046 or 37.2 per cent of total advances. Given that housing and personal loans comprise over 50 per cent of the Bank of Tonga's total advances, overdrafts would account for over 80 per cent of business and public sector loans. These commercial loans and overdrafts would generally be charged interest at a rate of 8.5 per cent.

Given past inflation rates, the Bank's interest charges in recent years have been effectively providing a negative real interest return on bank advances. Even so, the Bank has still had difficulty expanding local lending. Indeed, the position would have been much worse but for the national rebuilding programme required following Hurricane Isaac in 1982. This position is neither new nor unexpected, as an early Bank of Tonga report commented, the Bank can be 'little more than a catalyst, without which entrepreneurs, workers and other resources would tend to remain idle or only partially used':[27] the Bank cannot implement projects itself.

As was shown in Table 3.4, housing loans comprised 48.11 per cent of the Bank's loans in 1985. This was not always the case. For example, 'initially the Bank of Tonga was restricted in its domestic lending activities by a lack of security for loans, but recent changes in legislation have overcome this problem'.[28] Housing finance subsequently increased, particularly in 1982–3 following repairs and rebuilding from the cyclone. Indeed, through a National Office of Disaster Relief and Reconstruction programme, Tongans were provided with some 1000 homes on a loan or grant basis over 1982, with the Bank of Tonga administering the loan component.

Despite amendments to the Land Act in 1977 to allow a limited form of mortgage over local land and the extension of allowable mortgage terms in 1980 from 10 to 30 years, much of the Bank's home finance is still provided on very short terms. Indeed, as shown in Table 3.5, some 78 per cent of its outstanding advances are repayable within five years. These loans are normally charged 7.5 per cent interest, of which 0.5 per cent represents a Loan Protection Insurance premium.

TABLE 3.5   Bank of Tonga Housing Loans, by loan maturity, 31 December 1984

78.0	Repayable within 5 years	3,848,145
20.8	Repayable between 5 to 10 years	1,028,014
1.2	Repayable over 10 years	59,197
100.0	Total housing loans	4,935,356

Source: Bank of Tonga (1986).

At least one reason for the limited terms is the Bank's often adverse experiences with longer advances. For example, in many cases home loan 'borrowers fail to follow approved plans; the high percentage of salary which must go to repayments . . .; unexpected social obligations, particularly funerals; [and] dismissal from employment, migration, etc.'[29] The government has suggested that the Bank of Tonga could improve its housing lending, currently to middle-income families and permanent-salaried employees, by 'increasing the number of loans granted; providing longer-term loans; varying terms and interest rates; and easing the legal and other constraints governing the terms of loans'.[30] It has also indicated a willingness to assist the Bank to increase its lending to lower-income families, and a low-cost housing scheme was planned under the Fourth Development Plan. It would be operated by the Bank of Tonga, and be supported by an Australian government T$ 100,000 guarantee.[31] This plan, however, was never finalized.

As with housing loans, the Bank's personal loans are for relatively short periods, normally for two years or less. They are charged 8.5 per cent interest, which includes a 0.5 per cent Loan Protection Insurance premium that would pay the loan in full on the death of the borrower.

(iv) *Liabilities*

As was shown in Table 3.3, deposits accounted for some 70.5 per cent of the Bank of Tonga's total funding. These are raised in the form of cheque accounts, savings accounts and term deposits. As shown in Table 3.6, term deposits are the most important with 46 per cent of the total.

In early 1986, the Bank paid 5 per cent on savings deposits and 6.5 per cent on three-year term deposits under T$ 1,000,000: larger term deposits receive 6.75 per cent. Unfortunately, Tonga's inflation rates has meant that depositors have received negative real interest rates over the 1980s. This is in part a function of a government policy to limit lending rates to a maximum of 10 per cent. This has meant the Bank has been unable to pay higher rates to savers.

Despite these restraints, the Bank still experienced considerable growth. In 1974, for example, when it assumed the operations of the Treasury's Government Savings Bank, it had 14,990 savings accounts and 50 cheque accounts. Some ten years later, in 1984, the Bank had 2933 cheque accounts and 49,839 operating savings accounts.[32] By December 1985, though, the saving account numbers had dropped to 39,824, following a review of inactive accounts when the Bank of Tonga computerized its operations.

In 1985 virtually all of the Bank's deposits were from Tongan citizens or residents. The introduction of off-shore banking in 1984, though, may eventually result in some additional deposit business. Indeed, in 1974 the King of Tonga had announced plans for the Bank of Tonga to offer special secret numbered bank accounts for foreigners, not unlike those accounts offered by Swiss banks. While this announcement subsequently resulted in Tonga being treated as a tax

TABLE 3.6 Bank of Tonga: composition of deposits, 1984
(figures at 31 December 1984)

Deposits	%
Term deposits	46
Savings deposits	23
Non-interest-bearing deposits	31
	100

Source: Bank of Tonga (1985) *Annual Report: balance sheet and profit & loss account for the year ending 31 December 1984 for the twelfth annual general meeting, 25 June 1985*, p. 8.

haven by the Australian Tax Commissioner, these facilities were never introduced.

After deposits, the Bank's own capital and reserves are its most important source of funds, with some 23 per cent of the total in 1984. The Bank's paid-up capital is unusually structured into five equal, but different, classes of shares, each with the right to elect one representative on the Board of Directors: class A shares are owned by the Bank of Hawaii, B shares by the Bank of New South Wales (now Westpac Banking Corporation), C shares by the Bank of New Zealand and D and E shares by the Tongan government. The Tongan government's additional 20 per cent shareholding was also designed to 'have the right to sell to Tongan nationals at some future date'.[33]

(v) *Representation*

When the Bank of Tonga commenced operations in 1974, it was supported by agency arrangements through the government's sub-treasury offices at Vava'u, Ha'apai, 'Eua, Niuatoputapu and Niuafo'ou. As its business expanded, these agency operations were first supplemented, where possible through scheduled mobile bank visits, and then eventually a bank-run agency.

These agencies open savings, cheque and term deposits, receive deposits, accept withdrawals, provided limited cheque cashing services, sell bank cheques and drafts and arrange for telegraphic transfers.

Thus far, only one bank agency has subsequently been upgraded to branch status. The bank's current representations are shown in Table 3.7.

TABLE 3.7   Bank of Tonga: representation, 1985

Type	Location	Island	Established
Main office	Nuku'alofa	Tongatapu	1 July 1974
Daily agency	Ma'ufanga	Tongatapu	6 April 1980
Daily agency	mobile van[a]	Tongatapu	1980
Airport agency	Fua'amotu Airport	Tongatapu	1981
Branch	Neiafu	Vava'u	22 Feb. 1983[bc]
Sub-branch	Pangai	Ha'apai	27 Sept. 1982[c]
Agency	Tungi Arcade	Tongatapu	December 1985
Govt agency	'Eua	'Eua	1 July 1974
Govt agency	Niuatoputapu	Niuatoputapu	1 July 1974
Govt agency	Niuafo'ou	Niuafo'ou	1 July 1974

[a] Visits all main villages in Tongatapu on a daily schedule.
[b] Initially opened as a sub-branch on 1 July 1977.
[c] Represented by government agencies from 1 July 1974 until the sub-branches were opened.

Source: Bank of Tonga (1986).

(vi) *Staffing*

When the Bank of Tonga was established, the three commercial bank shareholders planned to provide the Bank of Tonga's chief manager on a rotating basis. In practice, though, following Westpac's provisions of the General Manager, and the other banks of the Manager International and Manager Lending, it proved more effective to retain the initial organizational structure and subsequent bank officers have been provided accordingly. No doubt the Bank of Hawaii's management of what was then the Pacific Savings and Loan (now Pacific Commercial Bank) in Western Samoa and the Bank of New Zealand's management of the Bank of Western Samoa may have influenced the end decision. In any case, in 1975, what is now Westpac was formally appointed as the Bank of Tonga's managing agents: a position it fulfills even in 1986. The other two bank shareholders, however, have generally provided one expatriate each, and expatriates are expected to continue as the General Manager and International Manager for the immediate future. The third traditional expatriate position, Manager Lending, is hoped to be localized by late 1986.

TABLE 3.8   Bank of Tonga: staffing levels, 1977–86

	1977	1978	1979	1980	1981	1982	1983	1984	1985	1986[a]
Staff	63	70	81	87	105	120	135	144	159	163

[a] May 1986.

Source: Bank of Tonga (1985) *Annual Report: balance sheet and profit & loss account for the year ending 31 December 1984 for the twelfth annual general meeting, 25 June 1985*, p. 19 and correspondence (1986).

The Bank of Tonga is active in training local staff, and since 1981 has conducted its own training operations through on-the-job schemes, video tapes, and occasional special in-house training courses. In addition to the Bank's programmes, some staff are enrolled in administrative and accounting studies at the Tonga Centre of the University of the the South Pacific, and are studying for the certificate and associate courses of the Bankers' Institute of New Zealand.

The result of this training is apparent, as the Bank of Tonga has been able to expand from its initial 18 staff members to 163 staff in May 1986 without the need of additional expatriate secondments. The recent growth in staff numbers is shown in Table 3.8.

Tonga Development Bank

The Tonga Development Bank was created on 30 June 1977 through the Tonga Development Bank Act 1977, and commenced business on 1 September 1977. It was created (Section 6(1)) to 'promote the expansion of the economy of Tonga for the economic and social advancement of the people of Tonga by giving financial and advisory assistance in its discretion to any enterprise operating or about to operate in Tonga'. It provides short-, medium- and long-term loans, equity participations, guarantees for other lenders, and technical, managerial and financial consultancy services; and is also active in identifying, formulating and promoting new projects within the Kingdom.

(i) *Development*

As with other Pacific island development finance institutions, the Tonga Development Bank was created to assume a variety of existing government lending operations. In Tonga these included the

TABLE 3.9   Tonga Development Bank: loans, equities and assets, 1980–84

	Loans & equities	Total assets
1980	1,874,248	3,218,513
1981	2,665,807	3,733,557
1982	3,518,422	5,176,396
1983	3,892,804	5,678,841
1984	5,319,134	7,045,810

Source: Tonga Development Bank' *Annual Report* (various years).

government's Agricultural Credit Scheme, Fisherman's Loan Scheme, and Small Scale Industries Fund. Not all of these programmes, though, were immediately assumed by the new Bank. The Fisherman's Loan Scheme, for example, initially established by the government's Fisheries Division in 1975, was not transferred to the Development Bank until 1978.

As shown in Table 3.9, the Development Bank has grown rapidly both in terms of advances and total assets. The main exception was between 1982 and 1983, when the costs of rebuilding the country following the damages of Hurricane Isaac absorbed most of the Bank's traditional government and overseas funding sources.

(ii) *Assets*

As shown in Table 3.10, loans account for approximately three-quarters of the Bank's assets. Its advances are divided almost equally between the agricultural and commercial sectors, and play an exceedingly important role in financing productive investment within the Kingdom. By the end of 1984, for example, the Tonga Development Bank's larger project financing had been credited to adding T\$ 7.1 million in gross value added to national income, T\$ 5.4 million to net foreign exchange earnings, T\$ 0.538 million to taxation, and 704 to employment numbers.[34]

In making its advances, the Development Bank must give due consideration to the proposal's use of local raw material, the employment and training of local people, the broadening of local entrepreneurship and ownership, the potential to increase exports or limit imports, the lowering of local costs or improvement of services, and the increase of incomes and living standards and incomes, particularly in rural areas.[35] Its over-all involvement with one client, by way

TABLE 3.10   Tonga Development Bank: assets and liabilities, 31
December 1984

%	Assets	T$
4.8	Cash on hand or at bank	340,600
7.1	Short-term deposits	500,000
1.0	Other debtors and prepayments	67,118
74.5	Loans	5,251,634
1.0	Equity investments	67,500
11.6	Net fixed assets	818,958
100.0	Total assets	7,045,810
%	Liabilities	T$
1.8	Bank overdraft	125,326
4.2	Creditors and accruals	295,713
2.8	Current borrowings	200,684
45.2	Other borrowings	3,187,419
44.1	Paid-up capital	3,105,120
1.9	General reserves	131,548
100.0	Total liabilities	7,045,810

Source: Tonga Development Bank (1984) *Annual Report*, p. ii.

TABLE 3.11   Tonga Development Bank advances, 1984

%	
19.3	Root crops
13.8	Beverages and spices
6.9	Fishing
6.1	Fruits
6.0	Vegetables
3.2	Livestock
0.5	Other agricultural
13.0	Retail trade
8.8	Transport & storage
6.0	Restaurants & hotels
4.7	Manufacturing
4.5	Wholesale trade
4.5	Other industrial & business
2.7	Development bank staff
100.0	Total advances

Source: Tonga Development Bank (1984) *Annual Report*, p. 6.

TABLE 3.12　Tonga Development Bank advances, by type of borrower, in 1984

Number		T$
3	Partnerships	94,535
180	Bank staff	97,637
2	Co-operatives	255,558
14	Companies	464,253
2,189	Small farmers	680,461
354	Single proprietors	917,952
352	Commercial farmers	1,016,539
3.094	Total	3,526,935

Source: Tonga Development Bank (1984) *Annual Report*, p. 7.

of loans, equity investment and guarantees should exceed neither 25 per cent of the Bank's own unimpaired capital and reserves nor 75 per cent of the client's tangible assets (including the Bank's own investments).

In respect to the specific types of lending, of the T$ 3.5 million lent by the Bank in 1984, approximately 55.8 per cent of the advances were made for agricultural purposes, 41.5 per cent for business and industry, and the remaining 2.7 per cent to Tonga Development Bank staff. A more specific breakdown of these sectors and their relative importance is shown in Table 3.11. Within the important root crop and beverages/spices areas, the major lending was for yams and taros and for vanilla and kava respectively.

The Bank's major involvement in agricultural lending, (particularly working capital for the purchase of seeds, fertilizers, and pesticides) has meant that some 85 per cent of its advances are for amounts of less than T$ 1000. For example, in 1984 some 2621 small borrowers of all types accounted for 85 per cent of the Bank's loan numbers, and nearly 25 per cent of the funds advanced. A special breakdown as to the number of loans and total advanced to each type of borrower is shown in Table 3.12.

This dominance of small loans within the Bank's portfolio results both in high initial lending costs and in administration costs. It also means that the Bank must carefully monitor repayments in order to avoid the substantial deliquency problems experienced by other Pacific development lenders. Besides good loan supervision, another method used by the Tonga Development Bank to lower deliquencies

TABLE 3.13   Tonga Development Bank advances in 1984 by area

Area	%
Tongatapu	72.4
Vava'u	20.2
Ha'apai	3.4
'Eua	3.4
Niuas	0.6
	100.0

Source: Tonga Development Bank (1984) *Annual Report, p. 6.*

is the 'Aim High' scheme. This programme gives borrowers who start with a small loan, which they repay successfully, special preference on subsequent larger loan applications. As an added incentive, the Bank provides each customer with a colour identification card system with first time borrowers receiving white cards; successful repayers, a blue card; and multiple successful repayers, a gold card. Reflecting the importance of religion within Tonga, each card also includes an appropriate quotation from the bible.

The significance of small loans in the Bank's portfolio, and the direction of at least half of this money to agricultural projects, suggests that the Bank has at least the correct orientation in its lending. Indeed one government report concluded, 'this institution, then, has managed most successfully to satisfy many of the immediately bankable demands of small farmers and fisherman both in Tongatapu and the outer islands'.[36] Unfortunately 3.13 shows that the importance of advances to the main island group is still considerable; this could be diversified further through greater bank representation in the more remote islands.

In addition to its loan activities, the Development Bank may also provide finance via equity investments. As was shown in Table 3.10, equity investments comprised only one per cent of the Development Bank's assets and as of 1985 it had shareholdings in only three firms (see Table 3.14). Thus far these investments appear successful, for the Bank's dividend income of T$ 6750 provided a 10 per cent return on the cost of its equity investments.

Equity finance will probably grow more important in the future, but at present it is limited both by local opportunities and, to a lesser extent, the Bank's own operational constraints. For example, the Bank's equity investment in a single firm is limited to an amount

TABLE 3.14   Tonga Development Bank equity investments, 1984

	T$
Mathews & Associates Tonga Ltd	7,500
Morris Hedstrom Tonga Ltd	25,000
Scan Tonga Engineering Co. Ltd	35,000
Total equity investments	67,500

Source: Tonga Development Bank (1984) *Annual Report*, p. v.

equal to ten per cent of the Bank's unimpaired share capital and reserves, and should not exceed more than 25 per cent of the client's paid-up capital. The latter requirement is to ensure that the Bank does not assume control of its client firms. The Bank's total equity investments are limited to an amount equal to 25 per cent of its shareholder funds.

The Bank's equity investments also play an important role in providing Tongan participation in foreign joint ventures, and provides the basis for future public share offering. Eventually, following

> consultations with the enterprises concerned, they will be disposed of to Tonga nationals, when appropriate, most probably to an investment company or unit trust to be managed by the Bank or to related employee trusts, because it is the Bank's general desire to broaden the base of local ownership over time.[37]

Besides providing loan and equity finance, bank staff often help clients prepare feasibility studies in support of loan proposals, establish book-keeping systems, and decide on appropriate technology and equipment. At a higher level, its officers also serve on the Board of Directors in those companies where the Bank is a shareholder. In the long run, though, this informal consultancy is expected to become a much more important part of the Bank's over-all operations, as well as a potential source of fee income.

As of 1985 the Development Bank provided housing finance only if directly related to a farming, commercial or industrial project. The 1980–85 Development Plan, however, calls for a T$ 500,000 'revolving housing fund to provide loans . . . for both rural and urban low-cost housing with a loan ceiling of T$ 5,000'. While the plan recognized that 'the provision of housing finance is strictly outside of that bank's functions', it nevertheless was considered a 'most appropriate' executive agency.[38] By early 1986, however, this programme had not been implemented.

(iii) *Funding*

As was shown in Table 3.10, the Tonga Development Bank is funded approximately equally from its own resources and borrowings.

Of the Bank's borrowings, most were at concessional interest rates ranging from 1.5 to 3 per cent. The Asian Development Bank, European Investment Bank, International Fund for Agricultural Development and the New Zealand government provide the Bank's major concessional credit facilities. In addition, the Australian government, British government, European Community, and certain United Nations agencies have also provided loan funds. In addition, the Bank has also borrowed some funds from the Bank of Tonga at 8 per cent per annum.

Most of these borrowings are designed to refinance specific types of productive projects rather than working capital purposes, and some include a range of special purpose revolving funds as well. The New Zealand government, for example, provided T$ 43,220 in 1984 for on-lending to horse-drawn-cart owners for the repair of existing carts and agricultural implements and T$ 29,000 for financing passion fruit cultivation and processing. The United Nations Development Programme similarly provided T$ 20,000 specifically to finance women-initiated income earning projects, and the United National Capital Development Fund, an additional T$ 118,000 to finance the construction of local fishing boats.[39]

As mentioned earlier, equity finance accounts for 46 per cent of the Bank's funding. The external funds are provided from the Bank's two shareholders, the Tongan government and the Bank of Tonga, in proportion to their ownership, 90 and 10 per cent respectively. In practice, though, the government moneys are generally provided through foreign government assistance grants. In 1984, for example, both the New Zealand government and the European Investment Bank provided funds for this purpose.

In 1985 the Tonga Development Bank's own cash flow in the form of retained earnings was its most important single source of funds. This has been particularly assisted by a ten-year exemption from local corporate tax. This exemption is scheduled to expire on 1 September 1987, but by that time the Bank is hoped to have more than sufficient retained earnings. This increase in shareholders' funds has also been

TABLE 3.15   Tonga Development Bank representation, by type, location and establishment dates

Type	Location	Island/Group	'Establishment date
Head office	Nuku'alofa	Tongatapu	1 September 1977
Branch	Neiafu	Vava'u	16 February 1979(a)
Rep. office	Pangai	Ha'apai	13 August 1981
Rep. office	Angaha	'Eua	30 July 1982
Rep. office	Hihifo	Niua	1 December 1985

(a) initially a representative office, upgrade to a branch in 1985
Source: Tonga Development Bank, 1986

assisted by the requirement that at least 50 per cent of the Bank's net income must be allocated to general reserves until such time as these reserves equal the Bank's paid-up capital.

The Bank's share capital and reserves are also important in determining its total funds, for its own longer-term borrowings are restricted to an amount equal to three times the Bank's unimpaired share capital and reserves.

(iv) *Representation*

As shown in Table 3.15, the Tonga Development Bank currently has three offices in addition to its head office in Nuku'alofa and Vava'u branch. At present these operations are responsible for education, processing loan applications, and conducting loan supervision. Their actual approval power is limited to T$ 1,000. In the longer term the Bank plans to upgrade these offices to branch status, and provide them with additional staff and higher local loan approval authority.

In addition to its own offices, the Development Bank is also assisted by government extension officers from the Ministry of Agriculture, Fisheries and Forests and the Ministry of Commerce and Industries. Church ministers are also important in educating potential borrowers about the Bank's services.

(v) *Staffing*

Unlike most Pacific island development banks, the Tonga Development Bank localized its managerial positions fairly rapidly with managing director position being localized on 31 March 1982. Indeed in May 1986, the only expatriate staff remaining were two officers provided by the US Peace Corps who act as the Bank's Chief Accountant and Insurance Officer.

This localization has been assisted by a range of overseas training courses provided by the Association of Development Financing Institutions in Asia and the Pacific, the Asia Productivity Agency, the University of the South Pacific, European Community, Australian Development Assistance Bureau, and the Commonwealth Fund for Technical Co-operation. These have been supplemented by special in-house training in accounting and economics as part of the Bankers' Institute of New Zealand, and from training consultants provided locally from overseas bodies.

Merchant Banks

Up to 1986 Tonga's experience with merchant banking has been limited to its short-lived merchant bank, the Bank of the South Pacific. This Bank was formed under its own ordinance on 21 June 1977 and given a 99-year monopoly on merchant banking within the Kingdom of Tonga.[40] It was also granted a wide range of operating powers to include normal banking, development banking, stock-broking and commodity dealing. It was also given an exemption from all exchange control over dealings in foreign currencies and, together with the government, would have sole access to the Kingdom's new telecommunication facilities.

While overseas the Bank of the South Pacific stressed the availability of Tonga as a tax haven, the Bank was also to help Tonga's local economy in 'the development of a totally integrated coconut utilization industry, the formation and promotion of a national and international airline, land development, and the establishment of an internal and international telecommunications system'.[41] As Tonga's Honorary Consul and Sydney racing bookmaker, Bill Waterhouse, explained, 'we have to attract money into the area which will help local business, I can't see any sense in letting the money go to Switzerland if we can do something with it in the South Pacific'.[42]

The driving force for the new institution was a John Meier who, among other positions, had served as a top aid to Howard Hughes between 1959 and 1970. His contacts within the United States were expected to raise substantial deposit funds which could then be used to finance a wide range of major development projects within the Kingdom. Unfortunately Mr Meier had apparently left the United States owing the Internal Revenue Service a substantial amount of unpaid taxes. This later resulted in the Bank's chief promoter, John Meier, being arrested in Sydney under tax evasion charges on 28 July. He actually avoided prison by claiming diplomatic immunity through his Tongan diplomatic passport, but with this event the Bank effectively came to an end. The Bank's ordinance was first withdrawn by the Kingdom's Chief Justice and then revoked by Parliament.[43]

Off-shore Banking

Though not yet an active part of Tonga's financial sector, the Off-shore Banking Act 1984 was passed on 11 October 1984 to provide the basis for such an industry. As with other off-shore centres, Tonga hopes to gain local income through taxes on staff incomes, hosting directors' meetings, and the expansion of accounting and legal services required for the new business. In return the banks need pay no income tax on the income, profits or gains from off-shore banking business. The same is also true for their clients and their deposits and other transactions. Both groups are also entitled to complete secrecy concerning their transactions, and it is perhaps reflective that the legislation's literal translation from Tongan is 'secret' rather than 'off-shore' banking act.

Under the legislation, registration as an off-shore bank in Tonga requires an annual license fee of US$ 3000 and a refundable security deposit of US$ 10,000 placed with the Tongan Treasury. In addition, those off-shore banks with a 'permanent establishment' within the Kingdom must also pay a royalty fee equal to 0.25 per cent of the institution's deposits received over the previous 12 months.

Both at the time of application and on annual license renewals, each off-shore bank must provide the Minister with a copy of its Act, charter, memorandum of association, articles of association, deed of settlement or other documentation under which the body is constituted; laws of the respective jurisdiction; the applicant's financial standing; and its management abilities and skills in regard to banking and financial transaction.

Otherwise there would be relatively few controls over off-shore bank operations, only that no off-shore banking transactions be denominated in pa'anga (Tongan-currency) without the prior written permission of the Minister of Finance, nor may these banks deal with

Tongan residents. There are tight controls, though, over the secrecy of these banks' operations, for under Section 18 any person who 'communicates to any other person any information which he has acquired by reason of his office, position or employment shall be guilty of an offense' and subject to a fine of up to US$ 10,000 or a one-year imprisonment. Similarly, in the case of fraud or embezzlement, those found guilty are subject to more severe penalties of 7 years' imprisonment and/or a fine of up to US$ 50,000.

It appears that, not only is information about the off-shore banks' clients and shareholders kept secret, but so apparently are the names of those institutions receiving off-shore banking licenses. It is understood, though, that two banks have received approval for off-shore banking licenses and five more had submitted applications.

If Tonga's off-shore banking centre is to be successful it will need to upgrade its existing accounting and legal services to an international standard. It will also probably need to establish local trust companies along similar lines of Vanuatu (see p. 266). Whether overseas private investors will feel such investments are warranted remains to be seen, but it is true that its political stability is unmatched within the region. As one overseas report commented, 'Tonga's political system ensures long periods of continuous government, whereas in other countries the government may change every few years'.[44] Internationally, too, Tonga's off-shore regulations compare favourably with its competitors, and Tonga's Minister of Finance, Cecil Cocker, considers these factors should provide the Kingdom of Tonga with an international rating of '87 per cent, the highest of 18 international banking centres, including Switzerland, the Bahamas, the Cayman Islands, and Ireland'.[45]

General Insurance

The Tonga's insurance industry as of 1985 was comprised totally of foreign companies, shown in Table 3.16, which are represented locally through part-time agents. New Zealand Insurance is currently the largest of the insurers with, some estimate, as much as 70 per cent of the existing premium business. They are followed in importance by QBE Insurance (represented locally by Burns Philp); Southern Pacific Insurance (a National Insurance subsidiary – sold locally by Morris Hedstrom) and Commercial Union (represented by Union Steam Ship); and the Sydney-based, Legal and General Insurance, which has traditionally serviced the Commodities Board and some

TABLE 3.16   Insurance companies in Tonga, 1985

Firm	Type of representation
Commercial Union Insurance	local agent
New Zealand Insurance Co.	local agent
QBE Insurance Co.	local agent
Southern Pacific Insurance Co.	local agent

Source: Industry interviews (1986).

other government business. In addition, a number of Tongan government agencies also use the services of Sidney Packett and Sons Ltd, a Lloyds broker in Bradford, England.

The industry's structure was subject to considerable uncertainty in the early 1980s following the visit of a UN consultant on insurance matters, Dr. A. R. B. Amerasinghe. He considered that the Kingdom could gain substantial foreign exchange savings and investment income through creating a state-owned insurance corporation. His view was that Tonga's annual premium income, estimated by industry sources to be less than T$ 500,000, was really too small to be shared by a number of companies. It would therefore be more efficient to have just the one company. This would also have the advantage of introducing full-time local insurance expertise to the local economy and help 'reduce the insecurity of private enterprises'.[46] Thus, as a result, the 1980–85 development plan, included a goal for the 'establishment of a state-owned or controlled insurance company'.[47]

This work resulted in the passage of the Insurance Ordinance 1981 on 22 May 1981. It was drafted to 'regulate the business of insurance to establish the Tonga Insurance Corporation and for purposes incidental thereto'.[48]

Under Section 26, the Tonga Insurance Corporation was to 'transact and carry on life insurance business, general insurance business, reinsurance business, risk management business and business related thereto whether in or outside of Tonga . . . to the best advantage of the community and economy of Tonga'. More significantly, under Sections 3, only the Tonga Insurance Corporation would be authorized to carry on insurance business in Tonga, and no new business should be conducted by other companies.

Given that the obligation effectively announced the eventual end of the private insurance industry in Tonga, those insurers with a well-established local client base were understandably upset. Thus most insurers made representations to the government, and in 1982, largely due to the efforts of the New Zealand Insurance Co., the concept was finally shelved. Instead the government would become more involved in insurance regulation and New Zealand Insurance, for its part, would commence a three-phase improvement in its Tonga operations.

The first phase was to second an experienced officer to the Kingdom to introduce a full range of insurance services. The second phase called for expansion into a branch operation. The third phase would establish a local company with, if desired, government participation.

These promises, combined with the impact of Hurricane Isaac, have apparently had some effect for, by 1983, the Bank of Tonga could report that the 'insurance business is growing as a result of the greater awareness of the need for improved risk management arising from recent natural disasters and other catastrophes'.[49]

In 1986 the government apparently still had some interest in establishing a Tonga Insurance Co. as it had held some discussions to this end with Pan Pacific Insurance, but no formal proposal has resulted. It is understood that the International Development Bureau of the International Co-operative Insurance Federation will visit Tonga in mid- to late 1986 to discuss the possibility of a co-operative based local insurance venture. This may also entail new insurance regulations and the New Zealand government is apparently providing some assistance in this regard.

Life Insurance

As with most Pacific countries, the life insurance business in Tonga is undeveloped and its potential premium income relatively small. In 1985, only one company was particularly active in this area, New Zealand Insurance. It has been selling both life and superannuation policies within Tonga since 1983. As one New Zealand Insurance Co. report predicted, 'there is considerable potential in the Kingdom for superannuation schemes as government, and most businesses, do not have any cover of this nature in existence'.[50]

Superannuation

By early 1986 the National Provident Fund had yet to be established, but it is expected to commence operations soon. As one government report concluded, the national provident fund 'will give employees the security and retirement benefits of Government and large companies not currently available generally to the private sector'.[51]

At present most superannuation or pension fund coverage is confined to Tongan government employees or other public sector bodies. The Tongan government, for example, has operated its own non-contributory retirement scheme since 1922, and most statutory bodies have similar forms of retirement plans. There is little private sector superannuation or pension coverage other than the Bank of Tonga which has had its own retirement fund since 1978.

Commodities Board

As with other South Pacific countries, Tonga has established a commodities board to assist in the promotion of its agricultural exports, and to operate a stabilization fund on behalf of the local producers of certain commodities. The Commodities Board in Tonga is also active in processing some agricultural products and operates the Kingdom's desiccated coconut plant, produces soap for local use and plans to produce a range of snack food based on traditional products to include taro, yam, breadfruit and bananas.

Marketing boards have had a long history in Tonga with the Tonga Copra Board and the Tonga Banana Board established under the Agricultural Organization Act of 1940. In October 1956, however, the Tonga Produce Board was created to assume the operations of the Tonga Banana Board and expanded them to include pineapple and watermelon exports. Finally, in 1974 these various bodies were merged into a new entity, the Commodities Board. In addition to produce marketing work, what is now the Commodities Board has also operated a construction division, both for its own building requirements, and those of other governments and local and private sector bodies since 1958.

With the European Community's STABEX (Stabilization of Export Earnings) payments for coconuts export assistance, the Commodities Board established the Copra Stabilization Fund in 1977. An additional fund, the Produce Stabilization Fund, was created in 1979 with New Zealand government assistance. These funds were 'to guarantee producers of selected viable export crops a minimum price in order to ensure that growers are protected from the worst effects of price fluctuations'.[52] Through these schemes the Commodities Board at times has accumulated substantial investment assets for short periods. Though the Produce Stabilization Fund is no longer in operation, the Copra Stabilization Fund, and possibly other such plans, may eventually prove an important longer-term investor within the Kingdom.

The Fund's main purpose is to ensure that coconut and, to a lesser extent, other agricultural products, are priced sufficiently high to attract small-holder production. When copra prices have been too low, for example, production has dropped dramatically as Tongan small-holders turning to fishing and other crops rather than collecting and processing the coconuts. While this results in lower exports, the impact has been more serious given the Kingdom's attempt to process its coconuts prior to export. Indeed, in recent years, particularly following Hurricane Isaac's damage, both the coconut oil mill and the desiccated coconut plant were forced to cease production due to insufficient raw materials.

Through its purchases the Board has also improved the quality as well as the reliability of Tongan agricultural exports. It has already had some success with vanilla and is working to improve other crops. It has also helped promote various government revitalization and rehabilitation schemes and intercropping vanilla, kava and other crops within copra plantations.

Unfortunately the Board's efforts have not always met with approval. A recent government plan, for example, listed among the major inhibiting factors in business development was the 'lack of sufficient flexibility in the trading policies of the Commodities Board'[53] and therefore the Board itself has instigated 'a review of the [existing] functions, structure and operations'.[54]

Co-operative Societies

The co-operative movement in Tonga is similar to that of other Pacific countries and is comprised of multipurpose, consumer, savings, industrial, handicraft, village development, and secondary co-operative societies. The multipurpose societies are by far the most important. In May 1986 they accounted for 65 of the 85 existing co-operative societies registered under Co-operatives Societies Act, 1973. The others include two secondary societies, one industrial co-operative society, six consumer co-operative societies, five thrift and credit co-operative societies, one development co-operative society and two handicraft co-operative societies.

Despite the existence of savings co-operatives and the fact that 'some retail societies also offer savings and loan facilities',[55] the co-operative movement has not been significant in local savings mobilization. The government, however, feels that it could prove an important force in rural areas and listed, among six objectives in a mid-term development plan review, 'the mobilisation of personal savings, deposited in co-operatives, into productive purposes'.[56]

While the first formal co-operative was only established in 1964, and the industry subject to formal regulation in 1973, the local co-operative movement has a much older history, for the first co-operative form of native trading company was attempted as early as 1909, the 'Tonga Ma'a Tonga Kautaha' or the 'Tonga for the Tongans Association'. It was intended to avoid the European middlemen involved in the copra trade.[57]

The individual co-operatives are supported at the national level by the Tonga Co-operative Federation. The Federation was established on 21 November 1977 to provide a centralized buying and selling point for its member co-operatives, as well as financial and managerial advice and training. Thus the Federation serves two key functions: first, as an importer to provide its members with consumer items at reasonable prices; and second, as an exporter to sell its members' produce under the best terms and conditions.

As an importer, the Federation deals in a range of consumer items to include sugar, snack foods, sweets, soap and curry powder from Fiji. But the main imports are mutton flaps, tinned fish and corned beef'.[58] This service is well developed and as one report commented, the Federation 'has been very successful in consumer goods wholesaling; channels, structures, and procedures for this activity are now well established'.[59]

In its marketing role, the Federation promotes the sale of its members' agricultural products such as coconuts, bananas, vanilla, fish and other vegetables, as well as handicraft items. The long existence of government marketing boards for coconut and bananas, though, have forced the co-operatives to concentrate on other items with vanilla and fish being the most important. More recently, the Federation has experienced some difficulty in these areas, too, with government fishery programmes and the Commodities Board's purchases of vanilla. In an attempt to develop its own vanilla and fish marketing business more effectively, the Federation planned in 1985–6 to split its present operations with 'the wholesale business retaining the TCF name and a new organization [Friendly Islands Marketing Cooperative Ltd] responsible for vanilla and fish marketing, as well as handicrafts, fishery supplies, and farm produce marketing'.[60] Unfortunately, some overseas aid agencies expressed 'much doubt as to whether the new organization will be able to survive independently'.[61] Nevertheless, the government still places a high priority on the development of the co-operative movement and in its most recent plan has hopes, for the provision of finance for the establishment and capitalization costs of the Tonga Co-operative Federation'.[62] and 'an integrated training and manpower placement programme for co-operatives and credit unions, together with the capacity to undertake investigations of likely future opportunities'.[63]

Credit Unions

Unlike many South Pacific countries, Tonga quickly developed it own credit union movement, and since 1973 the industry has operated under its own legislation, the Credit Union Act 1973. While it is administered by the same government department and the Registrar of Credit Unions is also the Registrar of Co-operatives, the industry's separate status has allowed it to develop its own national body, the Tonga Credit Union League, and in the process become much more significant than its savings and loan co-operative counterparts.

The Tonga Credit Union League serves as the industry's national body, and plays an important role in promoting the industry and providing assistance to its member credit unions. This includes field inspections, training, auditing, and some accounting and book-keeping services for its member credit unions. The League also arranges insurance coverage on member loans. By 1983 the League had some 32 member credit unions.

Unfortunately the League has little financial resources of its own and must rely either on its members or foreign assistance. These funds, though, have not proved adequate to cover its expenses and, over 1979 to 1983, the League's assets have declined from T$ 22,117 in 1979 down to only T$ 4,967 in 1983. This position would have been even more serious but for the managerial and technical assistance afforded by the World Council of Credit Unions and the Australian Credit Union Foundation.

As with savings co-operatives, the credit unions accept deposits from members in the form of shares: in June 1983 the movement had raised T$ 115,345 in member savings with an average of T$ 74 per share account. These funds are then loaned to other members: in June 1983 these loans totaled T$ 89,841. Of these advances, 69 per cent were for school fees, housing construction and family needs; and 32 per cent were for farming, fishing and other productive purposes.[64]

In 1973 the Vaiola Hospital Credit Union was the first to register under local regulations, but there were many credit unions in operation informally before that date.[65] The industry has since grown so that by 1980 there were 52 credit unions in Tonga: 31 in Tongatapu, 3 in 'Eua, 11 in Vava'u, and 8 in Ha'apai.[66] By 1982 the industry numbered 67, of which 56 were registered under the Credit Union Act. These had a total membership of 3800; some 60 per cent of these were female. The average membership stood at 50, the average assets at around T$ 2000, and the average loan size around T$ 50.[67] By May 1986 statistics from 28 of the then 53 credit unions showed an average membership of 33 (mostly family members), deposits averaging T$ 2576 per credit union and assets of T$ 4107.

Over recent years, the number of credit union members have declined sharply from 4128 in 1978 to an estimated 3000 in 1982 to only 1540 in 1983.[68] This reflects a past practice of letting inactive credit unions remain registered. The League and the Registrar have since undertaken an active programme of liquidating the inactive bodies, and the numbers have declined accordingly.

While it is the 'government's policy to encourage the growth of credit unions for strengthening the economic fabric of the community'[69] much action is required to improve local operations. In the raising of deposits, for example, the share savings were seldom withdrawable on demand, and in some cases the credit unions were unable to pay either dividends or interest on the funds. The maximum allowable was 6 per cent per annum. The problem, of course, is one of loan administration, and at least one report suggested that delinquencies in 1983 stood at least 30 per cent of loans outstanding and some suggested 75 per cent was more appropriate.[70] This has been a function of inadequate control procedures and poor loan selection. Indeed, 'little consideration appears to be given to the character of the member capacity to repay, and the collateral which could be offered.'[71]

Thus, in order to be successful, the credit union will first have to resolve its present difficulties in the 'training and education, credit union image, Tonga Credit Union Leage services and operations, attitudes (traditional, cultural and social), economic conditions (lack of opportunities) and funding and technical assistance'.[72] Another way credit unions might be more successful is to use employer-sponsored bodies. In other countries these credit unions have tended to be more successful than community-based institutions. In 1982, however, only one credit union, the Shipping Co. of Polynesia, was an employer-based body. The potential advantage of employer-sponsored credit unions have since been recognized for the government's most recent plan was to 'encourage the development of occupation-based credit unions in preference to geographical orientated credit unions'.[73]

FINANCIAL MARKETS

In early 1986, Tonga did not really have any markets which could be considered of a financial nature. There were not sufficient government securities for a government securities market and the lack of more than one commercial bank likewise precluded an interbank market or much foreign exchange business.

In the area of foreign exchange, the Bank of Tonga is responsible for maintaining the market in the Tongan currency, the pa'anga. As Tonga's Financial Secretary, Selwyn Jones, explained, the government has 'an agreement with the Bank of Tonga that we have to compensate them if we change the exchange rate between the Australian dollar and the pa'anga. If the value of their investment drops, we have to compensate them'.[74]

As mentioned in the development section, in its earliest days Tonga used a range of currency of which German currency became the most important. This was replaced by British and Australian coins in 1906 and following the Treasury Notes Act 1935, Tonga has issued its own notes. For a long period the Tonga pa'anga was tied to the Australian dollar, but more recently the government has switched its pegging operations to a basket of currencies and has generally tried to maintain the currency at artificially high levels in order to reduce the costs of imported goods.

ANALYSIS

Compared to other South Pacific countries, Tonga's financial sector still appears relatively undeveloped, and any improvements in this

TABLE 3.17   Inflation and Bank of Tonga savings rates, 1979–85

	1979	1980	1981	1982	1983	1984	1985
Inflation	5.5	22.4	14.9	10.8	9.7	0.7	18.8
Small savings	4.5	4.5	4.5 −5.0	5.0	5.0	5.0	5.0
Term deposits	6.5	6.5	6.5	6.5	6.5	6.5	6.5
Large deposits	6.5	6.5	6.5− 6.75	6.75	6.75	6.75	6.75
Max. loan rate	10.0	10.0	10.0	10.0	10.0	10.0	10.0

Source: Bank of Tonga (1986).

area should considerably assist (domestic savings) rates. The government has seemingly realized this position, hence its plans for a National Provident Fund and a central bank institution. The creation of a local insurance company would also assist local development. Other measures that deserve consideration are increasing domestic savings through more realistic interest rates, raising and using overseas remittances more effectively, expanding the degree of domestic financial institution representation, and improving the level of trained local staff.

(a) Improving Interest Rate Levels

As mentioned earlier, the interest rate structure adopted by the Tonga government has been far from conducive for local savings and there is little wonder that domestic savings rates have been less than desired. A quick examination of local inflation compared to the savings and lending rates, shown in Table 3.17, show that Tongan savers, through generally negative real interest rates on their savings, have effectively subsidized local borrowers. Given that these savings, particularly savings account money, are typically raised from rural and poorer family units, and the loans made to businesses and richer families, the impact is exactly the reverse of traditional government economic and social goals. Financial deregulation in a country where exchange rate management plays an important role in economic policy is probably not a true alternative, but there seems little question that the government could greatly increase local capital raisings by allowing the Bank of Tonga and other savings raising institutions to offer depositors real rates of return.

It could be argued that the higher lending rates which result may adversely affect future loan proposals, but economically it would seem better to allow at least the Bank of Tonga to allocate its funds on a market-determined basis and limit any concessional financing to the Development Bank.

(b) Increasing and More Effectively Utilizing Overseas Remittances

In most discussions of the Tongan economy, the importance of foreign remittances in balancing the Kingdom's balance of payments always receives a mention. In 1984, for example, an estimated T$ 16 million in foreign exchange was provided through remittances from Tongans overseas.[75] Interestingly, though, these flows have come solely from family connections between Tongan residents and Tongans overseas. Neither the government nor its financial institutions have taken actions to encourage these flows. What receives somewhat less discussion is the use to which these foreign inflows are put. Unfortunately interviews suggest that much of these monies are used to finance the purchase of consumer durables and generally increased consumption rather than productive use. The bulk of this spending, as it is primarily used to purchase imported goods, simply adds to the Kingdom's foreign exchange problems and does nothing to resolve the long-term problem.

There is a temptation to assume, as with foreign aid, that these funds will continue in the future, even at greater levels, but this is a dangerous assumption on which to base economic planning. A more correct approach would be a twofold action which would actively encourage the inflow of overseas remittances to the Kingdom, while at the same time ensuring that more of these funds are put to productive purposes rather than just consumption. Tongans overseas are obviously willing to save their incomes and provide support to the relations at home – the question is whether these same people can be encouraged to support their Kingdom's economic development.

There are really two sides to the approach. First, in raising more remittances, the government could easily provide much the same sort of tax benefits introduced for its off-shore banking centre to encourage Tongans to save their moneys at home rather than in New Zealand or elsewhere overseas. A combination of tax-free interest income and internationally competitive interest rates would do much to improve the attraction of Tonga-based savings. Similarly, special arrangements for these accounts might allow Tongans returning home to leave their funds there until needed for local purposes.

Given their relatively high disposable cash income compared to their local counterparts, the non-resident Tongan also represents a potential source of other than bank-account-type savings. Both Fiji and Papua New Guinea have had some success with unit trust operations for raising equity capital in the local market[76] and there would seem similar potential for investment by expatriate Tongans. At present the little institutional equity capital available through the Tongan Development Bank has been used sparingly, and an equity-based unit trust operation could do much to increase the flow of venture capital within the economy.

The second part of the foreign remittances question is to make better use of these funds within the Kingdom. Given the Bank of Tonga's current financial reporting, it is difficult to determine what portion of the Bank's overseas deposits are a function of the Kingdom's foreign exchange reserves, and what are from domestic deposits. If these deposits are to be used effectively in the Kingdom's development, then the Bank of Tonga must do more in development finance. It can be argued, of course, that this is the role of the Tonga Development Bank, but it seems illogical to suggest that, given the Bank of Tonga's foreign parents, more could not be done in development financing. Of course, if the government wishes to channel these monies through the Development Bank, this would present no difficulty. The funds could either be raised by the Bank of Tonga on behalf of the Development Bank or by the Development Bank itself, provided that the accounts were structured so that their administration would not present a burden.

(c) Expanding Domestic Institutional Representation

In conjuction with improved savings rates, financial development could be greatly improved by an expansion of savings institutions into local areas. The use of agencies and representative offices has certainly been one way to achieve a broader geographical coverage for the banking sector, but more could probably be accomplished in this area. In the Pacific there is not really the same need for modern office facilities or automatic teller machines to attract savings. Vanuatu's Co-operative Savings Bank, for example, has shown (see p. 225) that an extensive island representation need not be expensive if confined to simple savings deposit and withdrawal operations. Similarly, while the Bank of Tonga already uses some Sub-Treasury offices as its agents, there are post offices and similar government offices in other areas which might also be used for a simple savings operation purposes. These operations are obviously costly to administer and for that reason may not be attractive in a commercial sense to the Bank of Tonga, but this does not mean that they are not attractive in a national sense. It should be remembered that, besides any deposits raised, such rural banking operations add to the general monetization of the economy as well as performing an important educational role.

An expansion of rural services, coupled with a local education programme, might also result in a greater development of the Kingdom's outer islands and in the process reduce some of the current immigration pressures experienced on Tongatapu. As one government report concluded 'it is clear that improved accessibility to financial services, particularly to bank lending throughout the Kingdom would greatly benefit the inhabitants of the outlying regions and rural villages'.[77]

(d) Increasing the Trained Local Staff

As with other South Pacific countries, staffing is a serious limitation facing local financial development efforts. Even the simple transfer of certain Bank of Tonga and Treasury functions to the Kingdom's planned central banking institutions will in itself require more administrative staff than in the past. It is the expansion of this institution's activities to include financial development planning and eventually monetary policy implementation that will present problems for the Kingdom's resources, and it seems inevitable that an increase in expatriate staff numbers will be required. The creation of the National Provident Fund will similarly require considerable administrative and financial skills which are not necessarily easily available from within the local pool of labor.

The difficulty then is that while unemployment remains a problem, the availability of suitable trained and experienced staff is an even more serious restraint on the economy, and particularly on the financial sector's success. Not only does the Kingdom face the traditional problem of having a very limited number of suitable staff, there is also the danger that many of these individuals will choose to follow their relatives' example and accept higher paying positions overseas. Over 1984–5, for example, the Tonga government had to provide substantial rises in senior public servants' salaries in order to stem the emigration of experienced staff, and there is a similar, if not greater, danger of this attraction within the private sector.

One obvious solution is to increase the supply of adequately trained staff and the government, in its recent economic plan, has realized its responsibility to provide 'assistance to the private sector in developing the accounting legal, secretarial and other commercial professions'.[78] It could also do more to attract some well-trained Tongans back from overseas. Indeed, compared to many other developing countries, Tonga has a sizeable pool of skilled workers on which it could draw and, in fact, it might even be able to replace much of the Kingdom's dependence on certain expatriate skills. The problem, of course, is that most of these workers do not live in Tonga, but rather in New Zealand and other developed countries. If, some-how, they could all suddenly be transported back to Tonga, a large portion of the skilled staff problem would be resolved. How these workers could be encouraged to return is another matter and there is a danger in adopting a dual salary structure for formerly expatriate Tongans compared to those who have remained at home. There is also the added salary cost associated with paying wages competitive with those available in developed countries. There are other means, however, to improve the attraction of returning to the Kingdom, and possibly the access to special savings accounts and other fiscal bene-fits might prove sufficiently attractive to entice these workers.

Returning more specifically to the financial sector, it seems likely that in the short term at least, the Kingdom will require a substantial increase in expatriate numbers to assist both initially in the establish-ment, and then in the operation of these new financial institutions.

TRENDS AND PREDICTIONS

In terms of the future, Tonga's potential is often subject to substan-tial qualifications in the reports of international agencies. As one UN report commented 'the remoteness of the country from major econ-omic systems creates a serious burden with respect to imports, exports and tourism'.[79] Similarly, the Asian Development Bank has commented that Tonga 'has no known commercially exploitable minerals, little remaining forests, and not even a river or stream on its principle island'.[80] Despite these seemingly glum comments, the Tongan government has worked to overcome these disadvantages, concentrating first on its immediate problems of increasing trade deficits and unemployment. It has thus 'accorded high priority to measures aimed at stimulating and diversifying the economy, creation of employment opportunities and increasing foreign exchange earnings'.[81]

At present increased agricultural production and processing probably offers the best alternative to these interrelated problems, and the Kingdom could do much to improve both the quality and quantity of its agricultural output, Indeed, 'there is considerable under investment in farming, fisheries, and forestry which together account for almost 49 per cent of gross national product but are receiving less that 10 per cent of national investment'.[82] The government has therefore taken measures to encourage new investment in both traditional and other forms of production.

In the immediate future, at least, it is unlikely that coconuts will lose their dominance in the Kingdom's export figures, but there is little question that much can be done to improve their production value. Since 1966, for example, Tonga has tried to encourage smallholders to replace their aged trees with newer varieties, and to structure the new plantings to obtain the maximum value from their land. More recently a German-assisted programme to replace old trees resulted in some 287,000 trees being removed.[83] While this will reduce production in the short run, such measures not only ensure better copra production per tree, but also allow the effective interplanting of taro, bananas, sweet potatoes, watermelon, and tomatoes with the plantation. In addition, the resulting coconut palm stems can now be processed for use in local construction.

There is similarly a Banana Rehabilitation Scheme to replant those areas destroyed by natural causes. As with copra, the value of these new plants can be improved by using better varieties and planting methods.

In the longer term, however, there is much more potential in diversifying into other primary production. In this regard, one of Tonga's most promising aspects is the potential of its main island, Tongatapu, for non-tropical crops for Tongatapu's terrain, soil and climatic conditions should allow the cultivation of many otherwise temperate climate crops: an option not available for many of its Pacific neighbours.[84]

Besides providing more opportunities for produce diversification, temperate climate crops might also allow a broadening of export markets. Indeed, Tonga's traditional high dependence on New Zealand for its produce exports has recently had problems. Since 1951, for example, Tonga exports to that country have benefited through a New Zealand marketing arrangement whereby one company, Fruit Distributors Ltd, has the sole right to import bananas, citrus and other fruits. As part of the conditions, it is required to give some preference to Pacific island products. Even so, lower-priced and better quality bananas have recently enabled Ecuador to gain some 55 per cent of the New Zealand market largely at Tonga's expense. If the present monopoly is ended, and this was under consideration in 1985, Tonga's position would be even more difficult.[85]

Other areas include an expansion of the Kingdom's present fishing and other maritime-based operations, as well as better use of its forestry resources.

There is also more scope to expand the Kingdom's present manufacturing operations. Within the Small Industries Centre, for example, one knitware company alone, the South Pacific Manufacturing Co., with 100 employees, is already the largest, strictly private sector employer.[86] There are, no doubt, other potential successful employers awaiting their chance to commence business and the Centre plans to double its employment levels over 1986–7 with the addition of new factory buildings within an eight-acre extension. Similarly, a new small industries centre is now planned for Vava'u in northern Tonga. While it would be wrong to suggest that Tonga will develop into a manufacturing-based economy, these measures, coupled with a greater emphasis on processing the country's own primary products, should add a most helpful boost to future employment levels.

Another source of potential employment and foreign exchange is the tourism industry. Cruise ships are already an important source of foreign exchange, but Tonga could gain much more benefit from tourism. Since 1982, the government, through Polynesian Airlines, has tried to expand its attraction in countries such as New Zealand, Australia and the United States. In addition

> to make Tonga a more attractive tourist destination, Nuku'alofa and Neiafu have been declared 'duty free' ports in respect of a wide range of consumer items including perfumes, jewellery, fur and leather goods, portable typewriters, travel goods, electronic calculators and computers, radios, tape recorders and videos, small domestic electrical appliances, watches and cameras, toys and sporting goods'.[87]

More recently, the fiscal 1985 budget provided a 50 per cent tax concession on all overseas tourist promotion expenditures.

While there is little question that Tonga's geographical location, lack of natural endowments, and high population growth, will limit its development potential, there are alternatives available for dealing with such problems, and the Kingdom's long history of stable government should enable it to implement the necessary measures more readily than many of its South Pacific neighbours.

NOTES

1. Noel Rutherford (ed.) (1977) *Friendly Islands: a history of Tonga*, (Melbourne: Oxford University Press) pp. 173–89.
2. *Kingdom of Tonga Fourth Five-Year Development Plan, 1980–1985* (1981) (Nuku'alofa: Central Planning Department) p. 8.
3. *Kingdom of Tonga Fourth Five-Year Development Plan* (1981) p. 65.
4. These incentives were provided under the Industrial Development In centives Ordinance 1977. It provides a five-year corporate tax holiday, exemption from 15 per cent withholding tax during this period, depreciation on original value allowed at the end of the holiday, duty-free importation of capital goods and parts for two years, 50 per cent concession on port and services tax, unlimited loss carry forwards, local protection from imports in initial years, and the repatriation of profits, capital and capital gains.
5. *Kingdom of Tonga Fourth Five-Year Development Plan* (1981) p. 75.
6. *Kingdom of Tonga Fourth Five-Year Development Plan* (1981) p. 88.
7. *Kingdom of Tonga Fourth Five-Year Development Plan* (1981) p. 88.
8. *Kingdom of Tonga Fourth Five-Year Development Plan* (1981), p. 89.
9. A. E. Bollard (1981), 16 (1): 12.
10. Bollard, 'Financial adventures':14.
11. Bollard, 'Financial adventures':14.
12. Bollard, 'Financial adventures':14.
13. Noel Rutherford (1971) *Shirley Baker and the King of Tonga*, (Melbourne: Oxford University Press p. 55.
14. Rutherford, *Shirley Baker*, p. 54.
15. A. E. Bollard 'Financial adventures':16.
16. *Pacific Island Year Book and Who's Who*, 10th edn, (Sydney: Pacific Publications, 1968) p. 129.
17. The Treasury's private trader arrangements, for example, were never particularly numerous, and in the early 1970s provided for only around 50 traders (Bank of Tonga (1975) *Annual Report, Balance Sheet, and Profit & Loss Account for the year ending 31 December 1974*, p. 10.
18. Bank of Tonga (1982) *Annual Report 1982*, p. 5.
19. *Kingdom of Tonga Mid-Term Review: third development plan 1975–1977* (Nuku'alofa: Central Planning Department) p. 41.
20. *Kingdom of Tonga Fourth Five-Year Development Plan* (1981) p. 75.

200   *Financial Institutions and Markets in the South Pacific*

21. *Kingdom of Tonga Fourth Five-Year Development Plan* (1981) p. 89.
22. Bank of Tonga (1974) *Balance Sheet and Profit & Loss Account for the period ending 31 December 1973 and the Chairman's Report for the First Annual General Meeting, 16th September 1974* pp. 3–7.
23. 'Visiting Bankers Meeting Ends on Optimistic Note', *The Tonga Chronicle*, 18 November 1971, p. 1.
24. Bank of Tonga, *Balance Sheet 1974*, p. 4.
25. Bank of Tonga, *Balance Sheet 1974*, p. 5.
26. Bank of Tonga (1984) *Annual Report 1984*, p. 5.
27. Bank of Tonga, *Balance Sheet 1974*, p. 4.
28. *Kingdom of Tonga Fourth Five-Year Development Plan* (1981) p. 59.
29. Jeanette Ratcliffe and Rosemary Dillon (1982) *A Review and Study of the Human Settlement Situation in the Kingdom of Tonga: a paper prepared for the Economic and Social Commission for Asia and the Pacific*, (Nuku'alofa: Central Planning Department) p. 31.
30. *Kingdom of Tonga Fourth Five-Year Development Plan* (1981) p. 250.
31. Ratcliffe and Dillon, *A Review and Study of the Human Settlement Situation in the Kingdom of Tonga* p. 32.
32. Bank of Tonga (1975) *Annual Report, Balance Sheet, and Profit & Loss Account for the year ending 31 December 1974*, p. 10.
33. Bank of Tonga, *Balance Sheet 1974*, p. 4.
34. Tonga Development Bank (1984), *Annual Report* p. 4.
35. Tonga Development Bank, *Annual Report 1984*, p. 2.
36. Ratcliffe and Dillon *A Review and Study of the Human Settlement Situation in the Kingdom of Tonga*, p. 32.
37. 'Tonga Development Bank: how it can help you', undated paper, p. 2.
38. *Kingdom of Tonga Fourth Five-Year Development Plan* (1981) p. 249.
39. Tonga Development Bank (1984) *Annual Report*, pp. 11–12.
40. 'Pierpont' (1978) 'Controversial new bank's bookmaking connection', *The Bulletin*, 28 March, p. 88.
41. 'Pierpont', p. 88.
42. 'Howard Hughes' shadow over Tonga's new bank', *Pacific Islands Monthly*, February 1978:55.
43. 'Tonga's "South Sea Bubble" Burst', *Pacific Islands Monthly*, September 1978: 9. Mr Meier was later extradited from Canada and sentenced to imprisonment in the United States, Alan Merridew (1984) 'End of the road for the Bank of the South Pacific's Mr Meier?', *Pacific Island Monthly*, July:25–6.
44. Economist Intelligence Unit (1985) *Quarterly Economic Review*, 1:48.
45. Pesi Fonua (1985) 'Top Secret Banking', *Islands Business*, January:48.
46. *Kingdom of Tonga Fourth Five-Year Development Plan* (1981) p. 75. The plan, unfortunately, does not explain the cause of this insecurity or why a national insurance corporation would resolve it.
47. *Kingdom of Tonga Fourth Five-Year Development Plan* (1981) p. 244.
48. *Tonga Government Gazette Extraordinary*, 6, 22 May 1981, p. 1.
49. Bank of Tonga (1983) *Annual Report*, p. 16.
50. New Zealand Insurance Co. Ltd, undated materials provided in April 1986.
51. *Kingdom of Tonga Fourth Five-Year Development Plan* (1981) p. 75.

52. *Kingdom of Tonga Fourth Five-Year Development Plan* (1981) p. 126.
53. *Kingdom of Tonga Fourth Five-Year Development Plan* (1981) p. 243.
54. *Kingdom of Tonga Fourth Five-Year Development Plan* (1981) p. 244.
55. *Kingdom of Tonga Mid-Term Review: Third Development Plan* (1978) p. 121.
56. *Kingdom of Tonga Mid-Term Review: Third development plan* (1978) p. 121.
57. Noel Rutherford (1981) 'Tonga Ma'a Tonga Kautaha: a proto-co-operative in Tonga', *Journal of Pacific History* 16(1):20–41.
58. 'Beans mean money', *Island Business*, July 1983, p. 36.
59. *Evaluation Report: Tonga Co-operative Federation* (1985). (Washington, D.C.: Agricultural Co-operative Development International).
60. *Evaluation Report*.
61. *Evaluation Report*.
62. *Kingdom of Tonga Fouth Five-Year Development Plan* (1981) p. 244.
63. *Kingdom of Tonga Fourth Five-Year Development Plan* (1981) p. 239.
64. 'Tonga Credit Union Movement', an unpublished report to the World Council of Credit Unions, May 1984, pp. 1–2.
65. *Kingdom of Tonga Third Five-Year Development Plan 1975–80* (1975) (New Zealand: PA Management Consultants) December, p. 262.
66. *Kingdom of Tonga Fourth Five-Year Development Plan* (1981) p. 241.
67. 'Foundation News: Tonga', *Australian Credit Unions*, October 1982, p. 32.
68. 'Tonga Credit Union Movement', unpublished report to the World Council of Credit Unions, May 1984, p. 1.
69. *Kingdom of Tonga Third Five-Year Development Plan* (1975) p. 262.
70. 'Tonga Credit Union Movement', p. 2.
71. 'Tonga Credit Union Movement', p. 1.
72. 'Tonga Credit Union Movement', p. 3.
73. *Kingdom of Tonga Fourth Five-Year Development Plan* (1981) p. 239.
74. 'Cutting the cash cake', *Island Business*, July 1983, p. 38.
75. Economist Intelligence Unit (1985) *Quarterly Economic Review*, 1:47.
76. Michael T. Skully (ed.) (1985) *Financial Institutions and Markets in the Southwest Pacific* (London: Macmillan) pp. 133–4, 303–9.
77. *Kingdom of Tonga Fourth Five-Year Development Plan* (1981) p. 243.
78. *Kingdom of Tonga Fourth Five-Year Development Plan* (1981) p. 245.
79. As cited in Ted Morello (1982) 'Pacific quicksands', *Far Eastern Economic Review*, 17 December: 44.
80. 'Industry gently laps South Pacific shores', *ADB Quarterly Review*, January 1985: 17–18.
81. Bank of Tonga (1984) *Annual Report* p. 15.
82. Economist Intelligence Unit (1985) *Quarterly Economic Review*, 3:42.
83. Economist Intelligence Unit, *Quarterly Economic Review*, 2:43.
84. R. Gerard Ward and Andrew Proctor, (1980) *South Pacific Agriculture: choices and constraints* (Manila: Asian Development Bank) p. 384.
85. Economist Intelligence Unit (1985) No. 2, *Quarterly Economic Review*, 2:43.
86. 'Industry gently laps South Pacific shores',:17–18.
87. Bank of Tonga (1983) *Annual Report*, p. 15.

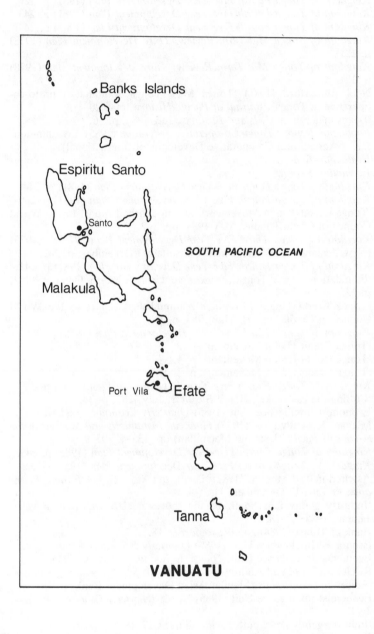

Banks Islands

Espiritu Santo

Santo

SOUTH PACIFIC OCEAN

Malakula

Port Vila Efate

Tanna

VANUATU

4 Financial Institutions and Markets in Vanuatu

INTRODUCTION

Located approximately 1750 kilometres north-east of Australia and north-north-east of New Caledonia, the Republic of Vanuatu consists of an archipelago of some 80 islands spread over 850 kilometres in a 'Y' shape running roughly north to south. The bulk of the country's 12,189 square kilometres land mass is made up by the eight larger islands of Efate, Espíritu Santo, Malakula, Tanna, Eromango, Aoba, Ambrym, and Pentecost. They also account for the bulk of the country's 140,000 population.

The native people, ni-Vanuatu, are of the Melanesian race and comprise 94 per cent of the population, Europeans 3 per cent, other Pacific island peoples 1 per cent, and other nationalities (mainly Chinese and Vietnamese) 2 per cent.

The distances between the various islands and the terrain of the islands themselves has meant that there are often strong cultural differences between the various island groups and the development of some 105 languages within the country. Belsima, the local form of pidgin English, has become the main language and it, together with French and English, are the official languages.

European contact first occurred on 1 May 1606, when the Portuguese explorer, Pedro Ferdinand de Queirós, in the belief that he had reached the bottom of the Australian continent, named his first land contact within the chain, what is now Espíritu Santo, Australia del Espíritu Santo.[1] Other European explorers subsequently visited the islands, including the French explorer, Bougainville, who in 1768 named the chain the Grandes Cyclades. It was Captain James Cook, though, who in 1774 finally named the group the New Hebrides, after the Scottish coast. This name remained in use until 1980 when the present name, Vanuatu ('our land') was adopted.

Despite its early discovery, Vanuatu was of little interest to the

European powers, and it was not until the early to mid-1800s that Europeans began regular contact with the group through the sandalwood trade, missionaries, and, later by recruiting natives for the Queensland and Fiji sugar plantations. With this latter 'blackbirding' trade came European government involvement in the islands; first, due to missionary complaints over the recruiting practices, and then in response to native retaliations against the *de facto* kidnapping.

Finally, in the late 1800s European plantations were established on some of the larger islands. Initially many grew cotton, but later turned to more tropical agriculture such as bananas, coffee, cocoa, and copra. At least part of this settlement was supported for political reasons, for Australia had expressed interest in the islands following the French settlement of a penal colony in New Caledonia, and hoped the British would annex the islands to curb any expansion of French influence. New Caledonia settlers, however, were equally keen for Vanuatu to be claimed by France. The Compagnie Calédonienne des Nouvelles-Hébrides was thus established in 1882 by a naturalized Frenchman, John Higginson, effectively to give land to French settlers with the hopes that their settlement would eventually result in French annexation. The Australians responded in turn with the Australasian New Hebrides Co. in 1884, which promoted British settlement and provided trading facilities within the region. Unfortunately these early settlements were not commercially successful and were also hurt by diseases and natural disasters.[2]

Neither government, however, actually claimed Vanuatu, and in 1878 both the French and British exchanged notes stating they had no plans for annexation. Both powers subsequently renewed this position in 1883. In 1886 though, the French sent soldiers from New Caledonia to the Vanuatu islands of Efate and Malekula following the murder of French settlers on those islands. This need for protection finally resulted in the Anglo-French Convention of 1887 (the Entente Cordiale), and the establishment of a Joint Naval Commission in 1888.

Five members comprised the Joint Naval Commission: a president, and two British and two French naval officers. The position of president rotated monthly between the local British and French naval commander. The Joint Commission, however, was not effective for administration and so was replaced under the Anglo-French Convention of 1906 with the Anglo-French Condominium.[3] Under this arrangement each power retained jurisdiction over its own subjects but neither could separately control the local people nor claim sovereignty over the islands.[4]

This system was later refined by the Anglo-French Protocol of 1914 (ratified on 18 March 1922), which allowed for a joint administration of matters concerning the native inhabitants. Thus there were three parallel administrative and legal systems (the British National, the French National and the Condominium or Joint Administration). Furthermore, each country retained the rights over its own nationals and businesses. Citizens from other countries had to choose either the British or French systems when operating in what is now Vanuatu. This Protocol served largely as the basis for government until the late 1970s.

While the French and British National Commissions dealt with their respective nationals, they also sought 'to hold up the dignity of their respective nations'.[5] This meant that whatever the French established, the British had to do the same, and thus in a short time there were quite separate sets of public servants, police forces, fire departments, military, prison systems, schools, hospitals, government buildings, and custom regulations.[6] The extravagance of this three-structured government is even more evident when one considers that in 1905 there were only some 500 settlers, other than missionaries, and these were mainly French. By 1927 there was still very few European settlers with only 777 French and 452 British.

This system could have been avoided by simply dividing the islands into a French and British Vanuatu, but neither country would agree over the division. Another alternative was for one power to exchange Vanuatu in return for control of another colony in Africa or elsewhere. Pressure from Australia and New Caledonia, however, ensured that neither country could politically make the exchange.

Nevertheless, the French actively encouraged their nationals to settle in Vanuatu and establish plantations. With special access to the French markets, better support from the New-Caledonia-based trading firms, and the availability of Indochinese workers, French settlers gradually assumed control of the foreign plantation sector.

Not surprisingly then, the French settlers were the most opposed to the Vanuaaku Party's policy to return all land to the traditional owners, and the positioning of these provisions in the 1979 constitution. The French were similarly concerned over the impact of Vanuatu's independence on nearby French New Caledonia. As Espíritu Santo had the largest French presence the settlers hoped that, with

French backing, partial self-government for the island could be achieved, and the French-owned plantations exempted from local ownership. Alternatively, they could try and form a separate island state much like the French settlers on Mayotte when the Comoro Islands gained their independence from France.[7]

There was thus local French support for the John Frum movement on Tanna and the Nagriamel movement on Espíritu Santo. The Tanna independence movement proved short lived, but Espíritu Santo had the advantage of more French settlers, as well as the support of a right-wing group from the US, the Phoenix Foundation. It also had a well-publicized leader, Jimmy Stevens who, on 27 May 1980, took control of Espíritu Santo and declared it the Vemarana Republic.

The timing was probably to delay Vanuatu's independence on 30 July 1980, and result in either a local self-government compromise or full independence. For various reasons, neither the French nor the British would stop the uprising, and while British troops were sent to Port Vila, they were not used due to French objections. Finally, in mid-July the French and British both sent troops to Espíritu Santo, but they did little to restore law and order and were taken by the independence movement as a sign of support.

Following Vanuatu's independence, Prime Minister Walter Lini signed a defence agreement with Papua New Guinea and then requested the French and British troops to be withdrawn. Papua New Guinea troops were then flown to Espíritu Santo with Australian assistance and ended the revolt.[8]

Unfortunately the revolt and its associated property destruction was still adversely affecting the country's economy some five years later. The copra oil-crushing plant on Espíritu Santo, for example, burnt down during the riots, had still not been replaced. Similarly, more than 1000 French nationals left the country, mainly for New Caledonia, and over 4000 people left Espíritu Santo and most have not returned. With them went most of Espíritu Santo's cattle and plantation expertize, and there has been a marked decline in productivity ever since. The events also placed relations with the French on a less friendly basis[9] and brought a reduction in over-all financial assistance.

Vanuatu is characterized by a dualist economy with a small, highly-developed, monetized sector dominated by expatriates and foreign ownership, and a much larger non-monetized traditional sector which includes most of the ni-Vanuatu population. The former is comprised mainly of plantations, retail trading, banking, shipping and tourism, while the latter is characterized by subsistence farming, and some small-holder copra and other cash crop agriculture. The modern sector has provided Vanuatu with a relatively high GNP in per capita terms compared to its neighbours, but the ni-Vanuatu in the traditional sector would have less than half of this average.

While copra is still the most important export, Vanuatu also earns substantial foreign exchange from fish and beef exports, from tourists visiting the islands, and from a range of other agricultural products. Cocoa, for example, is now the second-largest agricultural cash crop after copra, and coffee is of growing importance. Other exports include cardamom, ginger, turmeric, oil palm, pepper, rice, kava, vanilla, tea and limes. Vanuatu is also self-sufficient in beef, and in money terms exports of canned, frozen, and chilled beef have traditionally been second only to copra in terms of exports. Fish and fish-related products, as well as timber, are also important.

At present the local industry includes beef processing, soft drinks, bread, furniture, clothing, and small fishing boats, trochus shell buttons, frozen snails, sandals, toilet paper, cement roof-tiles, soap and detergents, biscuits, sails, furniture, leather goods, soft drinks, ice-cream, pottery, rattan furniture, meat-canning, jewelry, packaged coffee, upholstery, and handicraft items.

In addition to these industries, the lack of personal income tax, corporate tax, estate duties, capital gains tax, succession duties, gift duties, withholding taxes, and double taxation treaties has made Vanuatu an ideal base for off-shore investment management and international business transactions, and Vanuatu's Finance Centre is another source of government revenues and employment.

While initially the government concentrated on consolidating its three public services into a single administrative system, it is now more active in development projects which are largely financed under a range of aid programmes. In addition, grants from the United Kingdom and France account from some 30 per cent of the government's current expenditures. However, as this latter aid is gradually being phased out, the government has raised an increasing portion of its own funds, primarily through import duties. As these reductions will also reduce the flow of foreign exchange, the government has implemented a national programme 'to meet import requirements from foreign exchange earnings and fiscal requirements from domestic revenue'.[10]

The government's current development plan, the First National Development Plan 1982–6, is the first phase of a 15-year programme to promote balanced regional and economic growth, increase the utilization of local natural and human resources, promote the role of the private sector and economic self-reliance. Within this context, the financial sector should fulfill three major roles,

> 'to finance the residual balance of approximately 15–20 per cent of the total capital requirements; . . . mobilise domestic savings out of money income which will be generated during the implementation of the plan; and to control money supply in the economy conducive to monetary stabilisation.[11]

A mid-year review of the first plan in 1984, though, found that the government needed to do more to substitute domestic savings for its heavy reliance on aid money. Indeed, one of the major problems 'in the present economy . . . [is] . . . the lack of available investment funds for domestic savings'.[12] It is thus apparent that the financial sector must be used more for savings mobilization within the economy, and a range of activities are now under way to improve its effectiveness.

Overview of Financial Sector

As with its economy, Vanuatu also has a dual financial system with a domestic financial system dominated by the local commercial banks operating side by side with an off-shore system comprised of a wide range of exempted, as well as the local, financial institutions.

Vanuatu's experience with a formal financial sector, though, is a post-war phenomenon, with the first bank commencing operations in 1948. Prior to that time, financial services were largely restricted to expatriates and foreign business and operated either through the merchant finance services of the major trading companies, some minor services provided by the colonial administrations, or through bank accounts is Sydney or Noumea.

The entry of the first commercial bank, though, did little to change this position and savings facilities were not actively promoted until the opening of private saving bank agencies by the Commonwealth Bank of Australia in the early 1950s. These were later supplemented in rural areas through the co-operative movement, and in 1975 through the Vanuatu Co-operative Savings Bank.

The development of international banking operations did not develop until the early 1970s when a number of banks opened local

TABLE 4.1   Financial institutions in Vanuatu, by type, 1985

Central Bank of Vanuatu
Commercial banks
Co-operative Savings Bank of Vanuatu
Development Bank of Vanuatu
Merchant bank
Insurance companies
International trust companies
Exempt banks and financial institutions
Exempt insurance companies
Vanuatu Commodities Marketing Board[a]
Co-operative societies[a]
National Provident Fund[b]
State Housing Authority[a] [b]

[a] Are primarily active in non-financial matters.
[b] Expected to be established over 1986–7.

branches in the hope of gaining business from the recently-established Finance Centre. This allowed the licensing of exempt banks, financial institutions and insurance companies. As shown in Table 4.1, Vanuatu has a relatively large number of institutions active in financial matters and 1986–7 should see the establishment of its National Provident Fund.

FINANCIAL INSTITUTIONS

Central Bank of Vanuatu

The Central Bank of Vanuatu was established on 18 December 1980 under the Central Bank of Vanuatu Act 1980, to assume the central bank function for the new republic, and it commenced operations on 1 January 1981. Under its Act (Section 3) the Central Bank is required 'to regulate the issue, supply, availability and international exchange of money; to advise the government on banking and monetary matters; to promote monetary stability; to promote sound financial structure; and to foster economic conditions conducive to the orderly and balanced economic development of Vanuatu'.

The Central Bank's initial goal was to assume the currency issue role of the French agency, the Institut d'Emission d'Outre-Mer. While this took place on 1 January 1981, it was only an administrative change as the colonial currency continued much as before. The real objective was to replace the New Hebrides franc with a new national currency, the vatu. The first vatu notes were issued on 22 March 1982, and on 1 April 1983 both the old New Hebrides franc and its local co-circulating currency, the Australian dollar, ceased to be legal tender. Later, on 16 August 1983, this exercise was repeated for coinage with vatu coins being exchanged for the colonial FNH (New Hebrides Franc) coinage. By the end of 1984 over 92 per cent of FNH notes had been exchanged for vatu, compared with only 22 per cent of FNH coins: the low figures of the latter reflects the degree of hoarding in rural areas.

Under its own legislation and the Banking Regulations, the Central Bank has an extensive set of direct control measures which can be applied over both banking and non-bank financial institutions. Under Section 35(1)(b) for example, the Central Bank can 'aggregate ceilings and maximum amounts beyond which the approval of the Central Bank is necessary and the maximum maturity and maximum rates chargeable in respect of advances, discounts, letters of credit, acceptances and other forms of credit'. It can also differentiate between institutions and set reserve ratios as well as minimum cash margins or security required for bank lending.

In late 1985, for example, the Bank had issued informal guidelines for a maximum of 12 to 14 per cent interest to be charged on loans to productive sectors, and export promoting or import reducing projects. The banks were also to give favourable treatment to small businesses and locally-owned enterprises, and have an average weighted average lending rate of not more than 14 per cent per annum.

The Central Bank, however, is excluded under Section 35 (2) from applying these regulations to exempted banks and financial institutions.

As yet the Central Bank has been unable to implement any serious monetary measures other than by these direct controls. This is due, in part, to the openness of Vanuatu's financial sector, as well as the domestic bank's own off-shore operations. There is also a lack of government securities on which the Bank could mount an open-market approach. While a bond issue was planned for early 1986, it will take some time before the Bank will be in a position to use these securities for trading purposes.

As part of its functions, the Central Bank (Section 16) is required to buy and sell on demand convertible currencies for immediate delivery outside of Vanuatu against the vatu. In practice, however, it has delegated this role to Banque Indosuez. Thus, while it determines the over-all exchange rate, the day-to-day transactions are left to the commercial bank to implement. The Central Bank does hope to become active in foreign exchange management in 1987. Similarly, the government plans that 'in the immediate future the Bank will make more active use of exchange rate policy, and eventually assume responsibility for management of the nation's foreign currency reserves'.[13]

While it has the traditional powers of inspection and banking supervisory matters, the Central Bank was not active in actual banking supervision as of late 1985 for no staff were available for this purpose. This function will no doubt be developed in time, and with it should similarly come a greater emphasis on the development of a sound and stable financial sector within the country.

Other functions which will undertaken in the future include the role of banker to the government. It will serve as the depository for the forthcoming government bond issue and hopes to service the government bank accounts over 1986–7.

As shown in Table 4.2, the Central Bank holds the bulk of its assets in the form of foreign assets. This reflects the Bank's role as the holder of the government's foreign exchange reserves and the requirement to maintain an amount equal to at least 50 per cent of its currency issue in such assets. Currency issue is also the Bank's major source of funds.

The Bank's own retained earnings are also a growing source of funds, and its general reserves must be increased until they equal half the authorized capital. After that 'the balance of any profits over and above any other charges will be paid to the Development Bank'.[14]

Commercial Banks in Vanuatu

The commercial banks are both the oldest and largest of Vanuatu's financial institutions. The foreign bank branches and foreign-owned banking subsidiaries provide a full range of traditional banking services to include overdrafts, term loans, consumer finance, documentary letters of credit, guarantees, and immigration and customs bonds. In addition, the commercial banks in Vanuatu, like the economy itself, have a dualistic structure which includes a traditional

TABLE 4.2   Central Bank of Vanuatu: assets and liabilities, 1984
(in vatu)

Assets:		
13.5	Net International Monetary Fund subscription	159,075,045
0.7	Special drawing rights	8,613,068
11.2	Foreign Treasury notes	131,569,816
46.8	Short-term foreign deposits	551,844,151
1.0	Foreign current accounts	12,233,495
1.0	Other international bodies subscriptions	11,906,870
0.1	Fixed assets	1,579,589
4.4	Notes and coins	52,169,549
–	Prepayments	81,311
0.1	Interest receivable	1,595,162
11.1	Government securities	130,960,108
10.0	Current accounts	118,239,731
–	Other receivables	8,046
100.0	Total assets	1,179,875,941

Liabilities:		
8.5	Issued capital	100,000,000
–	Capital reserves	231,500
6.9	General reserves	81,645,716
76.3	Notes in circulation	900,084,800
6.8	Coins in circulation	80,026,022
0.2	Due to Vanuatu government	2,154,985
0.2	Due to International Monetary Fund	2,342,168
0.9	Due to Commission of European Communities	10,982,353
0.1	Due to Asian Development Bank	1,043,273
0.1	Accrued expenses	1,365,124
100.0	Total liabilities	1,179,875,941

Source: Central Bank of Vanuatu (1984) *Annual Report and Statement of Accounts for 1984*, pp. 26–7.

domestic operation coupled with off-shore banking in support of the country's Finance Centre.

(i) *Development*

Although the commercial banks are the oldest of the institutions there were none in local operation prior to 1948. The banking services were instead performed by local merchants. As one report commented, 'the main trading houses in the New Hebrides provided quasi-banking facilities, accepting deposits in current account and making advances but banking facilities proper had to be provided from outside'.[15] The bulk of the latter business went to Noumea in the case of the French or to Sydney for British business. Indeed, apparently the 'Condominium government, the National Administrations, commercial houses, most traders, and private individuals of any substance do their banking in Australia and New Caledonia'.[16] In addition, the Condominium's French Treasury also apparently provided some limited financial services for in 1930 it was reported that 'money transfers can be done very cheaply . . . to France and French colonies'.[17]

Banking commenced locally on 26 June 1948 with the opening of a branch in Port Vila by the Banque de l'Indochine, now Banque Indosuez Vanuatu. This reflected the importance of French trade with the Condominium and the Bank's own dominance of the New Caledonia market. The branch, though, had only a limited impact, for as a government report commented for that year, 'a great number of residents have continued their former practice of using local commercial houses as unofficial bankers, or banking in Sydney or Noumea or both'.[18] The Bank gradually grew in importance in the local economy and subsequently opened branches in Espiritu Santo in 1954, Malekula in 1973, and Tanna in 1973 (the last two were closed in 1981) and remains today the most important, although now not the largest, of Vanuatu's commercial banks.

The next entry into local banking, that of the Commonwealth Savings Bank, did not occur until 1950, and then in the form of private saving bank agencies rather than an actual branch. As shown in Table 4.3, most agents were established in the early 1960s, but some confusion remains over the exact opening dates and agency arrangements. Government reports of the day, for example, suggest that the Commonwealth's operations commenced earlier and were somewhat larger than Table 4.1 suggests. For example, the Condominium government in 1951 reported that 'in 1950, Messrs Burns Philp (New Hebrides) Ltd established an agency of the Commonwealth Savings Bank'.[19] Similarly, another government document in 1965 reported Commonwealth Savings Bank agencies at 'Vila and Santo and on Tanna, Aoba, Pentecost, Malekula and Tongoa'.[20] These agencies accepted savings deposits in Australian dollars and New Hebrides francs (the Condominium's dual authorized currencies), but converted the latter into its Australian dollar equivalent.[21] The agencies themselves were seemingly never a significant source of banking business and were probably unprofitable as

TABLE 4.3   Commonwealth Savings Bank agencies in the New Hebrides

Place	Opened	Closed	Operator
Landua (Aoba)	1964[a]	1974	Landua Training School
Lolowai (Aoba)	1958	1975	Melanesian Mission
Pentecost Island	1962[a]	1976	Melanesian Mission
Ranmawat (Pentecost)	1962	1974	Unknown
Espíritu Santo	1971[a]	1976	Burns Philp (New Hebrides) Ltd
Tanna	1958	1976	R. H. Paul (trader)
Vila (Efate)	1958[a]	1976	Burns Philp (New Hebrides) Ltd

[a] Indicates approximate dates.

Source: Commonwealth Bank of Australia, correspondence dated 17 February 1986.

well. They were thus either closed or subsequently taken over by a local institution, following the establishment of Vanuatu's Co-operative Savings Bank in 1975.

The Commonwealth Bank of Australia had actually been requested by local businesses to open a branch in the New Hebrides as early as 1947, and had even reconsidered the matter in 1950.[22] Given that it subsequently opened a branch in the nearby Solomon Islands in 1951, it is surprising that it did not proceed in the Condominium as well. This is particularly so as the Commonwealth's central banking division was very much involved with the Condominium's financial affairs. For example it, and later the Reserve Bank of Australia, served as the Condominium's exchange control agent and authorized foreign exchange dealers from 1941 until after independence.

Similarly, as the Australian dollar was used as the Condominium's main currency from at least 1935 until 1981, a local branch would have greatly assisted currency distribution. As one report commented, the problem of redeeming wornout Australian currency 'would not arise if the Commonwealth Trading Bank of Australia were to establish a branch in the New Hebrides'.[23] It would have also helped offset the French domination of local banking. Why the Commonwealth chose to open in the Solomons and not the New Hebrides is not documented. The potential profitability was certainly one factor as the Banque de l'Indochine had been operating for some years, and thus had most of the potential banking business. Similarly, whereas the Commonwealth was offered the Solomon government accounts as incentive, it would have been forced to compete with the

TABLE 4.4   Commercial banks in Vanuatu, by establishment date

Commercial bank	Establishment date
Australian and New Zealand Banking Corporation[a]	23 March 1970
Bank of New South Wales[b]	20 December 1971
Banque de l'Indochine[c]	26 June 1948
Barclays Bank International[a]	14 March 1972
Commercial Bank of Australia[b]	5 May 1972
Commercial Banking Co. of Sydney[d]	20 September 1971
Hongkong and Shanghai Banking Corporation	November 1972
National Bank of Australasia[d]	28 February 1972

[a] Merged with Barclays Bank Vanuatu to form ANZ Vanuatu Ltd.
[b] Merged to form the Westpac Banking Corporation.
[c] Was locally incorporated as Banque Indosuez Vanuatu Ltd on 29 September 1978.
[d] Merged to form the National Australia Bank, closed 30 September 1977.

Source: Industry interviews (1985).

Banque de l'Indochine for this business. Problems with the convertibility between the New Hebrides franc and the then Australian pound was probably another factor. Finally, the need to find French-speaking staff, and concern that the Bank could become involved in any political disputes between British and French interests also argued against a local branch.[24]

The lack of potential business also discouraged other banks from opening for, as shown in Table 4.4, it was not until after the passage of special banking legislation in 1970, as part of the government's off-shore financial centre efforts, that other banks established branches.

Of the new entries some, like the then Bank of New South Wales, Commercial Banking Co. of Sydney, and the National Bank of Australasia, concentrated almost solely on off-shore banking, with relatively little local deposit taking and lending. In contrast, what is now Banque Indosuez Vanuatu, Barclays, the ANZ and the Commercial Bank of Australia were actively involved in the domestic deposit and lending business. This business, however, contracted sharply with the coming of independence, as foreign investors postponed investment until the new government's economic policies were formalized. This was sufficient for some banks to close, and those that remained subsequently suffered substantial losses during the riots in Espíritu Santo in 1980, and the subsequent departure of many former European customers.

The after effects of the Espíritu Santo rebellion on the economy cannot be overstated, and the banking sector was similarly effected. With the departure of the European customers, the previous branch structure could no longer be justified. Thus Banque Indosuez closed its former branches in Malekula and Tanna in 1981, and while its Espíritu Santo branch remained, its business, which once required some 40 to 50 staff, was easily handled by only three.

Since independence there has been some improvement in lending levels, but generally most banks have stayed in Vanuatu more to support their off-shore banking business, and for the trade financing work, rather than for simple local deposit taking and lending. Indeed, most observers consider the country was over banked and those within the industry would like a reduction in the total numbers. The withdrawal of the Commercial Banking Co. of Sydney and its later merger partner, the National Bank of Australasia, meant at least two less competitors. The most recent rationalization, though, came in mid-1985 when Barclays Bank International sold its Vanuatu operations to the Australia and New Zealand Banking Group. The ANZ subsequently transferred its own Vanuatu operations into a local subsidiary, ANZ Bank (Vanuatu) Ltd, and then absorbed Barclays operations on 1 October 1985. As the *Australian Financial Review Review* commented, the acquisition gave the 'ANZ dominance in Vanuatu, combining its existing 10 per cent share with Barclays' approximately 50 per cent'.[25]

Though no longer the market leader in terms of deposits, Banque Indosuez is still Vanuatu's most important bank, for in many respects it remains the *de facto* central bank in terms of local banking services. For example, it is Bank Indosuez, not the Central Bank of Vanuatu, that still provides a limited lender of last resort support to the other banks, and handles all foreign exchange settlements. Indeed, even though the Central Bank handles the physical interbank clearing, the end settlements, in December 1985, were still handled through accounts with Banque Indosuez, not with the Central Bank. Similarly, as of December 1985, all government bank accounts were held at Banque Indosuez.

It seems quite logical that Banque Indosuez Vanuatu will retain some privileges, for on 1 August 1983 the Vanuatu government purchased 10,000 shares in Banque Indosuez Vanuatu Ltd at a price of 2200 vatu per share, and agreed to subscribe to an additional 10,000 shares. This purchase was financed with a loan of SDR 414,313 (denominated in the International Monetary Fund's Special Drawing Rights – SDRs) branch at an interest rate of the interbank offered rate plus $\frac{1}{8}$ per cent and the principle repayable in annual amounts of SDR 82,663 over 15 August 1984–8. This gives the government a 20 per cent ownership.

(ii) *Regulation*

Commercial banks in Vanuatu are regulated under the Queen's Regulation No. 4 of 1970. This legislation, introduced on 17 September 1970, is also a key part of the country's present off-shore financial system or 'Finance Centre'. It requires the licensing of financial institutions and stresses (in Section 2) that only a bank can accept deposits which are withdrawable by cheque. Licensed banks are the only ones allowed to use 'bank' in their name and, indeed, are required to include bank or one of its foreign derivatives in their title.

To obtain a local banking license (under Section 7), a bank head-quartered in Vanuatu must first have a paid-up capital and unimpaired reserves of at least A\$ 500,000, while a bank headquartered overseas must have at least A\$ 2,000,000: this compares to only A\$ 125,000 and A\$ 500,000 respectively for financial institutions.

In addition, it must also show itself to have adequate managerial abilities and no person who as a director or manager of a failed financial institutions, has been imprisoned by any country for dishonesty, or who has become a bankrupt, can serve as a director, manager or employee of any Vanuatu financial institution.

Once licensed, a bank (Section 14) must maintain a minimum liquid assets holding as a percentage of the bank's deposit liabilities set by the Central Bank of Vanuatu, but not to exceed 25 per cent. A locally-incorporated institution must also pay at least 25 per cent of its net profits into a reserve fund until the fund equals the firm's paid-up capital. Licensed institutions headquartered overseas must maintain a specified level of capital and reserves within Vanuatu similar to that for domestic institutions. Each institution is also required to be audited annually.

In terms of their operations, banks are precluded from lending or providing other forms of financing to one customer, or related group of customers, equal to more than 25 per cent of the institution's paid-up capital and published reserves. Transactions between banks, telegraphic transfers, or bills of exchange for the payment of exports from Vanuatu are exempted from this restriction. They are also prohibited from providing unsecured advances or other credit facilities the greater of A$ 300,000, or one per cent of the bank's paid-up capital and published reserve, to any director or firms associated with its directors or their families. Unsecured advances to bank staff are limited to an amount equal to their annual salary.

Finally, share investments are permissible, but these are limited to an aggregate amount of 25 per cent of the bank's paid-up capital and reserves. They may have wholly-owned subsidiaries for nominee, executor, trustee, or other functions incidental to banking business.

If the government is not satisfied with the institution's performance, it may revoke the license for a range of reasons to include where the institution is thought to be 'carrying on business in a manner detrimental to the public interest or to the interest of the depositors of such institution' (Section 5(4)(c)). It may also choose to appoint a qualified person to examine the books and affairs of the financial institution or require that certain information be provided.

In addition to these effectively prudential regulations, the Central Bank has also introduced a number of operational guidelines to ensure that bank operations conform to government monetary policy and economic objectives. These have included a number of informal measures on the cost and direction of bank advances.

In March 1981, for example, the Central Bank set an interest rate ceiling of 15 per cent on bank loans and advances. It was later raised to 18 per cent on 10 September 1981, and finally removed on 30 November 1982. However, it had only a limited impact on bank lending, for as one government report commented, the ceiling 'never acted as a serious constraint on the lending rate, and when it did come close in 1981, the ceiling was raised from 15.5 to 18.5 per cent'.[26]

In mid-1983, however, a more extensive set of guidelines were introduced. The most significant of these was the Central Bank's efforts to reduce the wide spread between the banks' deposit and lending rates. This was accomplished by stating that the margin between a bank's weighted average 1- to 12-month fixed deposit rate, and its weighted average lending rate, should not exceed 4.5 per cent. Given their high operating costs and bad loan provisions, the banks were particularly concerned over this limitation and, as mentioned elsewhere, lobbyed strongly for its removal: as a result the Central Bank later withdrew this restraint on 8 February, 1985.

The mid-1983 guidelines relating to the direction of bank lending, and the limitation of the bank's weighted average lending rate to 14 per cent per annum, though, still remain in force. The former provides that the rates on lending to productive sectors, tourist-orientated projects, and export promotion or import savings projects should range between 12 to 14 per cent (except in exceptional circumstances), and that the banks should favour particularly loan applications from small businesses and those local enterprises with ni-Vanuatu participation. The banks are also expected to limit their personal lending activities.[27]

(iii) *Deposits*

Due to the lack of exchange controls, commercial banks in Vanuatu may accept deposits in any currency from both residents and non-residents. As of the end of 1984, deposits from residents were the most important with 10,756.9 million vatu-worth of vatu and foreign currency deposits (or 62.3 per cent of the total) compared to 6506.1 million vatu-worth of non-resident vatu and foreign currency deposits (or 37.7 per cent). Not surprisingly, relatively few non-residents opt for vatu-denominated deposits. As of December 1984, for example, the non-residents had 237.6 million vatu in vatu-denominated deposits compared to 6,268.5 million vatu-worth of foreign currency deposits.[28]

Vanuatu residents have traditionally held a relatively high percentage of their deposits in foreign currencies. In particular after independence, their foreign exchange deposits rose, in 1981, to a high of 58.8 per cent, and then declined. Recently, concern over a possible vatu devaluation has caused resident foreign exchange holdings to rise again, and in mid-1985 they stood at 67.1 per cent of total deposits of 11,802 million vatu. As shown in Table 4.5, within these foreign currency deposits, Australian dollars have remained relatively important over recent years. This is due partly to the Australian dollar's previous use as local currency, and the significant trading links with Australia, as well as Australia's relatively high interest rates.

There are considerable differences in the interest rates afforded by the different banks in Vanuatu. In December 1985, for example, the

TABLE 4.5   Residents' deposits in Vanuatu commercial banks, by currency, 1984

	Demand deposits (%)	Savings and fixed deposits[a] (%)
Vatu	61.6	29.7
French francs	1.7	3.1
Australian dollars	11.5	28.8
US dollars	23.8	16.7
Other currencies	1.4	21.7
Total	100.0	100.0
Vatu millions	2,459.2	8,297.7

[a] No separate breakdown of savings deposits is available.

Source: Central Bank of Vanuatu (1984) *Annual Report and Statement of Accounts for 1984*, p. 18.

TABLE 4.6   Commercial bank rates for vatu deposits, 1985

	Australian and New Zealand Banking Group	Banque Indosuez Vanuatu	Hongkong and Shanghai Banking Corporation	Westpac Banking Corporation
Savings book	NA	5.5	6.5	4.0
1 month	NA	7.00	8.00	7.50
3 months	NA	–	8.25	8.25
6 months	NA	7.00	8.50	8.50
12 months	NA	7.50	9.00	9.00

Note: The above rates normally require a minimum deposit of 100,000 vatu.
Source: Industry interviews (December 1985).

rates on normal passbook savings accounts ranged from a low of 4 per cent (by Westpac) to a high of 6.5 per cent (by Hongkong and Shanghai). Differences in vatu-fixed deposit rates are shown in Table 4.6. These posted rates are for deposits ranging from between 100,000 to 500,000 vatu. Larger amounts, particularly 1,000,000 vatu or more, are subject to negotiation and depend largely on the individual bank's deposit and loan position and the world money-market rates on SDR-denominated deposits. Over-all, at the end of 1984 the weighted average interest rate paid by commercial banks on

TABLE 4.7   Commercial bank vatu and foreign currency loans and advances to residents, by type of sector, 31 December 1984

	Vatu (m)
Agriculture & fisheries	211.5
Mining & manufacturing	392.7
Wholesale & retail trade	907.3
Tourism	150.4
Entertainment & catering	81.4
Transport	260.3
Construction	462.6
Government	225.0
Financial institutions	70.7
Professional and other services	127.9
Personal	683.2
Miscellaneous	126.0
Total	3,699.0

Source: Central Bank of Vanuatu (1984) *Annual Report and Statement of Accounts for 1984*, p. 44.

savings deposits stood at 4.3 per cent compared to 8.3 per cent for fixed deposits.[29]

Foreign currency fixed deposits have a somewhat higher minimum, and most banks require at least the rough equivalent of US$ 10,000. Banque Indosuez Vanuatu, for example, would accept foreign deposits for as little as US$ 5000, but noted that really US$ 100,000 was required to obtain internationally competitive rates. This is apparently the minimum amount that they could in turn place off-shore.

In addition to the normal deposits, most banks will also accept large deposits on an overnight call basis. In December 1985 the rates varied between 4 to 5 per cent. Since November 1985 there has also been an interbank overnight deposit market in operation.

(iv) *Lending*

As with its deposit business, commercial banks may lend to residents either in vatu or foreign currencies. At one time most lending was in foreign currencies, but gradually vatu has become more important. In June 1985, for example, vatu-denominated loans accounted for 85.5 per cent of the loans to residents.

As shown in Table 4.7, loans to wholesale and retail industries and personal lending are the major advances to residents, and together accounted for 43 per cent of the loans outstanding at the end of 1984. More recently there has been some decline in the importance of the wholesale and retail business. In addition, construction finance has increased, reflecting new leases being issued in urban areas.

In terms of advances, most banks divide their business into three categories: commercial, housing, and personal lending. As indicated, commercial finance is by far the most important and is available both through medium-term advances or traditional overdrafts. Over 1985 the interest rates on this lending ranged between 12 and 18 per cent. Housing loans are available only for relatively short maturities with five years seemingly the maximum. As with other loans, the interest rate charged varies considerably ranging from 11.5 to 18 per cent. Consumer finance maturities depend largely on the loan's purpose but could be for up to three to five years. Interest is charged at rates between 14.5 to 19.5 per cent. In June 1985, the commercial banks weighted average lending rate stood at 13.9 per cent, just under the Central Bank's 14 per cent guideline.

While these rates are substantially above those on deposits, banks with long-standing loan portfolios incurred substantial losses following the 1980 riots and the subsequent departure of many former European clients. With the removal of the 4.5 per cent spread limitation in February 1985, the difference between the weight average lending and deposits rose, and in mid-1985 stood at approximately 6.4 per cent.

One concern among government planners is the relatively low growth in bank advances to residents. These increased by only 4.3 per cent in 1982, by 7.5 per cent in 1983 and by 2.7 per cent in 1984. 1984 in part reflects the high copra prices, which allowed many bank customers to pay off existing loans or reduce their potential borrowings.

The low rate of ni-Vanuatu borrowings is also notable. In 1984, for example, bank loans to ni-Vanuatu borrowers accounted for 801,649 million vatu or 23.3 per cent of total loans. In comparison, loans to expatriates totaled 2,383,956 million and loans to joint ventures, 258,403 million. In terms of loan numbers, though, ni-Vanuatu borrowers accounted for 1613 of the banks' 2686 loans, or 60.1 per cent of the total.

While each bank interviewed wished to make more vatu loans, they complained of a lack of viable projects in that currency. Questions over the leasing of formerly expatriate-held lands, particularly in the plantation sector, has also limited the scope for new projects and hence lending. As the Central Bank commented, 'certain structural characteristics such as dominance of trading activities, insufficient local entrepreneurship and urban-based structure of banking hinder more rapid deployment of deposits resources'[30] Given that there was little demand for larger loans, the banks understandably are not particularly aggressive bidders for vatu deposits. This attitude may change in the future, however, for the current development plan indicates that 'commercial banks will be encouraged to participate in specific development projects where possible'.[31]

In addition to the above advances, Banque Indosuez Vanuatu, in its quasi-lender of last resort role, also lends to the other banks on demand. In December 1985, for example, it would provide overnight funds via an overdraft at 13 per cent or longer-terms funds from one to six months at the international SDR interbank offered rate plus 0.25 per cent.

(v) *Other business*

In addition to domestic business, each commercial bank also conducts off-shore banking on behalf of their parent organizations. There is very little local Eurocurrency business. Instead, most Eurocurrency or off-shore business placed with the local banks is arranged and managed by the bank's head office or other off-shore branches, particularly Hong Kong. Those loans booked in Vanuatu are usually funded from Hong Kong. The Vanuatu branch simply handles the resulting documentation. As the Hongkong and Shanghai Banking Corporation reported, 'our small domestic branch achieved improved working profit from increased deposits, while our off-shore unit had a good year'.[32]

In addition to its own off-shore operations, local commercial banks may also represent other affiliated companies, either incorporated in, or with *de facto* branches, in Vanuatu. At the Hongkong and Shanghai Banking Corporation's Port Vila office, for example, there are name plaques for Wardley Services (New Hebrides) Ltd, Wardley International Bank (Vila) Ltd, Crorebridge Bank Ltd, SIH Bank (Vila) Ltd, and the Stanbridge International Bank Ltd. Thus even the off-shore business of domestic banks may not reflect their true importance in terms of an international bank's world activities. These other off-shore operations are discussed in the section on the Finance Centre and its exempt banks (see pp. 251–63).

(vi) *Representation*

In most countries it is usually worthwhile listing the various commercial banks and their respective types and numbers of local representation. In Vanuatu, unfortunately, this is not required as only two banks, the ANZ Bank (Vanuatu) Ltd and Banque Indosuez Vanuatu, have branch offices, and then only one each in Espíritu Santo. The other banks have only the one office in Port Vila. In addition, the ANZ also operates a part-time foreign exchange agency at the Intercontinental Hotel, and prior to its recent acquisition of Barclays' local operations, had a private agency in Espíritu Santo for both savings and limited cheque cashing purposes. This position, however, may change as the government's national development plan recommends the 'expansion of banking networks toward the outer islands'.[33] In practice, though, none of the bankers interviewed indicated a desire to expand outside of Port Vila and, without substantial government pressure, the Co-operative Savings Bank (see pp. 225–34) will be left to service these areas largely on its own.

(vii) *Staff*

As shown in Table 4.8, there are a relatively high number of expatriate staff given the total number of bank employees. It is tempting to suggest the large number reflects the more complex nature of Vanuatu's off-shore banking business, but in practice the banks themselves do little locally other than to administer overseas instructions, and much of this work is computerized. Instead it is a function of the lack of training provided for local nationals in banking operations. As a result, the highest ni-Vanuatu bank employee would only be at the supervisor level.

Each bank, though, is taking steps to correct this position. This is partly a function of government economic policies, but it is also simply a matter of economics. The present cost of expatriate banking staff is now exceedingly high for, despite the lack of personal taxation, a European's living costs in Port Vila is very high due to the extensive indirect taxes on most imported goods. In contrast, while the banks are considered relatively good payers, 800,000 vatu per annum (US$ 8000) is about the top salary for a ni-Vanuatu employee.

Overseas training programmes have featured highly in localization efforts, and those banks with representation in Papua New Guinea and Fiji have made good use of their training facilities in those

TABLE 4.8   Commercial banks in Vanuatu: staff numbers

	ni-Vanuatu	Expatriate	Total
Australian and New Zealand Banking Group Vila	70	15	85
Banque Indosuez Vanuatu Ltd	n.a.	n.a.[a]	83
Hongkong and Shanghai Banking Corporation	22	4[b]	24
Westpac Banking Corporation	18	8	26

[a] Only two expatriates are seconded bank staff, the others were hired locally. This allows the highest number of foreign staff, but the specific figure is not disclosed.
[b] This is comprised of two Europeans and two Chinese.

Source: Industry interviews (1985).

countries. Likewise, a more selective group of ni-Vanuatu employees have been sent for longer term head office training. Given the relatively small staff sizes, most local training is accomplished through video courses sent from home office. There would also seem some merit in organizing some centralized training courses through the Bankers' Association of Vanuatu, but as yet no action has been taken.

These various bank training programmes are gradually having their effects. Westpac training plans, for example, should reduce its expatriate numbers to six by the end of 1987.

Vanuatu Co-operative Savings Bank

The Vanuatu Co-operative Savings Bank is the trading name for the banking division of the Vanuatu Co-operative Federation Ltd and is not, as such, a separate financial institution. Its operations are limited to accepting passbook savings and fixed-term deposits, and investing these assets in deposits with commercial banks or other secure liquid assets. In addition, the Savings Bank also collects loan repayments on behalf of the Development Bank, pays wages and salaries to government employees in rural areas, provides an inter-island remittance service, and assists the Central Bank in distribution of currency in rural areas.

(i) *Development*

There had been calls for the co-operatives to provide banking services for some years prior to 1976, and in-house discussions had taken place between the Federation and the Co-operatives Department. In 1976, though, the high copra prices, and the expectation that these would continue, gave an added incentive finally to take action.[34] Previously some savings had already been mobilized through the sale and repurchase of co-operative shares, but these activities, while within the Act, were not particularly attractive either to potential depositors or the Co-operatives Department. Thus the British government and the Federation subsequently commissioned Barclays Bank International to conduct a feasibility study on the prospects of developing these informal arrangements into an actual financial institution.

The study found substantial untapped savings available in rural areas and suggested they could be tapped through a savings bank branch and agency network operating in conjunction with the Federation's member societies. The Savings Bank was initially formed as a division of what is now the Vanuatu Co-operatives Federation, to service the demand for a savings vehicle among its member co-operatives.

Based on these findings the Federation, with foreign assistance, established the administrative structure necessary for the savings operations, and by 1975 it had some 95 savings bank agencies at approximately half of its member societies. The secretary of each co-operative was responsible for maintaining customer account records on behalf of the bank, and periodically forwarding a record of savings and withdrawal transactions to the bank as well as any cash surpluses.

Unfortunately the Bank's initial deposit expectations of some A$ 2 million proved over-optimistic. Similarly, the large number of agencies proved too difficult to manage. In particular, the considerable distance between the agencies themselves made it impossible to supervise their operations adequately, and it was not cost effective, given the deposit levels, to expand the supervisory staff.

By 1976 the Bank clearly had operational problems, and new management support was provided under British technical co-operation assistance. The plan was for British officers to restructure the Bank so that it could be a profitable operation in its own right. To achieve this, it was decided that the Bank should become totally separate from the Federation, that the unprofitable agencies should be closed, and that the Bank should open its own branches where the potential business warranted. Unfortunately, on examination of the

Bank's records over 1977, the Savings Bank was found technically insolvent, and only through a A$ 222,000 trust fund established by the British with the British High Commission (to allow it to meet its potential deposit liabilities) was it able to continue business. Furthermore, it was also realized that, as the Bank was not licensed as a financial institution under the Banking Regulations, its operations were, in fact, illegal.

The rationalization process was conducted all the same and agencies either closed or replaced by the Bank's own branches. Thus, by mid-1984 some 55 agencies had closed and an additional 17 agencies were scheduled for closing. The UK's Overseas Development Administration, which had provided the Savings Bank management since 1977, was dissatisfied with the progress, and in 1983 indicated it wished to cease further assistance. Thus, in September 1983, the government decided that the Savings Bank would be best merged with one of the existing foreign banks operating in Vanuatu to form a joint venture national bank, the Commmercial Bank of Vanuatu. As government planners explained, such a merger would 'result in the provision of a more complete range of banking services while still maintaining ni-Vanuatu equity'.[35] The plan also received British support and they agreed to provide the Bank's management staff until the arrangements could be finalized.

The government, therefore, approached each of the commercial banks with the merger proposal. Of these only Barclays Bank International responded favourably. Under the arrangement Barclays domestic operations would be merged with the Savings Bank to form the Commercial Bank of Vanuatu: Barclays would retain its existing off-shore banking business as a separate entity. Agreement was almost reached and subject only to a final feasibility study by Barclays in June 1984. Unfortunately, further delays resulted and, in February 1985, Barclays withdrew from discussions, and in September 1985 subsequently sold its domestic banking operations to the ANZ Banking Group.

With the end of the discussions also came the end of the British technical support and the Bank's management is now conducted by a Canadian banker provided under the Canadian University Service Overseas (CUSO) scheme. While this has resolved the Bank's immediate management problem, the Bank has been forced to absorb much more management costs under this programme than under the former British scheme.

The establishment of the Commercial Bank of Vanuatu still remains the long-term goal of the Savings Bank and co-operative staff, but at present no foreign partners have been forthcoming. One alternative suggested was to give 'consideration of a merger with the [Development Bank of Vanuatu] in the medium term'.[36] Interestingly, neither the Savings Bank or Development Bank staff considered this likely. Instead, they could see some potential for a greater sharing of resources, premises and other services between the two institutions. In addition, the surplus funds raised by Savings Bank might also be used to some degree by the Development Bank as a means of recycling the savings back into rural areas.

An immediate government goal, however, should be to resolve the legality of the Savings Bank. At present both the Savings Bank and the Central Bank readily admit that the Savings Bank is an illegal operation in that it is accepting deposits from the public without registration under the Banking Regulations – a position that has existed since the Bank's establishment and certainly something that the government has known since 1977. Some suggest that the lack of action is a function of the Co-operatives Department and what is now the Central Bank, in that if the Bank registers as a company under the banking act, it would lose its present co-operative status and need to drop 'Co-operative' from its title. This has been seen by some as undesirable. If this really presents a problem, though, there would be little difficulty in amending existing legislation to allow for both the Bank's registration and the continuance of 'Co-operative' in its title, if not in its operations as well.

This present position is much more than a legal problem, for under its present structure the depositors are very much at potential risk. Given that the Savings Bank is part of the Federation rather than a separate legal entity, its assets and liabilities are really part of those of the Federation. This has the unfortunate effect of giving any secured creditors first call on the Bank's assets if the Federation should have financial problems. Worse still, the depositors would rank equally with the Federation's other unsecured creditors only after the secured claims were satisfied. It is doubtful if few Savings Bank customers are aware of their position. Any major realization of this problem might well result in mass withdrawals.

(ii) *Assets*

As shown in Table 4.9, the Savings Bank, as of mid-1985,confined its main investments to deposits in banks. Cash at bank or on hand accounted for over 96 per cent of the total assets. The relatively low rates paid on these vatu deposits greatly limit the Bank's potential income. In late 1985, for example, the bulk of its money was in 3- to 6-month deposits, which were rolled over at maturity: they were earning 8 per cent interest. As the commercial banks lack many acceptable vatu-denominated lending proposals, there has really been a surplus of vatu deposits, and hence the banks have not been willing to pay more for such funds. This position similarly effects the Bank's ability to attract a foreign banking partner, as they would face exactly the same problem with the resulting vatu deposits.

One alternative to the low vatu interest rates is to place the funds raised in the off-shore market. This would be a fairly realistic alternative, but unfortunately in the past the currency denomination chosen by the Bank was the Australian dollar. Given the one-time use of that currency throughout its operations, the choice is not surprising. Unfortunately since replacing the Australian dollar and New Hebrides franc with the vatu, and switching the vatu's linkage to the SDR, the Australian dollar has declined significantly in terms of vatu. As a result deposits, made when a A$ 1.00 equalled 100 vatu, are now worth only around 70 vatu. This problem is well reflected in the Savings Bank's income statement, for despite an operating profit over 1985 of 4,456,601 vatu, abnormal items involving exchange rate movements, and special provisions, together produced a net loss of VT 17,879,893.

Besides the potential foreign exchange loss and the low yield on commercial bank deposits, neither investment helps recycle the moneys raised back into the rural areas where they were collected. Similarly, the interest rate spread between its deposit rates and those on its commercial bank deposits is really too narrow to support any Saving Bank expansion into other banking areas. The Savings Bank's present structure can just about manage its straight deposit-taking operations, and any attempt at loan-making would require a considerable increase in managerial (probably all expatriate) staff.

There are nevertheless some areas where the government could assist the Savings Bank's operations. First, if it wishes an expansion of the Bank's rural banking services, it might provide a direct subsidy to support the additional costs. Secondly, it could provide a range of government or government-guaranteed securities through which the Savings Bank could invest on longer terms but with higher interest rates. Thirdly, it could make arrangements through which the Savings Bank could lend some surplus funds to both the Development

Bank and the soon-to-be-established National Housing Authority. However, with both the securities and loans, there must also be some rediscounting facility provided so that the Savings Bank could readily convert these investments into cash if required.

In addition to the normal assets and liabilities one might expect, the Savings Bank's agency rationalizations produced an accounting nightmare, and the time delays between the closure of the agencies and the receipt of the associated accounting records of those operations were considerable. Worse still, there were often substantial net unreconciled differences between the head office and agency savings account control cards. Many differences have been recovered, but there is currently a provision of some 4,000,000 vatu against the amounts owed by agencies to the Bank. As these are finalized, the bad debt portion has been written off, and in 1985 576,416 vatu was written off.

(iii) *Deposits*

As was shown in Table 4.9, deposits are the Savings Bank's major source of funds, and in 1985 accounted for some 96 per cent of total liabilities and capital. These may be accepted either in the form of a savings passbook account, or a term deposit. In late 1985 the Bank paid 4 per cent per annum on passbook savings and 5 per cent on term deposits: the maximum term deposit was for a one-year period. The passbook savings interest is calculated quarterly on the minimum balance and is credited to the account yearly: there is no compounding of the quarterly calculations.

As might be expected, the passbook is the key to the savings bank's success and it is used to transfer money throughout the island. The bulk of the Port Vila transactions, for example, are not with local residents, but rather with customers visiting the capital from the outer islands. In June 1985 the Savings Bank had some 15,000 customers. Indeed, as one government report commented, 'the Bank has become increasingly popular among the rural population to a point where a large portion of families in the country have at least one account'.[37]

While this customer base is seemingly desirable, the large number of accounts, small individual deposit levels, geographic spread of operations, and relatively poor interest-paying investment alternatives makes it difficult for the Bank to operate profitably. One alternative might be to lower the 4 per cent paid on savings deposits

TABLE 4.9   Vanuatu Co-operative Savings Bank: assets and liabilities,
30 June 1985

Assets:	
Fixed assets	683,539
Cash at bank or at hand	259,738,573
Sundry debtors	8,067,899
Owing from agencies	207,915
Owing from trading division	592,503
Commemorative coins	52,195
Total assets	269,342,624
Liabilities:	
Accumulated losses	(12,436,100)[a]
Fixed-asset revaluation reserve	634,336
Customer accounts	253,628,935
Provisions for future claims	1,000,000
Owing to agencies	894,853
Sundry creditors and accruals	25,620,600
Total liabilities	269,342,624

Note: The above accounts are preliminary figures and may be subject to adjustment.
[a] Figures in parentheses are losses.

Source: Vanuatu Co-operative Savings Bank (1985).

as there are little other alternatives available for rural savings. Indeed, as the commercial banks have withdrawn elsewhere within the islands, 'the savings bank has been able to take over business and provide some banking services, without which the commercial development of the various islands would probably have been seriously inhibited'.[38]

The Bank's expansion into rural areas, coupled with a growing rural involvement in the cash economy, has resulted, as shown in Table 4.10, in a steady growth of deposits, and by December 1985, these had reached around 260 million vatu. An equally important contributor to this growth has been the Bank's administration of the government salary payments in rural areas. Each fortnight the Savings Bank branches receives considerable funds, together with a listing of those government employees in its area. While the Savings Bank earns a fee of VT 100 per payment, more importantly, it gains potential access to the civil servant's savings.

As with the assets, the Bank's liabilities also reflect some of the

TABLE 4.10   Vanuatu Co-operative Savings Bank: deposits, 1980–85
(figures in millions of vatu for 30 June)

1980	118.8
1981	161.0
1982	163.6
1983	174.3
1984	213.3
1985	253.6

Source: Vanuatu Co-operative Savings Bank (1985).

unfinalized costs of agency rationalization. As of mid-1985, for example, the high level of sundry creditors reflects some VT 20, 802,964 of customer balances in suspense still not reconciled. There were similarly some moneys still owed to the former agencies which had also not been reconciled.

A major improvement in the Saving Bank's operations could be achieved through a restructuring in which the Bank would receive a substantial capital base. At present, as a division of the Federation, it does not have its own capital. This already presents a problem given the exchange losses on the Australian dollar deposits, and the pressure on margins caused by the sole reliance on vatu deposit-raising.

(iv) *Representation*

As shown in Table 4.11, the Vanuatu Co-operative Savings Bank operates some 20 branches in addition to its Vila head office, and as such has the greatest bank staff representation of any of domestic banks among the smaller Pacific island countries. The branches are somewhat different from what most Western bankers would expect, and to suggest they are modest establishments is something of an understatement. In a quite rational decision to keep rural network costs as low as possible, most branches operate from fairly simple rented premises. Indeed, often they just rent one room in the strongest permanent building in the village, install a secure door and a cash box, and the branch is in operation. While these facilities could easily be robbed by a determined thief, fortunately there is considerable honesty within rural areas, and theft is not expected to be a problem. Ideally, the Savings Bank would like to replace their cash boxes with safes and is currently seeking foreign aid assistance for this purpose.

TABLE 4.11   Vanuatu Co-operative Savings Bank branch locations and opening days, 1985

Branch	Location	Island area	Days open
Head Office	Port Vila	Efate	M T W Th F
Espíritu Santo	Luganville	Espíritu Santo	M T W Th F
Tanna	Lénakel	Tanna	M T W Th F
West Ambrm	Craig Cove	West Ambrm	- T - Th -
Ndui Ndui	Ndui Ndui	West Ambae	M - - - F
Port Olry	Port Olry	Espíritu Santo	M T W Th F
Lolowai	Lolowai	East Ambae	M T W Th F
North Ambrm	Magam	North Ambrm	M - W - F
Melsisi	Melsisi	Central Pentecost	- - W Th F
Abwatuntora	Abwatuntora	North Pentecost	- T W Th F
Panngi	Panngi	South Pentecost	- T - Th -
Paama	Liro	Paama	- T - Th -
Tongoa	Morua	Tongoa	M - W - F
Epi	Vaemali	Epi	- - - Th F
S.E. Ambrm	Utas	South-east Ambrm	- T - Th -
S.W. Bay	Wintua	South-west Malekula	- - - Th F
Mota Lava	Mota Lava	Mota Lava	M - - - F
Lamap	Lamap	South-east Malekula	- T - Th -
N. Malekula	Lakatoro	North Malekula	M T W Th F
East Tanna	Kitow	East Tanna	M - - - F

Source: Vanuatu Co-operative Savings Bank (December 1985).

In line with saving costs, and reflecting the level of local business, the branches are normally staffed with only one officer; the branches in Espíritu Santo, Lolowai, North Malekula and Tanna have two officers each. Similarly, not all branches open on a daily basis but rather twice, three, or four times a week. The specific positions are reflected in Table 4.11. As result, the smaller branches require relatively small amounts of operating cash, with a balance of 200,000 vatu or around US$ 2000 for most smaller branches. Only in the more active ones would amounts of up to 2,000,000 to 3,000,000 vatu be required.[39]

In addition to these permanent branches, the Savings Bank also operates a mobile banking service from their Espíritu Santo branch to a local high school, but poor road transport and small population centres would limit most potential mobile services to water rather than road transport.

While the Bank has no plans for additional branches in the immediate future, the National Development Plan calls for the Bank to open new offices in 'association with the DBV . . . where local Government Centres are to be established'.[40]

(vi) *Staffing*

In December 1985 the Savings Bank operated with a total of 39 staff of whom three were expatriates. Given the staffing requirements for the Bank's 20 branches, and the need to inspect their operations at least on a quarterly basis, it obviously operates with a very small head office staff. This is feasible as the Savings Bank only accepts a few fairly simple forms of deposits, and has no lending operations or other more complicated means of investing the resulting savings.

For the present it seems unlikely that the number of expatriate staff numbers will be reduced, as they are required to assist in the training and close supervision of the branch office operations. Indeed, a considerable expansion in expatriate numbers would be required before the Savings Bank could offer additional banking services.

In late 1985 it was hoped that a senior Savings Bank ni-Vanuatu employee, presently on a two-year banking course in the UK, will assume management of the Savings Bank in late 1986.

Development Bank of Vanuatu

The Development Bank of Vanuatu was established to provide loans for sound projects which were too small and lacked the size and security requirements for a commercial bank advance. In addition to normal lending, the Development Bank may also take equity positions, make guarantees, assist in project identification, evaluations, and promotion, and provide general consultancy work. More formally, under its revised legislation in 1983, the Bank is intended to 'facilitate and promote the economic development of the natural resources of Vanuatu with special regard to agriculture, forestry, fisheries, manufactures and tourism'.[41]

(i) *Development*

The Development Bank of Vanuatu was formed on 13 June 1979 as the Bank of Development of the New Hebrides under Joint Regulation No. 11 of 1979, and commenced operations on 1 September 1979. It assumed its present name in 1981 and is now regulated under the Development Bank of Vanuatu Act of 1983.

As with other Pacific countries, the Development Bank was created to absorb the specific lending operations of the colonial government. In the case of Vanuatu, these were the Agricultural and Industrial Loans Committee and the Housing Scheme for Colonial Officers.

The Agricultural and Industrial Loans Committee was established by Joint Standing Order No. 2 of 1965 to advise the government on loans

> to aid economic development by the provision of sound credit facilities of a nature not available from normal sources and to encourage the development of the land and industries by persons, companies or organizations to assist the production and revenues of the country.[42]

It was particularly active in making smaller loans for purchasing cattle and fencing wire, as well as some larger loans for a sawmill, prefabricated housing project, and an interisland trading vessel. Such lending was reportedly of 'great value in encouraging progressive farmers and stimulating production'.[43]

The Housing Scheme for Colonial Officers was less important as it was restricted only to government employees. It also never grew as large. It started with a small initial capital of 20,000 pounds sterling which had risen to 58,000 pounds sterling by 1968.

While these schemes provided the basis for the Bank's initial operations, it has since greatly expanded its loan portfolio, and as shown in Table 4.12, now has more than 518.3 million vatu in loans outstanding.

(ii) *Assets*

As shown in Table 4.13, the Development Bank holds approximately three-quarters of its assets in the form of loans and advances. These advances are generally for a longer term than normally available from a commercial bank, and often entail considerably more risk. Indeed, particularly with larger loans, the Bank is more concerned about the repayment capacity of the borrower than the collateral provided. It is also likely to place more stress on the borrower's past track record than a more conventional lending institution. Finally, its local evaluation procedures are often less complex than for a commercial bank loan. As one report explained these differences, 'the

TABLE 4.12   Development Bank of Vanuatu: loans outstanding, 1980–84
(figures in million of vatu)

1980	43.3
1981	150.8
1982	405.8
1983	423.9
1984	518.3

Source: Development Bank of Vanuatu (1985).

TABLE 4.13   Development Bank of Vanuatu: assets and liabilities,
31 December 1984

Assets:	
Fixed assets	8,822,086
Share investments	7,000,000
Deposits	12,804,536
Loans and advances	396,625,325
Other current assets	2,019,446
Sundry debtors	2,842,298
Interest receivable	1,968,640
Cash on deposit	91,320,725
Cash at bank or on hand	7,014,216
Total assets	530,417,272
Liabilities:	
Issued capital	200,000,000
Accumulated losses	(38,144,524)[a]
Grants	47,097,806
Guarantee funds	24,806,795
Other loans payable	194,628,379
Deferred exchange gains	69,984,957
Current loans payable	11,470,696
Accrued expenses	18,664,454
Other liabilities	1,908,709
Total liabilities	530,417,272

[a] Figures in parentheses are losses.

Source: Development Bank of Vanuatu (1984) *Fifth Annual Report*, pp. 22–3.

procedures followed by the Bank for granting of loans are simple, flexible, and far less time-consuming. The security insisted upon, for small but sound projects, is also the "minimal", and on the basis of which the commercial banks/lenders would generally hesitate to grant the loan'.[44]

The actual interest charge depends largely on the size of the loan and the purpose to which it is put. For example, loans for agricultural, fishing and cattle projects of less than 100,000 vatu are charged only 4 per cent interest, those up to 500,000 vatu, 5 per cent, and larger loans range between 8 and 12 per cent depending on whether they are refinanced or come from the Development Bank's own funds. Housing loans have a different interest rate schedule ranging from 6 per cent for housing loans under 500,000 vatu, to 8 per cent for loans up to 1,000,000 vatu, to 10 per cent for loans of 1,000,000 to 1,500,000 vatu. Finally the Bank's commercial loans charge between 12 to 14 per cent interest. In addition to the normal interest charges, the Development Bank also levies a service fee of 1 per cent of principal on all loans over 500,000 vatu. As a rule, 'the average amount per loan is highest in tourism, sea transport, and miscellaneous, and lowest in micro-loans, stock farming, fishing and agriculture'.[45]

The more aggressive stance in local lending, though, is not without its bad debts costs, and significantly in 1984 the Bank had provisions for doubtful debts of 100,542,765 vatu; an amount equal to over 20 per cent of its total portfolio of 497,168,090. It also has had to make provisions equal to 100 per cent of its remaining former Condominium loan portfolio of 21,099,954 vatu. While the Development Bank's advances are protected, in at least part, by a government guarantee fund, the Bank's experience with arrears, if not resolved, may present considerable future difficulties in educating rural borrowers about the banking system.

As the government's planners admit, some of the Bank's problems include the need to increase lending, setting aside large reserves for bad debt, 'inadequate loan recovery and other financial losses'.[46] The Bank, too, is ready to admit its difficulties are even more widespread and include 'general weakness of potential guarantees, the lack of clout of guarantee instruments themselves, the marginality and vulnerability of many projects which are financed, the mixed signals with respect to foreign investment and a generally poor mastery of business principles and management tools and skills'.[47] It will thus need to 'to be more prudent and diversify its risk better in the future'[48] as well as to adopt 'far more rigorous and conservative loan appraisal standards'.[49]

In terms of diversification, the Development Bank's past lending has been too concentrated in the Port Vila and Efate island areas, but it is now trying to increase its lending to other islands: in 1984 loans to Port Vila and Efate accounted for 24 per cent of new loan numbers and 46 per cent of the amount lent. For a major expansion in these areas the Bank will need to expand its branch representation considerably. Even with a extensive branch structure, such lending will be faced with the same basic problem that 'the fixed costs associated with any loan tend to be higher for loans outside of Efate [due to agency costs and follow-up tours] while smaller [and agricultural] loans generally represent lower interest rates and higher security risks'.[50] Even so, such expansion seems more than appropriate, for at present the Development Bank has not found sufficient projects on which to lend and as a result some 18.5 per cent of its assets were held in bank deposits.

As shown in Table 4.14, housing loans comprised the largest category of Development Bank outstandings in 1985 with 34 per cent of the total. This position reflects the Bank's assumption of the local housing loan portfolios of the Colonial government and Caisse Centrale de Cooperation Economique, rather than its current lending orientation. Thus this percentage is decreasing over time. For example, low cost housing loans accounted for some 48 per cent of total outstandings in 1983. Its emphasis today is instead on agricultural lending, and in 1984 agricultural-related projects accounted for 66 per cent of its new advances and 72 per cent of loan numbers. Indeed, once the National Housing Authority is established, the Development Bank is unlikely to provide additional housing finance.

While micro-loans account for only 3 per cent of the Bank's outstanding loans, they nevertheless are the most numerous form of the Bank's lending. They were introduced with government assistance in July 1981 for rural groups to borrow up to 50,000 vatu for up to two years at an interest rate of 6 per cent per annum. Since 3 June 1985 up to 75,000 vatu has been available for normal loans and 1,000,000 vatu for agricultural purposes. The funds are to be used to purchase materials for productive purposes such as copra driers, fences and buildings, outboard motors, lawn-mowers, sewing-machines, chain saws, barbed wire, wire netting, building materials, guttering, ovens, fishing nets, various tools, and agricultural spare parts.

The conditions for these loans are particularly attractive to rural borrowers as 'the Bank makes no stipulation at all for any personal contribution by the borrower. The only security asked for by the Bank in such cases is the personal guarantee of another villager or

TABLE 4.14   Development Bank of Vanuatu: loans outstanding, by type of borrower, 1985

	(%)
Housing	34
Industry and tourism	30
Transport	18
Agriculture and fishing	13
Micro-loans	3
Miscellaneous	2
Total	100

Source: Development Bank of Vanuatu (1985).

friend'.[51] Such an approach is probably a little too attractive for borrowers, and even the government admits that the Bank is taking 'high risks in granting many small loans on which the security is minimal'.[52] Perhaps not surprisingly, industry estimates suggest that almost half these micro-loans are in arrears.

As was shown in Table 4.13, the Development Bank's equity investments have been a very minor part of its operations and account for just over 1 per cent of Bank total assets. As shown in Table 4.15, most of these have been limited to a few million vatu and involve only five companies. Unfortunately these investments have not proved very successful and the Bank has since written off its total investments in both Vanuatu Cement Industry and Société SENAC.[53]

(iii) *Funding*

The Development Bank obtains a major portion of its funding (38.9 per cent in 1984) through loans from such bodies as the Asian Development Bank, Caisse Centrale de Cooperation Economique, European Investment Bank and European Development Fund. Such funds, though, are not available for general use but are rather provided through special refinancing schemes which are subject to special conditions. For example, the European Development Fund's facilities can only be used to finance small-scale agricultural projects. Most schemes also preclude housing finance or loans of over 30 million vatu. For larger loans the Bank must lend either from its own resources or co-finance the advance with off-shore institutions.

Besides being available only under certain conditions, most development bank facilities are subject to interest rate limitations on

TABLE 4.15   Development Bank of Vanuatu: equity investments, 1984

Firm	No. of shares	Cost in vatu
Vanuatu Cement Industries	– 4,000 B ordinary shares	4,000,000
Vanuatu Cement Industries	– 15,000 B pref. shares	15,000,000
Société SENAC SARL	– 21,600 ordinary shares	2,160,000
Island Products Ltd	– 20,000 ordinary shares	2,000,000
Less (Vanuatu) Ltd	– 20,000 redm. pref. shares	2,000,000
Melanesian Shell Products	– 30,000 ordinary shares	3,000,000

Source: Development Bank of Vanuatu (1984) *Fifth Annual Report*, p. 32.

advances made with these funds. For example, the Caisse Centrale de Cooperation Economique places a maximum of 8 per cent interest on the advances it refinances. The Asian Development Bank sets a maximum of 14 per cent.

After loan funds, the Bank's own capital resources are next in importance with 30.5 per cent of the total. This would obviously be much higher but for the effect of past losses. While the Bank's articles allow for up to 49 per cent private shareholdings, it remains wholly owned by the Vanuatu government.

The Development Bank has also received significant funds by way of special grants from the European Development Fund, the Caisse Centrale de Cooperation Economique of France and the Australian, French and New Zealand governments, as well as the Vanuatu government and the Central Bank of Vanuatu. As with the foreign loan facilities, most foreign grants were made for specific purposes. The New Zealand government grants, for example, were to fund small loans to rural ni-Vanuatu, while the Australian government grants were to acquire equity in locally incorporated industries.

Guarantee funds are another smaller source of funds and accounted for 4.7 per cent of the Bank's capital and liabilities in 1984. These are provided mainly by overseas agencies to support special project lending. The government also provides funds through this means and it is hoped that its current guarantee fund contribution of 5 million vatu will be expanded to 15 million vatu in 1986.

(iv) *Representation*

The Development Bank operates from its head office in Vila and, since 1981, from three branches in Espíritu Santo, Malakula and Tanna. The branches accept loan applications and assist potential borrowers with completing the forms. They are also responsible for loan recovery work. All actual loan processing, though, is done in the head office and mainly by ni-Vanuatu staff.

The lack of representation in more remote areas has been recognized by the government as inhibiting the Bank's development functions and it has wished 'to expand the National Development Bank network to major regional centres in order to assist local businessmen'.[54] Unfortunately, though, 'in spite of demand and of plans to that effect, further branch offices have not been set up basically because of staffing and cost constraints'.[55]

As a result, the Development Bank must work closely with a range of government agencies to supplement its own efforts. Understandably, the Department of Industry and the Directorate of Agriculture play the most important role in the Bank's evaluation process. More specific government sub-units include the Office for the Development of Enterprises and the Office for Extension Services.

One alternative for rapidly expanding the Bank's present representation, which has received at least some government consideration, is a possible merger between the Development Bank and the Co-operative Savings Bank. Industry interviews suggest that neither institution particularly supports this suggestion, but government development plans at least indicate that 'a merger of the VDB and the NCSB is envisaged in the medium term'.[56] It is unlikely, though, that any such merger will eventuate.

(v) *Staffing*

In late 1985 the Bank had a staff of 35 of which 5 were expatriates. These included the managing director, the accountant, the agricultural loans officer, the administrative officer, and the data processing manager. The accountant and data processing positions are expected to be localized over 1986 and 1987. Three of these positions have traditionally been filled by VSN (Volunteer of National Service) personnel. These are graduates providing a professional service to developing countries as their national service requirement to the French government, instead of serving in the military. The cost of the expatriates are covered mostly by their sponsoring organizations. As part of its localization programme, the Bank has been active in providing overseas training for its local staff and by late 1985 six staff members were on overseas training courses in France, Italy, Fiji and Western Samoa.

Other Development Institutions

In addition to the Development Bank of Vanuatu there are three foreign development finance institutions operating within the country: the Asian Development Bank, the Caisse Centrale de Cooperation Economique and the Commonwealth Development Corporation.

The Asian Development Bank, though headquartered in Manila, has established its regional representative office for the Pacific in Port Vila. Though the office itself is directly involved in lending operations, these are handled by Manila-based staff, and there is little question that local conditions are much better understood as a result of this full-time presence. The office also adds to Vanuatu's claim as the Pacific's major financial centre.

In terms of Vanuatu involvement, the Caisse Centrale de Cooperation Economique has been, and probably still is, the most important of the three institutions. It is the French government's development bank and is designed to assist French territories and former colonies as well as other developing countries. Within Vanuatu it has had a long lending history during the colonial period and was largely responsible for the establishment of the local Development Bank. It is still active in development lending and maintains a local branch or office in Port Vila to administer these loans.

The Commonwealth Development Corporation is the British government equivalent of the Caisse Centrale de Cooperation Economique and its involvement, too, dates back to the colonial period. In practice, though, it has had a more limited involvement and has tended to operate from its regional office in Suva rather than opening local branches. A representative office in Port Vila, though, is believed to be under consideration.

In 1985 the Corporation was in the process of a major agricultural development in Vanuatu's coffee and cocoa industries. At present its major investment is a 60 per cent shareholding in Metenesel Estates Ltd, a cocoa estate development on the island of Malakula. The Vanuatu government with 37 per cent, and the local landowners with 3 per cent, own the remaining shares. The end project will involve some 1700 hectares of planting as well as a processing factory. In addition to its 98.9 million vatu equity investment and the project's management, the Commonwealth Development Corporation will also lend some £3.4 million to the project and other foreign currency loans will similarly be available from the British Overseas Development Administration, and the Caisse Centrale de Cooperation Economique. The Commonwealth Development Corporation is also providing much of the financing and technical support for the Tanna Coffee Development Corporation coffee project on Tanna Island.

Merchant Banks

As of late 1985, there was one merchant bank in operation within Vanuatu, the Bank Gutzwiller, Kurz, Bungener (Overseas) Ltd. It was established in 1973 as a subsidiary of the Swiss banking firm of Banque Gutzwiller, Kurz, Bungener S. A., which is itself controlled by Bank Leu Ltd, one of Switzerland's five major domestic banks. Its Port Vila operations are primarily in the Euro-bond market where it has been particularly active as an underwriter of Euro-bond issues.

Over 1984 it served as lead manager to four Euro issues, co-manager of two, and an underwriter in 176 other Euro-bond issues. It has also been particularly active in marketing New Zealand dollar denominated issues, 'Kiwi bonds', within the European market. It has also conducted a number of specialized and fairly innovative capital raisings to include the first convertible, guaranteed zero bond issue (for a US company) and a serial note of US dollar floating-rate notes for a Dutch bank.

On 29 February 1984 the Bank had assets of US$ 11,700,000 and capital and reserves in excess of US$ 2,600,000.[57] In late 1985 the merchant bank had four staff, two of which were expatriates.

By early 1986 the merchant bank's future in Vanuatu seemed questionable. It is understood that with the recent tax incentives provided by the Cook Islands for off-shore financial institutions, together with that country's greater attraction with New Zealanders, the Bank Gutzwiller, Kurz, Bungener (Overseas) Ltd may well cease as an operational entity within Vanuatu and move its expatriate staff to Rarotonga. It will probably continue, at least as an exempt institution in Vanuatu, in that it has only recently established a local trust company subsidiary in Port Vila.

Insurance Companies

The insurance industry in Vanuatu is characterized by its complete domination by foreign insurance firms, with two operating as local branches and the others through local agents. By late 1985, as shown in Table 4.16, some ten companies were active in the market. Of these companies, QBE Insurance has had the longest involvement in

TABLE 4.16   Insurance companies licensed in Vanuatu, December 1985

Firm	Representation
Assurance Générale de France (AGF of France)	Agent
Commercial Union	Agent
General Accident	Agent
Groupement Français d'Assurances (GFA of France)	Agent
National of New Zealand	Branch
New Hampshire (an AIU affiliate)	Agent
QBE Insurance	Branch
Saravanua	Agent
Cigna (formerly INA)	Agent
UAP	Agent

Source: Industry interviews (1985).

the country. Initially it provided coverage through its agency arrangements with Burns Philp, and for the last 16 to 17 years it has also operated a branch office in Port Vila. Industry interviews indicate that QBE is certainly the market leader and some estimate it to have 60 to 65 per cent of the local premium market.

In addition to the direct insurers there are also three insurance brokerage companies in Vanuatu providing services both locally and on a regional basis. These include Melanesian Insurance Brokers, Bowring Burgess Marsh & McLennan (part of an international brokerage operation) and Vanuatu General Insurance Co. Ltd (affiliated with Ian Balfour's Panpacific Group). Most brokers place their business in London rather than with regional companies.

(i) *Regulation*

The insurance industry is regulated under Queen's Regulation No. 18 of 1973 and requires an annual license fee of A\$ 1,000. Insurance companies may register as either a local, external or an exempt insurer. An exempt insurer may neither cover risks within Vanuatu, nor solicit business for the public either in Vanuatu or overseas. In contrast both a local or external company can conduct public business. Locally-licensed insurers are subject to maintaining a minimum paid-up capital, minimum assets levels, investment restrictions, separate accounts for life and general business, and an actuarial evaluation at least every three years. Of these, the major requirement is the net asset requirement which is based on premium income. Those firms with premium income of less than A$ 700,000, for example, must have at least A$ 140,000 of assets in excess of their liabilities. Those with local premiums of A$ 700,000 to A$ 7 million should have assets in excess of their liabilities of at least one-fifth of their premium income. Finally, those firms with over A$ 7 million in premium income should have assets of at least A$ 1.4 million plus an amount equal to one-tenth of their premium income in excess of their liabilities.

As of late 1985 there was no insurance commissioner. Instead, the companies report quarterly to the Central Bank of Vanuatu as well as to the government statistical department. In addition to insurance companies themselves, the legislation also controls insurance agents, brokers, and salesmen, as well as reinsurance companies.

(ii) *Operations*

In 1985 industry interviews suggested that the local annual general insurance premium income was around A$2.5 million. Much of these funds, however, was directed overseas in the form of reinsurance coverage, as there is relatively little interchange between the companies within Vanuatu.

Of the premium income, motor-vehicle insurance is the most important with over a third of the total. Fire insurance and marine and hull and cargo would be next with around 20 to 25 per cent each. General accident and workers' compensation business would account for most of the remainder. At present, little life insurance business is written other than by some of the French companies.

Workers' compensation business, however, should pick up considerably as the government plans to pass a Workers' Compensation Act sometime in 1986, which will make such coverage compulsory for all employees in Vanuatu. It will probably be operated under a system of 'approved' insurers and possibly allow a cartel arrangement in regard to an approved set of rates.

Workers' compensation coverage presently operates through a dual system with different compensation cover provided for ni-Vanuatu and expatriate employees. In the case of ni-Vanuatu staff, for example, the policies are written so that any claims are based on the insurance laws of either Fiji or Papua New Guinea, and Papua New Guinea or New South Wales (Australia) in the case of expatriates.

The new workers' compensation legislation is believed to be based on a combination of the equivalent Papua New Guinea and Solomon Island legislation. It will hopefully be enforced more effectively than the current third party motor-vehicle coverage. Though third party coverage is required by the Joint Regulation No. 16 of 1967, it is apparently not enforced.

The fire insurance business has also undergone some recent changes due to bad underwriting experiences. Between 1980 and 1985 there have been nine cyclones in the Vanuatu group. In January 1985, for example, there were Eric, Nigel and Odette. While these, particularly Nigel, created substantial claims for the industry in early 1985, many residents of the most damaged urban area, on Espíritu Santo, had not bothered to take insurance cover. Indeed, few properties other than those required to do so as part of a bank mortgage were insured. With the reconstruction, these owners obviously had the funds to rebuild while the other owners did not: more owners may now seek coverage. Also the additional claims have been used to justify increased premium charges. For example, following cyclone Nigel, there has been an additional levy on fire insurance premiums for hurricane coverage as well as the requirement to have window storm-shutters in order to gain the coverage.

(iii) *Staffing*

Given the agency representation of most insurers, they are not presently a major source of employment. QBE is the largest employer with one expatriate and eighth ni-Vanuatu branch office staff. It also has two agents on Espíritu Santo and four other agents in Port Vila. In contrast, National of New Zealand has one expatriate and two ni-Vanuatu staff.

Superannuation

In late 1985, there were few private pension or superannuation plans in operation within Vanuatu. The largest of private plans was that for Burns Philp's Vanuatu employees. The scheme provides coverage for some 290 employees and was funded jointly by the employer and the employee with each contributing an amount equal to 5 per cent of the employee's salary. The money is then invested and the total contributions and related interest available on retirement.

While there was no formal decision on the matter in late 1985, those private plans offering employees equal or more attractive benefits than that provided under the new National Provident Fund would be allowed to continue in operation.

Vanuatu Commodities Marketing Board

While the Vanuatu Commodities Marketing Board is not a financial institution, through its Copra Stabilization Fund and STABEX payments deposits, it nevertheless controls considerable financial assets and is an important source of potential deposits within the financial sector.

The Board was established under the Vanuatu Commodities Marketing Board Act No. 10 of 1980 and commenced operations on 5 April 1982. Its main objectives were to rationalize 'the marketing of copra and getting the industry back into the hands of producers'.[58] The Board was to eliminate the profit spread previously taken by private, mainly expatriate, companies on copra exports, and thus provide higher prices to the producers. It also planned to 'direct its attention to other agricultural exports once the copra marketing situation is under control'[59] and now, in addition to handling copra, also authorizes private exports of cocoa and coffee.

As part of its marketing efforts, the Board established a price equalization scheme for copra in November 1982. This was funded with an initial grant from the EDF (European Development Fund) and has since received regular payments under the European Community's STABEX (Stabilization of Export Earnings) scheme.[60] By manipulating the domestic prices, the Board should accumulate sufficient funds during times of high copra prices to be able to pay higher prices when world prices are low. The latter position was in effect in late 1984, as it was paying the local equivalent of US$ 343 per ton compared to a world price of US$ 260 to 290. Hopefully the knowledge of a more stable price under the Fund will encourage small-holders to increase their production. It should also discourage them from deserting their trees in response to a large price reduction.

While the Board has thus far limited its stabilization fund to copra, it also receives STABEX payments for cocoa. A stabilization scheme will later be established for that crop. In the longer term, stabilization funds for coffee and kava are also possibilities.

Details of the Copra Stabilization Fund and its various other STABEX moneys are not publically available but are held mainly in overseas financial assets rather than vatu-denominated investments.

In addition to its marketing and stabilization fund efforts, the Board has also had a major impact on the over-all quality and hence saleability of Vanuatu's major export crop. The Board accomplished this by paying a premium for air- and sun-dried, as opposed to smoke-dried, copra.

Co-operative Societies

As in other Pacific island countries, the co-operative societies play an important role in Vanuatu's commercial life, particularly in rural areas. They include consumer retail and marketing, savings and loan societies (see credit unions), block-making societies, as well as a national apex society. The consumer retail and marketing societies are the most important group and account for 237 of Vanuatu's 246 societies. These are mostly dual-purpose societies involved with the marketing of their members' local produce (copra, cocoa and other products) and consumer retailing. Co-operatives, for example, distribute some 85 per cent of consumer goods within the islands.[61] In addition to these commercial functions, the co-operatives also help 'to train and educate in business methods people who have only recently entered business and the money economy'.[62]

The national apex organization for Vanuatu's co-operative movement is the Vanuatu Co-operative Federation Ltd. The Federation operates with two divisions, the trading division and the savings bank division, and is intended 'to market and distribute consumer goods and to provide shipping, wholesale and banking services'.[63] The banking functions are now performed solely by its Co-operative Savings Bank division (see pp. 225–34). Its trading division conducts bulk buying for its members and distributes these goods through a network of nine small warehouses. These are then sold by its some 200-member retail societies' village stores. This distribution is also assisted by the Federation's 51 per cent shareholding in Vanuatu Navigation Shipping Co. While the Vanuatu Commodities Marketing Board now handles the export of copra, the Federation is still active in the domestic collection of copra and other locally-produced commodities.

Historically, the co-operative movement in a formal sense dates to the passage of the country's first co-operative legislation. Joint Regulation No. 11 of 1962. As elsewhere in Vanuatu, the Registrar's function was performed jointly with the British supervising the English-speaking co-operatives with English rules and accounting methods, and the French supervising the French-speaking co-operatives with their rules and methods. There were similarly two apex-co-operative organizations established in 1973, one for the English (the New Hebrides Co-operative Federation) and one for the French (the Syndicat des Coopératives Autochtones sous Contrôle Français – SCAF). The New Hebrides Co-operative Federation subsequently changed its name to the Vanuatu Co-operative Federation Ltd in 1981 and the SCAF was liquidated when France withdrew much of its financial and technical assistance after Vanuatu's independence.

Prior to the Vanuatu Commodities Marketing Board's establishment in 1982, the Federation purchased much of Vanuatu's copra exports, but its operations differed from other co-operatives in that it 'was organized along company lines and profits were to be invested in local private enterprise rather than in further co-operative concerns'.[64] For example, through its New Hebrides Co-operative Investment Fund, the Federation invested directly in the shares of New Hebrides Abattoirs Ltd and Vila Timber Products.[65] These investments, though, were more related to furthering the Federation's own operations as it already had business dealings with these companies.

Partly as a result, the Federation has experienced financial problems over its life. For example, it is reported that 'only intervention by the British government saved the VCF from bankruptcy in 1976'.[66] The real problem, though, was basically due to the mismanagement of the opportunities created during the copra boom.[67] Similarly, in 1981 the government had to provide a A$ 60,000 grant so it could continue operations. New management was subsequently appointed in 1982 and the Federation today operates a trading profit.

There has also been progress on the industry's regulation, for in August 1982 a new Co-operative Society Act provided better regulation, and the two national services now operate as one department. At the individual society level, though, the movement still faces 'a legacy of 2 separate management and accounting systems'.[68]

Legally co-operatives, other than savings and loan societies, cannot provide credit to their members or accept deposits, but in the past many societies have nevertheless done both,[69] and even today credit purchases occur on a *de facto* basis in some organizations. Indeed, a common reason for failures within the co-operative movement is such members' credit.[70] While deposits would not present the same danger, there is still the difficulty of safeguarding the resulting money. With the closing of the Co-operative Savings Bank agencies, some co-operatives have returned to a previous practice of accepting member deposits on a *de facto* basis through share purchase and resale schemes. Under these arrangements a member can purchase shares in addition to his required allotment for membership. In contrast to the required shares, these extra shares then receive interest (technically a dividend) at a rate of 6 per cent per annum. When the member requires these extra funds, the shares themselves can then be repurchased by the society or by other members. While a number of societies utilize this system, the amount raised is not significant.

As with other Pacific countries, the co-operative movement offers considerable potential for business development at the village level and over time should become even more important as a vehicle for rural development. Various government extension programmes now assist the establishment of village enterprises and since 1984 the International Human Assistance Program's small business project has also helped in this area.

As co-operatives become used for additional business purposes, the existing legislation may require some modification and amendments to allow specialized fishing co-operatives, housing co-operatives, credit unions, handicrafts, and producer and land-use co-operatives are presently under consideration.

Credit Unions

As with other Pacific countries, the credit union movement in Vanuatu was established during the colonial period and initially operated as savings and loan co-operative societies rather than credit unions. This was because the co-operative legislation did not provide for the establishment of credit unions. In practice, however, there is really no difference in their respective operations.

The first of these savings and loan co-operative societies, the Vila Civil Servants' Savings and Loan Society, was established in Vila in 1964 with a membership limited to those civil servants working for one of the three government services. Its operations were initially a success, and by the end of 1964 it had accumulated deposits of £2800 loans of £1460, and investments overseas of £1200.[71]

Other savings and loans societies were later established, and by 1971 there were three urban savings and loan societies and two rural societies. The latter two had been established on the island of Aoba in 1970 and 1971.[72]

These societies were apparently sufficiently successful to be still in operation when the Co-operative Savings Bank was established in 1975. These operations, however, were not sufficient to justify competition with the new institution, and the Savings Bank effectively absorbed their business.[73]

In December 1985 there were no credit unions legally operating in Vanuatu. However, there has been some discussion of re-establishing the movement within the country. In this regard it is understood that the Catholic Church under Bishop Lambert has expressed particular interest in credit unions.

Finance Centre

The Finance Centre is probably the best known and least understood component of Vanuatu's financial sector. First, the Finance Centre itself does not exist as a specific institution, nor does it have any official standing within the country. It is simply the local name for Vanuatu's off-shore international financial activities. It reflects the marketing effort of the local professional association of firms active in this off-shore business, the Finance Centre Association. While there is no legal requirement for local firms to join this Association or for non-residents to use their services, in practice virtually all of Vanuatu's off-shore business involves Association members.

As an international financial centre Vanuatu is still relatively small, but it still must compete both regionally with other newer Pacific entrants, and internationally with the full range of off-shore financial centres or tax havens from Panama and the Cayman Islands to Singapore and Liechtenstein. It thus offers a substantial range of fiscal incentives to attract international business, to include the complete absence of personal or corporate taxation, capital gains tax, property tax, withholding tax, estate duties, inheritance taxes, exchange controls, gift taxes, or tax treaties with other countries. Unlike some other financial centres, these taxation measures apply to residents as well as non-residents.

Given that few people think of Vanuatu when discussing tax planning measures, the country might seemingly have little chance of competing for international business. In practice, though, it does offer some specific advantages over its competitors.

Oddly, what might appear a substantial disadvantage, its location in the mid-Pacific, is actually a great advantage. The significance is that Vanuatu's time zone spans the opening day of most of the world's major markets. Thus, when Port Vila's business day starts at

7:30 a.m., it is 3:30 p.m. on the previous day in New York City. Similarly, Vanuatu's afternoon extends to morning the same day in London. As it is also open during most of the East and South-east Asian business day, clients can easily conduct their business through Vanuatu. This position is particularly helpful in international foreign exchange trading, and is assisted by Vanuatu's excellent satellite-based telecommunications system.

Vanuatu also has the advantage of using what is basically a British set of business regulations as well as using English as an official language within government agencies and in its regulations.[74] There is also a good selection of licensed banks, financial institutions, solicitors[75], accountants[76] and trust companies to support these off-shore activities, and the cost of both these services and related government charges are competitive with similar off-shore centres. The country also has the advantage of a stable and democratic political system, and a domestic currency linked with the International Monetary Fund's Special Drawing Rights.

The various taxation measures and other concessions offered to attract off-shore business are not without their benefits and the government, through various registration fees and stamp duty charges, gains some US$ 1.5 million in direct revenues. Company registration, incorporation and licensing alone earned 121.8 million vatu in 1984 and shipping business fees another 11.5 million vatu. In addition, the Finance Centre provides employment for some 200 ni-Vanuatu and 148 expatriate staff. Besides providing additional expertise and training for the local economy, the latter group also contributes to government revenues through import duties and other charges and adds some US$ 10 million to the over-all economy.[77]

(i) *Development*

Vanuatu's off-shore business centre was created by the British National Service of the Condominium government in 1970 and is based on three principle pieces of legislation: the Banking Regulation of 1970, the Company Regulation of 1971, and the Trust Company Regulation of 1971. In terms of significance, the companies legislation is probably the most important. It replaced the Companies Act of 1948 and was patterned closely on the financial centre's regulations used in the British West Indies and Bermuda.

Though the new centre quickly attracted a number of international banks, its early period was characterized more by individual and

TABLE 4.17 Registered companies in Vanuatu, 1976–85[a]

	1976	1977	1978	1979	1980	1981	1982	1983	1984	1985[b]
Local	263	255	271	276	291	341	384	372	405	418
Exempt	469	480	480	473	505	555	584	516	600	642
Overseas	41	41	40	35	36	34	34	36	34	40
	773	776	791	784	832	930	1002	924	1039	1100

[a] In addition to those shown there are an additional 250 firms still registered under local French company law provisions.
[b] Registrar of Companies estimate for October 1985

Source: *Republic of Vanuatu First National Development Plan, 1982–1986* (1982) (Port Vila: National Planning Office) p. 79 and Central Bank of Vanuatu (1984) *Annual Report and Statement of Account for 1984*, p. 23.

small company tax avoidance rather than major international business. Indeed, it was apparently not uncommon for people to visit Vanuatu with 'suitcases full of money'.[78] In this early period Australian businessmen and investors provided a large portion of the business, and one study in 1982 estimated that 'twenty-five per cent of the Finance Centre clientele is made up of Australian companies'.[79] This dominance, however, quickly changed in 1974, when the Australian Taxation Commissioner made Vanuatu a scheduled category requiring special exchange control approval for any Australian transactions: a position which still applies today. Given its time zone position, Asia now dominate the Vanuatu market, and in recent years 'most business growth comes from Hong Kong (which in 1984 accounted for about half of Port Vila's foreign business) and to a lesser extent the rest of South East Asia'.[80]

This growth is reflected in the number of companies registered, as shown in Table 4.17. Of the 642 exempt firms in October 1985, 95 were exempt banks and financial institutions and 36 were exempt insurance companies.[81] Although the amount of business or assets of these companies is not publicly available, one estimate in 1982 suggested that 'three to four thousand million US dollars make their home in Vanuatu'[82] and industry interviews in late 1985 suggested that they are now in excess of US$ 5 billion.

While there has been an obvious commercial incentive to maintain client secrecy, the government's Confidential Relationships (Preservation) Act 1984 specially states that client information cannot be provided without the client's permission unless by order of Vanuatu's

Supreme Court. Violators are subject to a fine of 500,000 vatu and a two-year jail sentence. While information can be obtained through a Supreme Court action, it is significant that the Australian Tax Commisioners attempt to gain such information in March 1984 on certain accounts was unsuccessful. As the court commented, the secrecy provisions are 'one of the pillars of this part of our economic structure, the destruction of which would lead to the collapse of the whole structure which it supports'.[83]

(ii) *Operations*

Off-shore business in Vanuatu may be conducted through a corporation, trust, partnership, or an individual. There are no comparable statistics for these categories. Due to the costs and secrecy provisions, trusts are probably the most common form for conducting off-shore business, but most larger clients would operate through exempt companies or possibly a combination of trusts and exempt companies.

A book could literally be written on these various off-shore activities, but it is appropriate to give at least some flavour of the Centre's operations. Thus here are some very brief details on the exempt and local companies, trusts, shipping, and the Finance Centre Association. The Centre's exempt banks, exempt insurance companies, and trust companies, are treated separately in their own sections (see pp. 257–70).

1. *Exempt and local companies*   As with other countries, Vanuatu corporate law allows for the incorporation of local companies and the registration of branches of overseas incorporated firms. The Company Regulation of 1970, though, provides an additional alternative, that of an exempted company. An exempted company differs from the other categories as it is not allowed to conduct business in Vanuatu, except with other exempted companies. The advantage of this form is that an exempt company's share registers and other company documents are not open to the public inspection. Furthermore, through the use of nominee shareholders and directors, the beneficial ownership of the firm can be further concealed. Prior to 1984 the Registrar of Companies required the government be informed of the beneficial owners of each exempt company, but this is now applied only with an exempt bank, financial institution or insurance company.

Exempt companies serve a wide range of international business purposes but typically are used as an international holding or trading company for re-invoicing and commission payments; to bill professional, other services, and plant rental; to form international joint ventures; to hold patents, copyrights, royalty agreements and franchise fees; to conduct back-to-back lending. To provide one example, that of reinvoiced sales – an overseas exporter bills his Vanuatu company for $10,000 but the Vanuatu company then bills the ultimate purchaser with the agreed price of say $11,000 . . . This has the effect of reducing the tax planner's home country taxable income by $1,000 and accumulating $1,000 tax free'[84] in his Vanuatu subsidiary.

The incorporation of an exempt company is neither difficult nor costly and a firm can have as few as two shares with only a nominal par value (typically US$ 2.00 in paid-up capital). While the company's business is required to be outside of Vanuatu, the firm is required to have a local registered office. This office in turn must maintain a shareholder register, a register of officers and directors, and a register of charges. There must also be proper accounting records, and if these are not kept in Vanuatu, the local registered office must have sufficient details to prepare a balance sheet and profit and loss account on a six-monthly basis. None of these documents, though, need be available for public inspection. In addition, one director must be resident in Vanuatu and the company must hold at least one directors' meeting each year within Vanuatu: this requirement is normally fulfilled by the registered agent.

Most Finance Centre Association members have shelf companies on hand for immediate sale to clients, or can arrange for the incorporation of a new firm within 48 hours. The minimum direct costs of incorporation are approximately US$ 1059, with the government receiving at least US$ 400 of this as the registration fee. There would be at least an additional US$ 400 per year annual government registration fee plus some US$ 550 to 775 per year for a local agency to perform the annual management duties within Vanuatu. In addition, unless the shareholders give an unanimous agreement to waive the requirement, there is also an annual audit fee.

2. *Trusts*   As an alternative to incorporation, a discretionary or fixed trust offers a number of advantages. First, there is no incorporation or annual registration fees. Indeed, the Vanuatu government only receives some 7500 vatu (US$ 75) in stamp duties when the trust deed is established: there are no further payments. The costs, then, are really only related to those charged by a Finance Centre Association

member for the trust deed and for acting as the trustee. Most firms charge a fee based on a percentage of the trust's market value, with a minimum charge of around 35,000 to 40,000 vatu (US$ 350 to 400) per year.

The key advantage afforded by a Vanuatu trust is that there are no disclosure requirements in regards to a trust's principles or beneficiaries. These details are held in secretary by the trustee and even the Vanuatu government is not told the details. As a result, trusts can provide an additional layer of privacy in an exempt company by having the shares held by a trust rather than directly by the beneficial owner or his nominee.

Most trusts are discretionary or unit trusts with the trustee given a wide range of powers to accumulate and distribute the capital. The vesting power of trust can be postponed up to 89 years and the distribution of income postponed for up to 21 years.

3. *Shipping*   In addition to Vanuatu's more traditional off-shore business, it has also, since 1981, offered a ship registration service. This business is managed by Investors' Trust Ltd as the Vanuatu government's acting Maritime Administrator. Vanuatu Maritime Law and Regulations closely follow that of Liberia. Coopers & Lybrand offices act as the agents for the Maritime Commission overseas. The actual registration is conducted in New York City and the Deputy Commissioner of Maritime Affairs is formerly of the Liberian maritime service. In 1984 there were 56 ships registered on the Vanuatu register, compared with 22 in 1983.[85]

In support of these activities, Finance Centre Association members are active in the formation and management of exempt shipping companies. These firms offer a number of advantages to include secrecy of operations, no trade union agreements or regulations on crew engagements, low registration fees, no income tax payable, no stamp duties on ship mortgages, and no audit requirements.

4. *Finance Centre Association*   As mentioned, the Finance Centre Association has no formal legal status within Vanuatu. In practice, however, its members have a major influence on government policies in the off-shore business matters, and are involved in most off-shore transactions. The Association was created specifically as a lobby group so that the off-shore finance industry would be able to express a common viewpoint to the government.

There is little question that it has had a major impact on improving

Vanuatu's attractiveness compared to other off-shore centres, and since 1979 a special joint committee of Finance Centre Association and government representatives, chaired by the Ministry of Finance, has met monthly to discuss ways in which the Centre's operations could be improved, and must report its findings at least every six months to Vanuatu's *de facto* cabinet, the Council of Ministers.[86]

Association members are also active in promoting Vanuatu's off-shore services, and in 1983 a 13-man Joint Vanuatu Government-Finance Centre Association mission conducted seminars in both Hong Kong and Singapore. This mission, combined with other measures, was specifically designed to 'attract more business from South East Asia and particularly Hong Kong'.[87]

In December 1985, the Finance Centre Association consisted of 17 different members, each of which belonged to one of the Association's four sub-groups: licensed banks or financial institutions, solicitors, accountants and trust companies. The Association's chairman rotates between the four groups.

Exempt Banks

Exempt banks comprise another important aspect of Vanuatu's Finance Centre. As with other international banks, they are active in accepting deposits; lending; providing guarantees, letters of credit, and acceptances; nominee services; and financial advice. They differ from Vanuatu's domestic banks in that they may not accept deposits from, or otherwise conduct banking business with, Vanuatu residents; that they are exempt from Central Bank of Vanuatu regulations; and for the most part are operated by Vanuatu's trust companies, accounting firms, solicitors, and local commercial banks on the basis of telex and facsimile machine instructions from off-shore owners. By their nature, exempt banks in Vanuatu have no full-time local staffing.

The provision of exempt banking licenses is an important part of Vanuatu's role as international financial centre and as part of government policy, 'the expansion of offshore banking activities will be encouraged by continuing to provide a favourable commercial environment'.[88]

Given this interest in expansion, it might be thought that almost anyone could establish an exempt bank, and there is nothing in the legislation to suggest otherwise. In practice, Vanuatu has not been quite so free with its licenses. Only with those banks already licensed elsewhere overseas are the applications so straight forward. To a slightly lesser extent, a multinational company, who wishes to use an exempt bank for its internal use, also should have no problems. It is with individuals that the government is more selective. The potential loss of depositors' funds, even though these may be non-resident deposits, is the government's main concern. Few Vanuatu exempt banks deal with the public; they are strictly in the wholesale market. As the Minister of Finance, Kalpokor Kalsakau, commented on his Finance Centre regulations, 'to keep it clean banks, insurance companies, and trust companies all must make disclosures'.[89]

(i) *Development*

As with other aspects of Vanuatu's Finance Centre, the exempt banking and financial institution industry developed from the British National Service's efforts in the early 1970s. In the case of banking, this resulted from the Banking Regulation of 1970. Over time, the number of exempt banks and financial institutions have risen gradually. In 1981, for example, there were some 56 companies compared to 68 in 1982, 72 in 1983, and 84 in 1984.[90] Their assets have have similarly grown significantly from an estimated US$ 1.9 billion in 1981 to some US$ 2.9 billion in 1983.

Most of these exempt banks and financial institutions originate from Asia, American and Europe and, as shown in Table 4.18, many represent some the world's major banking and international business groups. While all may not have such an obvious direct connection, some find that a different named institution in Vanuatu affords them greater flexibility and more diversity in their international operations.

(ii) *Regulation*

In contrast to the locally-licensed banks, exempt banks are not controlled by the Central Bank of Vanuatu, and thus have no ratio requirements, liquid asset holdings, mandatory reserves, client lending restrictions, interest rate ceilings or qualitative operational guidelines. Exempt banks are, instead, controlled by the Registrar of Companies, but its requirements are not particularly difficult to fulfill.

The Registrar is concerned, however, with the initial licensing process, and more importantly with the bank's purpose and owners.

TABLE 4.18   Banks and financial institutions in Vanuatu registered under
the Banking Regulations, 31 December 1984

AAB Bank (Pacific) Ltd
Alta Pacific International Bank Ltd
American Alliance Bank Ltd
Anglo Asean Bank and Trust Ltd
Armour General Bank Ltd
Asean Investment Bank Ltd
Asia Credit International Bank Ltd
Asiac Bank Ltd
Asian and Pacific Commercial Bank Ltd
Asian Bank Ltd
Asian Oceanic Bank Ltd
Associated Bank Ltd
ATB International Bank Ltd
Australia and New Zealand Banking Group Ltd
Australia and New Zealand Savings Bank Ltd
Australian International Ltd
Australian United Corporation Ltd
Ayala International Capital (Vila) Ltd
Ayala International Finance (Vila) Ltd
Bank Gutzwiller, Kurz, Gungener (Overseas) Ltd
Bank of Earl International Ltd
Bankhaus Schneider and Munsing Ltd
Banque Nationale de Paris
Banque Nationale de Paris (Vila) Ltd
Barclays Asia (Vila) Ltd
Barclays Bank International Ltd
BBL International Bank Ltd
Binning Pacific Bank Ltd
Broad Rich Bank Ltd
Catham International Bank Ltd
Cathay International Pacific Bank Ltd
Commercial Bank of Hong Kong (Overseas) Ltd
Crorebridge Bank Ltd
Dao Heng Bank Vanuatu Ltd
Equities Bank Ltd
European Bank Ltd
European Commercial Bank Ltd
Far East Bank (Vanuatu) Ltd
First Bangkok City Bank (Overseas) Ltd
First Chicago Australia Ltd
First Europe Bank Ltd
First Financial Bank Ltd
First Pacific Bank Ltd
Global Bank Ltd

continued on page 260

TABLE 4.18   *continued*

Golden Peninsula Bank Ltd
GSP International Bank Ltd
Grand Credit Bank Ltd
Hongkong and Shanghai Banking Corporation
Indosuez Asia (Vanuatu) Merchant Bank Ltd
Industrial Development Banking Corporation Ltd
Intercontinental Bank Ltd
International Banking Co. IBC Ltd
International Commerce Bank Ltd
Investors Trust Ltd
JCG Bank Ltd
KG Bank Ltd
Kredietbank Luxembourg (Pacific) Ltd
Lincoln National Bank Ltd
Liu Chong Hing Bank (International) Ltd
McKenney Bank Ltd
Melanesia International Trust Co. Ltd
Meridian Financial Ltd
Middle East Arabian Banking Corporation Ltd
Mountain Credit Bank Ltd
Multilight Bank International Ltd
Multinational Bank (Vanuatu) Ltd
National Australia Bank Ltd
National Bank of Canada (Pacific) Ltd
National Security Bank Ltd
NMB Bank Pacific Ltd
Northwestern Bank of Commerce Ltd
Pacific Bank Ltd
Pacific International Bank Ltd
Pacific Investment Bank Ltd
Pacific Orient Bank Ltd
Security and General Bank Ltd
SHK Bank Ltd
SIH (Vila) Ltd
South East Asia Bank Ltd
Stanbridge International Bank Ltd
Suma International Bank Ltd
Trans Pacific International Bank Ltd
Transworld Bank Ltd
Union Credit Bank Ltd
Unipacific Bank Ltd
United National Bank Ltd
Unity International Bank Ltd
Universal Bank Ltd
Wardley International Bank (Vila) Ltd
Wardley Ltd
West European Bank Ltd

Western Pacific Bank Ltd
Westhan Bank Ltd
Westpac Banking Corporation
Westpac Savings Bank Ltd
WFI Banking Co. Ltd
Worldwide Guaranty Bank Ltd
Wuthelam International Bank Ltd
Yorker International Bank Ltd

Source: *Republic of Vanuatu Official Gazette* (1985).

In the case of an existing financial institutions from a recognized well-regulated country, it would find it very easy to establish a local banking subsidiary. Indeed, industry interviews suggest that a well-known and established financial institution might be able to incorporate an exempted bank or financial institution with as little as $ 2 in paid-up capital. In practice, though, one million vatu is considered the minimum amount: the capital can be denominated and paid in any currency and need not be deposited in Vanuatu.

An exempt bank or financial institution established by individuals or a normal company is another matter, and at least 15 million vatu (approximately US$ 150,000) in paid-up capital is required even if it is to be used only for in-house transactions: a considerably larger paid-up capital is required if the bank or financial institution plans to accept deposits from the public. In the case of a company, the Registrar must be provided with full details of its beneficial owners as well as past corporate and personal financial statements: these details, however, are kept secret. The principles or their managers must also provide evidence of their banking knowledge and experience as well as independent character references. Finally, they are required to sign a formal undertaking that their bank will deal only in-house and not with the public at large.

Once licensed, the exempt banks and financial institution must provide external audited accounts annually, but these reports are kept secret, even from the Central Bank of Vanuatu. They must also notify the Registrar of Companies of any change in the bank's beneficial ownership: the new owners must be approved by the Minister of Finance before the transfer can be allowed. As with other exempt companies, the exempt banks must maintain a registered office in Vanuatu (normally the office of an accounting firm, solicitor or trust Company), have at least one director resident in Vanuatu (normally a nominee provided by the register agent), maintain

TABLE 4.19   Costs for establishing an exempt bank in Vanuatu, 1985

Company Registrar's fee	400
Bank license	3,000
Trust company fee for incorporation	750
Other charges	50
Trust company first annual service fee	750
Total initial costs	US$ 4,950

Source: Investors' Trust Ltd (1985).

certain financial and corporate records, and hold at least one directors' meeting a year locally (again usually done via the registered agent). In practice, most exempt banks are technically managed, sometimes actually managed by a Finance Centre Association member firm. The major difference between a bank and a financial institution under the Banking Regulations is that a bank has the power to accept deposits withdrawable by cheque, while a financial institution does not. A bank must also include the word bank or a foreign derivative thereof in its name, while a financial institution cannot. The choice depends on the client's purpose, but most exempt institutions are locally-incorporated exempt banks. A foreign bank could chose to apply for an exempt licensed branch, but for most institutions the major tax advantages would be removed.

Most banking licenses are submitted though a Finance Centre Association member, and it said that on the receipt of all client's paperwork, they can establish a fully operational exempt bank or financial institution within two weeks. The costs involved vary from member to member firm, but seem to range between around US$ 5000 to 7000. A breakdown of the fees are shown in Table 4.19. In addition, each year US$ 400 must be paid to the Registrar for corporate registration, US$ 3000 for the banking license renewal, and US$ 750 to 1500 a year for the trust company or other registered agent. There will be additional fees, of course, if the exempt bank uses its local agent to manage the bank's affairs or otherwise becomes involved with its operations.

(iii) *Operations*

While it might appear that there would be little need for legitimate institutions to have banking subsidiaries in tax havens, they can provide many advantages both to international banks and business companies. For example, they can be used for intergroup financing, back-to-back loans, to gain interbank rates for on-lending funds to other group companies, showing bank deposits on company balance sheets, moving group international liquid assets into one tax and exchange controls free account, and gaining access to the international foreign exchange markets.

A captive bank is a particular advantage for a multinational company, for by using it for its international banking transactions, it, rather than an independent bank, can invest the international float these flows involve. In addition, the relatively few operational restrictions on exempt banks also allow them to act as a holding company, for group investments or other international trading operations, as well as traditional banking business.

Finally, wealthy individuals may use a captive bank for back-to-back lending of funds back to their home country, whereby the interest paid is tax deductible with local tax authorities, and the income earned by the Vanuatu bank, tax free.

A different approach to Vanuatu financial institutions has been used by Australian companies. These tended to operate as an overseas branch rather than as subsidiary. This is because the Australian Taxation Office is then more likely to approve the transactions. The advantage of Vanuatu for these companies was once the avoidance of interest-withholding tax and foreign exchange controls on international transactions. For the non-trading banks, it also gave them the advantage, prior to the wholesale granting of Australian foreign exchange licenses, of having a foreign exchange license which was unavailable to them in Australia. For the Australian trading banks, it also meant that these banks could establish an international loan portfolio without the costs of the then Statutory Reserve Deposits and Liquid and Government Securities ratios.

As mentioned, under law the Registrar of Companies can provide no details concerning the exempt banks' operations. The Minister of Finance, Mr Kalsakau, however, has commented publicly that 'exempted banks and trust companies are handling about $50 million each and every day'.[91]

Exempt Insurance Companies

The exempt insurance companies represent the least-developed aspect of Vanuatu's off-shore financial centre. As with other insurance

TABLE 4.20   Costs for establishing an exempt insurer in Vanuatu, 1985 (in US$)

Company Registrar's fee	400
Insurance license	1,000
Trust company's incorporation service	575
Miscellaneous disbursements	50
Trust company's annual statutory service	1,000
Total cost	3,025

Source: Investors' Ltd (January 1985).

companies, they are regulated under the Insurance Regulation of 1973 and, in October 1985, 36 companies were registered as exempt insurers.

While an exempt insurance company is not subject to Vanuatu's normal insurance regulations, and as exempt company operations are 'in-house' rather than with the public, there is not the same level of selectivity in exempt insurance licensing as there is for exempt banks and financial institutions. For example, there are no paid-up capital requirements or need for the beneficial owners to show experience in the area. There is a need to reflect management competence, but this is normally achieved by using a Finance Centre Association member experienced in this line of work.

The cost of establishing an exempt insurance company is shown in Table 4.20. In addition, there are annually costs of US$ 400 a year for the company registration and US$ 1000 a year for the insurance license. The trust company's annual management fee varies as to the work required. The basic fee reflects the normal statutory register agents duties required for exempt companies, as well as an agreement to provide the necessary experience in the insurance business. The actual cost of the latter depends on the type of service. One firm's charges, for example, ranged from US$ 20 to 70 per hour.

Exempt insurance companies operate as what are called captive insurance companies, in that they are created by their owners to cover their own 'in-house' insurance requirements. This activity is not limited to intracompany business. For example, certain professional groups, such as doctors or solicitors, may find it an advantage to provide their professional liability coverage through a captive company.

These companies provide the coverage their parents require and then generally offset their exposure through reinsurance with commercial insurers. Thus, through a captive insurer, the parent company can avoid the brokerage and most other administrative fees the commercial insurers normally include in the premium. As the captive deals in the wholesale market as an insurer itself, it may also be able to provide its owner with more suitable coverage than is normally available in commercial policies.

The concentration of an international firm's over-all insurance cover into one captive company has a number of advantages. First, at least some of the over-all risk exposure is reduced simply by the diversity of risks in the portfolio. Similarly, by providing potential reinsurers a much larger and more diversified portfolio, the captive will quite likely negotiate better terms and conditions than if the business was placed directly in each of the countries concerned.

In some cases, though, captive companies operate simply as a vehicle for self-insurance whereby the owner places sufficient funds aside each year in the captive to cover his potential claims. A company could always self-insure against most risks by creating internal reserves from its own profits, but a captive insurer would be more effective as premiums paid to the company are tax deductible whereas under the reserves method, deductions are available only when the loss occurs.

Once placed with their Vanuatu insurer, these investments are not subject to any foreign exchange controls, and any earnings are, of course, tax free. This in itself offers a substantial advantage over most self-cover schemes. Similarly, without the added cost of taxation, the captive can generate its reserves faster and hence retain a greater portion of the company's risks. A captive could, if managed properly, also undertake some reinsurance business in return to further reduce its over-all costs.

Besides the obvious tax advantages, the insurance laws in many countries make it difficult to establish new insurance companies even for simply captive business. Where new companies are possible, they would still be subject to considerable operational restrictions, all of which could be avoided by incorporating the captive off-shore. Vanuatu has a further advantage in that the exempt company's records are covered by the country's strict secrecy provisions.

Generally, captive insurers incorporated in Vanuatu are also managed from Port Vila through a registered agent. Unlike some other aspects of the Finance Centre's off-shore business, captive insurers offer the greatest potential for local management agreements, in that the owning companies (as they are not in the insurance industry themselves) are more likely to hire professional advisors than to undertake the business management directly.

Despite the numbers of exempt companies, off-shore insurance business is not yet one of Vanuatu's stronger areas. In late 1985, for example, there were really no local reinsurance companies operating within the country, nor underwriting expertise within the trust companies or other support bodies. This may change, however, in the near future. The internationally affiliated Bowring Burgess Marsh & McLennan of New Zealand incorporated a local Vanuatu insurance brokerage firm in 1985 to 'provide risk management and insurance broking services to not only the financial centre based here but also the surrounding Pacific islands'.[92]

Trust Companies

The local trust companies are among the most important components of Vanuatu's Finance Centre and provide a full range of financial and administrative services to potential clients. They are licensed under the Trust Company Regulation 1971 and, as with the Centre's solicitors and accounting firms, may deal with both off-shore and local business. Each of these firms are required to have an operational presence within the country and exempted companies cannot obtain a trust company license.

(i) *Development*

As with the other aspects of the Vanuatu Finance Centre, the local trust company developed in conjunction with the government's legislation of the early 1970s. In the case of the trust companies, the specific legislation was the Queen's Regulation No. 6 of 1971 (then the New Hebrides Trust Company Regulation of 1971). Even so, some firms, such as Investors' Trust Ltd, founded in 1969, were incorporated before the Act, but did not really commence business until 1972.

Many of the older trust companies were established by consortiums of domestic and off-shore banks, as well as other financial institutions. Melanesia International Trust Co. (Melitco), for example, was founded in 1970, with its shares held 45 per cent by the ANZ, 19 per cent by Barclays, 22 per cent by Hongkong and Shanghai Banking Corporation, 6 per cent by the Bank of Bermuda, and 8 per cent by Australian International Finance Corporation. Pacific International

TABLE 4.21   Major trust companies in Vanuatu, 1985

Asiaciti Trust Co. Ltd
Gestinpac
Helvetia Overseas Trust Co. Ltd
International Finance Trust Co. Ltd
Investors Trust Ltd
Melanesian International Trust Co. Ltd
Pacific International Trust Co. Ltd
Vanuatu International Trust Co.

Source: Industry interviews (1985).

Trust Co. (PITCO) was similarly founded as a consortium venture with 20 per cent held by what is now the Westpac Banking Corporation, 12.5 per cent by Perpetual Trustees, 20 per cent by Sumitomo Bank, 20 per cent by Bank of America, 12.5 per cent by Montreal Trust, 7.5 per cent by Hill Samuel (UK) and 7.5 per cent by Schroder Darling & Co.

More recently, as with many consortium ventures, the trend has been to consolidate trust company ownership. In 1980, for example, Hill Samuel acquired full control of PITCO from the other shareholders.[93] In Melitco, too, there has been considerable rationalization. The Hongkong and Shanghai Banking Corporation purchased Barclays shares in mid-1985. The ANZ has similarly acquired full ownership of Australian International Finance to raise its holding to 53 per cent. They are now the only shareholders.

The trend against consortium ventures is also reflected in the number of new trust companies which have developed out of the business interests of firms otherwise involved with Vanuatu's Finance Centre. Vanuatu International Trust, for example, was established in 1982 by the local partners of Coopers & Lybrand office to provide additional services for their accounting clients. Likewise the most recent firm, Helvetia Overseas Trust, was created in November 1985 to handle the trust business of the Bank Gutzwiller, Kurz, Bungener (Overseas) Ltd and is a wholly-owned subsidiary of the Bank.

As shown in Table 4.21, there are now eight trust companies as members of the Trust Company Association of Vanuatu. It in turn is one of the four member organizations of Vanuatu's Finance Centre Association.

(ii) *Regulation*

The trust companies are licensed under the Trust Company Regulation 1971. Among the Act's various provisions is one under Section 10 for the preservation of secrecy. It prohibits any person disclosing any information entrusted to him in confidence to other parties, even after he has ceased employment, and places a 100,000 vatu fine and/or a six-month prison sentence on such violations.

(iii) *Operations*

There are few limitations on trust company operations, but for practical purposes their business can be divided into six general categories: trustee work; corporate services; banking and deposit taking; insurance; accounting; and other services.

As mentioned in the Finance Centre section, overseas clients make frequent use of both trusts and exempt corporations to gain the maximum advantages of secrecy and convenience. In practice, though, there is little difference between the trust company activities in either area. Their services are much the same, only the names are slightly different. In the case of a trust, for example, the trust company helps with the establishment of the trust deed and then normally serves as its trustee. With a corporation, it assists with its articles and incorporation and then acts as the new company's registered agent. It may also act as the manager of the trust or company, or simply act on instructions from the beneficial owners. The trust company may also provide resident directors, shareholders, and officers for client companies. Most of these services, however, are also offered by local solicitors and accounting firms.

In banking services, trust companies can provide the local expertize and management services necessary to establish an exempt bank or financial institution. Some trust companies, though, are also locally-licensed financial institutions in their own right. Melanesian International Trust and Investor's Trust Ltd, for example, are both licensed under the Banking as well the Trust Company regulations. While they cannot use the word 'bank' in their names, or offer cheque accounts, they have all the other powers associated with the local commercial banks. In practice, neither accepts deposits from the general public, and they operate only on the directions of their clients. Indeed, acting on client investment instructions does not require banking regulation approval, and virtually all trust companies can effectively act as deposit-takers by using a special trust account to handle their customer banking transactions and other investments.

As discussed elsewhere, the insurance business is the least developed of Vanuatu's various off-shore businesses. While most trust companies would argue that they could, and probably do, provide corporate services for exempt insurers, just as they do for exempt companies and banks, there is not yet the same level of local expertize in this area. Insurance should nevertheless develop into a major service area for the trust companies, and by late 1985 a new brokerage company was to establish local operations specifically to service this market.

It is wrong to suggest that the trust companies are accounting firms. Even so, most are headed by qualified accountants and provide a full corporate accounting service as part of their general 'resident agent-corporate services' business. They are not particularly active in auditing, but with the recent change in regulations, few exempt companies other than exempt banks, financial institutions and insurance companies, will require external audit reports.

Combined with the previously discussed operations, trust companies are active in tax-planning and investment management. They also are involved in a range of other activities. As mentioned in the Finance Centre discussion, for example, Investors' Trust Ltd acts as Vanuatu's Maritime Administrator and administers its vessel registration register in addition to its normal trust company work.

Finally, it should be mentioned that the trust companies are not solely involved in off-shore business. Many are active in local business as well as advising foreign investors on local conditions.

(iv) *Representation*

Besides their Vanuatu operations, to be effective in international business most trust companies have a number of overseas subsidiaries which can be used for the maximum benefit of their customers. Each of the companies also have reciprocal arrangements with similar companies operating in other tax centres. In addition, some trust companies actually have their own operating companies overseas. PITCO, for example, has a representative office in London and Asiaciti advertises offices in Hong Kong, Singapore and Sydney.

In addition to their own direct representation, the larger firms are also indirectly represented through their shareholders' international business operations. The importance of these international connections cannot be overstated, and surprisingly these overseas affiliations play an important role in Vanuatu's own off-shore business operations. Indeed, while many might expect all off-shore business in Vanuatu to be done through Vanuatu exempt companies or trusts, this is not the case, as for various reasons other countries may be more attractive for certain business purposes.

(v) *Staff*

The trust companies vary considerably in size. The older firms with a background of consortium ownership are by far the largest. Of these PITCO is the largest by far. In late 1985 it had a staff of 9 expatriates and 20 ni-Vanuatu. Melitco was second with 4 expatriates and 9 ni-Vanuatu. Among the smaller firms it is difficult to calculate the exact number of employees as some staff work for the trust company's affiliated solicitor or accounting firm and handle trust company business on a part-time basis.

As with other aspects of law and accounting, the major limitation for employing ni-Vanuatu staff is their lack of professional training in these areas. Thus, for the most part their participation is limited to clerical duties.

Investment Companies

Another less developed aspect of the Finance Centre is a formalized structure for investment management operations. Each of the trust companies would conduct some investment management on behalf of their clients, but there are no active Vanuatu-based international unit trusts. As mentioned elsewhere, the present structure of local stamp duty has precluded the economic use of this vehicle.

One alternative, however, is to use a corporate structure for this purpose. In late 1985 the only major example of this style of management was Pacific International Currency Funds Ltd.

Pacific International Currency Funds is operated by the Pacific International Trust Co. for its clients. It offers a range of currency funds whose net assets are valued weekly. They require a minimum deposit of US$ 25,000 or its equivalent. There is an Australian Dollar Currency Fund, a Deutschmark Currency Fund, a Japanese Yen Currency Fund, a United States Dollar Currency Fund, the Pieces of

Eight Currency Fund (a defensive fund) and the Managed Currency Fund. The latter's trading and management is handled by the Macquarie Bank Ltd in Sydney under contract. There is a management charge of 0.75 per cent per year on each fund except for the Managed Currency Fund which has a 2.5 per cent annual charge.

Unlike most cash management trusts which involve units and distributions, these funds use shares, and all investment earnings are reinvested. As the manager will repurchase the shares at their net asset value, the holder can redeem the interest or principal at any time. While there is little difference whether the interest is paid out or reinvested, as Vanuatu has no tax on either form of income, there may be some advantages in other countries for the profit to come as a capital gain rather than interest income.

As yet there are no equity investment companies available, only fixed-interest currency investments, but this would seem a logical development in the not too distant future.

National Housing Authority

Another government entity planned, but not yet it in operation in late 1985, was the National Housing Corporation or National Housing Authority. Industry interviews suggest a number of possibilities, but it is certain that this body will be involved in the production of residential housing for ni-Vanuatus. There are also plans for these residences to be available on favourable credit terms, but it is not so clear as to how this would be accomplished. Some money would probably be raised under the new Economic and Social Development Loans (issue of bonds) Act 1985. These funds could then either be lent by the National Housing body, or the housing role could be split with the new body handling only the construction side and the Development Bank of Vanuatu administrating the actual lending. The Development Bank itself already apparently has some plans to help finance a low-cost housing scheme in conjunction with a foreign company, and the National Housing work would not be difficult to absorb within its current operations. On the other hand, though, few international development lenders are keen for development banks to provide housing finance, and it might be more effective in the long run for the new body to assume the Development Bank's housing loan portfolio as well as handling its own operations.

National Provident Fund

By early December 1985 plans were under way for the establishment of a National Provident Fund for Vanuatu. The Fund will be created and regulated under the Vanuatu National Provident Fund Act 1985.

It will initially commence operations by requiring employers to provide contributions equal to 6 per cent of each worker's salary, with the provision that half of this amount, 3 per cent, could be collected from the worker. Interestingly, the split was initially planned at 10 per cent, but its own budgetary problems gave the government a strong incentive to choose a lower contribution figure.

End benefits available are a function of the total contributions and their associated investment income over the period. It is presently planned that it be payable on a lump sum basis at the age of 55, or on permanently leaving the country or, on death, to one's estate. A pension option may be considered later once the Fund's initial administrative operations are well established.

The Fund will be run by a board comprised of two members appointed by the government, two by the employers, two by the employees, and a chairman appointed by the Minister of Finance.

Under its Act (Section 16), the Fund must invest these contributions in the 'interest of members on the one hand and also the needs for assisting the financing of balanced social and economic development on the other'. These investments are nevertheless restricted to bank deposits, other trustee investments, or securities and loans approved by the Minister of Finance.

FINANCIAL MARKETS

Vanuatu's financial sector has yet to develop any financial markets, outside some limited interbank deposit and foreign exchange transactions, nor is there any substantial securities trading within the Finance Centre. With a government Treasury bonds issue planned for 1986, some limited trading between the Central Bank and the commercial banks may eventually develop in these securities.

The local foreign exchange market is dominated by Banque Indosuez Vanuatu which manages Vanuatu's foreign exchange functions on behalf of the Central Bank. In this regard it must take positions in Special Drawing Rights (SDR) and to quote this against the vatu: the vatu has been linked to the SDR since 10 September 1981. The value of the vatu to other currencies is then determined on the basis of that currency's relation to the SDR. The SDR itself is comprised of a basket of currencies which since January 1981 has included five currencies in the following proportions: $ 0.54 in US dollars, DM 0.46 in German marks, 34 Japanese yen, FF 0.74 in French francs, and 0.071 in British pounds sterling.

Banque Indosuez also actively deals with the foreign exchange markets in Hong Kong and Singapore, and uses them to clear out all other foreign currency exposures into an SDR position at the end of the trading day. In addition to spot transactions, forward cover is also available for commercial transactions, both directly through off-shore SDR, or by constructing a similar cover through the SDR's composition currencies.

While the other banks can similarly deal in vatu as well as foreign currencies, they have tended to limit their involvement to customer transactions. More recently, though, the ANZ Bank is believed to have taken some positions in foreign currency. Westpac now has a similar, but very limited, exposure and the Hongkong and Shanghai Bank tends to deal only for clients. At least some foreign exchange business is a product of Finance Centre transactions.

Banque Indosuez has a substantial advantage over its competitors in taking a vatu position for, due to its foreign exchange duties, the Central Bank has agreed to cover any losses incurred by Banque Indosuez in case of a vatu devaluation; in return though Banque Indosuez must give the Central Bank any profits it gains in the event of a vatu revaluation.

As with most aspects of its colonial period, Vanuatu has an interesting history in terms of foreign currency use within the Condominium, and then the Republic. The Condominium's 1914 Protocol, Article 4, stated that, 'English and French money and bank notes authorized by either power shall be legal tender in the Group'. For the French, prior to 1941, this meant Bank of France notes and Pacific francs issued by the Banque de l'Indochine in Noumea. For the English, though, it was really a mix of Australian and British currencies, with most commercial transactions conducted in the former. Initially the choice was unimportant as they were of similar value. With the end of their interchangeability on 11 February 1935, though, the Australian dollar officially became an authorized currency within the islands.

This position continued until the Second World War when, in 1940, wartime conditions saw the introduction of a special French currency in the New Hebrides. These were, in fact, Banque de l'Indochine notes from Noumea overprinted with the the words 'Franc Neo-Hébridais'. Initially these notes were backed by a special foreign currency account located in Australia, and later by the guarantee of the French Treasury. This currency was finally replaced in 1969 by the New Hebrides franc issued under an arrangement with the French government body, the Institut d'Emission d'Outre-Mer.

Even after the introduction of the vatu, Australian currency remained important within Vanuatu's commercial life, and the vatu remained linked to the Australian dollar until 10 September 1981, when the vatu's linkage was changed to the Special Drawing Rights of the International Monetary Fund. As the government explained, 'the change in exchange rate arrangements was designed to give the vatu greater stability and to stabilize the rate of inflation'.[94] The current linkage is 110 vatu to one SDR.

ANALYSIS

There are certainly many problems facing Vanuatu and these have been compounded by the adverse effects of two competitive colonial masters often concentrating on their own status, rather than the development of the country. As one writer described, this produced a legacy comprised of

a numerically inflated civil service, inflated wage scales, duplication of services, lack of preparation of ni-Vanuatu administrators, lack of training of indigenous people in necessary job skills, misplaced emphasis in education, extravagant and unbalanced health care systems, lack of infrastructure, neglect of the rural sector and maintenance for over seventy years of a system assuming cultural, racial and class superiority.[95]

Given these difficulties, it is little wonder that financial development matters are only now being given careful consideration by government planners.

There are obviously many measures which are common to most Pacific island countries which could be adopted to promote financial development within Vanuatu but there a few specific measures where government action would be particularly effective. These include expanding the degree of financial services available in the rural areas, consolidating government shareholdings under one business-orientated body, taking further measures to improve the attractiveness of the Finance Centre, and making the most effective use of trained staff.

Improving Bank Representation

As mentioned earlier, Vanuatu's experiment with the Co-operative Savings Bank is a unique venture within the Pacific countries and could, if successful, serve as a very useful model for increased savings mobilization within other developing countries. There is little question that bank offices in Pacific island villages do not require the same degree of sophistication as in a developed country. A permanent building, some sort of safe, a record-keeping system, honest employees, and an effective supervisory system is really all that is required to operate a savings collection network. Admittedly the savings mobilized will be very small, and hence administratively costly, but that is the whole point of handling the collection through a modest branch network. If, as it appears, the Savings Bank cannot only collect rural savings but also accomplish this with an operational profit, or at least break even, this will a major achievement in itself.

Unfortunately the Savings Bank's major strength, that of deposit raising, will not in itself overcome another problem facing the banking system, that is, the poor demand for loans. The recent period of high copra prices, for example, generated considerable deposit funds but there was very little change in loan demand. As the Central Bank commented, the period 1982–4 was characterized by a 'fast growth of monetary liquidity without any commensurate increase in the economy's absorptive capacity'[96] for these funds. In other words, the banks succeeded in deposit collection, but not in the on-lending of these funds. There are many facets to this problem, but at least one aspect is the lack of commercial banking representation outside Port Vila and Luganville. Indeed, in late 1985 no commercial bank had either a branch or private agency arrangement outside of the country's two major cities.

It is difficult to argue for private sector institutions to open loss-making branch offices, but this is certainly one aspect of the lending problem. This position, of course, is not confined to the private banks, for the Development Bank has a similar problem. Government funding for the additional costs of increased rural representation is an obvious solution, but perhaps unnecessary. In the short run, at least, more could probably be accomplished by making more effective use of the bank staff and other government extension officers in rural banking education. The Papua New Guinea Banking Corporation, for example, has developed a very effective 'travelling show' to provide such services in remote areas, and it would not be difficult to adapt their methods for both Vanuatu and other island states. The Papua New Guinea Development Bank has similarly developed a number of educational devices to assist in rural banking education.

While it is unlikely that any one bank could justify such education effort on economic grounds, at the national level it would certainly be a worthwhile investment and help to change, at least in part, the Port Vila and Finance Centre mentality of the country's commercial bankers. If approached in conjunction with the Development Bank, it would be difficult for the Vanuatu Bankers' Association not to participate and support the government in such a national programme.

Consolidating Government Shareholdings

As shown in Table 4.22 the government presently has shareholdings in a number of commercial and quasi-commercial entities, and is in a good position to take additional equity positions in foreign joint ventures through the financial grant assistance afforded under bilateral government aid schemes, such as provided by the Australian and New Zealand governments.

At present, though, the constitution does not allow for the government to hold shares in its own right so the shares themselves are actually held by the government minister with responsibility for that company's operations. Thus, when the ministers change office, the various shareholdings must be transferred as well. These ministers are also the point of contact between the company and the government. Thus, with any negotiations, the respective department settles the matter first with its joint venture and then the process starts again with the other government departments actually regulating the matter concerned.

There would seem considerable merit in consolidating these various shareholdings either through the Development Bank or more likely a new body, such as the Vanuatu Investment Company. Such a move is much more important than simply saving administration costs. First, rather than having mainly government officers serving as

TABLE 4.22   Vanuatu government shareholdings, 1985

Air Vanuatu	60.0
Banque Indosuez Vanuatu Ltd	20.0
Central Bank of Vanuatu	100.0
Development Bank of Vanuatu	100.0
Luganville Urban Land Corporation	100.0
Metenesel Estates Ltd	37.1
Port Vila Urban Land Corporation	100.0
Port Vila Fisheries Ltd	100.0
Santo Abattoir/SASI	27.0
South Pacific Fishing Co.	10.0
Tanna Coffee Development Co. Ltd	99.0
Tour Vanuatu Ltd	51.0
Vanuatu Abattoirs Ltd	28.0
Vanuautu Aquacultural	40.0
Vanuatu Cement Industries	33.0
Vanuatu Livestock Development Ltd	100.0
Vanuatu Navigation	10.0
Vila Abattoir	28.0

Source: Ministry of Finance (1985).

directors, the new body could afford to hire professional, private-sector-orientated staff for this purpose. This would help remove government departmental influences from commercial decision-making, and ensure that the companies operate as an independent business venture rather than by government fiat. Second, the centralized body could also serve as an effective vehicle for the training of ni-Vanuatu staff on business procedures and other corporate matters so that they can participate on a more equal footing with their foreign partners. Third, it could also serve to centralize foreign joint-venture approaches to government within the one body. While its own operations could certainly be improved, the Government Shareholding Agency in the Solomon Islands has shown that there are advantages in using a consolidated agency and its benefits more than offset the costs involved.

Improving the Financial Centre's Attractiveness

As mentioned earlier, Vanuatu has thus far been fairly successful in attracting off-shore business to its financial sector and certainly changes in Hong Kong's taxation system coupled with its 1997 question[97] has assisted its development. The problem, however, is that other Pacific countries have seen the potential benefits that an off-shore banking centre could entail, and have introduced legislation and incentives accordingly. By 1985, for example, both Nauru and the Cook Islands were already very active in this area. Tonga similarly has some involvement and other countries are known to be considering such centres.

Unfortunately there is a finite supply of off-shore banking activity and what is more, the very nature of these operations means that the business can quickly move from one centre to another if there becomes any significant difference in relative incentives. An off-shore financial centre is not the same sort of industry as a steel mill for it takes little more than a telex to transfer the business elsewhere. There are, of course, advantages in being first in the Pacific market, and Vanuatu to date has had success as a financial centre, but this need not continue if better services are developed elsewhere.

The government and Finance Centre Association members must therefore keep an active watch on overseas developments to ensure that Vanuatu remains competitive with its counterparts overseas. It must also ensure that its existing operations are being conducted effectively. In this latter area, though, there are a number of seemingly minor matters where government action would greatly improve the Centre's international position.

Not all of these measures entail particularly difficult or costly actions. For example, a surprisingly common complaint among Finance Centre executives was the lack of a suitable Companies Act. At the most basic level, the Act has been out of print for some period, and despite the obvious need to supply copies to prospective clients, it has not yet been reprinted. Similarly, while the content is generally acceptable, the existing legislation is considered poorly worded by many international lawyers, and a simple redrafting would greatly improve its acceptability overseas. In contrast, the Cook Islands, in entering the off-shore tax haven business, has made sure that its legislation is well drafted and attractively presented on quality paper.

There could also, of course, be improvements to the legislation's content, and in July 1985 a British legal expert, Dr L S Sealy, was hired by the Vanuatu government to review its existing companies legislation and commercial regulations to ensure they are competitive with other centres, and such updating should be accomplished on a periodic basis.

Another area where the Centre could be made more attractive is in the structuring of stamp duty charges on unit trust operations. At present the costs on the purchase and sale of units has effectively precluded the establishment of a Vanuatu-based regional unit trust industry. The replacement of these charges with a flat government fee or annual running charge would make Vanuatu much more attractive for investment management.

Some consideration might also be given to granting residency status to individuals with significant Vanuatu investments. The option of dual residency is very attractive with some Asian investors. It has been used successfully to attract investment funds in a number of countries and Vanuatu could easily compete on this basis. One report has suggested that Vanuatu residency permits were available to those foreigners willing to invest US$ 120,000 by purchasing a retirement villa, or simply by opening a local investment account.[98]

The final area of concern for the Finance Centre is the temptation for the government to gain more revenue or to direct some off-shore funds into financing local investments. In the latter case, for example, one government paper comments that 'there is also the potential for some of the funds currently invested in off-shore trusts associated with the Finance Centre, to be directed toward investment in income producing projects'.[99] This may be true provided these local investments are sufficiently competitive with other investments. The users of off-shore financial centres are exceedingly adverse to taxes and government investment controls, and even rumours that such ideas were under consideration could cause potential investors to place their business elsewhere. Fortunately the Minister of Finance, Kalpokor Kalsakau, has been very supportive of the Finance Centre and predicted that this off-shore business 'will continue to grow, with government support . . . We plan to make it the best in the South Pacific'.[100]

Staffing Restraints

As with other developing countries, Vanuatu faces the problem of having too few trained and experienced staff. This is particularly true in the financial sector where ni-Vanuatu personnel occupy few, if any, senior positions. This position will certainly worsen in the short term as the government establishes its planned National Provident Fund and National Housing Authority. Both will require significant expatriate expertize for the immediate future.

Unfortunately, as with the Solomons, the Vanuatu government has adopted a major decentralization programme as a key plan of its development effort. This will entail the establishment of some 11 regional governments, in addition to the two independent townships of Port Vila and Luganville, each with its own President and Cabinet. Furthermore, these bodies will eventually gain responsibility for their own education, health and agricultural extension services, as well as raising their own taxes to supplement federal government funding. While there are perhaps many political and cultural reasons for implementing such a system, the financial decentralization will place an undue burden on the relatively small number of experienced personnel, and raise considerable administrative and financial difficulties. It would be better that such plans, if implemented, are accomplished under a schedule in keeping with the country's growing financial and administrative expertise.

TRENDS AND PREDICTIONS

In late 1985 Vanuatu's economy was suffering from the dual affects of low commodity prices and a marked decline in tourism. This, coupled with a gradual decline in foreign aid, resulted in the country's first current account deficit for some years and only a very small surplus in its over-all balance of payments. These factors have also reduced government funding, and unless current revenue constraints are overcome, the goverment will have serious problems fulfilling its future goals, particularly in education and decentralization. Indeed, in 1986 the goverment is expected to experience its first sizable deficit and may well have to resort to borrowings.

To overcome these difficulties, the government has adopted a multi-faceted approach to development, with the intention of diversifying its current dependence on copra sales into a broader-based export trade, as well as expanding the foreign exchange earnings of its tourism and Finance Centre operations.

In agriculture much can be done to improve both the quality and quantity of Vanuatu's exports. The Vanuatu Commodities Marketing Board has already significantly increased the quality of its copra exports and thus receives a much better price for its crop. Coconut production, however, still offers considerable scope for improvement, and since 1983 there has been a major expansion of government agricultural extension services and research both in copra and other suitable export crops.

Unfortunately, conflicts over land tenure following independence has meant that most of the plantation sector has made no major reinvestment or upgrading of copra plantations since the late 1970s. As a result, the total plantation industry 'is in a state of decline, due mainly to the ageing of the stands, reduction in the number of trees due to cyclones, and over grazing'.[101] The Land Records Office registration and leasing of land under the new Land Lease Act 1983, since 1 March 1984, should encourage plantation improvement efforts, but the current legislation is probably still too restrictive. For example, most agricultural leases are restricted to a maximum period to 30 years. As coconut palms generally do not reach their production peak for up to 15 years, and have a productive life of at least 50 years, a 30-year term is hardly attractive to investors. Only in the case of large projects where there is substantial ni-Vanuatu participation can a 75-year lease be granted.

Next to copra, cattle form the most important agricultural product, and here plantation-styled cattle stations have continued to supply the bulk of the export production. Their productivity, though, could be greatly expanded, and a major cattle project in South Espíritu Santo (delayed due to custom landownership disputes) should have a major impact on over-all production levels. Interestingly, Vanuatu has been relatively successful in both production and exporting. It has some advantages in exporting its beef to the EC (mainly France) due to its past French and British colonial connections.

As with other South Pacific countries, Vanuatu's sea resources could seemingly be used to more advantage both as a source of employment and as foreign exchange revenue. In addition to its own efforts, and those in conjunction with Japanese and Taiwanese interests, the recent agreement between Kiribati and the Soviet Union show that the fishing rights themselves can produce valuable foreign exchange.

Other than import replacement, Vanuatu's industrial potential is limited to those areas where it has a comparative advantage in terms of local supplies. In particular, more value added could be gained from current exports through the greater processing of coconuts, timber, and other agricultural products. The by-products of the existing exports, such as cattle hides and fish waste, could also be used as the basis for other local industries. The government would like to encourage more boatbuilding, coconut oil extraction, cement making, tannery and leather processing, and wood processing, as well as other agriculturally-based industries, timber, tourism and manufacturing. Special access to the Australian and New Zealand markets under the South Pacific Regional Trade Economic Co-operative Agreement (SPARTECA), coupled with special equity funding assistance from both governments, should make joint-venture arrangements in these areas particularly attractive to Australian or New Zealand entrepreneurs.

Though much less certain than agriculture and manufacturing, there is also a potential for mineral exports, for up until the early 1970s manganese was one of the country's major exports. While these resources have since been depleted, other commercial deposits of manganese, copper, gold and silver are certainly possible. This is the view of foreign mining companies, for foreign prospecting licenses increased from only 2 to about 90 over 1985.[102] One Australian firm, City and Suburban Properties, through its wholly-owned subsidiary, United Resources (Vanuatu) Ltd, holds 28 prospecting licenses or applications, and has located some new gold deposits and is searching for additional deposits using a ship, the MV United Venturer, as its mobile laboratory and equipment base. Other companies with a Vanuatu involvement include Canyon Resources, Mumbil Mines, Dominion Gold, Negri River Corporation, Jason Mining, Solomon Pacific Resources, Kia Ora Gold Corporation, and Austpac Resources.

The importance of tourism on the local economy cannot be overstressed, and its significance should increase in the short term as the 83 rooms of the Irririki Island hotel resort are added to Port Vila's current stock of 440 rooms. There are also plans to expand one of the existing large hotels, Le Lagon, as well as to construct a major 300-room hotel complex at Malapoa Point, also near Port Vila.

To ensure the expansion of the hotels, and gain full advantage of their facilities, will require an expansion of the airport facilities at Port Vila so that it could take larger aircraft. In 1984 it was limited to the Boeing 737 but hoped to take the larger 727 as well. In contrast, both Fiji and New Caledonia can handle 747 and their much larger passenger numbers. The provision of more frequent and direct air connections to other financial centres would equally assist the Finance Centre's development.

In 1985 the government also introduced a duty-free scheme in Port Vila for tourist purchases, where the goods taken out of the country by the purchaser were subject only to a custom service tax rather than full import duties. This operation has apparently proved successful in increasing tourist purchases and making Vanuatu more attractive for the duty-free shopping sector aspect of foreign tourism.

Nevertheless, tourist numbers were down considerably from recent years, and at least part of this is a function of Vanuatu's high dependence of Australian tourists. With the weakening of the Australian dollar, many Australians now prefer to holiday within Australia or in countries with similar currency problems. The vatu's 8.5 per cent devaluation on 1 April 1985 was partly to improve Vanuatu's attractiveness to Australian tourists: interviews with government officials, however, suggest this has had little effect on the industry. While a further devaluation was certainly rumoured for 1986, a major portion of the decline in tourists is the result of the recent bombings in nearby New Caledonia, and the infortunate tendency to view Vanuatu, possible due to the Espíritu Santo problems in 1980, as offering similar dangers.

In conclusion, while Vanuatu faces considerable potential difficulties in the short term, its current plans to improve its agricultural production and diversify into other products, coupled with a marked improvement in the quality of its tourist industry, and in the competitive of its Finance Centre, should ensure a relatively healthy current account surplus. It will also need to adjust its spending and revenue-raising capabilities in line with the expected decline in foreign aid.

NOTES

1. The actual voyage was funded by the Spanish as Portugal was then part of Spain. de Queirós had been the navigator of the Mendana expedition which had discovered the Solomon Islands in 1595.
2. Neither the Compagnie Calédoniènne des Nouvelles-Hébrides, or the Australasian New Hebrides Co., survived the 1890s depression. The defunct Australasian New Hebrides Co. was subsequently taken over by Burns Philp in 1896. The Compagnie Calédoniènne des Nouvelles-Hébrides in 1904 was reformed as the Société Française des Nouvelles-Hébrides with the support of the French government and the Banque de l'Indochine.
3. Given its unique position in international affairs, the condominium government has been the subject of much attention by politicians and international lawyers as well as much humourous treatment in plays and literature. Critics sometimes called it a 'pandemonium'.
4. At its highest level the Condominium was headed by the British and

French High Commissioners. In the case of disagreement between the two, the matter was to be settled by the arbitration of the King of Spain.

5. Cyril Belshaw (1950) *Island Administration in the South West Pacific: government and reconstruction in New Caledonia, the New Hebrides, and the British Solomon Islands* (London: Royal Institute of International Affairs) p. 110.

6. One reflection of the extent of the duality of French and British services was the fire departments where they naturally chose different equipment and had to install their own sets of fire hydrants as well. In theory a conversion device was created so that they could use the other's hydrants in an emergency, but as recently as 1985 a major fire in Port Vila continued to burn long after the fire department arrived, as they were unable to use a nearby older-style hydrant and had to modify it.

7. In 1974, Mayotte, one of the four main Indian Ocean islands which voted against independence, eventually did not join the others in Comoro's new republic, but rather remained as a special collectivity of France.

8. For a discussion of these events see Grace Molisa, Nike Nike Vurobaravu and Howard Van Trease, 'Background to "The Eve of Independence," the hidden agenda,' in Lini, Walter, (1980) *Beyond Pandemonium: from the New Hebrides to Vanuatu* (Wellington: Asia Pacific Books) pp. 56–9.

9. The French government and Vanuatu presently contest the ownership of two small uninhabited islands, Matthew and Hunter Islands, east of New Caledonia and south-east of Vanuatu.

10. *Investing in Vanuatu: a guide to entrepreneurs* (1983) (Port Vila: Government of Vanuatu), p. 11.

11. *Investing in Vanuatu*, p. 12.

12. *Republic of Vanuatu First National Development Plan, 1982–86* (1982) (Port Vila, National Planning Office) p. 73.

13. *The Mid-Term Review of Vanuatu's First National Development Plan* (1984) (Port Vila: National Planning and Statistical Office) December, p. 23.

14. *Republic of Vanuatu First National Development Plan* (1982) p. 82.

15. J. S. G. Wilson (1966) *Economic Survey of the New Hebrides* (London: HMSO) p. 188.

16. *New Hebrides, 1938* (1940) (London: HMSO) pp. 25–6.

17. *New Hebrides, 1930* (1931) (London: HMSO) p. 5.

18. *New Hebrides – Anglo-French Condominium, Annual Report for 1948* (1949) (London: HMSO) p. 24.

19. *Colonial Reports: Anglo-French Condominium; New Hebrides, 1949 and 1950* (1951) (London: HMSO) p. 24.

20. *Anglo-French Condominium – New Hebrides Condominium, Annual Report for the years 1965 and 1966* (1967) (London: HMSO) p. 26.

21. Wilson, *Economic Survey*, p. 182.

22. Commonwealth Bank of Australia, correspondence dated 17 February 1986.

23. Wilson, *Economic Survey*, p. 183.

24. Commonwealth Bank of Australia, correspondence dated 17 February 1986.

25. David Wheeler (1985) 'Barclays ends ties with Pacific Islands', *Australian Financial Review*, 13 August, p. 45.
26. *The Mid-Term Review of Vanuatu's First National Development Plan* (1984) p. 47.
27. Central Bank of Vanuatu (1983) *Annual Report and Statement of Accounts for 1983*, p. 18.
28. Central Bank of Vanuatu (1984) *Annual Report and Statment of Accounts for 1984*, p. 48.
29. Central Bank of Vanuatu, *Annual Report for 1984*, p. 22.
30. Central Bank of Vanuatu, *Annual Report for 1984*, p. 21.
31. *Republic of Vanuatu First National Development Plan* (1982) p. 82.
32. Hongkong and Shanghai Banking Corporation (1984) *Annual Report*, p. 18.
33. *Republic of Vanuatu First National Development Plan* (1982) p. 81.
34. Brian A. Ponter (1983) 'Co-operatives in Vanuatu, 1962–1980', Ph.D. thesis, University of the South Pacific, p. 202.
35. *The Mid-Term Review of Vanuatu's First National Development Plan* (1984) p. 55.
36. *Republic of Vanuatu First National Development Plan* (1982) p. 83.
37. *Investing in Vanuatu*, p. 41.
38. *Republic of Vanuatu First National Development Plan* (1982) p. 76.
39. Industry interviews, December 1985.
40. *Republic of Vanuatu First National Development Plan* (1982) p. 83.
41. Development Bank of Vanuatu (1984) *Fifth Annual Report*, p. 11.
42. *Anglo-French Condominium* (1967) p. 27.
43. *New Hebrides Joint Development Plan, 1971–75* (1971) (London: HMSO) p. 7.
44. *Investing in Vanuatu*, p. 77.
45. *Republic of Vanuatu First National Development Plan* (1982) p. 76.
46. *The Mid-Term Review of Vanuatu's First National Development Plan* (1984) p. 55.
47. Development Bank of Vanuatu, *Fifth Annual Report*, p. 17.
48. Development Bank of Vanuatu, *Fifth Annual Report*, p. 17.
49. Development Bank of Vanuatu, *Fifth Annual Report*, p. 18.
50. Development Bank of Vanuatu, *Fifth Annual Report*, p. 16.
51. *Investing in Vanuatu*, p. 77.
52. *Republic of Vanuatu First National Development Plan* (1982) p. 81.
53. Development Bank of Vanuatu, *Fifth Annual Report*, pp. 32–3.
54. *Investing in Vanuatu*, p. 20.
55. Development Bank of Vanuatu *Fifth Annual Report*, p. 13.
56. *Republic of Vanuatu First National Development Plan* (1982) p. 82.
57. Bank Gutzwiller, Kurz, Bungener (Overseas) Ltd (1984) *Annual Report*, p. 4.
58. *Republic of Vanuatu First National Development Plan* (1982) p. 187.
59. *Republic of Vanuatu First National Development Plan* (1982) p. 192.
60. *Republic of Vanuatu First National Development Plan* (1982) p. 192.
61. *Papua New Guinea, Solomon Islands and Vanuatu: a business profile* (1985) (Hong Kong: Hongkong and Shanghai Banking Corporation) p. 61.
62. *Republic of Vanuatu First National Development Plan* (1982) p. 188.

63. *Republic of Vanuatu First National Development Plan* (1982) p. 185.
64. Mike Bishop and Ann Wigglesworth (1982) *A Touch of Australian Enterprise: the Vanuatu experience* (Fitzroy (Vico): International Development Action) p. 10.
65. Ponter 'Co-operatives in Vanuatu', :203.
66. Bishop and Wigglesworth, *A Touch of Australian Enterprise*, p. 10.
67. Ponter 'Co-operatives in Vanuatu', :203.
68. *Republic of Vanuatu First National Development Plan* (1982) p. 188.
69. During the 1974 copra boom, the Co-operatives Department provided exemptions for certain co-operatives to make specific loans to specific members as a means to increase primary production levels and the societies' turnover in the New Hebrides boom-time economy.
70. In Ponter's 1975 survey he found only one British supervised co-operative paying interest on shares, but believed this facility to be much more common among French-run societies (B. A. Ponter, personal correspondence, May 1986).
71. *New Hebrides Anglo-French Condominium (1966) Annual Report for the years 1963 and 1964* – (London: HMSO) p. 42.
72. British Service of the New Hebrides (1973) *Biennial Report of New Hebrides Condominium, 1971–1972* (1966) (London: HMSO) p. 48.
73. Co-operative Department, Ministry of Finance, correspondence dated 14 January 1986.
74. In addition to its own legislation, Vanuatu's constitution states that those British and French laws existing prior to 30 July 1980 are still applicable in Vanuatu unless they have been specifically revoked, or are in direct contrast to subsequent local legislation.
75. In 1985 these solicitors firms included George Vasaris & Co.; Turner Hopkins Coombe & Partners; Hudson & Co.; and Preville (de) Armand.
76. In 1985 these accounting firms included Briggs Moore & Co.; Coopers & Lybrand; Moore Stephens & Co.; Pannell Kerr Forster; Peat Marwick Mitchell & Co., and Price Waterhouse.
77. Edna Carew (1984) 'Letter from Port Vila', *Far Eastern Economic Review*, 6 September. The government estimated 115 million vatu in fees alone over 1985 and 161 million for 1986.
78. Julie-Ann Ellis (1984) 'Port Vila's booming finance centre', *Pacific Island Monthly*, August.
79. Bishop and Wigglesworth (1982) op. cit. *A Touch of Australian Enterprise*, p. 26.
80. Economist Intelligence Unit (1985) *Economic Quarterly Review*, 1:44.
81. Registrar of Companies, Vanuatu, 1985.
82. James E. Winkler (1982) *Losing Control: toward an understanding of transnational corporations in the Pacific island context* (Suva: Pacific Conference of Churches) p. 41.
83. As cited in Julie-Ann Ellis, 'Port Vila's booming finance centre', :36.
84. *Vanuatu: the tax-free financial centre of the Pacific* (1983) (Port Vila: Peat Marwick Mitchell & Co.) p. 13.
85. Economist Intelligence Unit (1985) *Annual Summary*, p. 48.
86. Economist Intelligence Unit (1985) *Economic Quarterly Review*, 1:43.

87. Economist Intelligence Unit, *Economic Quarterly Review*, 1:43.
88. *Republic of Vanuatu First National Development Plan* (1982) p. 82.
89. 'Vanuatu gets the vaults ready', *Australian Business*, 4 July 1984, p. 102.
90. Unfortunately, government reports do not yet show which institutions are domestic and exempt license under the Banking Regulations, nor does it indicate which are banks and which are financial institutions. In 1984, for example, it was estimated that of the 95 registered institutions, 71 were registered banks of which 5 did local business.
91. 'Vanuatu gets the vaults ready', *Australian Business*, 4 July 1984, p. 102.
92. *PITCO Vanuatu Update*, No. 4, October 1985, p. 2.
93. Until the transformation of Hill Samuel's Australia operations into the Macquarie Bank, PITCO's managers reported directly to Hill Samuel Australia. PITCO's ownership is now in a transitional stage with a new major institutional owner expected in 1986.
94. *Republic of Vanuatu First National Development Plan* (1982) p. 75.
95. Bishop and Wigglesworth, *A Touch of Australian Enterprise*, p. 1.
96. Central Bank of Vanuatu (1984) *Annual Report and Statement of Accounts for 1984*, p. 21.
97. For a discussion of these matters see Michael T. Skully (ed.) (1982) *Financial Institutions and Markets in the Far East: a study of China, Hong Kong, Japan, South Korea and Taiwan* (London: Macmillan) p. 45–6, 70.
98. Robert Keith-Reid (1984) 'Vanuatu: a nation in gear', *Islands Business*, September, p. 14.
99. *Investing in Vanuatu*, p. 15. Certainly prior to independence, considerable off-shore funds were invested in Port Vila real estate.
100. 'Steady as she goes on Vanuatu economy, says Kalsakau', *Pacific Island Monthly*, July 1984, pp. 35–6.
101. *Investing in Vanuatu*, p. 15.
102. *Business Review Weekly*, 20 September 1985, p. 24.

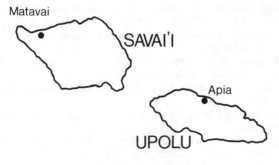

SOUTH PACIFIC OCEAN

Matavai

SAVAI'I

Apia

UPOLU

WESTERN SAMOA

5 Financial Institutions and Markets in Western Samoa

INTRODUCTION

Located 2575 kilometres north-east of New Zealand, Western Samoa consists of some 20 islands covering a land area of 2935 square kilometres. The two main islands, Savai'i and Upolu, account for most of the land area as well as the country's 160,000 population, of whom approximately 89 per cent are full Samoan, 10 per cent of mixed-race Samoan, and 1 per cent European and other races. In addition to its domestic population, Western Samoa has experienced extensive emigration, and some 40,000 Samoans now live in New Zealand, and there are many thousands within the United States.

European discovery came on 14 June 1722 when the Dutch Admiral, Jacob Roggeveen, first sighted the islands. Luis de Bougainville also passed the islands in 1768, calling them the 'Navigators Islands', but it was not until 1787 that François La Perouse became the first European actually to land.

The first missionaries came in 1830, and the first formal agreement between Europeans and Samoans occurred in 1838 between a British naval officer and local chiefs on a code of 'Commercial Regulations' covering the rules and harbor fees for European ships: these rules were later followed in 1839 by an American naval expedition. This set the basis for European recognition of the Samoan nation, and later governed the conduct between European settlers and the local rulers.

By 1840 European traders had permanent operations in Apia and they were followed in turn by diplomatic representation, with a British consul appointed in 1847, a United States Commercial Agent in 1853, and a German consul in 1861.

289

Though in some respects Samoa was then a unified nation, internally it was divided into four major districts and controlled by five major families. Unfortunately the various leaders frequently contested the key positions. In 1848 the death of one of Samoa's more important rulers started a major civil war. The fighting continued for years, and an expansion of the conflict in the 1860s finally brought the intervention of the British, German and American forces in 1873, and forced a power-sharing agreement between the two major factions.

This arrangement was finalized by a US negotiator, a Colonel Steinberger. He subsequently resigned from US service, and took an active part in Samoan life. He redrafted the country's constitution into a constitutional monarchy and served as Samoa's first premier until being deported by the British in 1876.

Shortly afterwards inter-island warfare resumed, and was often supported at various times by American, British, and German interests, each hoping to gain the greatest influence over local affairs. These rivalries continued to escalate with all three powers sending naval forces to Samoa. In the end direct conflict was avoided, due largely to a major naval disaster in Apia in 1889, when three German and two US warships were lost during a severe hurricane.

This loss gave a major incentive to settle the issue and resulted in the Berlin Treaty of June 1889. The Final Act of the Berlin Conference on Samoan Affairs reached between Britain, Germany and the United States, recognized King Malietoa Laupepa as the ruler of Samoa, as well as Samoan independence and neutrality, but gave the three countries' consuls power to run Apia on a joint basis.

With the death of the King in 1898 came a resumption of local leadership problems and renewed violence, but the European powers were no longer interested in supporting the various factions against each other. Instead, they simply divided the islands in 1899 between Germany and the United States: Germany was given Western Samoa, and the United States gained what is now American Samoa. Britain gave up all claims to both islands, but Germany in return withdrew all claims to Tonga, most of the Solomon Islands, and Niue. In addition to reaffirming British claims to these islands, the agreement also improved British-German relations which were strained due to the Boer War and lessened the prospect of German intervention.

The Germans subsequently took control of Western Samoa on 1 March 1900. While the Samoans objected, they were unable to prevent it. Over various periods, particularly in 1909, there were protests over German rule. Nevertheless the Germans maintained local control and expanded their existing plantation interests within the country.

With the outbreak of the First World War, a combination of New Zealand and allied forces occupied Apia unopposed on 29 August 1914 and Western Samoa became the first German Territory to fall to the Allied forces. The country was then ruled by a New Zealand led military government until 30 April 1920, when New Zealand received a formal mandate over the islands under the Treaty of Versailles and the League of Nations. Following the Second World War, New Zealand retained control of Western Samoa as a Trustee Territory of the United Nations in December 1946.

Also following the Second World War, Samoans were gradually given control of their local government. In 1947 a legislative assembly was established, and in 1954 a constitutional convention held. Local cabinet government commenced in 1959, and in 1961 a plebiscite was held on independence. The voting favoured an independent state, and on 1 January 1962 Western Samoa resumed its independence.

Western Samoan government is an interesting mixture of Western democracy and traditional Polynesian practices. The government's head of state is elected from one of the four Paramount Chiefs within the country. Initially, two of these were elected to hold the Office of Head of State jointly for life, but they will have only one successor and he will be elected for only a five-year term by the Legislative Assembly.

The Legislative Assembly is comprised of 47 members – 45 of these are elected by the local matai (traditional rulers) within the country, and the remaining two are elected by those citizens without an aiga affiliation. The matai and the aiga are the key to Samoan society for the aiga is the extended family to which most Samoans have a very strong affiliation. The aiga in turn elects its own traditional ruler, the matai, who generally serves for life. The title may be removed, though, if the holder does not fulfill his obligations to his aiga. The matai is responsible for the use of the aiga's traditional landholdings and the general welfare of its members. While the current electoral system may soon be replaced with one based on universal suffrage, this would have small effect on the power of the matai and aiga in Western Samoan life.[1]

In terms of its economy, Western Samoa in 1985 had the unfortunate status of ranking as the only 'Least Developed Country' in the South Pacific: a ranking similar to that of Bangladesh and Kampuchea.

Furthermore, it has been unable to show much improvement in recent years, with an actual decline in real GDP experienced over 1980–82. These economic figures, however, are not truly reflective of local living conditions, for as one researcher explained, 'in purely subsistence terms, Western Samoans enjoy a fairly high standard of living and it is only when we consider the economy in modern development terms that the situation alters'.[2]

As with other Pacific countries, Western Samoa's economy remains based on agriculture, with a heavy dependence on subsistence farming and coconut production. While it has been successful in processing much of its previous copra exports into higher-value-added products, such as coconut oil and coconut cream, coconut related products still comprised at least 56 per cent of Western Samoa's exports over 1985. It has nevertheless had some success in diversifying into other forms of agriculture, and over 1985 taro root exports, worth some WS$ 5,274,000, were the country's second largest single export product. Cocoa is also becoming important. As in Tonga, bananas were also once a major export but due to disease, hurricane damage, and competition in export markets, particularly New Zealand, they are no longer important exports. They are still important though as a local food item as are fish.

Western Samoa also has some degree of local manufacturing which has been encouraged under the Enterprises Incentive Act 1965 and the Industrial Free Zone Act 1974. It now produces such exports as desiccated coconut, canned coconut cream, frozen passion fruit pulp, canned tropical fruits and fruit drinks. Some locally-produced biscuits, bread, soap, soft drinks, ice cream, beer, cigarettes and matches are also exported. Other local manufacturing industries include building products, clothing, concrete products, copra-based stock feed, footwear, handicraft items, matches, paints, soap, and timber products. A wood veneer mill is one of its more recent industries, established in 1982, and it is now one of the larger employers.

Unfortunately, neither its agricultural nor manufactured exports provide sufficient foreign exchange, and Western Samoa experienced severe balance of payments problems following higher oil prices, poor commodity prices, and a higher consumption demand for imported items. This has resulted in excessive overseas borrowings which aggravated inflation and intensified the balance of payments problems. By 1982 a shortage of foreign exchange forced the government to implement significant import restrictions, and in 1983 it was forced to seek International Monetary Fund assistance to cover its external account problems and reschedule its finances. While the resulting austerity programme resolved the immediate crisis, major trade deficits, which are only just compensated for by the inflow of foreign aid and remittances from Samoans overseas, continue.

The government hopes to overcome these difficulties by increasing production through the more intensive utilization of the country's human and physical resources, particularly agricultural products that can replace current imports, produce foreign exchange, or diversify the present range of exports. Private sector investment is expected to play an important role in this process, as is an increased dependence on local savings mobilization. As one development plan emphasized, 'a strong financial sector is important in influencing the mobility and allocation of capital and in channelling savings into productive investment'.[3]

Overview of the Financial Sector

As with Tonga, Western Samoa's early financial history was closely linked with the firm of Johann Cesar Godeffroy and Sohn of Hamburg, Germany (commonly called J. C. Godeffroy and Son, or just Godeffroys) and its representative's arrival in August 1856. Godeffroy's international trading and financial links were unmatched among other traders, and in the end 'almost all the small Pacific traders were committed to using the Godeffroy banking network because they were too small to arrange their own bills of exchange. Meanwhile Godeffroys were financing their own imports by issuing bills on London or Sydney'.[4]

1874, though, was a turning point for Godeffroys position in Western Samoa, for it obtained a secret agreement for the Samoan government 'to sell all its copra and buy all its imports through Godeffroys'.[5] Furthermore the agreement appointed Godeffroys as the Samoan government's 'sole banker and fiscal agent'. A commercial bank was supposed to have been established and a new currency issued but, for various reasons, neither resulted.[6]

Godeffroys also expanded its plantations in Samoa, and at its peak had 6500 acres under cultivation, employed 880 labourers, and handled 75 per cent of Samoa's exports and 60 per cent of imports.[7] Unfortunately Godeffroys did not survive to enjoy the fruits of this investment for difficulties in Hamburg in 1879 caused its bankruptcy, and by 1880 the ownership of these interests were in the hands of the

Deutsche Handels und Plantagen Gesellschaft der Sudsee Inseln zu Hamburg (DH & PG).

With German control of Western Samoa in 1900, this German trading gained even greater importance, and DH & PG conducted much of the local banking during this period. The German colonial administration also provided some banking services as it collected small deposits though its native affairs office. It also apparently provided some credit in return. German records, for example, suggest 'small sporadic loans from the administration to Samoans, but these seem to be largely bribes for the good behaviour of high chiefs'.[8]

With the change in colonial governments, native deposit facilities continued much as before, for under the 'early New Zealand administrations money was deposited with the Department of Native Affairs for safe keeping, and most missions also accepted funds'.[9] These functions, though, became unnecessary with the establishment of the Apia branch of the Bank of New Zealand in 1915 and local Post Office Savings Bank in 1921.

As shown in Table 5.1, Western Samoa now has a wide range of financial institutions. Most were established in the 1970s and virtually all but those in the co-operative movement are either statutory government corporations or have the government or a government body among its shareholders.

In addition to the institutions shown in Table 5.1, the Western Samoa Treasury retains some central banking functions to include holding some foreign exchange reserves, the issuance of coins, and the provision of interest-bearing call-deposit accounts. It is expected, though, that the Central Bank of Samoa will eventually assume these functions.

Also not listed is the Western Samoan Trust Estates Corporation. Unlike the Commodity Boards, which actually provide for compulsory savings through the copra and cocoa price stabilization schemes, this company has no obvious financial institution function. Its operations nevertheless have a major impact on the Western Samoa economy as well as the financial sector. It is also an important investor in agricultural projects and in this regard fulfills a role not unlike a government investment corporation.

In addition to these formal sources, Western Samoa has a well-developed informal financial market, particularly in rural areas, which includes 'family and relatives, friends, rotating co-operatives, traders and money lenders'.[10] Some merchants also apparently operate a form of savings scheme for clients as well as loans.[11] These

TABLE 5.1   Financial institutions in Western Samoa, by total assets, 31 December 1985

	Establishment date	WS$M
Central Bank of Samoa[a]	1984	29.59
Monetary Board of Western Samoa[a, c]	1975	–
Bank of Western Samoa[b]	1959 ⎱	
Pacific Commercial Bank[b]	1977 ⎰	69.24
Post Office Savings Bank[a]	1921	1.58
Development Bank of Western Samoa[a]	1974	26.09
National Provident Fund[a]	1972	38.43
Western Samoa Life Assurance Corp[a]	1977	5.05
National Pacific Insurance Co.[b]	1977	7.02
Co-operatives	1954	n.a.
Credit unions	1955	n.a.
Commodity Marketing Boards[a]	1948	n.a.
Public Trust Office[a]	1921	3.44

[a] Wholly government-owned.
[b] Partly government (direct/indirect)-owned.
[c] Replaced by the Central Bank of Samoa.

Source: Central Bank of Samoa, (1986).

smaller traders, at least in the past, were in turn 'largely dependent on big firms for credit'.[12]

FINANCIAL INSTITUTIONS

Central Bank of Samoa

The Central Bank of Samoa was established on 1 May 1984 under the Central Bank of Samoa Act 1984. It was created to assume most functions of the Monetary Board of Western Samoa and serve as the country's central bank. Its functions are to regulate the issue, supply, availability, and convertibility of the tala; promote internal and external monetary stability; promote a sound financial system; promote credit and exchange conditions conducive to balanced economic development; to supervise the banking and credit business; and to advise the government on banking and monetary matters.[13] By 1985 it had begun to implement government monetary, credit and exchange rate policies and planned providing banking services to government agencies over 1986. The Treasury, however, has retained the right to issue coins and manage some government reserves.

Its predecessor, the Monetary Board of Western Samoa, had been established, under the Monetary Board of Western Samoa Act 1974, to assume the currency issue function of the Bank of Western Samoa, manage the foreign exchange rate, regulate the financial sector and advise the government on economic and financial matters. It also administered the foreign exchange control system and licensed financial institutions.

In terms of bank regulation, the Central Bank has the power to set reserve requirements, allocate credit, and fix interest rate levels. As the Monetary Board, it first introduced reserve requirements on the banking system in November 1975, with a reserve requirement of 5 and 3 per cent respectively on demand and time deposits. In December 1976 it also introduced a 3 per cent cash reserve requirement on savings deposits. Interest rates are also controlled and most recently, in February 1985, interest rates on bank deposits were reduced by 2 per cent to 15 per cent, and the maximum lending rate dropped to 18 per cent.

As shown in Table 5.2, the Central Bank holds the bulk of its assets, some 61.2 per cent in 1986, in foreign assets. These represent both Western Samoa official foreign exchange reserves, as well as providing the backing for the Western Samoa tala. The Bank began to hold some foreign reserves in September 1984, but did not purchase the full holdings of the commercial banks until April to July 1985. The government, though, still holds some foreign exchange reserves independently: 9.5 million of 31.65 million tala in December 1985.

The Central Bank's other major asset holdings include advances to the government and interest-bearing deposits with the Treasury.

Unlike many central banks, notes in circulation are not its major source of funds. Instead, some 42.1 per cent of the Bank's liabilities were in the form of deposits from commercial banks over and above their legal requirements. This reflected the high level of the liquidity within the economy traditionally experienced over the Christmas season. The Central Bank nevertheless has been responsible for the issue of the tala since 30 November 1984[14] and currency on issue provides some 30 per cent of its funds. Commercial bank reserve deposits and deposits from government bodies provide the other major funds.

TABLE 5.2   Central Bank of Samoa: assets and liabilities, 31 December
1985

Assets:	WS$ m
Foreign assets	18.12
Advances to government	3.78
Deposits with government	1.67
Government securities	0.54
Fixed assets	0.18
Other assets	5.30
Total assets	29.59
Liabilities:	WS$ m
Capital and reserves	2.08
Notes in circulation	9.02
Government deposits	2.59
Bank reserve deposits	2.73
Other bank deposits	12.47
Other liabilities	0.70
Total liabilities	29.59

Source: Central Bank of Samoa (1986) *Bulletin*, March, Table A-4.

Commercial Banks in Western Samoa

Commercial bank industry in Western Samoa is comprised of two
institutions; the Bank of Western Samoa and the Pacific Commercial
Bank. They both provide a fairly standard range of commercial and
savings bank services, but have a strong concentration on foreign-
trade-related business. In addition to its normal banking business,
the Bank of Western Samoa performed many quasi-central-bank
roles prior to the establishment of the Central Bank of Samoa. This
section examines the recent history, regulation, assets, funding, staff
and representation of the industry.

(i) *Development*

Commercial banking in Western Samoa commenced on 28 April
1915, when the Bank of New Zealand opened a branch in Apia
following the capture and occupation of Western Samoa by New
Zealand troops in August 1914.[15] While there were no specific
reasons for this opening, the New Zealand Administrator for

Western Samoa had apparently had some difficulties in local financial matters and the Bank would also improve the payment facilities for the New Zealand troops. In addition, from a commercial viewpoint there were a number of financial incentives for the Bank of New Zealand to include additional drafts, bills of exchange, foreign exchange, and deposit business.[16]

Initially, at least, the Bank was well received and had a marked effect on local commercial life. As one report in 1918 commented,

> hitherto banking methods had been unknown in Western Samoa; merchants however soon commenced to avail themselves of the institution; and the financial convenience afforded has proven a boon, not only to the community and the administration, but also to outsiders having business relations with Apia.[17]

The Bank of New Zealand services, however, did not expand much outside of the major business community, and its lack of business with the more general public forced them to rely on the Post Office or local merchants for their banking requirements. This was also true for even some planters. As one report in 1934 commented,

> apart from the favoured few, they also say, there is no financial assistance forthcoming from the government or from the Bank of New Zealand, a branch of which operates in Apia, so that the planters have to depend upon merchants for advances on their produce.[18]

There was probably some justification for these complaints, for even as late as 1957 the Bank of New Zealand's Apia branch was operated with only a staff of 12. A government report at that time found its business confined mainly to trade financing and documentation, with no provision for accepting fixed deposits, and it dealt mainly 'with the trading and planting communities, though it has some Samoans among its clients'.[19]

Both for political reasons and to expand local banking services, Western Samoan leaders had long sought their own Samoa institution, and as early as 1951 a Reserve Bank of New Zealand economist, V. D. Stace, was sent to Western Samoa to study the position and his findings were reported by the government in 1953.[20] Stace proposed that:

the government of Western Samoa and the Bank of New Zealand [the only bank operating in the Territory] should be the major shareholders in the new bank and that the Reserve Bank of New Zealand should be a minor shareholder.[21] Besides its planned

central banking and normal trading bank functions, the new bank should take over savings bank business from the Post Office and devote special attention to the development of rural credit facilities.[22]

These proposals, however, were not accepted, and the idea was postponed until 1956–7 when the Samoans again raised the issue. As one New Zealand government report concluded, 'there has developed among Samoan political leaders a strong desire for some measure of banking reform which would at least permit some direct Samoan participation in banking'.[23] This interest resulted in another market survey in February 1957. This time a team was sent with officers from the Bank of New Zealand, Reserve Bank of New Zealand, and New Zealand Treasury 'to examine fiscal and banking problems in the Territory of Western Samoa'.[24] The Committee considered four possible alternatives: a bank owned by the Samoan government and managed under contract by the Bank of New Zealand; a bank owned jointly by the Samoan government, the Bank of New Zealand and the Reserve Bank of New Zealand; the Bank of New Zealand could compete directly with a new Samoan government-owned bank; and a joint-venture bank owned 45 and 55 per cent by the Samoan government and the Bank of New Zealand.[25] This last alternative was favoured by the Committee and approved by the Legislative Council of Western Samoa on 22 May 1957.

The Bank of Western Samoa was created under the Bank of Western Samoa Ordinance 1958 in February 1959 and commenced business on 1 April 1959. Under the arrangement the new Bank purchased the assets and operations of the Bank of New Zealand's Apia branch and was owned 55 per cent by the Bank of New Zealand and 45 per cent by the Western Samoa government. Initially the Bank of New Zealand could appoint three directors and the Western Samoa government only two, but this was changed to two each in August 1975.

In line with its planned quasi-central-banking functions, the Bank of Western Samoa assumed the currency issue role from the Treasury as well as the management of most foreign exchange reserves. It had to hold at least 30 per cent of its notes and deposit liabilities in foreign assets and limit its advances to the government to not more than 25 per cent of government revenue. In addition to its normal commercial business, the Bank of Western Samoa also provided banking services to the government, statutory bodies and government-owned enterprises, and acted as the registrar for government securities. Finally, since 1 April 1964 the Bank has operated a savings bank division in competition with the Post Office Savings Bank. The Bank of Western Samoa continues as the largest bank and controls two-thirds to three-quarters of the local banking market.

As elsewhere in the Asia Pacific region, the late 1960s and early 1970s found foreign bankers, particularly from Japan and the United States, interested in opening local branches in Western Samoa. When evaluating the foreign bank applications, the Western Samoa government considered a number of factors to include the minimum capital (at least US$ 1,000,000), subsequent support of the branch in time of need, investment policies, foreign exchange business, localization and staff training policies, degree of local management powers, desire to open a branch or subsidiary, attitude on the purchase of government securities and financing government projects, range of banking services, attitude to lending with customary land security, representation outside of Apia, expected percentage of loan portfolio by sector, the bank's experiences in other similar countries, assistance afforded in trade and tourism promotion, and a range of other administrative matters.[26]

In April 1970 the Bank of Hawaii and First National City Bank of New York (now Citibank) both made approaches to the government to establish branches.[27] The National Bank of New Zealand also expressed interest, and successfully completed its negotiations for an Apia branch in May 1975 and planned to open in October 1975. Prior to the opening, however, a change in the conditions caused the National not to pursue the matter[28] and it is believed that Citibank had a fairly similar experience. Though this change in government policy is not publicly documented, it is believed that the government decided that another New-Zealand-operated institution would not provide the same advantage as other foreign representation. Similarly, rather than a foreign bank branch, a joint-venture bank between two non-New-Zealand foreign banks and local interests would be more desirable.

The joint-venture suggestion resulted in the Bank of Hawaii approaching the Australian-based Bank of New South Wales (now the Westpac Banking Corporation) and the incorporation on 18 July 1977 of the Pacific Commercial Bank Ltd. The Bank is owned 40.6 per cent by the Bank of Hawaii, 40.6 per cent by the Westpac Banking Corporation and the remaining 18.8 per cent by some 101 Western Samoan shareholders to include the National Provident Fund, National Pacific Insurance, and most major traders. These hold mostly 5000 share parcels.

While there was a public issue to help raise local capital, at least some of the smaller shareholdings resulted from Pacific Commercial's acquisition of the assets and liabilities of the Pacific Savings and Loan Co. through an exchange of shares based on 6.5 shares in Pacific Savings for one share of Pacific Commercial. Pacific Savings had operated effectively as a local finance company since 1969 and had been partly owned by the Bank of Hawaii since 1971. (See pp. 328–9.) Thus when the new bank opened for business on 22 August 1977, it had the advantage of an existing client list, deposit-based and loan portfolio from Pacific Savings.

(ii) *Regulation*

When the Bank of Western Samoa was established in 1959 there was no central bank or monetary board in operation and in the end the Bank was regulated under a combination of its Act and agreements between the Bank of New Zealand and the Western Samoa Treasury. Later, when the Pacific Commercial Bank commenced operations, there was still no specific legislation covering financial institutions, nor was Pacific Commercial created under a special ordinance. Instead much of its control was arranged between the government and the foreign bank shareholders when the license approval was first granted.

The government's first regulatory requirement was to set a reserve requirement on demand and time deposits. Initially these were equal to 5 per cent of the bank's demand deposits and 3 per cent of its time deposits. Later these percentages were raised to 7 per cent and 5 per cent respectively and expanded to cover savings account balances as well. While the commercial banks receive no interest on these reserve deposits, the Central Bank does pay interest, currently at 7 per cent per annum, on any excess deposits.

(iii) *Assets*

As shown in Table 5.3, the commercial banks hold approximately half of their assets in loans and other advances to the private sector, the government and government bodies. Of these the private sector is the most important. The commercial bank lending rates ranged between 15 per cent for agricultural and housing finance to 18 per cent for business advances and 21 per cent for import financing.

Reflecting its government ownership and status as initially the country's only bank, the Bank of Western Samoa gradually expanded from primarily a trade-financing operation into a broader-based banking business: it commenced its Small Loan Scheme for personal lending in 1965, Housing Mortgage Loan Scheme in 1966, and Term Loan Fund in 1970.

TABLE 5.3   Commercial banks in Western Samoa: assets and liabilities, 31 December 1985

%	Assets	WS$ m
2.1	Cash at bank	1.45
3.9	Reserve deposits with Central Bank	2.73
18.0	Other deposits with Central Bank	12.47
6.8	Foreign assets	4.68
32.3	Claims on the private sector	22.39
2.0	Claims on the government	1.38
17.5	Claims on public enterprises	12.08
17.4	Other assets	12.06
100.0	Total assets	69.24

%	Liabilities	WS$ m
12.4	Demand deposits – private	8.57
3.7	Demand deposits – public enterprises	2.53
1.2	Demand deposits – government	0.85
22.1	Time deposits – private	15.31
13.3	Time deposits – public enterprises	9.20
0.2	Time deposits – government	0.15
11.4	Savings deposits	7.93
16.1	Capital and reserves	11.12
0.9	Foreign liabilities	0.67
18.7	Other liabilities	12.91
100.0	Total liabilities	69.24

Source: Central Bank of Samoa (1986) *Bulletin*, March, Table A-5.

TABLE 5.4   Commercial bank advances to the private sector, by type of industry, December 1985

%	Industry	WS$ m
4.6	Agricultural	1.02
2.6	Manufacturing	0.58
11.0	Housing and construction	2.46
23.4	Distribution, exports, imports	5.23
1.8	Transportation	0.41
22.1	Other business	4.96
1.5	Non-profit organizations	0.34
33.0	Personal loans	7.39
100.0	Total advances	22.39

Source: Central Bank of Samoa (1986) *Bulletin*, March, Table A-7.

The Housing Mortgage Loan Scheme is probably the most interesting as its loans were initially funded by an amount equal to 20 per cent (later 40 per cent) of the Bank's savings account deposits. The loans were intended mainly for new home financing and extended for periods of 10 to 15 years.

These various programmes have diversified the banks' lending so that today, as shown in Table 5.4, personal loans now comprise the largest private sector lending category. Trade-related finance nevertheless remains second in importance.

Public sector lending is still very important, and absorbed some 37.5 per cent of total bank loans and advances in 1985. This percentage is relatively low as the public sector has typically accounted for more than half of the bank advances and reached over three-quarters in 1982. Of the public enterprise loans, the Western Samoa Trust Estate Corporation is the largest borrower as well as the largest public enterprise. Other major state enterprises with commercial bank financing included Copra Board, Cocoa Board and the Special Project Development Corporation.

(iv) *Funding*

As was shown in Table 5.3, the commercial banks raise most funds from deposits of which time deposits are the most important. In 1985, for example, time deposits from all sources accounted for 35.6 per cent of their total funding, demand deposits 17.3 per cent and savings

TABLE 5.5   Commercial banks in Western Samoa time deposits, by
source and type, December 1985 (figures in tala millions)

Months	Business enterprizes	Individuals	Public enterprizes	Total
One	0.94	1.62	0.43	2.99
Over one, up to three	1.43	1.39	0.65	3.47
Over three, up to six	0.58	1.62	1.20	3.40
Over six, up to 12	1.67	3.49	5.39	10.55
Over 12, up to 24	0.47	2.10	1.53	4.10
Totals	5.09	10.22	9.20	24.51

Source: Central Bank of Samoa (1986) *Bulletin*, March, Table A-8.

deposits 11.4 per cent. In 1985 the banks paid 7 per cent on savings
deposits, and interest on time deposits ranged from 10 per cent on
one-month deposits to 15 per cent on deposits for over three months.
Individuals provided the major portion of the time deposits, 41.6 per
cent at the end of 1985. Government bodies were the next important,
followed by business enterprises. The specific deposit figures and
their breakdown by depositor type and maturity are shown in Table
5.5.

Prior to 1981, bank notes issued by the Bank of Western Samoa
were also important funding for that institution, and thus the banking
system as a whole. The Monetary Board of Western Samoa, however, assumed this function on 1 June 1981, and the Bank of Western
Samoa notes were gradually withdrawn. By February 1985 Bank of
Western Samoa notes were no longer in circulation.

(v) *Representation*

Both commercial banks have representation on Western Samoa's two
main islands. The Bank of Western Samoa in addition to its main
office in Apia, has six full-time agencies and three part-time agencies.
The Pacific Commercial Bank operates three bank-staffed agencies in
addition to its Apia head office. In 1985 there were no private
banking agency arrangements in Western Samoa.

In addition to permanent offices, both banks use some mobile or
part-time bank-staffed agencies. Pacific Commercial has taken an
interesting approach to mobile banking and uses this method to
service its merchant clients rather than for savings deposits. These

visits are conducted daily within the greater Apia area, and weekly or bi-weekly in a number of other areas: it has apparently been very successful in gaining business.

(vi) *Staffing*

Western Samoa's two commercial banks are both headed by expatriate personnel and have other expatriates in key positions within each bank. Their number has declined over time due to the increased training and experience of local personnel and government pressure on localization. The Bank of Western Samoa, for example, had 6 of it 184 staff as secondments from the Bank of New Zealand in 1983, while in 1985 the Bank operated with only 4 expatriates. Similarly, the Pacific Commercial Bank, which had 3 expatriates, now has only 2 among a staff of 80: the Bank of Hawaii traditionally provides the Bank's general manager, and its other foreign shareholder, the Westpac Banking Corporation, the manager of the international department.

In addition to the bank's own in-house training programmes and support of their parent's overseas training facilities and job training work, bank staff are also encouraged to take the qualifying examinations of the Western Samoa Society of Accountants and the New Zealand Bankers' Institute.

Post Office Savings Bank

The Post Office Savings Bank operates as a branch of the Western Samoa Post Office under the Post Office Act 1972. It provides a basic passbook and term account savings as well as the sale and collection of internal and external postal remittance orders. In addition to its banking activities it also accepts payment of telephone and telex accounts.

The New Zealand government postal service traditionally has operated a postal savings division as an integral part of its operations and so, when a postal system was created following its League of Nations mandate, the New Zealand administration created a savings bank in 1921 as well. This position continued through independence. As one report in the late 1950s commented, 'the Post Office, while it is administered locally as a branch of the Samoan public service, is for accounting and investment purposes a part of the New Zealand Post Office'.[29]

Though the Post Office was never particularly aggressive in raising deposits, there were relatively few other alternatives for interest-paying deposits: the Bank of New Zealand in Apia, for example, did not encourage such business. Thus, when the Bank was converted into a joint venture with the Samoan government, these postal operations seemed a logical means of providing the new bank with an immediate local deposit base. In the end, though, the New Zealand officials, no doubt influenced by the position in New Zealand, argued that 'the existence of two institutions actively competing to maximise savings' could well benefit mobilization[30] and the Post Office Savings Bank retained its independence.

The Bank, however, never provided much competition, other than in terms of branch locations, for the Bank of Western Samoa, and from an account base of 36,000 in 1966 (an average balance of WS$ 25), there was little change over the mid-1970s to the early 1980s when the totals ranged between 37,000 and 38,000. In 1980, however, the Bank took a new direction and raised its rates to be competitive with commercial bank savings accounts, and it has subsequently retained this policy. For example, whereas its rates had increased to 6 per cent on savings accounts and 11 per cent on investment accounts in 1982, they were raised again significantly in 1983 to 8 and 17 per cent respectively. As a result its account numbers have grown significantly and by May 1986 had reached some 50,000.

As shown in Table 5.6, the Post Office Savings Bank invests its funds in either government securities or bank deposits. Its funding is similarly simple, and provided either from savings account deposits or 12-month term investment accounts. As indicated in the Table, the savings accounts are by far the most important. These deposits are withdrawable on demand and in May 1986 earned interest at 7.5 per cent per annum. The 12-month investment accounts paid interest at 15 per cent per annum.

Though not reflected in its balance sheet, the Post Office Savings Bank is very active in the foreign exchange business as many Samoans living overseas use foreign postal orders for remitting funds to their relatives at home. These payments are commonly handled through the Post Office Savings Bank, particularly in rural areas. In 1985 alone, it handled some 55,000 of these inward money orders worth a total of WS$ 6.7 million.

Its payment facility for telephone and telex accounts is also an important business and, over 1985 involved some 42,000 account payments worth WS$ 5 million.

TABLE 5.6   Post Office Savings Bank: assets and liabilities,
31 December 1985

Assets:	*WS$*
Government Development Loan Stock	1,433,000
Cash and bank balances	151,000
Total assets	1,584,000

Liabilities:	*WS$*
Savings deposits	1,406,000
Term deposits	136,000
Other liabilities	42,000
Total liabilities	1,584,000

Source: Central Bank of Samoa (1986) *Bulletin*, March, Table A-11.

Post office officials would like to expand these other financial services. As one report comments – the provision basically of only basic savings accounts and one-year term investment accounts 'obviously limits its opportunity to compete'. [31] Indeed, in the long term there is some concern that 'unless new services such as investment flexibility, cheque accounts, and small loans can be introduced in the near term, the bank cannot be expected to grow'.[32]

In terms of staffing, the Post Office Savings Bank's 18 employees are concentrated at its head office in Apia where they centrally maintain the Bank's some 50,000 account records, and the accounting and distribution of cash and payment records. Until 1983 a New Zealand Post Office Savings Bank officer served as the local manager under contract with the Bank, but this position has since been localized. Its current offices and island locations are shown in Table 5.7.

Development Bank of Western Samoa

The Development Bank of Western Samoa was established on 27 August 1974 under the Development Bank of Western Samoa Act 1974, and commenced operations on 1 October 1974. It was created to assume the operations of the Development Department of the Bank of Western Samoa. Under its Act (Section 5), the bank is

to promote the expansion of the economy of Western Samoa for the economic and social advancement of the people of Western

TABLE 5.7   Post Office Savings Bank representation, May 1986

Type	Location	Island
Head Office	Apia	Upolu
Branch	Faleulo	Upolu
Branch	Matautu-uta	Upolu
Branch	Salelologa	Savai'i
Branch	Tuasivi	Savai'i
Branch	Fagamalo	Savai'i
Branch	Asau	Savai'i

Source: Post Office Savings Bank (1986).

Samoa by making loans and giving financial, technical and advisory assistance in its discretion to any enterprises in Western Samoa.

While it is mainly a medium- and long-term lender for agricultural, industrial, and infrastructural purposes, it has a wide range of powers under its Act (Section 8). For example, it can make equity investments, underwrite securities, accept deposits, assist in project identification and promote new business projects and guarantee loans from other sources; provide technical, managerial, and financial advice; accept deposits; participate in the management of client enterprises; and conduct leasing business. While it has concentrated on lending in the past, the government would like it to 'adopt a more innovative, aggressive, and diversified role in identifying and promoting new projects'.[33]

(i) *Development*

The Development Bank's predecessor, the Development Department of the Bank of Western Samoa, was established in 1965 to administer the Government's Development Loan Fund. This fund was started with WS$ 20,000 to make small loans to Western Samoa agricultural and industrial projects. In 1966 the Department's operations were expanded to include a WS$ 160,000 Plantations Restoration Fund following major hurricane damage to the islands. Later, when the Development Bank became a separate body, the Development Loan Fund's operations were assumed by the Development Bank and the Plantation Restoration Fund absorbed by the Treasury Department.

TABLE 5.8   Development Bank of Western Samoa: assets and liabilities, 30 September 1982

Assets	WS$
Net fixed assets	389,731
Investments at cost	234,913
Net loans	10,883,636
Other assets	26,212
Cash and bank	541,945
Total assets	12,076,437

Liabilities	WS$
Issued capital	3,970,980
Reserves	237,027
Borrowings	7,341,107
Agency funds	36,563
Creditors and accruals	286,853
Government	16,250
Accrued interest	187,657
Total liabilities	12,076,437

Source: Development Bank of Western Samoa (1982) *Annual Report*, p. 14.

(ii) *Assets*

As shown in Table 5.8, the Development Bank holds mainly loans and advances, and these comprised some 90.1 per cent of assets in 1982. These loans can extend for long periods, but most are for a one- to three-year duration, and up to WS$ 5000 in amount. There are relatively few advances for more than WS$ 50,000.

In terms of advances and other assistance, the Development Bank's total commitment to any one client cannot exceed an amount equal to 25 per cent of the Development Bank's unimpaired shareholders' equity. Its commitment should also not be more than 65 per cent of an industrial client's total fixed assets or 80 per cent of an agricultural project's total assets. In allocating its funds, the Bank gives preference (under Section 6) to those projects using local raw materials, improving local employment or training, increasing local entrepreneurship, expanding exports, decreasing imports, lowering local costs, or improving efficiency or standards of local goods and services.

As with other development banks, its advances do not require the same level of security as a commercial bank advance. However, the

Development Bank does insist 'on a loan being adequately supported by a number of guarantors, preferably people with a certain level of kinship who could be expected to influence the borrower to work his project and honour his loan obligations'.[34] While this has worked with some success, recently loan arrears have grown to 20 per cent of the Bank's advances.

While the Bank has since introduced more detailed loan evaluations and monitoring (hence lower lending over 1985), its main constraints remain

> loan procedures; problems in supervision and follow-up; scattered lending, which makes loan supervision difficult and costly [the cost of credit is over 90 per cent of the interest earnings]; lack of security for loans; lack of co-ordination with line agencies; interest rate structure; and non-repayment of loans.[35]

The Bank's loans are primarily to private sector borrowers and can be divided into three general categories: loans to agriculture, group lending, and loans to industry. In late 1985, loans to agriculture accounted for approximately half of the Development Bank's loans outstanding, industry around 40 per cent and group lending projects, the remainder.

In terms of agricultural lending, the Development Bank is the major provider of agricultural credit within the country, and accounts for about 80 per cent of these compared to the Bank of Western Samoa's 12 and the National Provident Fund's 8 per cent.[36] These loans are generally for one to three years and involve an interest rate of 10 to 12 per cent. The advances provide assistance to a wide range of agricultural production, but have traditionally concentrated on mixed farming, taro and other root crops. Passion fruit farming has also been important, but since 1984 the Bank has tried to limit its exposure in that area.

Agricultural lending is by far the most important activity in terms of loan numbers, but most agricultural advances are for relatively small amounts and accounted for virtually all of the Bank's 2301 loans of WS$ 500 or less made over 1984. While these loans are meant to finance productive investment rather than consumption, loan officers find it 'difficult to recognize a small loan application for agricultural development purposes which is genuine from that which is really intended to meet some provident purpose, until after the event'.[37] Furthermore, 'because of the sheer volume of these small loans, the Development Bank finds itself unable to provide adequate time for client assessment, project evaluation, and project supervision and follow-up to guard against mis-use of funds and project failure'.[38] Due to high costs of small agricultural loans, the Development Bank helped establish the Samoa Credit Union League, with the hope that credit unions might assume the Development Bank's smaller loan functions. It intends to provide the League with a manager, office space, secretarial back up, and transportation support, at least through 1987.

Though group lending has never accounted for more that 10 per cent of Development Bank advances, it is nevertheless an important activity for the Bank. The village is the key economic unit within Samoan society and, in conjunction with the extended family, offers excellent development potential. At present most of these loans are for school buildings and health centres (often in conjunction with grants from the government's Rural Development Fund), but some also finance agricultural development projects. The Asian Development Bank at least believes that a greater use of group or village guarantees, streamlined loan appraisal procedures, and an area approach for administration, would greatly improve the Development Bank's operations.[39]

Development Bank advances to industry account for its larger loans. To date, most of these finance Western Samoan manufacturing and processing but it also funds transport and communications, equipment purchases, commerce, tourism and professional services. These advances are typically for a longer term than most agricultural loans, and involve a higher interest charge ranging from 16 to 18 per cent.

In addition to loans and guarantees, the Development Bank may also invest in the shares of client companies. Under Section 8, its participation in a single enterprise is limited to an amount equal to 5 per cent of the Bank's unimpaired shareholders equity, and total equity investments up to 20 per cent. In 1982 it had only one equity investment, WS$ 4913 in Polynesian Match shares, but hopes to expand its investments to include other companies.

(iii) *Funding*

As shown in Table 5.8, the Development Bank obtains most funding from borrowings, some 60.8 per cent in 1982. These come mainly from loans through the Asian Development Bank, but also includes borrowings from the European Community, and the Australian and

New Zealand governments. Locally, it also borrows tala from the National Provident Fund as well as through overdraft facilities with the two local banks.

In raising its funds, the Development Bank is precluded from assuming any foreign exchange risk on borrowings and must limit its long-term liabilities exposure to three times its unimpaired shareholders' equity. To build its equity position, the Bank must set aside at least 50 per cent of net income to its reserve account until this equals its paid-up capital.

The Bank's own capital and reserves is its second most important source of funding and accounted for 34.8 per cent of total funds in 1982. The initial funds were provided mainly through grants from the Western Samoan, Australian and New Zealand governments, and have been supplemented in part by the Bank's own retained earnings. While the Development Bank can both accept deposits and issue shares to non-government investors, by early 1986 it had not done either.

(iv) *Staffing*

The Development Bank of Western Samoa localized its management positions relatively quickly, and in May 1986 had a staff of 110. In addition to its own training officer, staff also benefit from special training courses run by the Asian Development Bank, Development Finance Corporation of New Zealand, and other bodies. More training, particularly through overseas secondments, is apparently still required, for as one study concluded, 'the restricted availability of trained and experienced manpower' remains a problem in the Bank's operations.[40]

(v) *Representation*

As yet the Development Bank has relatively limited representation within the country, with only two offices other than its main office. This is unfortunate for although Savai'i has the greatest potential for agricultural development, in mid-1985 it still accounted for only 21 per cent of Development Bank advances. While more should be done to diversify its lending, there remains the problem of servicing 'a population spread across a number of islands with poor communication facilities'.[41]

TABLE 5.9   Development Bank of Western Samoa representation, 1985

Type	Location	Island	Date opened
Head office	Apia	Upolu	1974
Branch	Salelologa	Savai'i	October 1979
Agency	Asau	Savai'i	March 1980

Source: Development Bank of Western Samoa (1985) *Annual Report*.

Off-shore Banks

As with other Pacific island countries, Western Samoa has at least considered the possibilities of an off-shore banking centre as a source of foreign exchange. In 1981, for example, there was some discussion about establishing an off-shore bank, and in 1983 Western Samoa briefly entered this area with the establishment of the Hong-Kong-owned, International Pacific Bank.[42] This bank was intended to bring substantial foreign investment funds from Hong Kong, but never really commenced business. Its lack of success has made the concept of off-shore banking less attractive to the local authorities.

Public Trust Office

The Public Trust Office was established initially in 1921 as the Samoa Public Trust Office, and now operates under the Public Trust Office Act 1975. Traditionally it assists in the preparation of wills, and in estate and trust administration to include acting as an executor, administrator, trustee, receiver, guardian, and arbitrator. In addition, it is also the major source of longer term housing finance within the country, and in late 1985 had assets of around WS$ 4 million.

Under Section 26, its Common Fund investments are limited to the government securities of Western Samoa, New Zealand, the United Kingdom, Australia or Australian states; first mortgage advances on real estate up to three-quarters of the appraised value; deposits with the commercial banks, Development Bank or Post Office Savings Bank; or by way of mortgages secured by debentures, stock, bonds, funds or other eligible government securities up to four-fifths of their value.

TABLE 5.10   Public Trust Office: assets and liabilities,
31 December 1979

Assets:	WS$
Cash at bank and on hand	34,234
Prepayments	1,190
Mortgages	2,087,810
Advances to beneficiaries	50,763
Deposits – Post Office Savings Bank	2,719
Deposits – Bank of Western Samoa	1,464
Government securities	5,000
Net Fixed assets	2,871
Total assets	2,186,051

Liabilities:	WS$
Mortgage payments due	26,286
Sundry creditors and accruals	1,668
Audit fee provisions	800
Common Fund	258,483
Enemy property estates	30,478
Public Trust Office Staff Fund	63
Deposits from Treasury Sinking Fund	300,000
Deposits from National Provident Fund	1,350,000
Deposits from Post Office	30,000
Deposits from Pacific Commercial Bank	3,100
Assurance and Reserve Fund	181,378
Legal Expenses Reserve Fund	3,795
Total liabilities	2,186,051

Source: Public Trust Office (1979) *Accounts and Report for the Year Ending 31 December 1979*, p. 8.

As shown in Table 5.10, most of its advances were in the form of mortgages, and these are confined primarily to residential housing finance. Its over-all rates in 1985, however, ranged between 12 to 15 per cent per annum.

In addition to its mortgage lending, the Public Trust Office also provides financing under certain circumstances to its clients. For example, when an estate has assets but not sufficient cash to meet necessary expenses, the Fund may lend it the necessary funds against a charge over the estate's assets. Similarly, it may lend funds to an estate's beneficiaries up to two-thirds the value of their share as determined by the Public Trustee.

As shown in Table 5.10, the Public Trust Office actually receives relatively little of its funds from Common Fund deposits: money held by the Trust Office on behalf of estates. Instead, most of its money is provided through deposits from the National Provident Fund, and to a lesser extent the Treasury and the Post Office Savings Bank. The funds from the National Provident Fund are provided specifically in support of Public Trust Office mortgage lending.

Western Samoa National Provident Fund

The Western Samoa National Provident Fund was established on 13 August 1972 under the National Provident Fund Act 1972, to provide compulsory coverage for all wage and salary earners. The Fund also administers benefits under the Government Superannuation Act 1972, the Parliamentary Retirement Fund and the Judiciary Retirement Fund and acts as the local paying agents for the New Zealand Superannuation Fund. In late 1985 the Fund had assets of some WS$ 36 million, and a membership in excess of 55,000.

The Fund initially operated as part of the New Zealand National Provident Fund, but was eventually restructured as a separate body some years after Samoa's independence. An associated fund, the Government Superannuation Scheme, was also initially established under the New Zealand Government National Provident Fund, as the Western Samoa Superannuation Scheme, to provide coverage to employees of the Western Samoa government, Western Samoa Trust Estates Corporation and the Bank of Western Samoa.

The Fund covers all wage and salary earners with the exception of certain plantation workers, domestic servants, and self-employed persons. It requires that an amount, currently equal to 10 per cent of the employee's wages, be contributed by the employer to the Fund. The employer in turn may recover half of this contribution from the employee except where the employee is under the age of 15 and does not earn more than the minimum labour wage of 62.5 sene an hour. Due to this coverage the Fund, as shown in Table 5.11, has grown steadily both in terms of assets and membership numbers.

This money is then invested by the Fund on the member's behalf and each year an interest payment is declared based on the contributor's account balance. Under its Act (Section 9) the Fund is limited to a maximum payment of 2.5 per cent unless it can fulfil all its obligations. In practice, however, this restriction has not proved a problem and the Fund has declared interest payments of 5.5 per cent in 1981, 6

TABLE 5.11   Western Samoa National Provident Fund: assets, members and employers, 1979–84

Year	Assets	Members	Employers
1979	13,602,384	41,231	401
1980	16,688,732	46,073	414
1981	19,782,991	49,478	486
1982	23,364,238	52,416	538
1983	27,362,581	55,414	586
1984	31,765,519	58,607	641

Source: Western Samoa National Provident Fund (1986).

per cent in both 1982 and 1983, and 6.5 per cent in both 1984 and 1985.

The contributions and their accumulated interest is available on reaching the age 55, on death payable to one's estate, to those permanently leaving Western Samoa, or when physical or mental incapacitation precludes further employment. In the case of death before age 55, a special death benefit is also paid. With normal retirement at 55, the member can choose a full pension based on his account balance, or receive a quarter of his account in cash and the remainder via a reduced pension. Alternatively, where the balance is less than WS$ 1600 or the person is leaving the country, the full balance may be paid in cash. As the pension payable is calculated using an assumption that the contributor will live for an additional eight years, the member's account balance is divided by eight to find the annual entitlement. This amount is then divided by 26 and paid fortnightly. In contrast, pensions paid under the Government Superannuation scheme are calculated on the contributor's total salary over the last five years rather than his contribution.

In practice, the pensions payable by the Fund have not been fixed to the initial calculation but rather have been adjusted upward as part of the Board's social welfare responsibilities. This first commenced in June 1981 when a 15 per cent increase to all pensions was declared. The Board has since conducted an annual review of pension benefits.

(i) *Assets*

Under its Act (Section 6) the Fund may invest its fund in

Western Samoa and elsewhere after giving due consideration to the economic soundness and viability of the undertaking . . . [and

TABLE 5.12   Western Samoa National Provident Fund: assets and
liabilities, 31 December 1982

%	Assets	WS$
15.7	Net fixed assets	3,697,021
35.9	Western Samoa govt securities	8,455,050
7.0	Public Trustee Common Fund	1,650,000
1.3	Development Bank	300,000
2.1	W. Samoa Trust Estates Corporation	500,000
2.2	GSF Small Loans	513,797
30.0	Advances to private sector	7,056,308
1.1	Shares	265,000
0.8	Cash on hand and at bank	199,219
2.1	Short-term deposits	500,000
1.3	Accrued interest	306,216
0.3	Other current assets	76,287
0.2	Intangible assets	54,000
100.0	Total assets	23,572,898

%	Liabilities	WS$
8.0	Member funds – GSF[a]	1,904,633
0.2	Member funds – JRF[b]	36,580
0.3	Member funds – PRF[c]	64,343
62.1	Member funds – NPF[d]	14,644,589
22.9	Reserves – GSF[a]	5,403,196
5.6	Reserves – NPF[d]	1,310,897
0.9	Current liabilities	208,660
100.0	Total liabilities	23,572,398

[a] Government Superannuation Fund.
[b] Judiciary Retirement Fund.
[c] Parliamentary Retirement Fund.
[d] National Provident Fund.

Source: Western Samoa National Provident Fund (1982) *Annual Report and Statement of Accounts*, p. 7.

its ability]. . . . if brought forward to maturity, to provide for a yield on the investment commensurate with the degree of risk associated with it and to provide if necessary for the repayment of the capital invested whenever due.

As shown in Table 5.12, Western Samoan government securities comprise its major investment, with some 35.9 per cent of total assets. Of similar importance are its advances to the private sector (30 per cent). These together have seen the Fund 'become one of the most important sources of long-term investment capital in Western Samoa'.[43]

In terms of its lending, the National Provident Fund in late 1985 charged between 10 and 17 per cent per annum on its advances, with the lower rates for loans to individuals and the higher rates for commercial purposes, normally 15 to 17 per cent. As shown in Table 5.13, the Fund's lending to the private sector is dominated by construction finance with such loans accounting for 56.7 per cent of the total.

Traditionally the Fund has concentrated on making larger loans, and most lending is for a minimum of WS$ 20,000. Since 1984, though, contributors have been able to borrow small amounts from the Fund. Provided they have been contributors for at least five years and have more than WS$ 1000, members can borrow up to 45 per cent of their account balance for investment purposes. These loans are made at a concessional interest rate of 10 per cent, and repayable over ten years. The Fund has allocated a maximum loan portfolio of WS$ 2 million under this scheme, but this has not presented any difficulties.

TABLE 5.13   Western Samoa National Provident Fund: advances to the private sector, by industry, 31 December 1982

%		WS$
2.4	Agricultural	183,513
8.9	Industry	673,518
10.8	Trade and commerce	815,275
14.4	Services	1,089,351
56.7	Construction	4,294,651
6.8	GSF Small Loans	513,797
100.0	Total	7,570,105

Source: Western Samoa National Provident Fund (1982) *Annual Report and Statement of Accounts*, p. 4.

In addition to its lending and deposits, the National Provident Fund may also invest in equity securities, but in 1982 these comprised only 1.1 per cent of Fund assets. The shares included investments in the Western Samoa Hotel Co. Ltd and Western Samoa Match Factory Ltd.

(ii) *Funding*

As indicated, the National Provident Fund obtains its money from employers and employee contributors as well as the interest and investment income from its portfolio. In 1982, for example, it received WS$ 3,696,784 in contributions from employers and members and paid out WS$ 1,204,840 to members leaving the Fund and WS$ 288,680 in pensions over 1982. Its investment income over the same period amounted to WS$ 1,623,774.

Accident Compensation Board

The Accident Compensation Board of Western Samoa was established on 20 March 1978 under the Accident Compensation Act 1978 to administer the government's workers compensation and motor-vehicle accident insurance schemes. These were created as part of the government's social welfare programme so 'that compensation would be available to all persons suffering personal injury by accident in Western Samoa whether the injury occurred at work or on the road, and it abolished the notion that compensation should be based on fault'.[44] In addition to direct financial compensation, the Board also emphasizes safety promotion, rehabilitation, and the protection of dependents.

Though not a financial institution in a strict sense, the Accident Compensation Board, through its two compensation funds, the Workers' Compensation Fund and the Motor Vehicle Fund, is nevertheless an important longer term investor within the Samoan economy. Under its Act (Section 42), the Board may invest 'on fixed deposit with any bank in Western Samoa approved by the Board or in public securities' and receive the resulting income free of tax. As shown in Table 5.14 most assets were held in Western Samoa government securities, 63.8 per cent in 1984, and deposits with commercial banks, 32 per cent.

The Workers' Compensation Fund is the most important of the two funds, and in 1984 had assets of WS$ 2,474,350 and an investment income of WS$ 301,807. It is funded by contributions from employers equal to 1 per cent of every complete tala of gross wages paid to employees, and collected by the National Provident Fund. Over 1984 it obtained WS$ 488,604 from employers' contributions, compared to total expenditures of WS$ 148,524.

The Motor Vehicle Fund had assets of WS$ 1,090,071 and an

TABLE 5.14   Western Samoa Accident Compensation Board: assets and
liabilities, 31 December 1984

Assets	WS$
Cash in hand and at bank	3,458
Accrued interest	123,939
Net fixed assets	28,086
Fixed deposit – Bank of Western Samoa	660,000
Fixed deposit – Pacific Commercial Bank	520,000
Western Samoa Government Loan Stock	2,350,000
Total assets	3,685,483

Liabilities	WS$
Workers' Compensation Fund	2,474,350
Motor Vehicle Compensation Fund	1,090,071
Other	121,062
Total liabilities	3,685,483

Source: Western Samoa Accident Compensation Board (1984) *Annual Report*, p. 12.

investment income of WS$ 132,961 in 1984. It is funded by a levy of 5
sene per gallon on all fuel imported for motor vehicles. This is
collected by the government's Customs Department and over 1984
(after refunds for non-motor-vehicle use) amounted to WS$ 273,873.

The compensation provided under either scheme covers economic
loss up to 60 per cent of the injured person's earnings with a
minimum of WS$ 10 and a maximum of WS$ 75 per week; permanent
loss of body functions obtain compensation of between WS$ 20 to
2000; and for death, a payment to dependents equal to four year's
earnings with a maximum of WS$ 7500. In addition, the Board pays
transportation expenses to hospital or a medical doctor, up to WS$
100 for medical expenses, and up to WS$ 200 in funeral expenses, in
the case of death.

General Insurance

As with the life insurance industry, the Western Samoa government
has established a statutory general insurance company to service the
local market. This company, the National Pacific Insurance Corporation, was established in 1977. Initially it was wholly government
owned, but in November 1980 National Pacific was floated as a public

company and the National Insurance Co. of New Zealand acquired a major interest. National Insurance of New Zealand is also the company's managing agent and has been since its founding. In 1985 the Western Samoan government and National Insurance had a 30 per cent shareholding each with the remaining 40 per cent held by other investors.

Prior to National Pacific, the local insurance market was dominated by foreign insurers, and in 1971 there were some 26 agents representing foreign insurance companies. Today, foreign general insurance companies are still allowed to underwrite business within Western Samoa provided they register under the Insurance Act 1976. This requires the lodging of a non-interest bearing deposit of WS\$ 40,000 (reinsure Western Samoa risks, WS\$ 10,000) with the Western Samoa government. As Western Samoa has an annual premium income of only around WS\$ 3.5 million, few foreign companies have been interested in competing against the government owned firm. Thus as of early 1986 only American Home Insurance and QBE Insurance remain active with local agency operations.

National Pacific's major savings is in foreign exchange. As one government report commented, it 'will undoubtedly transact the bulk of the local insurance business thereby drastically reducing large overseas remittances of insurance premiums for Samoan nationals and business insured with foreign insurance companies', and to a lesser extent also 'encourage the mobilization of savings for investment purposes'.[45]

National Pacific has also been successful in raising premium income from outside of Western Samoa. It currently operates a branch office in American Samoa, agencies in Niue and Tonga, and participates in reinsurance arrangements with Fiji, the Solomon Islands, and Kiribati.

By mid-1985 National Pacific Insurance Corporation had assets of some WS\$ 6 million and was an active investor in government securities, bank deposits, and mortgages. A more detailed but rather dated idea of its asset holdings is shown in Table 5.15.

Western Samoa Life Assurance Corporation

The Western Samoa Life Assurance Corporation was established on 1 January 1977 under the Western Samoa Life Assurance Corporation Act 1976 and commenced operations on 1 July 1977. Though a government-owned and guaranteed statutory corporation, Western

TABLE 5.15   National Pacific Insurance: assets and liabilities, 31
December 1981

Assets:	*WS$*
Fixed Assets	265,670
Statutory deposits	102,500
Government securities	130,000
Secured loans	3,780
Share investments	157,000
Cash at bank	122,738
Short-term deposits	720,380
Trade debtors	796,655
Sundry debtors and prepayments	38,437
Income tax paid	8,255
Total assets	2,345,415

Liabilities:	*WS$*
Amounts owing reinsurers	484,591
Sundry creditors	246,561
Provisions – unearned premiums	534,413
Provisions – claims outstanding	463,514
Issued capital	525,000
Exchange fluctuations account	36,434
Retained earnings	54,902
Total liabilities	2,345,415

Source: National Pacific Insurance Ltd (1981) *Annual Report*, pp. 6–7.

Samoa Life operates as a mutual company in that all profits are distributed to its policy holders.

Under its Act (Section 17), the Corporation may conduct life assurance business in Western Samoa and elsewhere. It may provide policies to insure any life with or without sickness and accident disability benefits, grant endowment policies, sell life annuities or any other policies, or policy combinations, which are dependent on the termination or continuance of human life. Of the various types of policies, endowment policies are generally the most popular and at the end of 1985 the company had 8224 policies in force with a value of WS$ 3,375,991. The company had a premium income of WS$ 994,000 in 1984 and is estimated to save at least some WS$ 500,000 in foreign exchange outflow each year. In mid-1985 it had assets of some WS$ 4.7 million.

It should be stressed that Western Samoa Life does not have a monopoly on the local insurance. Foreign life insurance companies may still write life business within Western Samoa provided they lodge a deposit of WS$ 100,000. In practice, the potential premium income is much too low to justify the investment. One recent exception is the American-based company, Grand Pacific Insurance. It sells on an agency basis to expatriates only, and denominates both the policy cover and premiums in US dollars.

(i) *Development*

Western Samoa Life was established with the assistance of the New Zealand office of the Colonial Mutual Life Assurance Co., a major Australian mutual life insurance company. Colonial Mutual had pioneered the sale of life polices within Samoa as part of its New Zealand operations and, given its mutual status, was agreeable to helping Samoan policy-holders establish their own company. Thus Western Samoa Life commenced business with the assumption of 2715 former Colonial Mutual policies.[46]

(ii) *Assets*

As shown in Table 5.16, Western Samoa Life holds most of its assets in real estate holdings, government securities and loans to policy-holders. These are subject to Section 30 of its Act which restricts its investments to government securities, deposits with the Public Trustee, loans to policy-holders, through first mortgage finance, deposits with the commercial banks, development bank or savings bank, or other investments authorized by the Minister of Finance.

By 1985 its most important single asset was its headquarters building (37.5 per cent of total assets). Government securities were next in importance followed by loans to policy-holders. These have an interest rate of 12.5 per cent. Mortgage loans were also important and earned between 9.5 and 15.5 per cent per annum. The New Zealand investments reflect excess funds collected from policy-holders now residing in New Zealand.

Though the Minister of Finance will authorize share investments, these have not yet been important, and in 1985 included only three companies: Morris Hedstrom Ltd, a trading company, National Pacific Insurance Ltd, and Computer Services Ltd.

TABLE 5.16   Western Samoa Life Assurance Corporation: assets and liabilities, 31 December 1984

%	Assets	WS$
1.3	Cash on hand and at bank	57,416
7.1	Other current assets	316,504
–	Treasury premium account	1,736
0.7	Treasury call deposits	30,000
1.2	BNZ Finance deposits	53,019
1.3	Bank term deposits	60,000
23.4	Government securities	1,049,808
11.5	Loans on policies	515,254
2.7	Shares	118,950
7.9	Mortgages	353,950
3.8	Net fixed assets	170,219
37.5	WSLAC house	1,675,466
1.6	Net other assets	70,788
100.0	Total assets	4,473,110

%	Liabilities	WS$
3.0	Sundry creditors and charges	132,456
3.2	Loan from National Pacific Insurance	144,690
5.6	Mortality & contingencies	250,000
88.2	Net assurance funds	3,945,964
100.0	Total liabilities	4,473,110

Source: Western Samoa Life Assurance Corporation (1984) *Annual Report*, pp. 8–9.

(iii) *Funding*

Given its mutual company status, Western Samoa Life receives virtually all of its funds from policy-holders, and any earnings from its investments are credited against these clients' accounts less a small mortality and contingency reserve. The loan reflected in the current balance sheet is part of the mortgage finance raised for the purchase and construction of its new headquarters building, WSLAC House.

Commodity Marketing Boards

Commodity marketing in Western Samoa is conducted by four government bodies: the Copra Board, the Cocoa Board, the Banana Board and the Produce Marketing Division. As in other Pacific countries, these bodies have a marked effect on the local economy and, through the price stablization funds of the Copra and Cocoa boards, the local financial sector as well.

Their operations have recently been criticised as being both ineffective and expensive. As one government report complained, 'the present organisations are virtually export monopolies with high operating costs resulting in low returns to growers'.[47] One Asian Development Bank study recommended the creation of an Export Development Board to assume their marketing functions and expand them to include timber and processed goods.[48]

The new Export Development Board would have four divisions (coconut products, tree crops, fresh fruits, and vegetables) and would export 'cocoa, fresh produce and processed products, monitor the procurement of copra by the coconut oil mill and regulate copra exports', but not have any exclusive rights to market these products:[49] the role of the private sector in this process would be greatly expanded. The Board would also operate the cocoa and copra price stablization schemes, centralize the copra and cocoa processing centres, and promote quality control. By 1985 the government had basically accepted these recommendations and the Board should be in operation in late 1986.

Traditionally the Copra Board has been the most important of the four. It was established in 1948 to fix the price paid to growers; to secure the best arrangements for purchasing, exporting and marketing copra; to establish a price stablization fund; and to license buyers, exporters and manufacturers of coconut products.[50] Since the establishment of the Copra Oil Mill in 1982 the level of copra exports dropped significantly, and today the Copra Board no longer exports its purchases, but rather sells the crop to the plant at the then international price.

It terms of its stablization role, the Copra Board did not begin its stabilization fund until 1981. Initially with good copra prices, it built up sizeable reserves which were invested with the banking system. More recently the Copra Board did not adjust the price paid to local producers appropriately. When world copra prices dropped over 1985, the local price stayed much above world levels. Thus, despite record crops in 1983 and 1984, the Board needed commercial bank borrowings to fulfil its 1985 obligations, and in early 1986 had substantial overdrafts outstanding rather than reserves. As one government report commented, 'the present pricing systems for copra and cocoa are therefore not adequate and need to be simplified with the objective of increasing agricultural income to the growers'.[51]

Second in importance of the present boards is the Cocoa Board. It was established in 1972 to assist in the export and sale of cocoa, and in 1975 assumed control of Western Samoa's cocoa marketing. It also represents Western Samoa as a member of the International Cocoa Organization. In support of its marketing, the Board supposedly assists in improving the quantity and quality of local production. Unfortunately in recent years it has not purchased cocoa beans on the basis of quality. This lack of quality control has lead to an inferior crop and poorer world prices.

The Cocoa Board's price stabilization fund for cocoa was established in 1981. The Cocoa Board has been more market oriented in its pricing policies, and as a result still had surplus reserves in early 1986.

Neither the Produce Marketing Division nor the Banana Board operate a stabilization programme, and as such are not significant in the financial sector. The Produce Marketing Division exports a range of products, particularly taro, in competition with private growers, and acts as the agent for the Banana Board for banana purchasing and exporting.

Co-operative Societies

The co-operative movement represents one of the older aspects of Western Samoa finance. A Registrar of Co-operative Societies, for example, was appointed in 1954 and by 1958 there were some 39 co-operative societies within Western Samoa: three of these were savings and loan societies. These savings societies had a total membership of 172, but by 1960 only one society was listed as still active.[52] Nevertheless, a study a decade later still commented that 'considerable sums of money are also deposited with co-operative thrift societies, in credit unions, in merchants' savings schemes, and particularly in the compulsory savings held by the Banana and Copra Boards'.[53]

Today, while co-operative societies can hold funds on behalf of members, the credit union movement has become the major vehicle for co-operative savings.

Credit Unions

As with the co-operative societies, the credit union movement developed after 1954 when a Registrar was appointed by the Western

Samoa government. It resulted from a request by Bishop Dieter to Father Marion Ganey in Suva in 1954 to assist in developing a local movement.[54] A pilot project was subsequently conducted and the first Western Samoan credit union, the Apia Parish Credit Union, was founded in 1955, and the Western Samoan Credit Union League was founded in 1958.[55]

Initially credit unions experienced excellent success as they made full use of the village and extended family orientation of Samoan society. As one government report concluded, 'the Samoans have shown an outstanding capacity for group savings and investment in non-productive social capital in the form of churches and pastors' dwellings . . . [as well as] . . . in financing the construction of village and district schools and hospitals'.[56]

The credit union movement was subsequently 'taken over officially by the Justice Department in 1960' under the Credit Union Ordinance 1960.[57] Unfortunately, though, by the mid-1960s the initial overseas assistance which had been instrumental in the industry's growth was discontinued, and 'consequently, the credit union movement stagnated and declined to a stage where the Credit Union League of Western Samoa and all except one credit union became inoperative'.[58] Thus, as one study concluded, by 1964 they were only of minor importance.[59]

Besides the loss of foreign assistance, a major reason for the industry's early success and then failure was that 'most people imagined at first that their credit union would, in some mysterious way, usher in a new age of prosperity. Societies are called "paradise" (parataiso) or "riches" (fa'a moni). When paradise or riches does not materialize, people lose interest'.[60]

Even so, credit unions and other co-operatives have major advantages over commercial banks in dealing with small lending at the village level. As one banker commented,

> credit unions enable small loans to be made quickly and cheaply for both development and provident purposes. Members are well known to credit union officials and the fact that disclosure of members borrowings are allowed enables the credit unions to use traditional social pressures effectively to ensure loan repayments are adhered to by its members.[61]

These advantages, coupled with the high costs of the Development Bank's own small agricultural loan programme, caused it to assist in the rebirth of the local credit union industry in the late 1970s, and the re-establishment of the Samoa Credit Union League. With the over-seas assistance from the Credit Union National Association of the United States, the Catholic Bishops of Samoa and others bodies, as well as the Development Bank of Western Samoa, credit unions again became active and by 1981 there were eight credit unions in operation covering a number of six religious-based bodies, the Development Bank of Western Samoa Staff Credit Union and the Polynesian Airlines Staff Credit Union.[62]

By mid-1985 some 20 credit unions has been established and by the end of 1986, one plan, optimistically, called for a total of 150 credit unions in operation each with an average membership of 100.[63] By April 1986 the credit union industry was comprised of 31 credit unions with a membership totalling 2655. It had share deposits of WS$ 572,408 and loans of WS$ 550,995. The interest charged on loans is restricted to 1 per cent per month under the industry's standard by-laws.

Finance Companies

Though there are no finance companies in operation at present in Western Samoa, the predecessor of the Pacific Commercial Bank, the Pacific Savings and Loan Co., operated basically in consumer finance. It collected deposits and made small loans for home improvements, school fees, travel expenses, ceremonial costs, consumer durables and farm implements.

This lending was potentially very profitable as Pacific Savings charged very high rates of interest as it was reported to obtain a 'return of 48 per cent per annum from the loans'.[64] It also limited its potential losses by arranging much of its lending to be repaid through payroll deductions plans arranged with a number of local employers to include some government departments.

On the funding side it paid a tiered set of interest rates of 4 per cent per annum on balances of WS$ 50 or less; 4.5 per cent for balances over WS$ 50 up to WS$ 100; 5.0 per cent for balances over WS$ 100 up to WS$ 200; and 6 per cent on amounts of WS$ 200 or more. All rates were computed monthly and paid quarterly.

Despite the obvious margins, when the Pacific Savings and Loan Co. commenced business on 29 September 1969 there were 'many residents of the community who felt that the new company would fail after six months or less'.[65] It did have difficulties in screening appropriate loan applicants and supervising collection of repayments, and partly for this reason encouraged the Bank of Hawaii to become a shareholder in 1971.

Besides introducing the concept of a publicly-owned company to many individual Samoans and promoting personal lending, Pacific Savings also had a major impact on local savings rates and 'the increase in interest rates paid on savings accounts at the Bank of Western Samoa and the Post Office were influenced in part by the current rates paid by Pacific Savings and Loan'.[66]

Western Samoa Trust Estates Corporation

The Western Samoa Trust Estates Corporation was established in 1957 to administer the New Zealand Reparation Estates. These estates were acquired by New Zealand as part of the war damages paid by Germany after the First World War. Its main business still is plantation related and in 1985 it operated 14 plantations with 30,100 acres, or approximately 20 per cent of the country's total cultivated land. These properties export copra, coffee, cocoa, taro and other produce worth some WS$ 7 million per annum. In addition, the Corporation also operates a dairy farm, beef cattle, a piggery, meat processing, a bakery, a coconut timber factory, a retail business, a coconut mill, and a soap factory. Current plans will double its present soap production and expand into detergents as well as laundry and toilet varieties. It also plans to increase its copra and cocoa production as well as diversification into a range of other activities.

While it would be wrong to consider this Corporation as a formal or even informal financial institution, it is nevertheless 'the largest single productive enterprise in the country',[67] and in some respects acts as the government's agricultural investment agency. Rather than seek foreign partners to establish a local coconut oil mill or soap factory, for example, the government turned to the Corporation to create such businesses.

Unfortunately the Corporation has suffered as a government-run rather than private sector operation. It is not adequately funded, and many of its plantations have run down and now need replacement. As result it has been characterized by 'indifferent management, low export earnings and deteriorating assets'.[68] Indeed, due to large operating losses, its 'financial structure has become increasingly weak, which has caused delays in the implementation of its plantation development programme'.[69]

In the longer term, the Corporation has the potential as the major source of investment capital in agricultural production and processing activities.

FINANCIAL MARKETS

As yet there are no financial markets in Western Samoa other than in foreign exchange and, to a very nominal extent, interbank transactions.

Foreign Exchange Market

Unlike some Pacific countries, Western Samoa issued its own currency during most the colonial period. Under New Zealand administration these were Samoan pounds issued by the Treasury. Under the Samoa Act 1921, these Treasury notes required full backing with the investment mainly in New Zealand government securities. With the establishment of the Bank of Western Samoa in 1961, the Treasury relinquished its note-issuing powers but retained its coinage operations. Initially, the Bank of Western Samoa issued Treasury notes overprinted with the 'Bank of Western Samoa', but in August 1963 introduced its own notes.

With independence on 1 January 1962, the New Zealand dollar, which had previously been legal tender within Western Samoa, was withdrawn from circulation, leaving the Western Samoa pound as the local currency. New Zealand coins, however, continued in use until 10 July 1967 when they and the currency were replaced by the Western Samoa sense and tala. In June 1980 the Monetary Board of Western Samoa assumed the Bank's note issuing functions, and on 1 June 1981 Bank of Western Samoa notes were no longer legal tender.

The tala was fixed to the US dollar from 1973 until October 1975 and from 1979 to 1985 the tala had a fixed link with the New Zealand dollar. Since 1 March 1985 the tala's value has been determined from a fixed linkage to a basket of five currencies. They are weighted in the following importance, the New Zealand dollar, US dollar, Australian dollar, Japanese yen, and the German mark, and reflect these country's relative importance as trading partners.

With the change to the basket system, the US dollar is now the settlement currency and the tala is determined daily in terms of US dollars. The Central Bank of Samoa issues a mid-rate quotation for the tala against US dollars at which it will buy or sell with a 0.2 per cent margin either way. The banks can then set their margins on other currencies. While the banks are free to trade during the business day, they cannot keep a foreign currency position, and must close out their holdings with the Central Bank at the US dollar rate by the end of the trading day. In practice, however, the 0.2 per cent margin has encouraged the two banks to net their own positions at a lower rate prior to approaching the Central Bank.

In addition to the trade- and travel-related foreign exchange business, there is also a substantial level in actual foreign currency notes. Industry interviews suggest that much of this money is in New Zealand currency sent through the postal system or brought by visitors. This flow is particularly heavy over the Christmas period, and one bank alone was receiving in excess of WS$ 200,000 in New Zealand notes each day over much of December 1985. There was also a considerable inflow of US currency and the outflow of notes from American Samoa was such that special arrangements were required to ship the notes back to Pago Pago daily during the peak of the season.

Other Financial Markets

With only two banks, there is a limit to the level of interbank transactions, and most interbank business is related to foreign exchange matters. Significantly, the banks have traditionally had a surplus of deposit funds and have relied on extra deposits with the Central Bank for an interest-earning alternative. Government securities, however, may eventually become a more important alternative, and legislation to provide the basis for a Treasury bill market was under consideration in 1985.

Though there are a few companies, such as the Pacific Commercial Bank, with a number of local shareholders, there is very little, if any, secondary trading in these securities.

ANALYSIS

While Western Samoa is fortunate to have a fairly wide range of financial institutions already in operation within the country, there are nevertheless many areas where government action could greatly improve financial development and market effectiveness. Some of these measures would include improved local savings mobilization,

TABLE 5.17   Interest rates and inflation in Western Samoa, 1980–84

	1980	*1981*	*1982*	*1983*	*1984*
One-year bank deposit rate	8.0	10.0	11.0	17.0	17.0
Annual inflation rate (CPI)	33.0	20.5	18.3	16.4	12.0
Real interest rates	(25.0)	(10.5)	(7.3)	0.6	5.0

[a] Figures in parentheses are negative.

Source: International Monetary Fund and Western Samoa Department of Economic Development, as cited in Shahid Yusuf and R. Kyle Peters (1985) *Western Samoa: the experience of slow growth and resource imbalance*, (Washington, DC: World Bank) p. 12.

increased banking representation, greater overseas Samoan savings and investment, better management of public enterprises, and the creation of a National Investment Corporation and Investment Fund.

Improved Local Savings Mobilization

As mentioned, increased savings mobilization is a key·part of the government's current development plan, but until recently Samoans had relatively little incentive to save. First, Western Samoa has suffered a long history of high inflation, and over most of this period interest rates were not adjusted accordingly. Indeed, only in 1983 were savers afforded a positive real return on their savings. This position is worse if considered in respect to US dollars or most other currencies as the tala has been devalued frequently over recent years. As major consumer purchases rely heavily on imported items, the real loss in purchasing power is much worse than suggested in Table 5.17.

As a result, individual Samoan savings are often placed overseas through relatives, and returned through the postal system or visits only when required. Overseas savings is also desirable for social reasons for well. As one World Bank study concluded, in 'a society with the ethic of sharing and communal living so firmly entrenched, accumulation of wealth is difficult to achieve and beyond a point would be considered inimical to the basic values of the community'.[70] It is therefore rational that, if accumulated, these funds be kept outside the village.

The need to share with, and otherwise support, one's extended family is certainly one disadvantage for local savings as there can be strong pressure to support one's poorer relatives. This sharing concept also reduces the perceived need for 'rainy day' savings. As the same World Bank study found, 'the social configuration of individual villages and the highly developed system of exchange in the form of money and kind also serves to attentuate risk perception and the precautionary motive for savings'.[71]

Another problem is that the concept of banking is not particularly understood at the village level. There is therefore a heavy dependence on cash in business transactions rather than cheques, and a surprising number of cash transactions actually take place at the banking counter with the buyer withdrawing the money, paying the cash to the seller, and the seller then re-depositing the funds. This suggests that even more Samoans avoid the banking system completely and that a banking education programme would greatly assist local savings efforts.

Finally, even if an individual did decide to save locally, there are only a 'limited range of financial choices available to savers in what remains only a partially monetized economy with limited banking facilities'.[72] Expanding the current banking network into more remote areas should help correct part of this problem as would the sale of government securities and term deposits as well as passbook savings.

Expanded Banking Representation

As mentioned in the banking section, commercial banks have only a limited exposure in rural areas, and have relied exclusively on bank-staffed branches and full-time and part-time agencies. Mobile banking services are also used to service more remote areas but past experience, probably as a result of the negative real interest rates then offered, has not been particularly favourable. Pacific Commercial Bank, for example, has continued the concept, but now services merchant clients rather than savers through this method. Given the much higher interest rates in 1985–6, these mobile services, coupled with a banking education, could again be considered.

Another fairly obvious means to expand local representation would be to use private banking agencies to service clients in more remote areas. Private banking agencies have been used successfully in Australia and other Pacific countries, and local traders, particularly those already serviced through mobile banking visits, would seemingly be ideal candidates for this purpose.

There is also merit in encouraging the co-operative movement as a more economic means of raising local savings and providing small loan financing in more remote areas.

Attracting Overseas Samoan Savings and Investment

As with Tonga, Western Samoa is dependent on a large inflow of foreign exchange from those living overseas. Indeed one World Bank study estimated that 'besides the US$ 20 million that enters financial channels each year, an equal amount may find its way into the country in the form of currency sent by post or brought back by Samoan visitors'.[73] Besides helping to offset the country's traditional trade deficit, these inflows have a major impact throughout the economy and as another study found, 'the benefit of sizeable remittances incomes are now available very widely within the rural sector'.[74] While seemingly beneficial, these remittances unfortunately also remove the need for many Samoans to work in the cash economy in order to purchase desired consumer items. Furthermore, a large portion of this remitted savings is spent on imported consumer items rather than for productive purposes.

There appears to be substantial savings placed in overseas financial institutions, both by Samoans resident overseas and on the behalf of local Samoans, which might be attracted to return and finance Samoan investment. The government has already improved the attractiveness of the banking system through higher interest rates combined with a lowering of inflation. However, as long as a foreign exchange risk is perceived, it may be difficult to attract these foreign funds into tala.

Samoa, however, is not the only country with difficulties in attracting expatriate savings to the home country and experiences of other countries such as India and Pakistan provide a number of examples of special savings and investment programmes for this purpose. Special tax-free, high interest, non-resident external savings accounts in tala and US or New Zealand dollars for expatriates would certainly be one alternative as might be a special issue of government securities designed to tap this market. More also needs to be done to channel these funds into productive investment. At present, for example, the banking system still has an excess of local savings so the immediate benefits of attracting additional money might not be so attractive. The alternative is to attract these funds into local business enterprises. Special tax incentives have proved very successful in attracting non-resident investment into priority industries in India, and it would seem possible that such a programme might work in Samoa. Similarly, although Samoa lacks the diversity of India's financial markets, special treatment could be afforded equity investments, and at least a version of the National Investment Fund (see pp. 336–7) could be designed to the specific requirement of overseas Samoan investors.

Improved Management of Public Sector Enterprises

As mentioned earlier, public sector corporations such as the Western Samoa Estates Trust Corporation, play a very important role in the economy and through their actions have a major impact on the financial sector as well. As was shown in the banking section, these public sector bodies have traditionally accounted for a large portion of bank advances, and in the early 1980s 'excessive public sector borrowings from the banking system, resulting in high growth in domestic credit and the money supply',[75] worked very much against the government's over-all economic policies.

Unfortunately, while these companies have traditionally absorbed a fairly large portion of bank credit, their success in using these funds has been less than desired. Instead of development purposes, inadequate control and monitoring of expenses has seen the financing of growing operational deficits.[76] Worse still, rather than taking corrective action, many of these problems are being resolved by other means. In the building of the new airport extensions, for example, the government's Special Projects Development Corporation received the contract, despite the fact that it was not the lowest bidder.

A major problem in correcting these public sector enterprises is that political factors play a very important role in their operations. Besides examples such as the airport extension contracts, director appointments to these companies have been considered as an appropriate political reward, and thus many appointees have been selected on their political or family connections rather managerial abilities. This is perhaps not unusual in itself. However, when coupled with the instability of Western Samoa politics, the combination is exceedingly damaging for the firms' success. It is only a slight exaggeration to say that the public enterprise directors change with a change of government. Given that in the early 1980s Western Samoa had four prime ministers in less than one year, such a practice is hardly conducive to good planning. Instead it would not be surprising if directors chose instead to maximize any benefits of office as soon as possible.

Public enterprises, if to be retained under government ownership, must at least be restructured to run, not for political purposes, but as commercial enterprises. In regard to the largest of these bodies, the Western Samoa Trust Estate Corporation, the Asian Development Bank has recommended that in order to be perceived by the public as being above politics and structured along commercial lines, only persons with a commercial agricultural background should be appointed to its Board. As a matter of policy, the terms of Board members should be staggered in order to ensure continuity and no excessive turnover of Board members at any time.[77] There is no question but that the same rules and recommendations should be applied to all government-owned commercial enterprises.

The Creation of a National Investment Corporation

In line with the suggested separation of state enterprises from political influences, the government could do well to follow the Solomon Islands and establish an investment-styled company to hold its shares in commercial enterprises. In the Solomons at least, this slight separation of ownership has allowed directors to be selected more on their business abilities than for political reasons and to build the level of professionalism within these companies. Eventually this company could also sell some of these shares to Samoa investors. This would both provide additional capital for the investment company as well as increase the level of individual Samoan participation in the local economy.

Interestingly, the above suggestion appeared in government plans as early as 1981. They called for the establishment of a National Investment Corporation to acquire the then government shareholdings in commercial enterprises. As the plan explained, this Corporation's function was 'to rationalise government's equity participation in industrial investment, and to facilitate the small saver's participation'.[78] While the latter was not stated in full, this would have probably entailed the sale of units in an associated body, the National Investment Fund. Each unit would represent a share in the Corporation's over-all investment portfolio. Investors would then 'be able to sell their holdings in the Fund at market value, but underpinned by a government guarantee initially so that investors will be able to recover at least the money they put in'.[79] It was envisioned that the National Investment Corporation would also later sell some shares directly to the private investors.

While both the Corporation and the Fund were to be established over the 1980–84 development plan, no action was taken and neither body was mentioned in the subsequent plan for 1985–1987.

TRENDS AND PREDICTIONS

Given Western Samoa's recent economic history, most commentators have been less than optimistic concerning its potential. As one Asian Development study concluded, 'in the absence of a marked improvement in the level of foreign exchange earnings, Western Samoa has little prospect of being anything other than an increasingly dependent economy'.[80] Similarly, the World Bank has stated that without an expansion and diversification of its agricultural exports, 'the prospects of an economy totally dependent on the remittances derived from exporting young males abroad, are indeed dim'.[81] Finally, as the government itself admits, any potential development will be limited as 'the local market is small, no mineral resources of commercial value are available, shipping and transport costs are high, and the administration and financial support given by the government has not always been adequate'.[82]

Fortunately these quotations are not totally reflective of the country's true potential and there seems some scope for improving both the quality and quantity of Western Samoa's agricultural production as well as diversifying and gaining more value added from these efforts.

First, in increasing quantity, copra production has had no long-term growth over the last 20 years. Cocoa production is currently around half of its peak and banana exports are only at 5 per cent of their one-time high. As previously discussed, this is largely a function of poor agricultural practices, inadequate re-investment and ineffective marketing, as well as natural causes. Through its Coconut Suspensory Loan Scheme and Cocoa Suspensory Loan Scheme the government has tried to encourage small-holders and plantation owners to expand existing facilities or to replant older trees with better hybrid stock. The Cocoa scheme, for example, provides a government loan equal to 60 per cent of the costs of cocoa plantation establishment, which under certain conditions can later be converted into a grant. Such programmes should result in increased plantings, and in time higher production figures. Better use of agricultural extension services and local agricultural research is needed, though, to ensure these plantings are used to their best advantage.

Similarly, plantations have good scope for diversifying into other areas as well. Some recent tree crops include avocado, coffee, limes, macadamia nuts, mango, and pawpaw. There is also potential to combine certain of these plantations with beef cattle raising. Such intercropping has worked with some success in other Pacific countries and could help reduce meat imports.

There is also scope for greater exports of other traditional products. Taro is now an important export to New Zealand, Australia and the United States (American Samoa, Hawaii and the West coast). Yams, breadfruit, and whole coconuts are now also being exported to Australia, New Zealand and the United States.

In terms of crop diversification, beans, cabbages, lettuce, passion fruit, pineapples, and tomatoes are now also exported. There would seem more scope for similar exports, primarily in fresh vegetables, to markets such as Hawaii and the US West Coast, as well as Australia and New Zealand.

The recent wood veneer plant also suggests that more could be done to utilize the country's forest reserves, and Western Samoa's sea-based resources have as yet had little impact on export totals.

Besides a greater and more diversified agricultural product base, existing exports could be processed locally to improve their value added. The switch from simply copra exporting to coconut oil and coconut cream was an important step in this process, but more can be done with good effect. At present, for example, Samoa does not refine its coconut oil. While traditional purchasers may prefer to do this process themselves, other markets may welcome better quality oil exports.

Another important innovation in existing products would be to utilize coconut husks and shells. These by-products are currently not used other than for fuel, but apparently if wet processed with the whole coconut, the quality of the resulting coconut cream is much improved. If the whole coconut could be used in this manner, the husk and shell by-products could then be used in coir or charcoal production.[83]

Taro exports could also be expanded by increasing their shelf life through freeze-drying, and by local processing into baby food and other products. Other traditional products could similarly be used for new purposes. The production of ethanol from local breadfruit, for example, might reduce the need for imported motor fuels, as well as producing saleable by-products.

A further suggestion to gain more from existing products might be to establish a can or other packaging manufacturer. This would allow Western Samoa to produce the containers now imported for its present beer, soft drinks, fruit juice and coconut cream exports.[84] Other future export products might include soap, desiccated coconuts, timber, fishing, ice cream, butter, tallow and corolite. A local Small-Scale Industries Centre to provide factory buildings for these industries,[85] as well as export incentives and tax concessions, are under consideration.

Tourism, which offers the other major potential for foreign exchange, has hardly been developed, but new efforts within Australia and other nearby markets could greatly expand this source of income. A new run way for Boeing 747s is almost completed, and a new terminal under construction. More importantly, the Royal Samoan Hotel, which was planned initially in the mid-1970s, finally commenced building in 1985, and should eventually employ up to 1000 people.[86] Also of significance in 1985 was the government's announced plans to sell 62 per cent of Apia's Tusitala Hotel to a private consortium which includes Australia's Ansett Airlines as a participant.[87]

The importance of tourism and other labour-intensive activities cannot be overemphasized, for in the long run unemployment will probably rate as Western Samoa's major domestic economic problem. The country has traditionally had a very high birth rate with a natural population growth of round 3 per cent per annum. Thus far, however, an extensive migration of Samoans to New Zealand and American Samoa has largely resolved the immediate problem. Since 1975 New Zealand has gradually placed restrictions on Samoan migration, and further restraints can be expected. With more than 42 per cent of its present population under 15 years old, population growth will continue to present problems for economic planners for the foreseeable future.

In conclusion, Western Samoa has faced, and will continue to face, significant economic problems, but in recent years its ability to deal with these matter has greatly improved. In particular it has been making better use of International Monetary Fund and World Bank advice and taking strong measures against imports to conserve foreign exchange. The government has also tried to increase its domestic earnings through higher charges and more effective spending and to reduce its foreign debts. As one report explained, current government includes

> import control through a new foreign exchange allocation system; concessionary loans for export promotion; a flexible exchange rate policy; increased interest rate levels; reduced government borrowings from the commercial banks; strict guidelines on banking lending to the private sector; and careful watch over public enterprise activity.[88]

These measures, coupled with the previously discussed diversification plans, should do much to improve Western Samoa's economic management, and hopefully provide the basis for trading self-sufficiency, before overseas remittance and foreign aid assistance prove insufficient.

NOTES

1. Lee Anderson (1985) 'Poll may be last under old rule', *Australian Financial Review*, 22 February, p. 16.
2. Te'o Ian J. Fairbairn (1985) *Island Economies: studies from the South Pacific*, (Suva: Institute of Pacific Studies, University of South Pacific) p. 304.
3. *Western Samoa's Fourth Five-Year Development Plan 1980–1984* (1980) (Apia: Economic Development Department) p. 51.
4. A. E. Bollard (1981) 'The Financial adventures of J. C. Godeffroy and Son in the Pacific', *Journal of Pacific History*, 16 (1):12. Also see Stewart Firth (1973) 'German firms in the Western Pacific islands, 1857–1914', *Journal of Pacific History*, 8:10–28.
5. Bollard, 'Financial adventures':15.
6. Bollard, 'Financial adventures':15–16.
7. Bollard, 'Financial adventures':16.
8. David Pitt (1970) *Tradition and Economic Progress in Samoa: a case study of the role of traditional social institutions in economic development*, (Oxford: Clarendon Press) p. 207.
9. Pitt, *Tradition and Economic Progress*, p. 203.
10. P. G. H. Carroll (1984) *Development Bank of Western Samoa: a profile*, (Canberra: Development Studies Centre) p. 4.
11. Pitt, *Tradition and Economic Progress*, p. 203.
12. *Western Samoa Second Five-Year Development Plan 1971–1975* (1970) (Apia: Department of Economic Development) November, p. 49.
13. Central Bank of Samoa (1984) *Annual Report*, p. 11.
14. Central Bank of Samoa (1984), *Annual Report*, p. 11.

15. N. M. Chappell (1961) *New Zealand Banker's Hundred: a history of the Bank of New Zealand, 1861–1961*, (Wellington: Bank of New Zealand) p. 281.
16. Bank of New Zealand, personal correspondence, May 1986.
17. Robert W. Watson (1918) *History of Samoa*, (Wellington: Whitcombe & Tombs Ltd) p. 145.
18. Felix M. Keesing (1934) *Modern Samoa: its government and changing life*, (London: Allen & Unwin) p. 309.
19. *Western Samoa Financial and Banking Survey* (1957) (Wellington: Government Printer) pp. 28–9.
20. See the *Report of the Select Committee of the Legislative Assembly on Currency and Banking* (1953) (Apia: Government Printer).
21. J. W. Davidson (1967) *Samoa Mo Samoa: the emergence of the independent state of Western Samoa*, (Melbourne: Oxford University Press) p. 251.
22. Davidson, *Samoa Mo Samoa*, p. 251.
23. *Western Samoa Financial and Banking Survey* (1957) pp. 28–9.
24. Davidson, *Samoa Mo Samoa*, p. 252.
25. *Western Samoa Financial and Banking Survey* (1957) p. 33.
26. 'Questionnaire for any foreign bank wanting to establish a branch or unit bank in Western Samoa', undated two-page paper.
27. 'Second bank is real possibility', *Samoa Times*, 10 April 1970, p. 2.
28. The National Bank of New Zealand Ltd, correspondence dated 14 May 1986.
29. *Western Samoa Financial and Banking Survey* (1957) p. 39.
30. *Western Samoa Financial and Banking Survey* (1957), p. 40.
31. Post Office Department (1983) *Annual Report*, p. 6.
32. Post Office Department (1983), *Annual Report*, p. 6.
33. *Western Samoa's Fourth Five-Year Development Plan, 1980–1984* (1980) p. 51.
34. P. Leumaga (1983) 'Social and cultural considerations in rural lending in Western Samoa', in Jim Lamont (ed.) *Development Bank Credit in Rural Areas of the Pacific – the implications for rural development: proceedings of a workshop held in Tonga, July 1982* (Tonga: Rural Development Centre, University of South Pacific) p. 183.
35. *Western Samoa Agricultural Sector Survey* (1985) (Manila: Asian Development Bank), pp. 34–5.
36. *Western Samoa Agricultural Sector Survey*, p. 34.
37. Sam Leung Wai (1983) 'Western Samoan Position Paper', in Jim Lamont (ed.) *Development Bank Credit in Rural Areas of the Pacific – the implications for rural development: proceedings of a workshop held in Tonga, July 1982*, (Tonga: Rural Development Centre, University of South Pacific) p. 100.
38. Sam Leung Wai (1981) 'Credit Unions in Western Samoa Five-Year Development Programme, 1981–1985', unpublished paper dated 27 May, p. 3.
39. *Western Samoa Agricultural Sector Survey*, p. 35.
40. Carroll, *Development Bank of Western Samoa*, p. 2.
41. Carroll, *Development Bank of Western Samoa*, p. 2.

42. Fairbairn, *Island Economies*, p. 89.
43. Western Samoa National Provident Fund (1982) *Annual Report and Statement of Accounts*, p. 5.
44. Western Samoa Accident Compensation Board (1978) *Annual Report*, p. 2.
45. *Western Samoa's Fourth Five-Year Development Plan* (1980) p. 50.
46. Western Samoa Life Assurance Corporation, correspondence dated 15 July 1983.
47. *Western Samoa's Fifth Development Plan 1985–1987* (1984) (Apia: Department of Economic Development) p. 88.
48. *Western Samoa Agricultural Sector Survey*, p. 34.
49. *Western Samoa's Fifth Development Plan* (1984) p. 88.
50. *Western Samoa's Fifth Development Plan* (1984) p. 85.
51. *Western Samoa's Fifth Development Plan* (1984) p. 87.
52. *Western Samoa 1959* (1960) (Wellington: Government Printer) p. 138, and *Western Samoa 1960* (1961) (Wellington: Government Printer) p. 135.
53. Pitt, *Tradition and Economic Progress*, p. 203.
54. Leung Wai, 'Credit Unions in Western Samoa', p. 1.
55. Stanley F. Arneil (1979) *Forming and Running a Credit Union*, 2nd edn (Sydney: Alternative Publishing Co-operative) p. 145.
56. *Western Samoa Financial and Banking Survey* (1957) pp. 23–4.
57. Pitt, *Tradition and Economic Progress*, p. 209.
58. Leung Wai, 'Credit Unions in Western Samoa', p. 1.
59. Pitt, *Tradition and Economic Progress*, p. 209.
60. Pitt, *Tradition and Economic Progress*, p. 209.
61. Leung Wai, 'Western Samoan Position Paper', p. 101.
62. Leung Wai, 'Credit Unions in Western Samoa', p. 1.
63. Leung Wai, 'Credit Unions in Western Samoa', pp. 2–3.
64. Pacific Savings and Loan Co. Ltd (1971) *First Annual General Meeting of Shareholders*, 1 April, p. 4.
65. Pacific Savings and Loan Co. Ltd, *First Annual General Meeting of Shareholders*, p. 1.
66. Pacific Savings and Loan Co. Ltd, *First Annual General Meeting of Shareholders*, p. 1.
67. *Western Samoa's Fifth Development Plan* (1984) p. 1.
68. Fairbairn, *Island Economies*, p. 307.
69. *Western Samoa's Fifth Development Plan* (1984) pp. 54–5.
70. Shahid Yusuf and R. Kyle Peters (1985) *Western Samoa: the experience of slow growth and resource imbalance*, (Washington, DC: World Bank) p. 11.
71. Yusuf and Peters, *Western Samoa*, p. 12.
72. Yusuf and Peters, *Western Samoa*, p. 12.
73. R. Gerard Ward and Andrew Proctor (1980) *South Pacific Agriculture: choices and constraints*, (Manila: Asian Development Bank) p. 399.
74. Yusuf and Peters, *Western Samoa*, p. 13.
75. *Western Samoa Agricultural Sector Survey* (1985) p. 4.
76. *Western Samoa Agricultural Sector Survey* (1985) p. 4.
77. *Western Samoa Agricultural Sector Survey* (1985) p. 37.

78. *Western Samoa's Fourth Five-Year Development Plan* (1984) p. 51.
79. *Western Samoa's Fourth Five-Year Development Plan* (1984) p. 51.
80. Ward and Proctor, *South Pacific Agriculture*, p. 398.
81. Yusuf and Peters, *Western Samoa*, p. iii.
82. *Western Samoa's Fifth Development Plan* (1984) p. 71.
83. *Western Samoa's Fifth Development Plan* (1984) pp. 77–8.
84. *Western Samoa's Fifth Development Plan* (1984) p. 78.
85. *Western Samoa's Fifth Development Plan* (1984).
86. Economist Intelligence Unit (1985) *Quarterly Economic Review*, 2:38.
87. The hotel's former owners (50 per cent by the Western Samoa government, 25 per cent by the National Provident Fund and 25 per cent by the Nauru government) will together own 38 per cent under the new arrangements. Besides Ansett Airlines, the new consortium includes the South Pacific Investment Corporation and a local group, the Retzlaff Estate. South Pacific Investment, itself, is a consortium venture involving Wormald International Ltd, Development Finance Corporation of New Zealand, Westfield Holdings, and Yuills Australia Ltd among its shareholders. Peter Starr (1985) 'Ansett to join W Samoan hotel takeover consortium', *Australian Financial Review*, 5 February, p. 13.
88. *Western Samoa's Fifth Development Plan* (1984) p. 6.

Select Bibliography

SOUTH PACIFIC (GENERAL)

Alley, Roderic (ed.) (1982) *New Zealand and the South Pacific* (Boulder: Westview).

American University (1971) *Area Handbook for Oceania* (Washington, DC: US Government Printing Office).

'Australasia '79' (special survey), *Far Eastern Economic Review*, 8 June 1979.

'Australasia & Oceania '77', *Far Eastern Economic Review*, 17 June 1977.

'Australasia & Oceania '78', *Far Eastern Economic Review*, 9 June 1978.

'Banking in Asia '77', *Far Eastern Economic Review*, 8 April 1977.

Belshaw, Cyril S. (1947) *Post-war Development in Central Melanesia* (New York: Institute of Pacific Relations).

Belshaw, Cyril S. (1976) *Changing Melanesia* (Westport, Conn.: Greenwood Press).

Boyan, R. H. (1961) *What Kind of Co-operative Society?* (Noumea: SPC Co-Operatives Booklet, no. 1).

Boyan, R. H. (1962) *Guide to Book-keeping for Credit Unions in the Pacific* (Noumea: South Pacific Commission).

Brookes, Jean Ingram (1972) *International Rivalry in the Pacific Islands 1800–1875* (New York: Russell & Russell).

Brookfield, H. C. ed. (1969) *Pacific Market Places* (Canberra: Australian National University).

Brookfield, H. C. and Hart, Doreen (1971) *Melanesia: A Geographical Interpretation of an Island World* (London: Methuen).

Brookfield, H. C. (1972) *Colonialism, Development and Independence: the case of the Melanesian Islands in the South Pacific* (Cambridge: Cambridge University Press).

Brookfield, H. C. (1973) *The Pacific in Transition: geographical perspectives on adaptation and change* (London: Edward Arnold).

Buckley, K. and Klugman, K. (1981) *The History of Burns Philp: the Australian company in the South Pacific* (Sydney: Burns Philp & Co. Ltd).

Buckley, K. and Klugman, K. (1983) *The Australian Presence in the Pacific: Burns Philp, 1914–1946* (Sydney: George Allen & Unwin).

Carter, John (ed.) (1981) *Pacific Islands Yearbook*, 14th ed. (Sydney: Pacific Publications).

Castle, Leslie V. and Holmes, Sir Frank (eds) (1976) *Co-operation and Development in the Asia/Pacific Countries – relations between large and small countries* (Tokyo: Japan Economic Research Centre).

Coats, Austin (1970) *Western Pacific Islands* (London: HMSO).

Cole, R. V. (1977) 'Encouragement of the Inflow of Capital to the Smaller Countries or Territories of the South Pacific Region', a report to the Secretary-General, South Pacific Commission, 30 April.

Cole, R. V. and Thompson, G. J. (1981) *Proposal for a Pacific Island Fund: an evaluation* (Noumea/Suva: South Pacific Commission/South Pacific Bureau for Economic Co-operation) 7 July.

Crawford, Sir John G. (1982) *Australia-Japan and the Pacific Community in the year 2000* (Canberra: Australian National University).

Crawford, Sir John G. and Seow, Greg (eds) (1981) *Pacific Economic Co-operation – suggestions for actions* (Petaling: Heineman Asia).

'Credit Unions in the South Pacific', *The Credit Union Magazine*, April 1965.

Crick, W. F. (ed.) (1965) *Commonwealth Banking Systems* (Oxford: Clarendon Press).

Crocombe, R. G. (1973) *The New South Pacific* (Canberra: Australian National University Press).

Crocombe, R. G. (1976) *Rural Development in the Pacific Islands: past disasters and future hopes* (Suva: University of the South Pacific).

Crocombe, R. G. (1983) *The South Pacific: an introduction* (Auckland: Longman Paul).

Cumberland, Kenneth B. (1969) *South-West Pacific*, rev. edn (New York: Praeger).

Economist Intelligence Unit, *Quarterly Economic Review of Pacific Islands: Papua New Guinea, Fiji, Solomon Islands, Western Samoa, Vanuatu, Tonga*, various issues.

Fairbairn, Te'o Ian 'Pacific Islands Economies', (1971) *Journal of the Polynesian Society*, 80(1):74–118.

Fairbairn, Te'o Ian (1977) *The Exploitation and Development of Pacific Islands Resources* (Noumea: South Pacific Commission).

Fairbairn, Te'o Ian (1978) *Industrial Incentives in the South Pacific* (Noumea: South Pacific Commission).

Fairbairn, Te'o Ian (1985) *Island Economies: studies from the South Pacific* (Suva: Institute of Pacific Studies, University of the South Pacific).

Fairbairn, Te'o Ian and Bollard, Alan (1978) *South Pacific Economies – statistical summary* (Noumea: South Pacific Commission).

Firth, R. and Yamey, B. S. (eds) (1965) *Capital, Savings and Credit in Peasant Societies* (London: George Allen & Unwin).

Fisk, E. K. (1982) 'Development and Aid in the South Pacific in the 1980s', *Australian Outlook*, 36(2):32–7.

Fry, Maxwell, J. (1981) 'Financial Intermediation in Small Island Developing Countries', a paper for the Commonwealth Secretariat, 15 June.

Herr, R. A. (1982) 'Economic Co-operation in the South Pacific', in Roderic Alley (ed.) (1982) *New Zealand and the South Pacific* (Boulder: Westview).

Inder, Stuart (ed.) (1978) *Pacific Islands Year Book*, 13th edn (Sydney: Pacific Publications).

'Insurance: covering the Pacific', *Island Business*, April 1985, pp. 58–9.

Island Business, various issues.

Lamont, Jim (ed.) (1983) *Development Bank Credit in Rural Areas of the*

Pacific – the implications for rural development: proceedings of a workshop held in Tonga, July, 1982 (Tonga: Rural Development Centre, University of South Pacific).

Luke, Sir Harry (1962) *Islands of the South Pacific* (London: Harrap).

McBride, Jo (1982) 'Pacific Prospects I: sovereign borrowers and off-shore banking centres', *Asian Banking*, February, p. 42.

McIlroy, Robert Harbison (1985) 'The New Hebrides and the Emergence of Condominium', Ph.D. thesis, Columbia University.

Mara, Ratu Sir Kamisese (1974) 'Regional Co-operation in the South Pacific', *New Zealand Foreign Affairs Review*, 24(5):19–28.

Maynard, D. (1978) 'Monetary Policy in Small Developing Economies', in S. Schiavo-Campo (ed.) (1978) *Monetary Policy in a Small Developing Country* (Suva: University of the South Pacific) pp. 74–91.

Maynard, D. (1981) *Sources of Change in the Money Supply: Fiji, Tonga and Western Samoa* (Suva: Centre for Applied Studies in Development, University of the South Pacific).

Meeting on Problems of External Finance for Small Islands, Western Samoa, 1979: report and documentation (London: Commonwealth Secretariat, 1979).

Oliver, Douglas L. (1975) *The Pacific Islands*, rev. edn (Honolulu: University of Hawaii Press).

Osborne, Charles (ed.) (1970) *Australia, New Zealand and the South Pacific: a handbook* (New York: Praeger).

Pacific Islands Monthly, various issues.

Pacific Islands Yearbook, 15th edn (Sydney: Pacific Publications, 1984).

Peters, C. W. (1974) *Rural Credit in the South Pacific Region* (Suva: UNDAT Report).

Report on Capital Formation Methods and Credit Facilities for Islands in the South Pacific (Noumea: South Pacific Commission, 1962).

Report on the Regional Seminar for South-West Pacific on Agricultural Credit for Small Farmers (Rome: F.A.O., 1975).

Ross, Angus (ed.) (1969) *New Zealand's Record on the Pacific Islands in the Twentieth Century* (Auckland: Longman).

Runcie, N. (ed.) (1969) *Credit Unions in the South Pacific* (London: University of London Press).

Sevele, Feleti V. (1979) *South Pacific Economies* (Noumea: South Pacific Commission).

Shand, T. (ed.) (1980) *The Island States of the Pacific and Indian Oceans: anatomy of development* (Canberra: Development Studies Centre, Australian National University).

Shineberg, Dorothy L. (1967) *They Came for Sandalwood: a study of the sandalwood trade in the Southwest Pacific, 1830–1865* (Melbourne: Melbourne University Press).

Simkin, C. G. F. (1980) 'The South Pacific Islands – patterns and strategies of economic development, 1975–1990', *Economic Bulletin for Asia and the Pacific* December, pp. 77–113.

Skully, Michael T. (ed.), (1985) *Financial Institutions and Markets in the Southwest Pacific* (London: Macmillan).

A Socio-economic Survey of Selected Melanesian and Polynesian Areas (New York: Foundation for the Peoples of the South Pacific, 1967).

Stace, V. D. (1954) *The Pacific Islander and Modern Commerce* (Nouméa: South Pacific Commission).

Stanley, David (1982) *South Pacific Handbook* (Chico, Calif.: Moon Publications).

Stanner, W. E. H. (1953) *The South Seas in Transition – a study of post-war rehabilitation and reconstruction in three British Pacific Dependencies* (Sydney: Australasian Publishing Co.).

Steeves, Jeff S. (1984) *Decentralisation and Political Change in Melanesia* (Suva: USP Sociological Society).

Sutherland, William M. (1986) 'Microstates and unequal trade in the South Pacific: the SPARTEC agreement of 1980,' *Journal of World Trade Law* 20, May–June:313–28.

Task Force Report on the Study of the Bank's Role in the South Pacific Developing Member Countries in the 1980s (Manila: Asian Development Bank, 1983).

Thompson, Roger G. (1980) *Australian Imperialism in the Pacific: the Pacific expansionist era, 1820–1920* (Melbourne: Melbourne University Press).

Ward, R. Gerard and Proctor, Andrew (1980) *South Pacific Agriculture: choices and constraints* (Manila: Asian Development Bank).

NEW CALEDONIA

'Banks merge in New Caledonia', *Pacific Islands Monthly*, November 1975, p. 77.

Beer, Patrice de (1982) 'Like it or Lump it', *Far Eastern Economic Review*, 12 November p. 25.

Beer, Patrice de (1983) 'A Coup in the Countryside', *Far Eastern Economic Review*, 11 August, pp. 24–5.

Belshaw, Cyril S. (1950) *Island Administration in the South West Pacific: government and reconstruction in New Caledonia, the New Hebrides, and the British Solomon Islands* (London: Royal Institute of International Affairs).

Burchett, Wilfred (1941) *Pacific Treasure Island* (Melbourne: F. W. Cheshire).

Businessman's Guide to New Caledonia (Suva: Office of the Australian Trade Commissioner for the Pacific Islands, September 1985).

Dornoy, Myriam (1984) *Politics of New Caledonia, 1950–1977* (Sydney: Sydney University Press).

Ferris, Paul (1984) *Gentlemen of Fortune: the world's merchant and investment bankers* (London: Weidenfeld and Nicolson).

French Possessions in Oceania (London: HMSO, 1920).

'French Right's plans for New Caledonia', *Australian Financial Review*, 2 May 1986, p. 11.

Guiart, Jean (1982) 'One of the Last Colonies: New Caledonia', *Journal of International Affairs*, 36, Spring–summer,:105–12.

Hastings, Peter (1982) 'Outcasts in the Islands', *Far Eastern Economic Review*, 12 November, pp. 25–6.

Inder, Stuart (1983) 'New Caledonia's Future – how Paris plays racial roulette', *The Bulletin*, 26 July, pp. 66–9.

Inder, Stuart (1984) 'Big Trouble is Brewing in Aussies' Holiday Island', *The Bulletin*, 14 August, pp. 116–7.

Institut d'Emission d'Outre Mer (1985) *Bulletin Trimestriel*, December 1985.

Institut d'Emission d'Outre Mer (1984) *Nouvelle-Calédonie Exercice 1984 Rapport d'Activité*.

Jacob, Alain (1985) 'New Caledonia: the strategic implications', *The Guardian*, 3 February, p. 12.

Lawrey, John (1982) *The Cross of Lorraine in the South Pacific: Australia and the Free French Movement, 1940–1942* (Canberra: Journal of Pacific History).

Lehmann, Jean-Pierre (1985) 'The Second Front', *Far Eastern Economic Review*, 24 January, pp. 9–11.

Loans and Financial Assistance to Private Investment (Noumea: Territorial Statistics and Economic Research Department, 1984).

Lyons, Martyn (1986) *The Totem and the Tricolour: a short history of New Caledonia since 1774* (Sydney: UNSW Press).

Macrae, John T. (1972) *The Structure and Evolution of the Caledonian Economy, 1967–1970* (Auckland: University of Auckland).

Macrae, John T. (1974a) 'New Caledonia: a summary of recent economic developments with special reference to "le problème Melanesian"', *Pacific Viewpoint*, 15, (1):33–50.

Macrae, John T. (1974b) 'The New Caledonia Economy, 1967–72', *New Zealand Economic Papers*, 8:23–57.

McDonald, Hamish (1985) 'Caught in the Trap', *Far Eastern Economic Review*, 10 October 1985, pp. 14–15.

McDonald, Hamish (1984a) 'Independence Minded', *Far Eastern Economic Review*, 1 November 1984, p. 39.

McDonald, Hamish (1984b) 'Far from Pacific Isles', *Far Eastern Economic Review*, 29 November 1984, 14–15.

McDonald, Hamish (1984c) 'More Rouge than Noir', *Far Eastern Economic Review*, 13 December 1984, pp. 56–7.

McDonald, Hamish (1985) 'Le Nickel goes Local', *Far Eastern Economic Review*, 31 October 1985, pp. 122–4.

McDonald, Hamish (1986) 'Tangle over Tripoli', *Far Eastern Economic Review*, 16 January 1986, p. 40.

McTaggart, William D. (1963) 'Noumea: a study in social geography', Ph.D. thesis, Australian National University, March.

Moorehead, Alan (1966) *The Fatal Impact* (London: Hamilton).

Naldi, Gino J. (1985) 'Self-determination in the South Pacific: the case of New Caledonia', *World Today*, 41, August–September:170–2.

New Caledonia: a background (1985) (Canberra: French Embassy).

'New Caledonia: now for the tricky part', *The Economist*, 6 October 1985, p. 30.

Osborne, Robin (1985) 'The Island People Begin to make Waves', *The Guardian*, 10 February, p. 8.

Outline on New Caledonia (Canberra: Department of Foreign Affairs, Australian Government, February 1985).

'Pisani Plan', *Pacific Islands Monthly*, February 1985, p. 17.

Reinhart, Denis (1983) 'New Trouble in Noumea', *Far Eastern Economic Review*, 1 December, p. 32.

Roff, Sue Rabbitt (1986) 'New Caledonia: decolonization and denuclearization in the Pacific', *Third World Quarterly*, 8, April: 621–38.

Rollat, Alain (1984) 'Edgard Pisani's Mission Impossible', *The Guardian*, 16 December, pp. 13–14.

Saussol, Alain, (1971) 'New Caledonia: colonization and reaction', in R. G. Cromcombe (ed.) (1971) *Land Tenure in the Pacific* (Melbourne: Oxford University Press), pp. 227–47.

Shineberg, Dorothy L. (1967) *They came for Sandalwood: a study of the sandalwood trade in the Southwest Pacific, 1830–1865* (Melbourne: Melbourne University Press).

Schneiderman, Daniel (1984) 'Capital Independence says Kanak Leader', *The Guardian* 16 December, p. 13.

Spencer, Michael C. (1985) *New Caledonia in Crisis* (Canberra: Australian Institute of International Affairs).

Starr, Peter (1985a) 'Growing Unrest a Poser for Canberra', *Australian Financial Review*, 25 July, p. 14

Starr, Peter (1985b) 'Power Play to be Fought in the Economy', *Australian Financial Review*, 26 July, pp. 14–15.

Starr, Peter (1985c) 'Trade Slides Further into the Red', *Australian Financial Review*, 2 October, p. 15.

Starr, Peter (1986) 'Rise in Nickel Exports Fails to Lift the Gloom', *Australian Financial Review*, 14 March, p. 13.

Thompson, Virginia and Adloff, Richard (1971) *The French Pacific Islands: French Polynesia and New Caledonia* (Berkeley: University of California Press).

Ward, Alan (1982) *Land and Politics of New Caledonia* (Canberra: Department of Political and Social Change, Australian National University).

Ward, Alan (1984) *New Caledonia – the immediate prospects* (Caberra: Parliament of Australia Legislative Research Service).

Waterman, Peter (1986) 'Kanaks Rethink Strategy in Freedom Campaign', *Australian Financial Review*, 7 December, p. 52.

Williams, Sue (1985) 'Bitter French Backlash in Latest Bombings', *The Bulletin*, 17 December, p. 92.

Woodstock, George (1976) *South Sea Journey* (London: Faber).

SOLOMON ISLANDS

'Agriculture: Pitfalls in a Promising Solomon Science', *Pacific Islands Monthly*, May 1979, pp. 73–5.

Amherst, Lord and Thompson, B. (1967) *The Discovery of the Solomon Islands in 1568* (London: Hakluyt Society).

Ayton, K. J. (1982) 'Solomon Islands – the country and its people', *Bankers Magazine of Australasia*, February, pp. 10–11.

Bathgate, M. A. (1978) *The Structure of Rural Supply to the Honiara Market in the Solomon Islands* (Canberra: Development Studies Centre, Australian National University).

Bathgate, M. A., Frazer, I. L. and McKinnon J. M. (1973) *Socio-Economic Change in Solomon Island Villages* (Wellington: Dept of Geography, Victoria University at Wellington).

Beaglehole, J. C. (1966) *The Exploration of the Pacific*, 3rd edn (London, A. & C. Black).

Bornemeier, Wayne M. (1985) *Development Plan for the Solomon Islands Credit Union League 1986–1990* (Washington, DC: Volunteers in Overseas Cooperative Assistance).

Central Bank of Solomon Islands (1982), (1984) *Annual Reports*.

Central Bank of Solomon Islands, *Mid-Year Economic Review*, various years.

Clarence, Margaret (1982) *Yield not to the Wind* (Sydney: Management Development Publishers).

Cochrane, G. (1970) *Big Men and Cargo Cults* (Oxford: Clarendon Press).

Connel, John (1983) *Migration, Employment and Development in the South Pacific: country report no. 16, Solomon Islands* (Noumea: South Pacific Commission).

Corris, Peter (1973) *Passage, Port and Plantations: a History of Solomon Island Labour Migration 1820–1914* (Melbourne: Oxford University Press).

Deans, Alan (1985) 'The Pacific Islands Gold Rush', *Business Review Weekly*, 20 September, pp. 22, 24.

Development Bank of Solomon Islands, *Annual Report*, various years.

Dommen, Edward C. (1972) *A Proposal for a Solomon Islands Currency* (Suva: United Nations Development Advisory Team for the Pacific).

Economist Intelligence Unit, *Quarterly Economic Review of Pacific Islands: Papua New Guinea, Fiji, Solomon Islands, Western Samoa, Vanuatu, Tonga*, various issues.

Eale, G. J. (1978) *Indigenous Agriculture in the Solomon Islands* (Canberra: Development Studies Centre, Australian National University).

Firth, Raymond (1959) *Social Change in Tikopia* (London: Allen & Unwin).

Foreign Investment Act No. 10 of 1984, and Foreign Investment Regulations 1984 (Honiara: Foreign Investment Division, Prime Minister's Office, August 1984).

Fox, C. E. (1976) *Story of the Solomons* (Taroaniare: Diocese of Melanesia Press).

Fox, Morris G. (1971) *Development of the Social Welfare Service in the British Solomon Islands Protectorate: initial observations* (Nomuea: South Pacific Commission).

Fox, Morris G. (1972) *Second Report on the Development of the Social Welfare in the British Solomon Island Protectorate: followup observations* (Noumea: South Pacific Commission).

The Government Shareholding Agency, *Annual Reports*, 1980 to 1984.

Hansell, J. F. R. and Wall, J. R. D. (1974) *The British Solomon Islands Protectorate* (London: HMSO).

Hansell, J. F. R. and Wall, J. R. D. (1976) *Land Resources of the Solomons*, (London: Ministry of Overseas Development).

Hardman, D. J. (1983) *Solomon Islands: accounting shibboleths and no-strums* (Broadway (NSW): Faculty of Business, New South Wales Institute of Technology).

Hawkins, Edward K. (1980) *The Solomon Islands: an introductory economic report* (Washington: World Bank).

Hawkins, Irene (1979) 'Solomon Islands: a pervasive but nowhere dominant, presence', *Pacific Islands Monthly*, October, pp. 49–50, 52.

Hinton, Colin Jack (1969) *The Search for the Islands of Solomon 1567–1838* (Oxford: Clarendon Press).

Hoyt, Edwin P. (1983) *The Glory of the Solomons* (New York: Stein & Day).

Hughes, A. V. (1983) 'Monetary Policy in Perspective', a speech by the Governor of the Central Bank of Solomon Islands, 24 January.

Hughes, A. R. (1985) 'Coming back to earth . . . return to economic reality and prospects for growth', a speech, 19 August.

Ifunaoa, Wilson (1984) 'Planning of Provincial Government System in Solomon Islands', in *Second Regional Conference of Development Planners: collected papers* (Noumea: South Pacific Commission, November) pp. 27–38.

Information Book (Honiara: Development Bank of Solomon Islands, undated).

Investment in Solomon Islands, 2nd edn (Honiara: Peat Marwick Mitchell & Co., 1985).

Investors Guide to Investment Possibilities in Solomon Islands (Honiara: Foreign Investment Division, Prime Minister's Office, June 1984).

Kent, Janet (1972) *The Solomon Islands* (Melbourne: Wren).

Kick, Charles G. (ed.) (1986) *Development Services Exchange of the Solomon Islands: directory* (Honiara: Development Services Exchange).

Larmour, Peter (ed.) (1979) *Land in Solomon Islands* (Honiara: Institute of Pacific Studies, University of South Pacific).

National Bank of Solomon Islands Ltd, *Annual Reports*, 1981 to 1985.

National Provident Fund *1983 Budget Speech* (Honiara: Government of the Solomon Islands, November, 1982).

Oliver, D. L. (1955) *A Solomon Island Society* (Cambridge: Harvard University Press).

'Pacific Island Peoples', *Current Affairs Bulletin*, 44 (6) (1969): 82–95.

Papua New Guinea, Solomon Islands and Vanuatu: A business profile (1985) (Hongkong: Hongkong and Shanghai Banking Corporation).

Pettman, Ralph (1977) 'The Solomon Islands – a developing neo-colony?' *Australian Outlook*, August, pp. 268–78.

Pickering, George F. (1978) *Basic Banking Facilities in Rural Areas of the Solomon Islands* (Suva: United Nations Development Advisory Team for the Pacific).

Pitaduna Stainer (1965) 'Savings and Loan Societies and the Western District Association in the Western Solomons', *Co-operatives Newsletter* (Nouméa: South Pacific Commission).

Potterton, Peter (1979) 'The Solomon Islands Today', *Current Affairs Bulletin*, November, pp. 24–31.

Premdas, Ralph R. (1985) *The Solomon Islands: an experiment in decentralization* (Manoa: Center for Asian and Pacific Studies, University of Hawaii).

Premdas, Ralph B. and Steeves, Jeffery S. (1981) 'The Solomon Islands: the first elections after independence', *Journal of Pacific History*, October, pp. 190–202.

Programme of Action, 1981–84 (Honiara: Government of Solomon Islands, November 1981).

A Review of the Solomon Islands National Development Plan (1975 to 1979) (Honiara: Central Planning Office, 1977).

Richardson, John (1985a) 'End of the Tuna War', *Islands Business*, February, p. 39.

Richardson, John (1985b) 'The Land and that Nature Blessed', *Islands Business*, April, pp. 13–14.

Ringshall, J. R. (1984) 'Report of the SIHA and overall housing policy and funding', a paper to the Solomon Islands Housing Authority, dated November.

Rural Financial Services in Solomon Islands (Honiara: Central Bank of Solomon Islands, October 1984).

Saemala, Francis J. (1979) *Our Independent Solomon Islands* (Suva: Institute of Pacific Studies, University of South Pacific).

Sheffler Harold W. (1971) 'The Solomon Islands: seeking a new land custom', in R. G. Crocombe (ed.) (1971) *Land Tenure in the Pacific* (Melbourne: Oxford University Press) pp. 273–91.

Sixth Development Plan, 1971–1973 (1971) (Honiara: British Solomon Islands Protectorate).

Solomon Islands (London HMSO, 1978).

Solomon Islands: background notes (Washington, DC.: US Department of State, April 1985)

Solomon Islands Copra Board, *Annual Reports*, 1980–1984.

Solomon Islands Handbook (Honiara: Government Printing Works, 1983).

Solomon Islands Monetary Authority, *Annual Report*, various years.

Solomon Islands National Development Plan, 1975–1979 (Honiara: Office of the Chief Minister, April 1975).

Solomon Islands National Development Plan, 1980–84, vol. II, Financial Plan (Honiara: Ministry of Economic Planning, 1980).

Solomon Islands National Development Plan, 1985–1989 (1989) (Honiara: Ministry of Economic Planning).

Solomon Islands National Provident Fund, *Annual Reports*, 1977 to 1985.

Solomon Islands 1981 Statistical Yearbook (Honiara: Statistics Office, Ministry of Finance, December 1981).

'Solomon Islands – outlook better than most', *Asian Banking*, August 1984, pp. 104–5.

'Solomon Islands – roads to independence', *Australian Foreign Affairs Record*, January 1976, p. 36.

Some Information of Credit Unions: the credit union idea is born, 1854 (1985) (Honiara: Solomon Islands Credit Union League).

Standish, Bill (1984) *Melanesian Neighbours: the politics of Papua New Guinea, the Solomon Islands, and the Republic of Vanuatu* (Canberra: Department of the Parliamentary Library).

Statement of General Business Policies (Honiara: Development Bank of Solomon Islands, 1978).

Sunga, Selwyn (1983) 'How DBSI works', *Solomon Islands Monthly Magazine*, 30 April.
'The Investors line-up', *Islands Business*, April 1985, p. 15.
The Money System (Honiara: Central Bank of Solomon Islands, 1984).
The Solomon Islands: an introductory economic report (Washington, DC: World Bank, April 1980).
Thornton, Nicholas (1985) 'Sir Peter Faces Kwaio Challenge', *Pacific Islands Monthly*, January, pp. 22–3.
Tregaskis, Richard (1955) *Guadalcanal Diary* (New York: Random House).
Trumbull, Robert (1978) *Tin Roofs and Palm Trees* (Seattle: University of Washington Press).
'Zanex Gets Mining Go-ahead in Solomons: performance promising', *Rydges*, September 1985, p. 44.

TONGA

Ashton, Chris (1978) 'The Bank that Died of Shame', *The Bulletin*, 12 December, pp. 105–6.
'A Banker's Paradise', *Island Business*, January 1985, p. 52.
Bain. K. R. (1967) *The Friendly Islanders* (London: Hodder & Stoughton).
Bank of Tonga, *Annual Reports*, various years.
'Beans Mean Money', *Island Business*, July 1983, p. 36.
Beer, Patrice de (1983) 'Tonga and Fiji – racial tensions and a generation gap', *The Guardian*, 25 September, p. 12.
Biennial Report: Tonga 1956 and 1957 (London: HMSO, 1959).
Bollard, A. E. (1976) 'Dualism in Tonga Commerce', *Pacific Viewpoint*, 17 (1):75–81.
Bollard, A. E. (1981) 'The Financial Adventures of J. C. Godeffroy and Son in the Pacific', (1981) *Journal of Pacific History*, 16 (1):3–19.
Bollard, A. E. (1977) 'The Role of Money in Development: the Tonga Experience', *New Zealand Economic Papers*, 11:122–34.
Bres, Joris de (1975) *Worth Their Weight in Gold* (Auckland: Auckland Resource Centre for World Development).
Colonial Reports: Tonga, 1952 and 1953 (London: HMSO, 1954).
'Credit Unions in Tonga', *Australian Credit Union Foundation News*, 1983.
Crocombe, R. G. (1975) 'Land Tenure in Tonga: the process of change, past and present', paper to the Tonga Council of Churches Seminar on Land Tenure and Migration, 21–26 September, Nuku' alofa.
'Cutting the Cash Cake', *Islands Business*, July 1983, pp. 35–8.
Dommen, E. C. (1972) *Tonga: a twenty-five year prospect* (Suva: United Nations Development Advisory Team for the Pacific).
Economist Intelligence Unit, *Quarterly Economic Review of Pacific Islands: Papua New Guinea, Fiji, Solomon Islands, Western Samoa, Vanuatu, Tonga*, various issues.
Evaluation Report: Tonga Cooperative Federation (Washington, DC: Agricultural Cooperative Development International, 1985).
Fairbairn, Ian (1972) 'Economic Planning: Tonga Style', *Pacific Perspectives* (1):38–45

Farmer, Sarah Stock (1976) *Tonga and the Friendly Islands* (Canberra: Kalia Press).

Firth, Stewart (1973) 'German Firms in the Western Pacific Islands, 1857–1914', *Journal of Pacific History*, 8:10–28.

Fonua, Pesi (1975), (ed.) *Tonga: land and migration* (Nuku'alofa: Tonga Council of Churches).

Fonua, Pesi (1985) 'Top Secret Banking', *Islands Business*, January, pp. 48–9.

Fonua, Pesi (1985) 'Industrial Revolution', *Islands Business*, April, pp. 43–4.

'Foundation News: Tonga', *Australian Credit Unions*, October 1982, p. 32.

Guide to the Market – Tonga (Canberra: Australian Department of Trade, October 1974).

Hardaker, J. B. (1975) *Agriculture and Development in the Kingdom of Tonga* (Armidale: University of New England).

'Howard Hughes' Shadow over Tonga's New Bank', *Pacific Islands Monthly*, February 1978, p. 55.

Jehle, Eugen (1983) 'The Tax System of the kingdom of Tonga: a brief survey', *Bulletin of International Fiscal Documentation*, 37, December: 553–6.

'Industry gently laps South Pacific shores' (1982), *ADB Quarterly*, pp. 17–18.

Johns, Graham (1978) 'Tonga Development Bank: Pangike Fakalakalaka 'o Tonga', *The Bankers' Magazine of Australasia*, June, pp. 112–13.

Kingdom of Tonga: Mid-Term Review, Third Development Plan 1975–1977 (Nuku'alofa: Central Planning Department, 1978).

Kingdom of Tonga First Five-Year Development Plan 1965–1970 (Nuku'alofa: Government Printing Office, 1965).

Kingdom of Tonga Second Five-Year Development Plan 1970–1975 (Naku'alofa: Government Press, 1970).

Kingdom of Tonga Fourth Five-Year Development Plan 1980–1985 (Naku'alofa: Central Planning Department, October 1981).

Kingdom of Tonga Third Five-Year Development Plan 1975–1980, (Naku'alofa: Central Planning Office, February 1976).

Kingston, A., Fleming, E. and Antony, G. (1986) 'Effects of price and income on rural household demand in Tonga', a paper presented to the Australian Agricultural Economics Society Conference, Canberra, February.

'Know Your Bank', *The Tonga Chronicle*, (four-part article), 30 May, 7 June, 13 June and 20 June 1974.

Latukefu, S. (1974) *Church and State in Tonga* (Canberra: Australian National University).

Maude, Alaric (1971) 'Tonga: equality overtaking privilege', in R. G. Crocombe (ed.) (1971) *Land Tenure in the Pacific* (Melbourne: Oxford University Press) pp. 106–28.

Maude, Alaric (1973) 'Land Shortage and Population Pressure in Tonga', in H. Brookfield (ed.) *The Pacific in Transition: Geographical Perspectives on Adaptation and Change* (New York: St. Martin's Press) pp. 163–85.

Maynard, David L. (1981) *Sources of change in the money supply: Fiji, Tonga and Western Samoa* (Suva: Centre for Applied Studies in Development, University of South Pacific).

Marridew, Alan (1984) 'End of the Road for the Bank of the South Pacific's Mr Meier?' *Pacific Islands Monthly*, July, pp. 25–6.

Morello, Ted (1982) 'Pacific Quicksands', *Far Eastern Economic Review*, 17 December, p. 44.

Oliver, John (1982) *Isaac: cyclone impact in the context of the society and economy of the Kingdom of Tonga* (Townsville: Centre for Disaster Studies, James Cook University of North Queensland).

'Pierpont' (1978) 'Controversial New Bank's Bookmaking Connection', *The Bulletin*, 28 March, pp. 88–9.

Popper, J. B. A. (1980) *Recent Developments and Problems in the Financial Sector in Tonga* (Nuku'alofa: Central Planning Department, April).

Ratcliffe, Jeanette and Dillon, Rosemary (1982) *A Review and Study of the Human Settlement Situation in the Kingdom of Tonga: a paper prepared for the Economic and Social Commission for Asia and the Pacific* (Nuku'alofa: Central Planning Department, May).

Report of the Ministry of Finance and the Custom, Post Office, Inland Revenue, Statistics, and Harbours and Wharfs Department for the year 1984 (Government of Tonga, 25 July 1985).

Rew, A. W. (1979) *Housing Options for Tonga 1980–85* (London: British Technical Cooperation).

Richardson, John (1983) 'The world of the Sun King', *Island Business*, July, pp. 32–3.

Rutherford, Noel (1971) *Shirley Baker and the King of Tonga* (Melbourne: Oxford University Press).

Rutherford, Noel (1981) 'Tonga Ma'a Tonga Kautaha: a proto-co-operative in Tonga', *Journal of Pacific History* 16 (1):20–41.

Rutherford, Noel (ed.) (1977) *Friendly Islands: a history of Tonga* (Melbourne: Oxford University Press).

Snow, P. A. (1969) *Bibliography of Fiji, Tonga and Rotuma* (Canberra: Australian National University).

'The Cyclopedia of Tonga', in *Cyclopedia of Samoa, Tonga, Tahiti, and the Cook Islands*' (Sydney: McCarron, Stewart & Co., 1907).

Tonga: background notes (Washington, D.C. US Department of State, April 1985).

'Tonga Credit Union Movement', an unpublished report to the World Council of Credit Unions, May 1984.

Tonga Development Bank, *Annual Report*, various years.

'Tonga Making Opportunities', *Australian Financial Review*, 11 October 1982, p. 28.

Tonga: a trade and investment guide (Wellington: Asia Pacific Research Unit, 1982).

'Tonga's "South Sea Bubble" bursts', *Pacific Islands Monthly*, September 1978, p. 9.

'Visiting Bankers Meeting Ends on Optimistic Note', *The Tonga Chronicle*, 18 November 1971, pp. 1, 10.

Walsh, A. C. (1972) *Nuku'alofa: a study of urban life in the Pacific islands* (Wellington: Reed Education).

Ward, R. Gerard, and Proctor, Andrew (1980) *South Pacific Agriculture: choices and constraints* (Manila: Asian Development Bank) pp. 381–94.

VANUATU

Allen, Michael (1981) *Vanuatu: politics, economics and ritual in island Melanesia* (Sydney: Academic Press).

Anglo-French Condominium–New Hebrides Condominium, Annual Report for the years 1965 and 1966 (London: HMSO, 1967).

Bank Gutzwiller, Kurz, Bungener (Overseas) Ltd (1984) *Annual Report.*

Barrau, Jacques (1960) *Outline of an Agricultural Programme for the New Hebrides Condominium* (Noumea: South Pacific Commission).

Beasant, John (1984) *Santo Rebellion: an imperial reckoning* (Richmond (Vic.): Heinemann).

Bishop, Mike, and Wigglesworth, Ann (1982) *A Touch of Australian Enterprise: the Vanuatu experience* (Fitzroy (Vic.): International Development Action).

Bonnemaison, J. (1977) 'Custom, Cash and Compromise: Melanesian systems of food production in the New Hebrides', a paper presented at the 'Adaptation of Traditional Systems of Agriculture' seminar, Honiara, 3–7 October.

Carew, Edna (1984a) 'Investors in Hellish Rush to Vanuatu's Tax Heaven', *Australian Financial Review*, 20 July, p. 37.

Casew, Edna (1984b), 'Letter from Port Vila', *Far Eastern Economic Review*, 6 September.

Central Bank of Vanuatu, *Annual Report*, various years.

Clark, Alan (1980a) 'Vanuatu: independence but still the French connection', *NZ International Review*, 5 (3), pp. 12–14.

Clark, Alan (1980b) 'The French Way: toward integration?' *NZ Internal Review*, 5 (5), pp. 18–20.

Colonial Reports: Anglo-French Condominium; New Hebrides, 1949 and 1950 (London: HMSO, 1951).

'Coordination of Donor Activities: a paper presented by Vanuatu', in *Second Regional Conference of Development Planners: collected papers* (Nouméa: South Pacific Commission, November 1984) pp. 9–14.

Crocombe, R. G. (1970) 'Land Tenure in the New Hebrides', in *Land Tenure in the South Pacific* (Melbourne: Oxford University Press).

Dean, Alan (1985) 'The Pacific Islands Gold Rush', *Business Review Weekly*, 20 September, pp. 22, 24.

Development Bank of Vanuatu, *Annual Report*, various years.

Economist Intelligence Unit, *Quarterly Economic Review of Pacific Islands: Papua New Guinea, Fiji, Solomon Islands, Western Samoa, Vanuatu, Tonga*, various issues.

Ellis, Julie-Ann (1984a) 'Looking at Kava as an Export Crop', *Pacific Islands Monthly*, February, pp. 27–8.

Ellis, Julie-Ann (1984b) 'Port Vila's Booming Finance Centre', *Pacific Island Monthly*, August, p. 36.

Forster, R. A. S. (1980) 'Vanuatu: The end of an episode of schizophrenic colonialism', *Round Table*, 280, October, pp. 367–73.

Hours, B. (1979) 'Custom and Politics in the New Hebrides', *Pacific Perspectives*, 8 (1), pp. 15–20.

Howard, Michael C., (1983) 'Vanuatu: the myth of Melanesian socialism', *Labour, Capital and Society*, 16 (2):189–92.

Investing in Vanuatu: a guide to entrepreneurs (Port Vila: Government of Vanuatu, 1983).

Jupp, James and Sewer, Marian (1979), 'The New Hebrides: from condominium to independence', *Australian Outlook*, 33, April: 15–26.

Keith-Reid, Robert (1984a) 'Vanuatu: a nation in gear', *Island Business*, September, pp. 13–16.

Keith-Reid, Robert (1984b) 'No to the Superpowers', *Islands Business*, September, p. 16.

Lambert, Michel (1971) *Requirements for the Development and Improvement of Coffee Production on the Island of Tanna* (Noumea: South Pacific Commission).

Lamont, Jim (1983) *A Little Bit of Everything: a study of rural entrepreneurs financed by the Development Bank of Vanuatu* (Naku'alofa: Rural Development Centre, University of South Pacific).

Latham, Richard T. E. (1927) 'The New Hebrides Condominium', Masters thesis, University of Melbourne.

Leversedge, J. M. (1977) 'New Hebrides – financial centre on a Pacific Island', *The Banker*, April, pp. 131–3.

Lini, Walter (1980) *Beyond Pandemonium: from the New Hebrides to Vanuatu* (Wellington: Asia Pacific Books).

Lini, Walter (1982), 'Australia and the South Pacific: A Vanuatu perspective', *Australian Outlook*, 36, August: 29–31.

MacClancy, J. V. (1981a) 'From New Hebrides to Vanuatu, 1979–80', *Journal of Pacific History*, 16 (1):92–104.

MacClancy, J. V. (1981b) *To kill a bird with two stones: a short history of Vanuatu* (Port Vila: Vanuatu Cultural Centre Publications).

MacDonald-Milne, Brian and Thomas, Pamela (1981) *Yumi Stanap: leaders and leadership of a new nation* (Suva: Institute of Pacific Studies, University of South Pacific).

McGee, T. G., Ward, R. G. and Drakakis-Smith, D. W., (1980) *Food Distribution in the New Hebrides* (Canberra: Development Studies Centre, Australian National University).

McIlroy, Robert H. (1951) 'The New Hebrides and the Emergence of Condominium', PhD thesis, Columbia University.

New Hebrides, 1938 (London: HMSO, 1940).

New Hebrides, – Anglo-French Condominium, Annual Report for 1948 (London: HMSO, 1949).

Papua New Guinea, Solomon Islands and Vanuatu: a business profile (1985) (Hongkong: Hongkong and Shanghai Banking Corporation).

Philibert, Jean-Marc (1981) 'Living Under Two Flags: selective modernization in Erakor village, Efate', in Michael Allen (ed.) (1981) *Vanuatu politics, economics, and ritual in island Melanesia* (Sydney: Academic Press).

PITCO Vanuatu Update, various issues.

Plant, Chris (ed.) (1977) *New Hebrides: the road to independence* (Suva: Institute of Pacific Studies, University of South Pacific).

Ponter, Brian A. (1983) 'Co-operatives in Vanuatu, 1962–1980', PhD thesis, University of the South Pacific.

Ponter, Brian A. (1985) 'The Development of Co-operatives in Vanuatu', *Year Book of Agricultural Co-operation, 1984*, (Oxford: Plunkett Foundation for Co-operative Studies).

Ponter, Brian A. (1986) *Co-operatives in Vanuatu* (Suva: Institute of Pacific Studies, University of South Pacific).

Premdas, Ralph R. 1984 'Secession and Decentralization in Political Change: the case of Vanuatu', *South Pacific Forum*, 1 (1): 41–75.

Premdas, Ralph R. and Howard, Michael C. (1985) 'Vanuatu's Foreign Policy: contradictions and constraints', *Australian Outlook*, December, pp. 189–92.

Republic of Vanuatu First National Development Plan, 1982–1986 (Port Vila: National Planning Office, 1982).

Roadman, Margaret (1984) 'Masters of Tradition: customary land tenure and new forms of social inequality in a Vanuatu peasantry', *American Ethnologist*, February.

Shears, Richard (1980) *The Coconut War: the Crisis on Espiritu Santo* (North Ryde: Cassell Australia).

Sope, Barak (1975) *Land and Politics in the New Hebrides* (Suva: South Pacific Social Sciences Association).

Standish, Bill (1984) *Melanesian Neighbours: the politics of Papua New Guinea, the Solomon Islands, and the Republic of Vanuatu* (Canberra: Department of the Parliamentary Library).

'Steady as She Goes on Vanuatu Economy, says Kalsakau', *Pacific Island Monthly*, July 1984, pp. 35–6.

The First Vanuatu Industrial Products Fair 1985 (Port Vila: Chamber of Commerce of Vanuatu, 1985).

The Mid-Term Review of Vanuatu's First National Development Plan (Port Vila: National Planning and Statistics Office, 1984).

Theroux, Eugene A. (1977), 'Transferred Corporate Domicile: New Hebrides refuge from calamities', *Tax Executive*, 29 January:91–8, 184–5.

Thompson, Roger C. (1970) 'Australian Imperialism and the New Hebrides, 1862–1922', PhD thesis, Australian National University.

Vanuatu: an international tax-free financial centre, 2nd edn (Port Vila: Coopers & Lybrand, 1983).

Vanuatu: a trade and investment guide (Wellington: Asia Pacific Research Unit Ltd, 1982).

'Vanuatu Gets the Vaults Ready', *Australian Business*, 4 July 1984, pp. 101–2.

'Vanuatu: independent and steady', *Asian Banking*, August 1984, p. 103.

Vanuatu: the tax-free financial centre of the Pacific (Port Vila: Peat Marwick Mitchell & Co., March 1983).

Vanuatu: twenti wan lingling long team blong independence (Suva: Institute of Pacific Studies, University of South Pacific, 1980).

Wheeler, David (1985) 'Barclays Ends Ties with Pacific Islands', *Australian Financial Review*, 13 August, p. 45.

Wilson, J. S. G. (1966) *Economic Survey of the New Hebrides* (London: HMSO).

Winkler, James E. (1982) *Losing Control: toward an understanding of transnational corporations in the Pacific Islands context* (Suva: Pacific Conference of Churches).

Wise, Colin (1985) 'Banking in Vanuatu', a speech to the Vanuatu Law Congress, Port Vila.

WESTERN SAMOA

Afxentiou, Panayiotis (1977) 'A Social Instrument of Economic Development – an opportunity for Western Samoa', *New Zealand Economic Papers*, 11:135–50.

Altman, Joh C. (1978) 'Export Instability and its Consequences for Economic Growth and Development: Western Samoa', *Pacific Viewpoint*, 19 (1):26–46.

Anderson, Lee (1985a) 'Poll May Be Last Under Old Rule', *Australian Financial Review*, 22 February, p. 16.

Anderson, Lee (1985b) 'Is Samoa really an LDC?' *Islands Business*, June, p. 44.

Background Notes: Western Samoa (Washington, DC: Department of State, May 1979).

Bank of Western Samoa, *Annual Reports*, various years.

Beer, Patrice de (1983) 'Paradise Threatened by the 20th century?' *The Guardian*, 18 September, pp. 12, 14.

Bollard, A. E. (1981) 'The Financial adventures of J. C. Godeffroy and Son in the Pacific' *Journal of Pacific History*, 16 (1):3–19.

Boyd, Mary (1968) 'Independent Western Samoa', *Pacific Viewpoint*, 9 (2): 154–72.

Carroll, P. G. H. (1984) *The Development Bank of Western Samoa: a profile* (Canberra: Development Studies Centre, Australian National University).

Central Bank of Samoa (1984) *Annual Report*.

Central Bank of Samoa (1986) *Bulletin*, March.

Chappell, N. M. (1961) *New Zealand Banker's Hundred: a history of the Bank of New Zealand, 1861–1961* (Wellington: Bank of New Zealand).

Davidson, J. W. (1967) *Samoa Mo Samoa: the Emergence of the Independent State of Western Samoa* (Melbourne: Oxford University Press).

Desai, Ashok (1975) *Island Economies of the South Pacific: comparative statistics* (Suva: University of the South Pacific).

Development Bank of Western Samoa, *Annual Report*, various years.

Doing Business in Western Samoa (Apia: Price Waterhouse, 1977).

Economist Intelligence Unit, *Quarterly Economic Review of Pacific Islands: Papua New Guinea, Fiji, Solomon Islands, Western Samoa, Vanuatu, Tonga*, various issues.

Fairbairn, Te'o Ian J. (1971) 'A Survey of Local Industries in Western Samoa', *Pacific Viewpoint*, 12 (2):103–22.

Fairbairn, Te'o Ian J. (1973) *The National Income of Western Samoa* (Melbourne: Oxford University Press).

Fairbairn, Te'o Ian J. (1985) *Island Economies: studies from the South Pacific* (Suva: Institute of Pacific Studies, University of South Pacific).

Field, Michael J. (1984) *Mau: Samoa's struggle against New Zealand oppression* (Wellington: A. H. & A. W. Reed Ltd).

Select Bibliography

361

Firth, Stewart (1973) 'German Firms in the Western Pacific Islands, 1857–1914', *Journal of Pacific History*, 8:10–28.

'Fish, Timber, Minerals are Bases for Economy of the Solomon Island', *IMF Survey*, 5 March 1977, pp. 66–80.

Fletcher, Charles Brunsdon (1970) *Stevenson's Germany: the case against Germany in the Pacific* (New York: Arno Press).

Fox, James W. (1962) *Western Samoa: land, life and agriculture in tropical Polynesia* (Christchurch: Whitecombe & Tombs).

Gilson, Richard Philip (1970) *Samoa 1830–1900: the politics of a multi-cultural community* (Melbourne: Oxford University Press).

Haas, Anthony (ed.) (1977) *New Zealand and the South Pacific Islands: a guide to economic development in the Cook Islands, Fiji, Niue, Tonga and Western Samoa* (Wellington: Asia Pacific Research Unit).

Holmes, Lowell Don (1974) *Samoa Village* (New York: Holt, Rinehart & Winston).

Inder, Stuart (1983) 'On the Road from Crisis to Stability', *The Bulletin*, 8 February, p. 80.

'Industry Gently Laps South Pacific Shores', *ADB Quarterly Review*, January 1985, pp. 17–18.

Keesing, Felix M. (1934) *Modern Samoa: its government and changing life* (London: George Allen & Unwin Ltd).

Keesing, Felix M. (1973) *Elite Communication in Samoa: a study of leadership* (New York: Octagon Books).

Kennedy, Paul M. (1974) *The Samoa Triangle: a study in anglo-german-american relations, 1878–1900* (Dublin: Irish University Press).

Leumaga, P. (1983) 'Social and Cultural Considerations in Rural Lending in Western Samoa', in Jim Lamont (ed.) (1983) *Development Bank Credit in Rural Areas of the Pacific – the implications for rural development: proceedings of a workshop held in Tonga, July, 1982* (Tonga: Rural Development Centre, University of South Pacific) pp. 180–90.

Lockwood, Brian A. (1968) *A Comparative Study of Market Participation and Monetization in Four Subsistence-based Villages in Western Samoa* (Melbourne: Oxford University Press).

Lockwood, Brian A. (1970a) *Economic Statistics of Samoan Village Households* (Canberra: Research School of Pacific Studies Economics Department, Australian National University).

Lockwood, Brian A. (1970b) 'Market Accessibility and Economic Development in Western Samoa', *Pacific Viewpoint*, 11 (1):47–65.

Lockwood, Brian A. (1971) *Samoa Village Economy* (Melbourne: Oxford University Press).

McKay, Cyril G. R. (1969) *Samoana: a personal history of the Samoan Islands* (Wellington: Reed).

Malifa, Sano (1984) 'Economy Recovers – on Paper', *Pacific Islands Monthly*, March, p. 27.

Materman, Sylvia M. (1966) *Western Samoa* (Wellington: Government Printer).

Maynard, David L. (1981) *Sources of Change in the Money Supply: Fiji, Tonga and Western Samoa* (Suva: Centre for Applied Studies in Development, University of South Pacific).

Meleisea, M. and P. (1982) 'The Best Kept Secret: Tourism in Western Samoa', in R. G. Crocombe and F. Rajotte (eds) (1982) *Pacific Tourism: As Islanders See It* (Suva: Fiji Times and Herald Ltd) pp. 35–46.

Monetary Board of Western Samoa, *Annual Reports*, various years.

National Pacific Insurance Ltd, *Annual Report*, various years.

O'Grady, John P. (1960) *No Kava for Johnny* (Sydney: Smith).

Pacific Commercial Bank Ltd, *Annual Reports*, various years.

Pacific Savings and Loan Co. Ltd (1971) *First Annual General Meeting of Shareholders*, 1 April.

Pitt, David (1970) *Tradition and Economic Progress in Samoa: A Case Study of the Role of Traditional Social Institutions in Economic Development* (Oxford: Clarendon Press).

Post Office Department (1983) *Annual Report*.

Report of the Select Committee on the Legislative Assembly on Currency and Banking (1953) (Apia: Government Printer).

Rowe, J. W. (1965) 'Western Samoa', in Crick, W. F. (ed.) (1965) *Commonwealth Banking Systems* (Oxford: Clarendon Press) pp. 140–2.

'Second bank is Real Possibility', *Samoa Times*, 10 April 1970, p. 2.

Seuse, F. (1983) 'Book-keeping and Record keeping Systems for Small Rural Business – the Western Samoa Experience', in Jim Lamont (ed.) (1983) *Development Bank Credit in Rural Areas of the Pacific – the implications for rural development: proceedings of a workshop help in Tonga, July 1982* (Tonga: Rural Development Centre, University of South Pacific) pp. 247–60.

Shadbolt, Maurice (1962) 'Western Samoa, The Pacific's Newest Nation', *National Geographic*, October.

Shankman, Paul (1976) *Migration and Underdevelopment: the case of Western Samoa* (Boulder: Westview Press).

Shankman, Paul (1973) 'Remittances and Underdevelopment in Western Samoa', PhD thesis, Harvard University.

Spoehr, F. M. (1963) *White Falcon: the house of Godeffroy and its commercial and scientific role in the Pacific* (Palo Alto: Pacific Books).

Stace, V. D. (1956) *Samoa – an economic survey* (Nouméa: South Pacific Commission.

Stace, V. D. (1957) 'Problems of the Money Economy in Western Samoa', *ANZAAS Paper, 1957*.

Starr, Peter (1985) 'Ansett to Join W. Samoa Hotel Takeover Consortium', *Australian Financial Review*, 5 February, p. 13.

Su'apa'lia, Kipeni (1962) *Samoa: the Polynesian Paradise* (New York: Exposition Press).

The Development of Western Samoa 1971–1972 (Apia: Department of Economic Development, May 1972).

Third Five-Year Development Plan, 1975–1979 (Apia: Department of Economic Development, 1975).

Wai, Sam Leung (1981) 'Credit Unions in Western Samoa Five-Year Development Programme, 1981–1985', an unpublished paper dated 27 May.

Wai, Sam Leung (1983) 'Western Samoan Position Paper', in Jim Lamont (ed.) (1983) *Development Bank Credit in Rural Areas of the Pacific – the implications for rural development: proceedings of a workshop held in Tonga, July 1982* (Tonga: Rural Development Centre, University of South Pacific), pp. 91–108.

Ward, R. Gerard and Proctor, Andrew (1980) *South Pacific Agriculture: choices and constraints* (Manila: Asian Development Bank) pp. 395–406.

Watson, Robert W. (1918) *History of Samoa* (Wellington: Whitcombe & Tombs Ltd).

Western Samoa Accident Compensation Board, *Annual Reports*, various years.

Western Samoa Agricultural Sector Survey (Manila: Asian Development Bank, 1985).

Western Samoa, an Economic Survey (Noumea: South Pacific Commission, 1956).

Western Samoa Financial and Banking Survey (Wellington: Government Printer, 1957).

Western Samoa Life Assurance Corporation, *Annual Reports*, various years.

Western Samoa National Provident Fund, *Annual Report and Statement of Accounts*, 1981–1982.

Western Samoa Planning Project: a supplementary report on major projects, policies and institutional issues (Washington, DC: Robert R. Nathan Associates, Inc.) November 1975.

Western Samoa Second Five-Year Development Plan 1971–1975 (Apia: Department of Economic Development, November 1970).

Western Samoa's Economic Development Programme 1966–1970 (Apia: Economic Development Board, September 1966).

Western Samoa's Fifth Development Plan 1985–1987 (Apia: Department of Economic Development, December 1984).

Western Samoa's Fourth Five-Year Development Plan 1980–1984 (Apia: Economic Development Department, January 1980).

Yusuf, Shahid and Peters, R. Kyle (1985) *Western Samoa: the experience of slow growth and resource imbalance* World Bank Staff working paper, no. 754 (Washington, DC: World Bank).

Index